LA FRONTERA

LA FRONTERA

THE UNITED STATES BORDER WITH MEXICO

BY ALAN WEISMAN

PHOTOGRAPHS BY

JAY DUSARD

HARCOURT BRACE JOVANOVICH, PUBLISHERS

SAN DIEGO   NEW YORK   LONDON

HBJ

*Copyright © 1986, 1984 by Jay Dusard and Alan Weisman
All rights reserved. No part of this publication
may be reproduced or transmitted in any form or
by any means, electronic or mechanical, including
photocopy, recording, or any information storage
and retrieval system, without permission in
writing from the publisher.*

*Requests for permission to make copies of any
part of the work should be mailed to:
Permissions, Harcourt Brace Jovanovich, Publishers,
Orlando, Florida 32887.*

*A portion of this book previously appeared in a
different form in the* Atlantic.

*"Tragedias de Ojinaga" and "El Corrido de Fermín Arévalo"
by Los Rebeldes del Bravo; reprinted by permission of
El Zaz Music Publishing Co. "El Prieto Moro Manchado"
by Leonardo "El Nano" Yáñez, copyright © 1985 by
Intersong, S.A.; reprinted by permission of Intersong, S.A.
"Juan's Last Trail," by Drummond Hadley, copyright © 1986
by Drummond Hadley; reprinted by permission of the author.*

*Library of Congress Cataloging-in-Publication Data
Weisman, Alan.
La frontera.
Bibliography: p.
Includes index.
1. United States—Boundaries—Mexico.   2. Mexico—
Boundaries—United States.   I. Dusard, Jay.   II. Title.
F786.W375   1986   976.4'4   86-14837
ISBN 0-15-147315-3*

*Production supervision by Warren Wallerstein
Designed by Joy Chu and Jay Dusard
Printed in the United States of America
First edition*
A B C D E

FOR JOHN LOEGERING AND FREDERICK SOMMER

CONTENTS

LIST OF PHOTOGRAPHIC PLATES

Following page 30

PLATE 1: Artists, Matamoros, Tamaulipas

PLATE 2: Shrimpers, Brownsville, Texas

PLATE 3: Trio Astral: Pharr, Texas

PLATE 4: Casa Oscar Romero, San Benito, Texas

PLATE 5: Churches, Plaza de Armas, Reynosa, Tamaulipas

PLATE 6: Rodríguez family, Las Milpas, Texas

PLATE 7: Calle Hidalgo, Reynosa, Tamaulipas

Following page 126

Following page 150

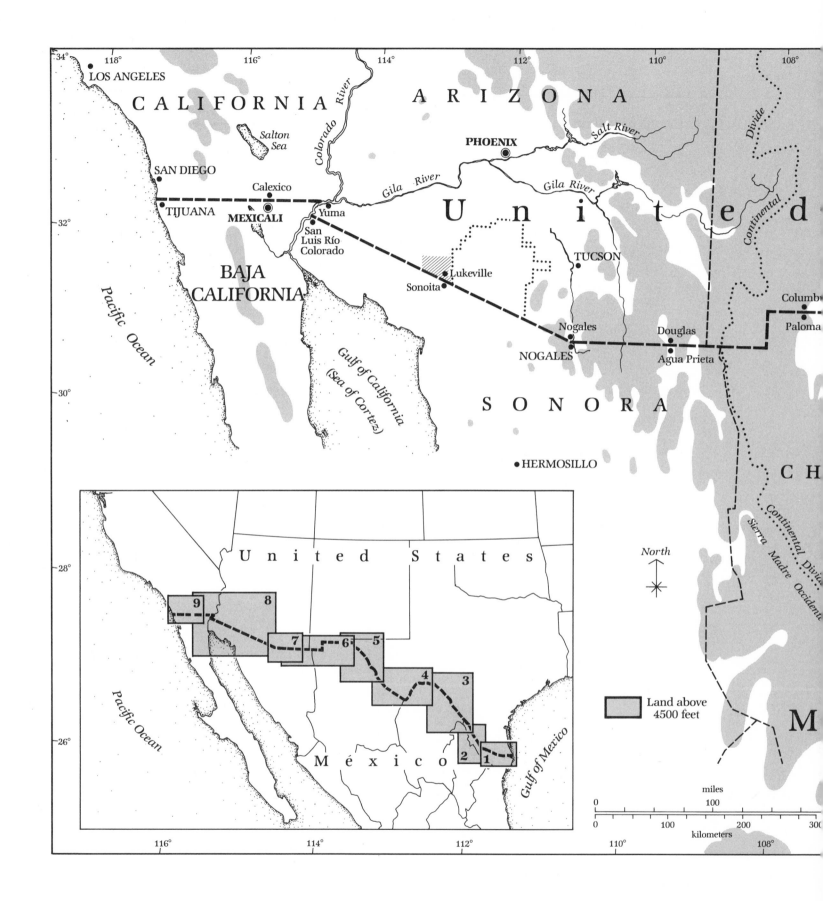

34°   118°   116°   114°   112°   110°   108°

• LOS ANGELES

C A L I F O R N I A   A R I Z O N A

Salton
Sea   Colorado River   PHOENIX   Salt River   Continental   Divide

• SAN DIEGO
          Calexico   Gila   River   Gila River   U n i t e d

32°   • TIJUANA   MEXICALI   • Yuma   TUCSON
          San
          Luis Río
          Colorado

BAJA   Sonoita   • Lukeville   Columb
CALIFORNIA   Paloma

Pacific
Ocean   Nogales
          Gulf of California   NOGALES   Douglas
          (Sea of Cortez)   Agua Prieta

30°   S O N O R A

     • HERMOSILLO   C H

North   Continental Divide
                              Sierra Madre Occidental
     U n i t e d   S t a t e s

28°

     9   8

          7   6   5
                              M

          4   3   Land above
                              4500 feet
     M é x i c o   2   1   *Gulf of Mexico*

26°
          Pacific Ocean

                              miles
                         0   100

                         0   100   200   300
                              kilometers

116°   114°   112°   110°   108°

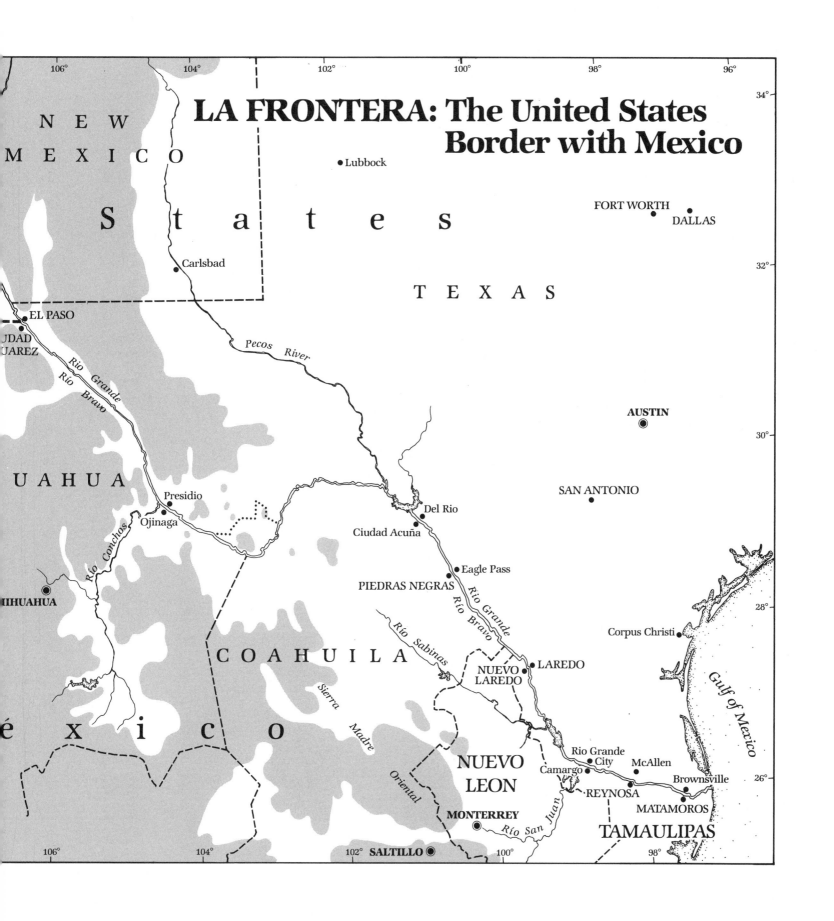

PREFACE

I grew up within a day's drive of the Canadian border. My closest connections to Mexico were some futile years of high school Spanish. So it remains a mystery to me why, during a newspaper assignment a decade later, I suddenly felt impelled to embrace that country. I was not satisfied to visit, but I had to live there, absorb its language and colloquialisms, master its local gossip, learn to drive in its cities, to seek Mexican comrades, and fall in Mexican love.

At various times, I displaced a brood of laying hens to find quarters in a poor agricultural village; I lived in a walled garden among poinsettias and Spanish jasmine; I moved into a shabby apartment complex inhabited by a descending middle class, whose national coin was corroding into fragments. I wrote, I traveled, I worked for charity, I commuted to Mexico City to serve on a project with the Mexican government.

I drank toasts with friends who sipped agave spirits, Baja California varietal wines, Kahlúa con crema, and the best commercial beer brewed in the Americas. I broke their bread, their pan dulce, their tortillas, their nothing. I became sick of it. I missed things in my own country I formerly would have never thought about—absurd items like American brands of crackers or shampoo, obtainable only if friends could be induced to smuggle them out of the bountiful stores in the basement of the U.S. Embassy. I missed cleanliness, technical prowess, and the firm cadence of the English language.

I returned home and gorged on a North American feast; antiknock gasoline, racquetball clubs, data bases. I soon got over it. I returned to Mexico, and eventually learned that when I was in one country, I missed the other.

In 1985, I spent a year exploring an area of both nations I'd mostly ignored: the common ground between them. I felt amazingly at home. Being in two familiar places at once was a little like seeing double, and I am grateful that I had a companion who perceived relationships in the borderlands I would have never seen on my own. Twenty-two years earlier, before photographer Jay Dusard began serving a life sentence in a darkroom, he took a $7.00-a-day detour from his career, working as a cowboy on a ranch whose southern fence was the border itself. It was an abbreviated reality, but it has remained for him an extended dream, and he was willing to sign on for another stint in this edge country.

Our intention was to learn what this region meant to the two worlds that held it like a vise and whether it had metamorphosed under this pressure into a new, separate entity. Educated as an architect, Jay was best known among his colleagues for his landscape photographs, and had received a Guggenheim fellowship for his skill as a portrait maker. This was an auspicious combination for recording the swirl of cultures found in border dwellings, in the shared spaces, and in the souls of border people.

Over several journeys, we saw both sides of the entire border twice. We learned that in some ways, la frontera is thoroughly bicultural. Distances on both sides are expressed interchangeably in miles and kilometers. Whether we used the precision of metric measurement or the convenience of the English system, we were always correct. In many instances, whichever language most easily expressed a given idea was the one to use, even if that meant multiple jumps between Spanish and English in the space of a single sentence.

Language in general is in flux: The term *American* applies to both norteamericanos and latinoamericanos—except when it only refers to gringos. After a while, which one is meant becomes apparent.

In the text, readers will encounter words such as *wetbacks, aliens, illegals, wets, mojados*—terms proscribed by many who prefer the political neutrality of *undocumented,* or *indocumentado.* The latter two are appropriate and precise, but they are not fully representative of the border's idiom. Various fronterizos, including the undocumented themselves, use the former terms frequently, with or without malice intended. Another example on the other side of the issue is the expression *migra,* sometimes uttered pejoratively, sometimes not, when referring to the Immigration and Naturalization Service.

By using such words here, not only in conversation but also in context, I expose myself to criticism but more accurately portray the range of attitudes found along, and caused by, the border.

The borderlands are nearly two thousand miles long, vast enough so that the term *Chicano* is imbued with pride in some places and is an insult in others. As anywhere else, part of its history is shameful, but to conclude that la frontera is merely sleazy is ridiculous. Most of it is a stunningly beautiful international treasure. To some, it divides two countries; to others, it unites them. We discovered the truth to be a bit of both, but it is still the former more than the latter. This will ultimately reverse. The "third country" between the United States and Mexico, a notion popularized recently by the press, has yet to congeal, but it will probably happen more quickly than many believe.

When it does, we suggest it will encompass much more territory than the narrow ribbon we refer to today.

Alan Weisman
Groom Creek, Arizona
May, 1986

LA FRONTERA

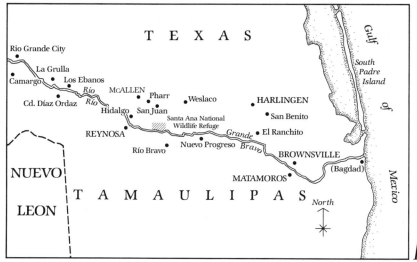

CHAPTER ONE

THE VALLEY

Aprehurricane dew, thick enough to condense on the fireflies, hangs over the river and resacas and the Brownsville ship channel. The July humidity smudges the luminous insects into bluish halos, which float and dissolve above the shrimp basin like spirit bubbles. Their winking, and the heat, continue damply through the night.

A little after dawn, when Jorge González's attention is first drawn to the sky, the fireflies have vanished. In their place, a pale green Piper Super Cub makes methodic, clockwise circuits, flying just thirty miles per hour, its right wing dipped steadily into the turn. González leaves his desk at the boatworks trailer, hitches the silver dollar belt buckle that keeps his khakis attached to his mizzenmast of a frame, and goes out for a better look. "Again," he mumbles, kicking at the oyster shell debris. No use calling anyone. The buses, he's sure, are already at the basin's entrance.

Half a block up Fisherman's Street, the crew of a shrimper, the *Compadre*, has been provisioning, stocking the hold with onions, beef, chops, tortillas, and apples. Eusebio, Jorge Luis, and Antonio, three men in their early twenties from Veracruz, Matamoros, and Brownsville, respectively, gut a thirty-pound bluefin tuna netted two days ago as they pulled in from Aransas for clutch repairs. Green eels and needlefish skitter around the trawler, feeding on chunks of fish entrails tossed over the stern. Sebastián Domínguez emerges from the cabin just as another fixed-wing aircraft appears. Up the dirt street he can see cars and vans filing past the green buses. He steals an apple for breakfast and relaxes against the bulkhead. "Vacación," he informs his crewmates. Eusebio and Jorge Luis look around and groan.

Channel 4's newsmen are busy everywhere, including up in one of the planes. Jorge González has nothing pleasant to tell them. The INS's public affairs guy had called a few days ago to make sure they could be there. "Tonight at six, George. Watch it."

Instead, González is watching border patrolmen splinter their way into one of his net sheds with a crowbar. "There's no one in there," he repeats. But they hear something and force the door anyhow, finding only a radio. They'll pay the damages, but not for the two or three days lost until the crews wander back across the border. As if Brownsville shrimping didn't have enough troubles.

"Domínguez," Sebastián answers the agent filling out his voluntary repatriation papers. "From Tampico." He has a Texas driver's license, showing a happy grin under sea-combed Medusa curls. He always uses his real name, because he is proud to be an illegal alien. The word *illegal* is supposed to make him feel undignified, but it does just the opposite, because such distinctions are made by governments, which don't know any better. His own government took the bread from his mouth, Sebastián explains to whomever wants to listen at the detention center.

"They took our boats, started their cooperativos and then chose who they wanted to be in them, turning the rest of us into thieves if we want to work in México. So we come here to support our families." Sebastián is glad his taxes go to the United States and not to Mexico, which, he is convinced, doesn't deserve them.

That afternoon the migra takes him, his two wet shipmates, and thirty other chronic cases a hundred miles upriver. Sebastián and the border patrolman have been on a first-name basis for the past three years. No hard feelings on either side; each man knows the other is just earning his living. At the low, flat bridge leading south from Rio Grande City, Texas, they shake hands. Carrying plastic bags containing their changes of clothing, Sebastián and the rest stroll across to fields of brown milo that lie between the river and Camargo, Tamaulipas. The finite American dream, which some say lately has an infinite number of dreamers, remains on the bank behind them.

The *Compadre* crew members stop for a bottle of Corona and a bowl of snook chowder in el Restaurante Colonial, and then walk out to Carretera 2, Mexico's border highway. Two trucks later, they camp at the edge of an okra field along the Río Bravo, east of McAllen and Reynosa. Overhead, the fireflies sparkle like Christmas lights in the feathery retama branches. By the next evening, they have white-knuckled their way through the girders of the Brownsville-Matamoros railroad bridge and rejoined Antonio aboard the *Compadre*. The following morning, they finish packing the hold. Helping them is Antonio's cousin Roberto, who is studying to take the Border Patrol exam. It's a good job, they say, and offer him some pointers.

"I don't hire wets," Jorge González explains. "I hire a captain with at least a green card, and he hires his crew. What does the government expect, though? They've made it impossible for shrimping to survive without illegals."

Jorge González, who started here when the industry began in the thirties, has watched the government progressively undermine his livelihood. The Port of Brownsville was once the world's largest shrimping fleet. Once they worked the Texas and Louisiana coast from July to October, then headed for the warm waters off Veracruz and Campeche. But then the United States agreed to honor Mexico's claim to a two-hundred-mile limit, and by 1980 Brownsville lost its shrimping rights to Mexican waters.

"That treaty came when the Mexican fleet was still growing. Then México nationalized its shrimp industry and it all turned to shit. Maybe 20 percent still operate—their government doesn't have managers to run a hundred million peso business." Jorge's fatigued eyes roll at the thought of what goes on down there. "The co-ops steal parts off each other's boats. And none of the scale-species fishermen want to invest anymore because they fear the government will expropriate them next."

What really rankles him is that Mexico probably wouldn't even notice where his boats go, but the United States fines any shrimper found in Mexican waters $10,000 and confiscates its catch. González has eleven such fines pending; the entire Brownsville fleet's infractions total over $5 million. He has no idea what will happen.

"No one can pay. Guys'll have to sell off their boats at twenty-five cents on the dollar to Africa. No one can afford insurance. You can't stop shipmasters from going over the line—they know the surplus is there, and they know they're making half of what they used to and splitting it thirty-seventy with their crew. Hell, we used to be ship captains. We'd do the same."

For a while, when they could still get Mexican permits for species like red snapper, they could pretend they were looking for scalefish and take their chances. But since 1981, the United States and Mexico have been waging naval wars over tuna, and now nobody ventures into the other's waters for anything. According to Washington, tuna belongs to neither country, because it roams from Fiji to the Aleutian Islands, visiting the Mexican and U.S. coasts but not actually breeding there. A welcoming committee of San Diego fishermen used to greet that migration along the coast of Baja California. Unhappy about competing with sleek American rigs, Mexico decided that its two-hundred-mile limit also applied to tuna.

The U.S. response is a mixed signal, something border people have learned to expect. It punishes the Mexicans with a tuna embargo, but takes pains to stop its Gulf shrimp boats from antagonizing them further. "This last time," González says, "they seized $7,000 worth of shrimp. And that particular boat had been out longest: I'd paid $6,000 for fuel, $500 for groceries, plus crew's salaries for thirteen days at sea when they're allegedly caught in Mexican waters. The

captain is off Port Isabel at the time, and he's dumb enough to come in and argue the point. Never come in, I told him. Don't make it easy on them."

He sighs. "So we go to court and the Coast Guard shows up with satellite charts proving where the boat was, and all we've got are the Port Isabel jetties to go by. My captain has sailed from Campeche to Florida by stars and landmarks and can dock a boat in the dead of night, but they get him confused. You're dealing with a Mexican mentality in a U.S. court. Because he's been brought up under the Napoleonic Code, he automatically assumes he's guilty and that they intend to hang him. He's never been in a courtroom before; the judge is screaming like Jesus Christ; there's a court-appointed translator who, I don't care how good he is, doesn't know half the nautical terms and everything my captain says comes out upside down. I sit there thinking, please, don't be so dumb, say this, don't say that, all the while watching him hang his head and stare down at the grave that his completely different mentality is digging for us."

The door to his office bangs open and a blond man in faded shorts enters, chewing a toothpick. "Hey, Joe," says González, switching to English. Joe Gayman has been looking into farming shrimp in artificial ponds as a way to stay in the market. The National Marine Fisheries Service is checking him pretty hard lately, and he's down to five boats.

Jorge doesn't know. An experimental shrimp farm up the road isn't doing so hot. But something has to happen. "Because three-fourths of the shrimp the U.S. eats comes from Thailand, the Philippines, Mexico, Russia, Cuba, Nicaragua—the communists launder it in Panama or Mexico and send it up here. That's what our government has done for us. Set all our foreign competition up in industries and gave them the gun to shoot us." González points a finger to his forehead and fires. His boats are all paid for; he was born here and has done nothing else in his life, so he'll probably hang around the basin and the courtrooms for a few years to see if things come back to normal. But in Brownsville nothing's been very normal since early in the decade when the rudderless Mexican peso drifted into a vortex and keeled over broadside. The maelstrom has yet to stop sucking; it keeps widening, threatening even to undercut the pilings of the country to the north.

Across the river, Matamoros harbors no fishing fleet. The Tamaulipan Gulf shoreline, just thirty kilometers east, lacks a natural bay such as Padre Island forms for the tip of Texas, and no artificial ship channel slices inland on the Mexican side. With its waters deflected by farms and cities of both nations upstream, the Río Bravo rarely runs deeper than a fathom now between Matamoros and the coast. Mexico's old attempt to have a port at the unprotected mouth of the river succumbed in the 1880s to too many hurricanes.

Like a myth built on sand, the port was called Bagdad. Among dunes and sea-colored halophytes, fifteen thousand Bagdad traders and brokers reaped a jackpot during the American Civil War. The North had every Confederate harbor on the Gulf of Mexico blockaded, but could not continue south of the Rio Grande without driving Mexico into an official alliance with the rebels. Matamoros and Bagdad became the portals to the American South, through which the Confederacy traded the harvests of slavery for European goods and weapons. For a time, more cotton passed through salty Bagdad than anywhere else in the world. Customs houses charging 50-percent duties provided Matamoros with unaccustomed windfalls.

Its sudden prominence was further enhanced by disruptions in Mexico's interior. By the second half of the nineteenth century, after years of Antonio López de Santa Anna's ruinous dictatorship, Mexico had lost half its territory to the United States and owed countries in Europe more money than its bankrupt treasury had ever held. With that pretext, and with the United States too occupied with the Civil War to enforce its Monroe Doctrine, Napoleon III invaded and conquered Mexico with little difficulty. He installed Ferdinand Maximilian of Hapsburg as Mexico's emperor, and suddenly France had a foothold in the New World again.

For Matamoros, named for a martyr of Mexico's independence, the change was an affront. Still, its closest North American ties were not to the Texas town rising around Fort Brown across the river but to New Orleans. French mercantile families had businesses in both Gulf cities; genteel Matamorans educated their children in New Orleans convents, and the language in which they addressed one another was French. During the 1860s, the blockade diverted both goods and culture from the Mississippi Delta to the Rio Grande. The French Mexican Empire was drawn toward Matamoros by language, capital, and by a convenient arrangement with the Confederacy.

Appomattox ended France's dream along with the South's. Louisiana became a base of support for Benito Juárez, a Zapotec Indian lawyer who was Mexico's president-in-exile. The Baton Rouge arsenal delivered thousands of muskets to his cause, and his liberation force swelled with mustered-out Union Army veterans. By mid-1867, Napoleon's troops were gone; Maximilian was executed and Juárez was reinstalled in Mexico City, wondering how to resuscitate his debt-ridden nation.

"Since then," sorrows Eliseo Paredes, "Matamoros's population has increased twentyfold, but we will never regain the importance we held during the Civil War." Shaking his whitened head, he wheels his chair down stone corridors that contain the relics of that glory. "We were the port. Brownsville was just a small suburb."

In 1910, when Paredes was eleven, his father took his family to Brownsville to wait out the Mexican Revolution. During the next seven years, more than a million other Mexican refugees crossed to the United States. "It was not unpatriotic to take refuge in Texas.

All Mexicans know that Texas was México's. One half of México is now in the U.S. But it was still México."

He attended high school in Brownsville. His brother Américo went to the University of Texas and became a respected professor and authority on Texas-Mexican culture. But Eliseo returned with his father to Matamoros to become a merchant and to reconstruct its once heroic image. His mania for recollection took him through the stifling streets of his city, into its Parisian architecture of wrought iron balconies and porch columns, into salt-washed neighborhoods filled with rows of wooden gabled cottages, reminiscent of poor sections of New Orleans. He combed the cemeteries, his watery blue eyes peering through oblong, wire-rimmed glasses at icons rising over carved vaults in whose crypts lay families named Bouchard, Legrand, and Cassagne. He sat for hours in Juárez Plaza talking to old survivors taking shade under laurel trees filled with chattering, yellow-eyed grackles. He gathered artifacts and histories, and converted Casa Mata, a fortress that once guarded Mexico against Zachary Taylor's invaders, into a museum for Matamoros.

Often his wanderings took him to where the Río Bravo merges with the Gulf tide, to where his grandfather, scion of a New Orleans family, was once mayor of Bagdad. Nothing remains, but Paredes has found where wells just a meter deep provided sand-filtered water for the former town. When the bonanza of war and cotton ended, there was no need to keep rebuilding Bagdad after each huracán took a turn at leveling it. The Tamaulipan maritime activities shifted south to Tampico, and dunes covered the rest.

Those dunes now look across the gray current to Boca Chica Beach and the United States, where the river is known by another of its historic Spanish names: Rio Grande. By either designation, Rio Grande or Rio Bravo, here begins the world's—perhaps history's—most compelling boundary. Yet nothing—no marker, no facing armies—indicates that it's anything of the sort. From both sides, fishermen in two- and four-wheel-drive vehicles chug through clay and sand to cast for redfish and flounder. Sometimes their lines tangle across the gaping political chasm, but nobody pauses to consider that; except for Coors on one side and Carta Blanca on the other, both banks and their respective anglers look much the same.

Yet these looks deceive, because the relationship between these two peoples, and the distinction between the two innocuous sandbars into which they prop their spinning rods, is momentous. Nowhere else on earth do two worlds so dissimilar and unequal meet for such a sustained distance. Here live the heirs to a legacy of southern Europeans who founded Latin America and northern Europeans who settled North America. At the time they began to do so, they were engaged in physical and philosophical conflict, Spain sending armadas against Britain, England severing ties with the church of Rome. Both societies became distracted by the potential of the New World and began to recreate themselves here.

Their differences were evident in their response to the discovery that the New World was already inhabited. One, here to enrich a distant kingdom and church, originally came with no women. Its conquistadors bred with the locals, and its missionaries shepherded them into its religion. The other arrived with entire colonies, and either killed the natives who were in the way or fenced them off.

For more than two hundred years, the inheritors of transplanted European history remained mostly separated by deserts, by sparsely settled colonial frontiers, and by terrorist aborigines known as Comanches and Apaches. When the new nations of the United States and Mexico emerged, they bordered each other less than the United States and Russia do today across the Bering Straits. But conquest drew them nearer, and transcontinental railroads and adjoining spurs built cities along their shared margin. Their distinctions became apparent. For reasons and traditions extending across centuries and an ocean, one was largely wealthy and the other was not.

By the 1980s, their border had become a brink, an edge cutting forward to the future and backward toward both societies' origins. Previous world history had been most concerned with the deeds of powerful and wealthy nations. Now, by the strength of numbers, the poor had become a mounting force, a Third World that the first two could neither ignore nor easily control. The long boundary between the so-called developed and developing worlds that runs from the Gulf of Mexico to the Pacific is less than 150 years old. As the history of European boundaries has frequently demonstrated, it can hardly be judged as permanent. Some believe that its fleeting reality is already revealed.

A little north of Boca Chica, beyond a strait flowing into the Laguna Madre, South Padre Island is the golden terminus of an arc of new residential development gleaming across the once-exclusively agricultural Rio Grande Valley. Miami Beach provided South Padre's model and Houston its down payment. But the open secret is that at least half of it belongs to Mexicans. After the 1982 peso devaluations, the rush of families from Monterrey buying entire condominium complexes slowed, but subsequent currency disruptions have actually had the opposite effect. "The idea," one investor told realtor Katharine Butler, "is to spend it before it's not worth anything at all." So, to Butler's immense delight, out come the money belts.

"When I say they pay in cash," she marvels, "I don't mean by check. I mean in $5,000 and $10,000 bills."

Along South Padre Island Boulevard, immigrants lean against Porsches with license plates from the Mexican state of Nuevo León and glumly swap war tales about how "la crisis"—the Mexican economic debacle of the 1980s—has driven them and their savings to find sanctuary across the border. "I used to be worth hundreds of millions," laments one, whose Porsche is painted a choleric red, "but now I am only worth tens of millions." Soon, the Mexican exiles of South Padre predict, there will be a revolution. By coming here, they affirm a tradition carried over from the last revolution.

Just across the causeway in Port Isabel, neighborhoods bulge with extralegal fishermen, including Mexicans, Miskito Indians from Nicaragua, and Bay Islanders from Honduras. Locals protest that the schools can't hold, much less teach, the multitudes of children spilling from cottages intended for single families. Ten minutes up Texas Farm Road 510, the Immigration and Naturalization Service's detention facility for unwelcome aliens, the Port Isabel Service Processing Center, has no room for Mexicans at all, so crammed is it with Central Americans. Nor does it have space for all of the OTMs ("Other Than Mexicans"). Because of numbers, because it doesn't know what to do with children and pregnant women, the INS has taken to releasing OTMs from El Salvador, Guatemala, and Nicaragua on their own recognizance.

The agreement is that they aren't to leave the area until the clogged courts get around to their hearings. As a result, Central Americans without immigration papers roam in stateless limbo all over the Rio Grande Valley, which has become a vast minimum-security detention center.

Rising out of cotton fields a few miles inland, the Port Isabel Service Processing Center is a loose compound of colorless block structures and cyclone fence partitions. Detainees have been encouraged to pass the time enlivening its exterior walls with murals of boats gliding dreamily across palm-lined lakes. The results, executed in government-issue basic tones, cheer nobody. El corralón—the big corral, as the refugees call it—inspires different sentiments.

Inside, green-uniformed INS officers, suave immigration attorneys, and bondsmen in knit shirts and reptile-skin cowboy boots shoulder past each other through buzzing security doors. A bank of thirty TV screens monitors dormitories filled with silent figures that stand, pace the passageways, and lie on beds.

Nearly everyone here—lawyers, guards, captives—is Hispanic. The main exceptions are eastern European aliens, mostly Poles and Czechs, whose organizations free them within hours, and paralegals from groups like Proyecto Libertad. Pale and bearded, some of them clergymen, these arrive with scuffed briefcases bearing request-for-asylum forms, bond agreements, petitions for change of venue to destination cities— anything to get their bewildered clients out of the Valley and farther from deportation proceedings. In flat, earnest Spanish, they help Central Americans clad in orange prisoner jumpsuits phrase answers to questions like "Have you or any member of your immediate family ever belonged to any organization in your home country?" or "What do you think would happen to you if you returned?" or "What specific skills do you have?"

In a featureless, white stucco house in San Benito, equally twenty minutes west of Port Isabel and northwest of Brownsville, there are problems. Casa Oscar Romero, sponsored by the sanctuary movement and shelter to Central American refugees, originally was limited to 40 residents. By the summer of 1985, it had 100. By fall, it had 220. Families sleep in shifts, on floors and in single beds. Every evening, 60 men parade through streets filled with the windblown residue of cotton fields to spend the night in the basement of the parish church.

Recently, many Nicaraguans dodging the draft have appeared. A year ago it was mostly Salvadorans. In the yard, a soccer field sustains three games simultaneously, with players of various age levels and nationalities. Despite the impossible conditions, residents get along reasonably well—except with their Mexican American neighbors, who are tired of the noise, of cars driving by filled with gawking white people, of the public displays of affection by frustrated couples who have lost not just their homes but also any chance for privacy. At the convenience store across the street, fights have occurred between refugees and taunting

locals. The latest Oscar Romero director, a no-nonsense nun named Sister Ninfa Garza, was sent by the Brownsville diocese to instill discipline. But nobody knows what to do about the numbers.

The Justice Department claims they are sheltering illegal job seekers, not political refugees. Meanwhile, vans from the INS's corralón keep showing up, not arresting people but delivering their overflow. At Casa Oscar Romero, arguments about who's responsible for Latin America's problems become pointless. The real question is, how are they going to end?

Leah Morrón, twenty and pregnant, with black hair hanging to her waist, left Nicaragua with her family six months ago when the army came to conscript her husband. To cross the Mexican-Guatemalan border, they paid a $600 bribe. Despite their bona fide Mexican visas, three more checkpoints cost $160 apiece. Only by threatening to call the Nicaraguan Embassy did they make it to Mexico City.

From there, they worked out a plan: She went ahead by train to earn enough money working as a domestic with her aunt in Houston to bring the rest over. The coyote she paid in Matamoros cost their last $1,000. Her bus to Houston was stopped by the migra, and she ended up in Casa Oscar Romero. By the time her husband and baby daughter reached the border, Leah knew enough to not bother with $1,000 coyotes. She took a taxi across the bridge to Matamoros, bribing the Mexican customs guard $3.00 to let her in. She crossed her family under the Brownsville railroad bridge, and they took another cab back to San Benito.

"We had to leave Nicaragua," she tells the nuns, adjusting her maternity outfit, an extra-large Texas Longhorns jersey. They are outside; she is seated on a picnic bench. A six o'clock breeze eases the pounding summer heat, and an impending thunderstorm has dissolved into a rainbow. But nothing quite relieves the whiff of humans living in close quarters. "They wanted Efraín to be a soldier. They take all the young men out of the schools, out of movie theaters, train them for two months, and send them to the mountains or the Honduran border to die. There's no milk for the children, no medicine—almost nothing in Nicaragua. My mother has a grocery, but she can't get goods. Everything is for the government. Supposedly, it's for the people, but they take the campesinos' sugar and beans and export them. All to buy more arms."

When she was fourteen, Leah Morrón became a revolutionary. Three drunken members of Somoza's National Guard had murdered her father while he was walking home from his store. Now she is disillusioned. "At least under Somoza we had things. The campesinos planted and sold freely. Somoza stole, but he let others do the same. Now only the Sandinistas get anything." Her hope is not to stay in the United States but to go home. "But not to kill or be killed."

Standing behind her bench so she can lean against him, Efraín shakes his head. He is slight, fine featured, and wears plaid pants and a white t-shirt. "I don't blame the government," he says. "The U.S. is arming la contrarevolución to overthrow them. What choice do the Sandinistas have?"

"In the U.S. people can at least live," she says.

He stares at the soccer balls flying by, at the dust. "Ay, Lita," he asks, "you like living like this?"

.   .   .

Antonio Zavaleta, Ph.D. sounds a little torn these days. At thirty-eight, he is a Brownsville city commissioner and a rising Hispanic hopeful in Texas Democratic politics who wants to champion the poor and create jobs and businesses that don't disappear each time the peso devalues. But he is caught between the long horns of opposing dilemmas: proposed immigration reforms that he finds abhorrent and the ominous growth of Mexico—especially Matamoros.

He teaches anthropology at Brownsville's Texas Southmost College, whose yellow stone buildings were formerly Fort Brown. Dozens of Mexican masks cover the walls of his office where he sits, sleeves rolled up and disdain tugging at his straight jaw, as he examines immigration bills sponsored by Senator Alan Simpson and Congressmen Romano Mazzoli and Peter Rodino. The current joke on the border is that had there always been such laws, Simpson would be around but Mazzoli and Rodino would be pressing olives in Sicily.

"The brains in Washington," Zavaleta assures his constituency, "come up with big plans for sanctions against employers. If they ever pass, we'll see a big flurry. Lots of press. Then everything will die down and we'll be back to normal. Except there'll be more bureaucracy, more expenses, and a lot of employers will suddenly be criminals. Ronald Reagan knows that—it would put a bunch of Republicans out of business. Too many people depend on illegals. If it were ever enforced, it would be devastating."

On the other hand: "Matamoros is a demographic time bomb. We have 100,000 people, and they'll have seven times that by the year 2000. They stream across the border to work and then stop at the currency exchanges on International Boulevard on the way back. Meanwhile, over half of our people are under the federal poverty line. Downtown merchants, land developers, and import-export people have conspired to keep unions out and wages low, and keep hiring illegals."

Zavaleta once asked Brownsville's police chief what the town's contingency plans were in the event that riot or revolution in Matamoros spilled twenty thousand people across the bridge. He didn't know.

"He hadn't ever thought about it. We have a handful of border patrolmen and the Cameron County sheriff's posse. I don't have many illusions about how many they'll be able to hold back."

At the United Nations World Population Conference in 1974 in Bucharest, the United States argued so forcefully for birth control that Third World countries protested, saying that the United States was again interfering in their affairs, that it was a racist ploy to limit the number of non-Caucasians in the world.

But during the next decade, most critics came to their economic senses. Even Mexico, whose numbers were nearly doubling each generation, abandoned its former opinion that multiplying was patriotic and fruitful and instituted its Planificación Familial program. Statistics being the plastic art they are in developing countries, no one is certain, but the average guess is that Mexico's birthrate lowered from 3.2 percent to 2.9 percent in this period.

Mexico's hopeful prediction is that the rate will go even lower, but some people like Tony Zavaleta aren't terribly reassured. Even at 2.9 percent, so the horror stories go, there would be more than a billion Mexicans by the year 2100—more Mexicans than Americans and Russians combined. Or in another generation, more Mexican babies born each year than in the United States and Canada together.

World Population Conferences are held every ten years. In 1984, appropriately, the site was Mexico City. To everyone's confusion, the Reagan administration appeared to reverse the United States' policy. Part of the issue was that the U.S. would no longer support agencies that fund abortions. But James Buckley, the American delegate, also stated, "We reject the notion that we are caught up in a world population crisis." Large populations, he explained, mean growing opportunities for developing economies and living standards, which lead to lower birthrates.

To its credit, Mexico joined most of the rest of the planet in finding this reasoning preposterous. The event did little to alter a Third World opinion that the United States meddles in world affairs for the sheer joy of it.

Antonio Zavaleta worries that we may be nearing the forbidding dawn of the Malthusian era and that the border is where the first dark glimmers will appear. "Poverty," he tells his students, "is a normal byproduct as capitalism produces wealth and a high standard of living. But if growth is too fast, poverty may become the *direct* product."

Right now, he believes, in terms of services, agencies, and unemployment, poverty is the number one industry of the Rio Grande Valley. Yet he can't help a feeling of optimism for Brownsville, assuming it survives all this. "Our destiny is geography. We're on the border with Latin America. We have a deep-water port aimed at the Caribbean."

Like the rest of the Valley, Brownsville is 90 percent Hispanic. The combination of distance from Washington and minority status has limited border opportunities in the past, but demographics is changing that. "In 1990, when we redistrict, we'll have a congressional seat. Hispanics like me are demanding our place in the sun. We're educated, we go to the statehouse in three-piece suits, not like little Mexicans with our sombreros in our hand. We've got doctorates, law degrees, and votes."

Tony Zavaleta would like to be Brownsville's mayor someday soon, and from there maybe its first native U.S. congressman. Like most educated Hispanics, his politics developed around Democratic populism.

"The Republicans lately are offering me lots of money to run for them. It's very tempting, of course, but I don't know how it would compromise my values." Toying with his necktie, he gazes at the ceiling fan that barely stirs the atmosphere of his second-story office. "Sometimes," he muses, "I wonder what it'd be like to have the money to implement some of the ideas . . . geez, they've got a lot of money."

.   .   .

The wealth of the Valley began with cattle from Jamaica, Puerto Rico, Hispaniola, Cuba—descendants of the original stock brought to the New World by Christopher Columbus. Here the first cowboys rode in what is now the United States; Tony Zavaleta's ancestors were among them.

The land was ribboned with oxbow resacas left behind by the river where hurricanes had whipped it from former courses. In the decades after 1848, with Texas now part of the United States, land-grant ranchers were joined in Brownsville by New York and

New Orleans merchants who built Victorian and brick classic revival homes along palm-lined boulevards, adorning them with French lampposts and iron hitching rails.

Some of the old moneyed families of Brownsville still hang on in the retail district, which has been staggered by the devalued buying power of their Mexican clientele. The Mexican American majority that one day may even inherit the Republican party is now in the process of inheriting the city from them. At Sams Memorial Stadium, the typically elaborate monument to that most Texan American activity of all—high school football—the hopefuls sweating through mid-August practice are often just a generation or two removed from la tierra to the south. On the surrounding Tartan track, Hispanic girls out for cross-country jog warm-up laps. Their parents now have representatives like Tony Zavaleta, who help them dismantle their outhouses and hook up to city sewers.

The first white Americans here endured the incursions of Juan "Cheno" Cortina, who harassed border settlements in the name of justice for Hispanics on both sides of the line. In 1859, he took brief possession of Brownsville, but was chased off by the Texas Rangers. Anglos rejoiced, but the rangers earned no love among the majority of the Valley's population. The disregard of "los rinches" for the border whenever they were in the mood for hunting Mexicans remains a stain on race relations in southern Texas and northern Mexico a century later. Their prey were often Hispanics who had been run off their ancestral lands. Whole Mexican families were sometimes found hanging from trees. Depending on which color Texan is doing the talking, raiders like Cortina are remembered as either bandits or heroes in the Rio Grande Valley.

The ranches eventually moved north and west, because the Rio Grande bottomlands were too rich to waste on pasture. Agriculture and irrigation spread as quickly as fields could be cleared and ditches dug.

Until the arctic freeze of January 1983, which beheaded half the region's Texas palms and froze citrus orchards to the ground, the fortune of the Valley was in its soil.

That has changed. Family farms are anachronisms; most of the cotton and grain operations belong to corporations whose profits leave for Dallas, New York, or Paris. Over the past decade, a winter tourism and retirement industry has created a nearly continuous band of development along U.S. Highway 83 out of rural communities like Harlingen, San Juan, Weslaco, Pharr, and McAllen. Resorts such as Rancho Viejo, whose water tower is a giant golf ball resting on a fifty-foot tee, generate more dollars than the loam beneath them could ever match. Much of the crops have gone over to the Mexican side. Eliseo Paredes, wistful for his city's Civil War glory, sees agriculture as Matamoros's less spectacular destiny.

But at eighty-six, Paredes may not witness what will change El Valle del Río Bravo as dramatically as the expanses of sorghum. Paralleling the great urban swath a few miles north of the border, which developers have christened the Magic Valley, is a chain of industries representing another form of wizardry: From Matamoros to Tijuana, America is creating its own Taiwan on its southern frontier.

Along Avenida Lauro Villar in Matamoros, where people once returned from siesta for one last earnest stab at work before quitting for home and supper, hundreds begin their jobs at three-thirty in the afternoon and go until midnight, when hundreds more replace them. At the evening shift at Thompson Industries, skeins of colored wires wave like battle standards, while machines sweep back and forth on belts and women furiously wind and knit cables for automobile electrical systems.

Outside, makeshift food booths line the muddy driveway leading to Industrias Thompson, to Fisher-Price Toys, to Zenith. Throngs of women on their breaks buy cigarettes, corn on the cob, oranges, pumpkin seeds, and Hershey bars smuggled across from Brownsville. In alleyways between factories, señoritas in Mexican designer jeans they've purchased with their minimum wages meet their lovers. Holding hands, they share Coca Colas and tostadas at the crowded tables. The atmosphere is reminiscent of a schoolyard: An airhorn blasts, and they snatch final kisses and bites of food. The mostly female tide of humanity that a half-hour earlier foamed from the low, windowless buildings now streams back. Vendors count the peso bonanza the maquiladoras—the American assembly plants—have reaped for them, and set about preparing for the night shift's arrival.

.   .   .

Nezahualcóyotl, the Aztec poet-king, once advised, "When you have nothing to eat, sing."

"So," sighs Jaime Garza, who does look a little emaciated, "while we go hungry, we sing. We dance. We paint."

In 1970, when he was twenty-two, Jaime Garza began Matamoros's Instituto Regional de Bellas Artes in the ruins of a 150-year-old military hospital. On budgets that seemed impossible then, the relic slowly became functional. Infirmaries where heroes died from trying to keep General Zachary Taylor's men out of Matamoros became classrooms and studios. Chamber musicians played in the courtyard where final bugle notes once sounded for the first martyrs in the 1846–48 Mexican-American War.

Those impossible budgets are now recalled with great longing. During these critical times, the Instituto is simply broke. Oils, brushes, canvas, sketchpads, strings for instruments—who can afford them when the peso buys one-twentieth of what it used to? The Instituto supposedly receives government funds, but Mexico has little to spare for the arts these days. "We need sewers before we need more culture," they tell Jaime in the presidencia municipal.

"Without culture," he replies, "you would never have had sewers in the first place."

Beauty being irrepressible in Mexico, in some places even poverty has a sweetness about it. The Instituto's courtyard is shaded by rubber and banana trees; the arches of its portico rest on pillars inlaid with Puebla tiles depicting wildflowers and bluebirds. Piano chords drift through open windows, providentially harmonizing with scales picked by guitar students in the garden.

There is no money, but art is a mystery that sometimes ignores the facts. Jaime is hard pressed to explain it, but the Instituto is awash in a torrent of inspiration. Paintings lean against walls, dry on gallery floors, clutter the music salons and the dance studio. Sculptures of wire and fiberglass, collages of feather and straw, triptych folding screens and ceramic creatures engulf his office, the secretary's cubicle, and the hallways. In the airy workshops, two of his artists, Lorenzo Rivera and Daniel Maldonado, direct students to model and draw, all the while sketching more overflowing ideas.

In his teens, Jaime Garza left Matamoros to study painting and design in Mexico City. He learned that the capital's art community considered border culture irretrievably *pocho*—literally, bleached white by the glare of its proximity to the United States. He returned anyway, to inhabit the cutting edge that exposes the nerve endings of two cultures. Resolving the border's natural tensions became his aesthetic fascination.

Surrealism meets Mexican folk traditions in the work lining these walls. Shadows of Mayan pyramids streak in deliberately different directions; shining automobiles levitate through desert skies; wizened Indian gods parade in modern dress. The influences of Mexico's genius muralists—Rivera, Siqueiros, Orozco—interlock with European impressions, New York experiments, and Oriental spells. Class struggles share canvases with unconstrained humor.

Jaime speaks proudly of Matamoros artists who have gone on to exhibit and perform in Monterrey and Mexico City. Reaching audiences in the United States is a different matter. His secretary hands him an invitation to take a folkloric ensemble to Brownsville. Dance shoes now cost 5,000 pesos a pair—"How can we afford to take twelve bailarines for a fifteen-minute show?" She shrugs. Then there's the migra: They know nothing about music. He's been through this: no visas for dance groups, because they might be taking jobs away from Americans. "We'll have to go through the consulates," he tells her, knowing that can take months.

These are just the technical difficulties. The less penetrable questions deal with identity, the fragile membrane enveloping an artist's consciousness. "Imagine being a Mexican child and waking up to Captain Kangaroo every morning. How does that relate to who you are?" Garza strokes his trim beard with the temples of his sunglasses, darkly recalling his puerile confusions. It's a border koan; he has no idea what the answer is, and senses that to try solving it would be an error.

He runs a design studio a block away that creates dresses for fiesta queens, coming-out gowns for quinceañeras, and folkloric ballet costumes. Amid yards of crinoline, a man and two women add sequins, ribbons, and lace while watching the Yankees play the Texas Rangers on a black-and-white TV. Upstairs, where Jaime lives, canvases line corridors so narrow that a viewer must plaster himself against the wall to see them. Sculptures, ranging from indigenous to inexplicable, have overtaken the living room. An immense charcoal portrait of a young man, flattened under glass, forms a kitchen tabletop—nowhere else to put it. The bathroom walls are paintings, some executed while Jaime was in the shower. Out on the balcony, grinning papier-mâché skeletons and giant skulls await completion for a forthcoming Day of the Dead exhibition.

Jaime Garza is part of a border culture that transcends the kitsch of the curio shops, creating medleys of rancheras, polkas, mariachis, tropicales, rock and roll, and Rodgers and Hart in fertile accompaniment to the rhythms of creative minds. But he knows the threat inherent in living on a double edge. Distrac-

tions like VCRs, Calvin Klein, and plastic garbage sacks tempt relentlessly. Fronterizos exchange birthrights for dollars.

"Now U.S. corporations come right across the line. They take our energy but leave nothing. The maquiladoras haven't donated buildings, parks, or anything else. General Motors squeezes Mexican brains and pays vassal wages for the privilege of inhaling paint thinner. Women go crazy attaching gray polyester sleeves over and over, never learning how to make the whole blouse. Fluoride factories that no city in the U.S. will accept come here. Companies pull out overnight if they feel like it. The people have no say in what happens to them."

From his balcony, Jaime Garza watches the people of Matamoros emerge from their wooden and concrete houses as the temperature cools with the twilight. Little boys on roofs call down to others playing with soccer balls. Women converse quietly in doorways. The border artist has to contend with a nagging obsession that he must justify himself to Mexico's interior, even as the frontera is its line of defense against an impending cultural rout. Looking down at his city, Jaime realizes that the very poverty that threatens their art is ensuring that no one will confuse them with their affluent American neighbors. He picks up a papier-mâché skull, contemplates it under the pale light of a streetlamp, and then goes to find some paint.

.　　.　　.

West of Brownsville, old Military Highway 281 slips beneath the juggernaut of Magic Valley subdivisions amassing a few miles to the north. Never more than a mile or two away from the tangled Rio Grande, it passes through La Paloma, Bluetown, Relampago—rural border outposts thus far spared the clatter of urbanization.

In fields backed up to the river, men who have come over from Mexico gather yellow and crookneck squash, bell peppers, cucumbers, zucchini, and okra.

It is quiet work, done to the rustling of vines and garter snakes. Despite the unceasing heat, the pickers wear long sleeves. They carry wicker hampers padded with leather, fastened to their backs with strips of sacking. They are fluid and efficient, each appearing to hoist an entire row of squash over his shoulders and move along under its great length, dropping its fruit into the hampers and laying it down behind him. At the end of the row awaits a tractor towing a stake-bed wagon with a canvas sunshade, a scale, and a twenty-gallon plastic water jug. The men empty their vegetables, drink, lift the end of another row and go again. For their pain, they earn seven cents per pound.

A mile away, at the weathered frame headquarters of Esparza Farms, J. D. Esparza argues on the phone with the Department of Labor. At the government's insistence, Esparza Produce, one of the few viable family operations along this part of the river, has punch cards for the workers, which everyone knows is silly. "An hourly wage is no incentive for pickers. They'll just lie around," J. D. repeats. "You feds work eight-to-five and assume that everyone else does, too."

He hangs up and looks at his cousin. "I know," Romeo Esparza says. "They don't understand. Pickers are individuals. Some here are making $10 an hour." Like J. D., Romeo is in his twenties. Both wear knit shirts and blue jeans; they have tanned, round faces, and have grown up working their fathers' farm. The government, they agree, doesn't help people anymore, but is just trying to refill the U.S. treasury.

It seems that whenever it's budget time at the INS, suddenly the Border Patrol appears, apprehending the same ones day after day. It makes the numbers look better, the Esparzas assume. Then the United Farm Workers raises periodic hell, demanding they hire U.S. labor. The last time, a local TV crew brought a woman and her babies from up the road at Progreso; she claimed they wouldn't hire her. Nicho, J. D.'s dad, promised her a job on camera, but then a livid Romeo came bursting out of the office. He confronted the woman, who weighed 220 pounds. "Are you telling me you're gonna drive thirty miles round trip to slip and slide in this mud, bent over seven days a week, for minimum wage?" he demanded.

"Well . . ." she said slowly, and finally shook her head.

"No U.S. citizen will pick okra," Romeo insists. "It has little spines that eat you raw. When it scratches, you break out in a rash. It has to be picked when it's fresh, early in the day, because the heat makes it irritate even more. Locals would rather sit around on food stamps."

But three hundred Mexican pickers can smoke their way through a hundred acres, picking them clean in a couple of hours. J. D. and Romeo Esparza have known the ones in their fields all their lives. While the cousins were growing up, every Sunday they would swim the río to visit their workers' little ranchitos— El Capote, San Luisito, La Barranca. Someone would slit a baby goat's jugular and stew the cabrito in its own blood, and they'd feast and watch the cockfights and horse races.

For generations now, the same families have slipped across the river, worked, and gone back home. The INS tells the Esparzas that they're earning money to head north. "We've seen these people all our lives," they reply. "If we stop employing them, then they will head north."

But if the government doesn't get you one way, they'll get you another, the Esparzas figure. Their mainstay crop, okra, has been threatened by the surprise elimination of tariffs on certain Mexican vegetables. No one knows why this occurred. J. D. talked to a farm lobbyist in Washington, who said that Mexico hired a big U.S. attorney to get rid of them. "American companies like Bird's Eye and Green Giant have huge farms and processing plants down there," he was told. "They're probably in on it." The price of labor in Mexico is two-and-a-half cents a pound, compared with eight cents in Texas. Without the tariff, competing is impossible.

So Esparza Produce is now buying from Mexico. The company has had a good year too. Mexico anticipated large profits with the relaxed tariff, so it overproduced and the Esparzas bought okra cheaper than they could grow it. J. D. and Romeo have decided they will phase out farming altogether when the place becomes theirs, and just be produce brokers.

And Nicho Esparza has subdivided their first twenty-four acres, into lots ranging in price up to $12,000 for three-quarter-acre plots. "This soil can grow just about anything," says J. D. "But there's no question what the best long-term investment in the Valley is going to be from now on. We all know it."

.   .   .

Evening winds carry Gulf moisture inland, where it combines with evaporation from the irrigated valley. Red-orange cumulus anvils appear at dusk, gathering heat but failing to turn to summer rain. For the first hundred miles westward, these clouds add the only vertical dimension to the landscape of the border.

On the Mexican side, the state of Tamaulipas extends a narrow arm along the border all the way to the uplifted plains of Nuevo Laredo. Carretera 2 pulsates like an artery along its length, its corpuscles the grain trucks and fleets of bonded semitrailers bringing components down from U.S. parent factories, to be assembled by Mexican hands and returned north. The highway passes through Nuevo Progreso, a city that materialized thirty years ago when a grower in Progreso, Texas, decided to build his own bridge across the river to import Mexican vegetables. U.S. Customs scrambled to collect duties; by then, thousands of hectares of former brushland were in corn, cherry tomatoes, broccoli, and okra. Curio shops and restaurants followed, bringing retired day tourists across the bridge to experience an "Old Mexico" far younger than themselves.

Thirty kilometers further, Río Bravo is the first of two significant Mexican border cities that lack U.S. counterparts. Barely ten years older than Nuevo Progreso, Río Bravo formed around a bureaucracy. Mexico's Ministry of Agriculture and Hydraulic Resources put an office here in the 1940s, and farmers needing permits began to flock and settle. Without an international bridge and the nightclubbing U.S. trade, Río Bravo's flashiest image is a crackling electrical generating plant at one end of town, cranking the machinery of new American maquiladora plants that keep arriving. Rows of seed hoppers outside Río Bravo give way to two busy commercial boulevards in town, lined with curbside markets, movie theaters, and outlets for John Deere, Nissan, Goodyear, Dodge, and Uniroyal.

Despite la crisis, they are all doing business. With 100,000 inhabitants, Río Bravo is the modern Mexican border town, built because Mexican agriculture has claimed its share of the river of two names and growing because gringo factories have linked it to the north.

The older border towns, once romantically shabby and lurid, have become border cities. Along a boundary between two unequal economies, a reversal occurs: Cities like Laredo, McAllen, and El Paso are the poorest urban areas in the United States, whereas Mexico's northern boundary is its most prosperous zone. Twenty kilometers upriver from Río Bravo, continuous traffic approaches Reynosa from the interior of Mexico. It passes the cardboard jacales of new squatters and continues through an industrial belt of junkyards, auto parts concessions, petroleum storage depots, supply houses, and a cluster of pastel prisms housing maquiladoras. The air is smoky; rouge powder puffs form around tail lights in the suspended dust. A statue looms in a glorieta, but traffic rushes around the circle too rapidly to determine whom it honors. Beyond, far too many trucks and buses funnel into a long boulevard, its new asphalt already cracking from overuse. Gradually, bigger vehicles yield places in the lanes to passenger cars. The plaza appears, and then the fancy bars and clubs that announce the border itself.

.   .   .

Ten miles north of Reynosa, DC-3s and C-47s leave the runway at Miller International Airport in McAllen and disappear beyond the black horizon to the south. These are large, blunt-nosed tail draggers, capable of lifting eight thousand pounds of cargo, with fat tires ideal for landing on dirt airstrips. Although there are no officially scheduled flights, every night six to ten of them rumble over Reynosa. They head deep into Mexico, stuffed with color televisions, Sony VCRs, and microwave ovens. Before departing, their pilots dutifully complete export declaration forms, required by the United States to monitor the all-important balance of trade. They do this in the presence of U.S. Customs officials, who know that as soon as they enter Mexican airspace, they are illegal. But the United States can't enforce another country's laws—and besides, there's the balance of trade to consider.

Backing them up is the McAllen rat pack, young free-lances in Cessna 206s and 207s, who make short hops down to Tampico, Monterrey, and Ciudad Victoria. For $500 per voyage, they haul 1,200 pounds of car stereos, cases of whiskey, or bolts of Korean rayon in a 1,000 pound capacity aircraft stripped of passenger seats. They top off their cargo with some domestic item, perhaps a load of ceiling fans, to pay for the gasoline. The pack often flies in groups of at least four, so that, should Mexican customs give chase, they can scramble and lose them in a cloud formation.

On this particular Monday night, a DC-6 two hours out of McAllen begins its descent toward a murky strip in the desert north of San Luis Potosí. The pilot is ex-CIA. The copilot flew in Vietnam. Neither has any connection to the merchandise they are hauling— Cutty Sark—except for the $1,000 and $500, respectively, they'll collect for the evening's work. Two or three runs a week adds up to a decent enough living; McAllen, supposedly the most impoverished city in the United States, is feeling nearly suburban and pricey, with winter tourists and its two new skyscrapers.

Some nights are so busy here they've had to hold their pattern for fifteen minutes before they can get on the ground. Once down, fifty unloaders can have them emptied and away in forty-five minutes. But the strip is on the ranch of somebody big in Mexico City, and with so many workers, all the pilots are nervous because it's just a matter of time before talk gets warm enough to heat some comandante's ear.

Tonight they glide right in. One C-46 is already on the ground. They stay in the cockpit, windows open, sharing a thermos of coffee. About the time they are half unpacked, beams of light suddenly flicker across the runway. Flashlights, and the military police holding them, have everyone surrounded.

The capitán instructs the workers to keep unloading. Things become very quiet. Except there is a third aircraft, a Lockheed Lodestar transport, circa 1940, coming in without radio contact. It hits the caliche, kicking up the usual fifteen seconds of tremendous dust, and a soldier gets too excited and pumps a round through the windshield, just above the Lodestar copilot's head.

The pilot—no one is even sure who it is—full-throttles, trying to get airborne. Half on the strip, half off, he struggles against the weight of five thousand pounds of VCRs. The soldiers and everybody else just stare, as though a great pterodactyl someone has just winged is flopping around the desert floor. Yet he actually lifts off, starts to raise his landing gear—and then a wing clips a fifty-foot cardón cactus, which tears into the fuel tank.

With gasoline spraying over its aluminum skin, the pilot belly-dives the Lodestar in the sand and kicks out the windshield just as the fuselage ignites. He and the copilot run into the desert, but no one gives chase because it's an engrossing sight to watch tons of aluminum and solid-state components explode on a moonless night.

While the army is thus occupied, the other two crews also flee. After running for about fifteen minutes, they realize nobody is chasing them. "If they catch us they'd have to take us to Mexico City with the goods," reasons CIA. "We'd know how much we were carrying and how much they ripped off for themselves." So they zip their flight suits against the desert's night wind and walk in the direction of the highway. By morning they have thumbed their way to San Luis Potosí and caught a bus for the border.

"Everybody expects to lose at least one load one time or other," Carlos Mejía explains to the orthodontist in his office. His smiling, dark-haired wife, Beatriz, enters, and places a glass of Johnnie Walker over ice in front of each.

"Gracias," says their slightly edgy guest.

"Salud," offers Mejía, raising his drink. He has a soft voice and reddish hair, and wears a long-sleeved blue guayabera over his slender frame. From a storefront in a shopping mall near the Reynosa bridge, he exports hospital supply equipment. He was once the vice president of a major American wholesaler, and started this as a hobby for his wife. The hobby's income soon surpassed his salary.

A one-way mirror overlooks their display room from his office, where he has a drawerful of fake Rolexes his men bring him up from Mexico. He gets them for acquaintances; they're good copies, worth $250 apiece. The diamond-trimmed, eighteen-karat president's model on his own wrist is no phony—just obligatory equipment for doing business in Latin America.

"You can't insure your shipments," he continues. "If it's caught, the seller and buyer split the cost of the mordida to get it back. The pilots don't get charged, because they're taking the risk." The risk that night outside San Luis Potosí was especially costly. Hangar 10 at the McAllen airfield lost $700,000 worth of aircraft in one evening. Nine months later, the DC-6 was still down there waiting for everybody to be paid off, and the Mexican military had put in a bid for it.

Early in his business, Carlos Mejía tried sending merchandise legitimately. A dentist from Puebla wanted $8,000 worth of high-speed drills and agreed to pay the duties. Mejía couldn't get a Mexican cus-

toms broker to touch it. "It's a waste of time," he was told. "It won't get through."

He should have known better. As a boy, he ran errands for his father's forwarding agency, making payoffs to Mexican feds. "Everybody does it," he advises distributors new to the border. "There's no way to take things legally into Mexico. Mexican customs officials prefer it this way, because they make something too. It spreads the money around a little."

During normal times—the lulls occurring between devaluations or earthquakes—he packs several thousand dollars' worth of orders a week. His three Mexican shippers pick them up, charging by the box. Their fee amounts to around 5 percent, which Mejía passes on to the customer and legally reports to the IRS as freight charges. One of his men works for Mexican customs, so there's no worry about having to pay extra at checkpoints. In 1984, a decent year, he paid his men $65,000.

Profits aside, he has no trouble justifying what some call smuggling. "They have no other way of getting these products, and there is no way of practicing twentieth-century dentistry or medicine without them." Government agencies in Mexico, despairing of the glacial pace of official channels, routinely go the streamlined route—Mejía's first shipment was $16,000 worth of microscopes to the state university of Tamaulipas.

It doesn't always work perfectly: Over the years, he's had loads confiscated twice in Mexico, and it cost $5,000 each time to bribe back the shipments. But at $40,000 per consignment, he still ended up ahead, so the risk is worth the price. The volume is so high—some border Sony dealers sell nearly at cost, simply for the 7 percent rebates on sales over $1 million—that contraband is arguably the smoothest form of communication between the two nations.

"It's bad for México, though," contends a former mayor of Reynosa. "Our industries can't compete. All it does is hurt international relations. The United States doesn't want to stop it because Americans are greedy."

"He oughta know," remarks a U.S. Customs official

at the McAllen airport. "While he was in office he had three planes flying out of his ranch. Johnny over there was one of his pilots."

Not far from the airport, a row of metal warehouses make up U.S. Free Trade Zone 12. Shipments of four hundred bales of synthetic fabrics arrive regularly from the Orient and are broken down into lots and loaded aboard southbound DC-3s. None of it stays in the United States, and no duties get paid; McAllen is just a trampoline for the Far East to bounce goods into Mexico. Customs agents earn overtime checking fabric and other bonded items that pass through the zone. "The U.S. doesn't lose any money providing this convenience," agent Steve Johnson explains, "because the Mexican merchants who profit bank their dollars in the United States. Nobody keeps money in Mexico. If you earn it there, you put it in McAllen State Bank, not in Veracruz."

When Johnson isn't looking over polyester or washing machines being loaded into World War II-vintage cargo planes, he works the international bridge connecting Hidalgo, Texas, a buffer village between McAllen and the border, to Reynosa. A tall, wire-haired Texan with a voice like grits and honey, after twenty-two years in customs, Johnson makes nearly $42,000 a year. His counterparts on the Mexican side earn the peso equivalent of around $8,000, but he figures their real income is several times that amount. "The comandante gets the biggest cut—he'll make up to a hundred grand. There's a constant change of comandantes in Mexican customs because Mexico City never believes it's getting a big enough percentage of the take."

Night duty on the bridge: A pickup with Tamaulipas plates carrying a family and six cases of tamarind candy is sent over to the naked fluorescence of secondary inspection, where customs officials probe vehicles for exotic cargo. Tamarind is duty-free, but Food and Drug needs to take samples, and they're off at five o'clock. The driver explains it was delivered

late to him, and there's a restaurant in Pharr, Texas, that needs it for tonight. Johnson and his comrades know he's a hardship case, so they let him go. It's a judgment call: Some people bring in food and other items that get taxed if they're to be resold. These days, a lot of what is claimed for personal use is actually headed to flea markets.

Some of the traffic consists of U.S. citizens coming back from dinner in Reynosa. It's impossible to check each, but any day the probability is high that at least one of those walking back with a bottle of Kahlúa or Mexican vanilla was in Bogotá the day before and has flown to Reynosa via Mexico City. The agents make eye contact, watch for throbbing neck veins and tap car doors.

"Why're you searching me and you let those cars through?" a bald Texan in a blue Mercury Marquis demands.

There's really no reason; random checks are part of the routine. "We got word," Steve Johnson tells him, "that something's coming through in a Marquis and we're inspecting them all." Next comes a silver Chevy Astro van with Mexican plates and the legend "Let's Party" airbrushed in dark green on the panels. The driver is a known narcotics dealer, so they take their time checking the vehicle and doing a personal search, updating his file. Dressed in a white summer pullover and blue chambray slacks, he looks like someone's father, and he is: His children are fussing inside, and his wife, resigned, waits in the passenger seat.

They delay long enough for a Drug Enforcement agent to arrive and take his picture through a gap in the drapes of the customs office and also to see if he gets nervous because they won't let him go to the bathroom. Body carriers who swallow condoms filled with cocaine have only so long to expel the contents of their intestines before the bags deteriorate and a fatal overdose leaks out. But the guy is calm tonight, so after an hour he drives on into Texas; the DEA man gets a drink of water and follows.

In a fenced lot adjacent to the inspection station, a row of seized vehicles await the next customs auction. Except for the IRS, the U.S. Customs Service is the only federal agency that makes a profit. Most of its revenue comes from tariffs, but confiscations represent another dependable source. Several pickup trucks here have butane tanks that conceal a second, smaller chamber within. These hold enough butane so that an agent testing the valve will smell gas and hear it fizz, leaving the main tank free for transporting valuables such as snowy white powder.

On a recent Saturday night, a new beige truck with Texas plates pulled into agent Rosa María Barraza'a booth. The driver, a deeply tanned blond man about twenty-five, smirked when she asked his citizenship, as if to imply that this Hispanic woman with her braided black hair had some nerve to question his nationality. Around the back of the pickup, Rosa María rapped the butane tank. Instead of ringing, it thudded. Walking slowly alongside, she escorted him to the secondary inspection area and stood there until other agents noticed and came over. Eventually, they located the hidden trap door. Inside was $25 million worth of cocaine.

All border agents dream of a big bust. Young Rosa María's catch that August night in Hidalgo, Texas, turned out to be the biggest of them all.

After 11:00 P.M., the traffic slows and only two booths are working. Occasionally, a Border Patrol van brings some indocumentados under the canopy, writes them up, and drops them at the bridge. The big excitement is a woman smuggling a comatose parrot, drugged with tequila-soaked corn, inside a diaper. One of the agents noticed that her baby had sprouted tailfeathers.

The rest of the vehicles are late-night drinkers and diners. A pair of trailers carrying fifty-five gallon drums of bonded Brazilian orange pulp head into Reynosa. There it will be diluted and brought back to be canned and sold as American orange juice.

At 4:00 A.M. things will begin to get busy, as hundreds of field workers enter the United States to look for a day's labor. But at midnight, nearly nothing. A tired pickup rolls up, loaded with a family. Rosa María can see that they're barely getting by. They're Mexican but they have green cards, making them legal residents of the United States. Rosa María, herself a naturalized U.S. citizen born in Chihuahua, checks their IDs and pauses. One of the two women has shown a birth certificate, and something doesn't match. She doesn't answer the questions right, doesn't even know where it was issued. An INS agent comes over. A little while later, the driver breaks down and confesses.

"She is my sister. She has no work." They were trying to bring her over to bake and sell cookies with his wife.

The law reads that any vehicle caught transporting an illegal alien into the United States must be seized. So now they take all their belongings out of the truck. The children hug their aunt; she, her brother, and his wife sob and embrace. She picks up her small suitcase and heads over the bridge into Mexico. The family turns; everyone, including the four-year-old, gathers up a bundle. On foot they set off toward McAllen.

•   •   •

Dr. Efraín Martínez, former mayor, sits with Pepe Elias Maciel in the gold-toned main dining room of Sam's Restaurant in Reynosa's Pink Zone. Maciel, a sallow, nervous man, is the manager here and he is upset. Tourism has collapsed during the past year, ever since an American drug agent, Enrique Camarena, was murdered in Guadalajara. That was regrettable, but the United States's reaction only worsened things. First, a massive slowdown at border crossings was ordered; for two weeks, all vehicles were searched, paralyzing the normal flow of goods and business. Then U.S. Ambassador John Gavin made a series of what the protesting Mexican press termed "irresponsible declarations" regarding the wisdom of travel in Mexico.

Mexicans were outraged. Ever since 1822, when the first American envoy, Joel Poinsett, schemed to redesign Mexico along the lines of the United States, they've put up with gringo interference. Now Gavin, a former actor who used to appear in rum commercials on Mexican television, was at it again. Maciel, president of the Reynosa Good Neighbor Council, delivered a speech in Monterrey citing the effect Gavin's comments have had on tourism and calling for him to shut up or go back to his own country.

"Ten thousand Americans came through here last year. Now we'll be lucky if we get two thousand. At noon we used to be full of Texans. Look." Martínez does. "Even the flies don't come now."

"Germany and Japan had difficulties with the United States once, and they bounced back," he offers. "Maybe there's hope for México."

Maciel also has had it with Reynosa police who assume that tourists were born to be extorted. "When is the party going to do something about this?" he wants to know.

The party is the PRI, the Partido Revolucionario Institucional, which controls nearly every political office and human activity in Mexico. Ensconced in its familiar green, white, and red insignia, the PRI's initials deface walls, buildings, and entire mountainsides from the U.S. border to the Guatemalan frontier. Martínez, a square-faced man with a thick, gray mustache, was, of course, a PRI mayor.

He shrugs. He has, after all, seen some improvements. Reynosa no longer dumps its sewage raw into the Río Bravo, as does Nuevo Laredo upstream. The oil refinery doesn't hand out jobs as it once did, but during his administration the maquiladoras arrived. He was able to negotiate a truce when union and nonunion factions, vying to transport maquiladora workers, took turns burning each other's buses. In a city where the newspapers earn more for what they don't publish—editorials forced one mayor to resign in 1975 the day after his inauguration—Martínez made it through politics relatively undespised. But he has

no quick solution for the perennial dilemma of border cities, dangling forever between the vagaries of Mexico City and the United States.

Down the street in Treviño's, Reynosa's most eminent nightclub, waiters in black ties and red dinner jackets morosely scan the rococo lounge, empty except for a Mexican immigration official and his party. The official, Emilio Garza, is pleased—he enjoys having the place all to himself. "Reynosa," he says, hoisting a crocodile-skin cowboy boot onto the edge of the table, "is a little more like México and a little less like the United States lately."

The waiters nod. They've noticed.

.   .   .

In 1623, in the village of San Juan del Lago in what is now the Mexican state of Jalisco, an Indian girl named Ana found work cleaning a mission chapel. She grew fond of a statue of the Virgin, which she talked to like a doll. One day a circus came to town. It featured a family who performed on a tightrope suspended over daggers. Ana went to see and witnessed a horror when the daughter slipped and was speared through the heart.

The grief-stricken family and spectators gathered around her corpse, except for Ana, who raced to the church. She returned with the statue and placed it on the dead girl's breast. The family swooned as their daughter sat up, alive and unmarked.

Centuries passed, during which New Spain became Mexico. The legacy of Spanish rule was Mexico's centralized feudal hierarchy, which responded sluggishly to the needs of a vast nation in the Americas. Within two generations, its entire northern territory belonged to the United States. Beset by their difficult birthright, many Mexicans followed, seeking a chance that, after centuries, still eluded them.

In 1949, Father José María Azpiazu, pastor to their descendants in the town of San Juan in the Rio Grande Valley of Texas, prayed over his peasant flock and wondered if that chance would ever come. After three hundred years, their dirt poverty remained. Spain, Mexico, the United States—none of them had mattered.

With no other foreseeable hope, he resorted to miracles. He drove south into the desert, a thousand miles to the village of San Juan del Lago, Jalisco. He prayed at the shrine erected where a circus had once played, and carried back with him a replica of La Virgen who had interceded there. En route, his vehicle ran off the road and was wrecked; he and the statue escaped untouched.

Back in Texas, he requested permission from his bishop to erect a shrine. When it was dedicated five years later, sixty thousand pilgrims genuflected before the image of the saint of San Juan del Lago.

In 1970, a religious fanatic kamikazied his light plane into the sanctuary, demolishing it. La Virgen's image emerged unharmed. They built a bigger church, which rises from the Valley like a stadium, its parking lots so extensive that the rows have street names. Instead of a choir loft, the Virgen de San Juan del Valle Shrine has a virtual orchestra pit, and the priest delivers the homily over a cordless microphone. Behind him, surrounded by a large bas-relief mandala depicting the people of the Valley themselves, is the image of the Virgin.

She wears a blue spangled gown and stands on a golden crescent surrounded by angels. An entire room holds offerings and supplications for her continued intercession, its walls hidden beneath handwritten prayers, photographs of parishioners, crutches, dollars, and peso bills. Every week, twenty thousand people attend the Spanish language masses.

During the 1980s, the steadfast Mexican faith led the poor people of the Valley to an improbable spiritual benefactor: a Jew from Chicago. It was no miracle this time, only the sort of thing that may happen in a country awash with so many cultures. But nothing like it had ever happened to them before, and many in the Valley conclude that their chance has now arrived.

Saul Alinsky began organizing Chicago's stockyards communities during the 1940s. His Industrial Area Foundation was regarded variously as a triumph of social justice or a communist foothold in the heartland. Its success owed to elementary arithmetic: A lot of people are poor. Organize them, and they have a lot of power and votes.

The bishop of Brownsville knew the only thing the people of his diocese had a lot of was troubles. At his invitation, Industrial Area Foundation organizers came to the Valley. In a year, they conducted one thousand interviews. "What are your problems?" they asked. "What are your hopes?"

Then they left. Behind them remained ten thousand volunteers for a new social order: the Valley Interfaith.

Slim, dark-haired Ofelia de los Santos, daughter of a mojado, was among them. She had a degree in political science; she had returned from college with her husband to her native Valley for jobs in a local school district. Her childhood surroundings rushed back to her. Americans were living without plumbing, without pavement, without sewers. Neighbors contracted forgotten diseases like leprosy and diphtheria. Too few people worked. They huddled around the church for what little warmth they could find. They were a Third World nation in a wealthy state.

When the organizers held a meeting in her parish, Ofelia doubted they could teach her much about politics. Instead, she learned that until then, she had known little about politics that was practical. They taught her that churches represented already assembled political cells, waiting to be activated. They taught her that her little Valley community of La Joya wasn't isolated and powerless, because it could join with San Benito and Pharr and the other towns in the four Valley counties to get what was needed. They connected her with other plain citizens, like graying storekeeper Carmen Anaya, who had believed that because she spoke no English, her voice could never be heard in the United States.

By agreement, none of them ran for office. None became leaders, indispensable to the cause. They supported no candidates or party, but worked with politicians already in office. They learned to pack city meetings, to charter buses to Austin, to hound legislators, to register voters in alarming numbers just to make it very clear they had power. They dressed in skirts and heels and business suits, wore makeup, and learned to meet power brokers on an equal footing. "We need for our kids what Dallas and Houston are getting," they told millionaire H. Ross Perot. "Texas is third in per capita income and forty-eighth in education." Perot listened and later lobbied. They got it.

They established five priorities: jobs, health care, education, environment, and colonias—neighborhoods. They dumped on a federal plan to hand out relief funds after the 1983 freeze instead of using the same money to create jobs. "We don't want people on welfare," Ofelia explained to the delegation from Washington. "Women stand in lines for slabs of cheese the government gives us while their men wait in cars, embarrassed that they don't have work. Our kids will grow mouse ears. We want jobs, not cheese."

They won mandatory hospital care for indigents who before would either go over to Mexico or to a midwife or just die. To prove they could do it, they picked Las Milpas, a community south of McAllen that overflowed with mud and wastes whenever it rained, and muscled Hidalgo County into applying to the state for sewers. When a county commissioner claimed credit and held a ground-breaking ceremony without inviting them, 100 of them showed up anyway. He apologized.

For such efforts, Valley Interfaith has been accused of harassing officials. Letters in newspapers have stated that Ofelia de los Santos and others have trained in Libya, and a pamphlet circulating through the Valley suggested that Interfaith was fomenting mass riots. Its cover bore the silhouette of a Hasidic Jew, supposedly Alinsky.

"What about this?" Ofelia was asked in a meeting by a worried gardener. "Are we communists?"

"The dictionary," she answered, "says that word means 'community.' I don't know anything about Castro or Russia and I don't really care about them. I'm not interested in anybody's regime. I'm just interested in our community."

Heads nodded. "Look," she said, "everyone who comes here—senior citizens, condominium owners—forms associations to protect their interests. When we do it, they suddenly suspect us. They think they have something and we are trying to get it. We don't want what they have. We just want a decent quality life."

In Las Milpas, Carmen Anaya and Ofelia visit the family of Crescencio Rodríguez. They live in a two-room shed of a house—an uninsulated, bare wood frame covered with unrelated scraps of sheathing and metal roofing. Like the 150 other houses in their neighborhood, there is no plumbing or sewage. There is also no work; Crescencio's car died on the last trip to the Lubbock onion fields. He sometimes mixes plaster at a nearby snowbird subdivision, but $10 a day doesn't feed the seven of them. Why, he wonders, are U.S. companies putting maquiladoras across the river and not here? He's willing to work.

His question is fundamental. This is the United States, and that is Mexico, where the minimum wage is far below even the absurd ten dollars he earns for twelve hours of labor. But the privy in his yard could be in either country. "I can't conceive," Carmen Anaya says in eloquent Spanish, "that here in the most powerful nation on earth our kids have to sit in an outhouse. How can a rich country send kids through knee-deep mud to school? Is it just because they are brown? These are American children."

Crescencio bows his head. Behind him, his kids play on the backhoe that has miraculously appeared to dig real sewers at last. Valley Interfaith brought it, he knows, and now it plans to do the same for twenty-nine more Valley colonias. If there's any way he can help, he will.

A mile or so behind the backhoe is Mexico. As their work spreads across the Valley, as people learn to think and organize regionally, the reality of Mexico, always *right over there*, quietly poses a question. Does it somehow enter into their plan? Do all those people remain disenfranchised because an accident of birth located them on the south bank of a slow, shallow river? Is there a Mexican solution for them? Should the border really matter?

·   ·   ·

Along the very bottom of this lower Rio Grande Valley, a boy from Tamaulipas waits under a deciduous canopy until the Border Patrol plane flies by. The smooth, orange bark of the tepaguaje is pleasant to lean against; a nearby shaggy brasil tree yields handfuls of sweet purple berries. Bouquets of red and yellow Texas lantana grow near the river he crossed moments before. When he continues on his northward way, setting off the clacking of pearl-gray chachalaca birds, he follows a trail set down by the ancestors of the coyotes that watch him from the underbrush, which are in turn studied by a secretive jaguarundi.

These remaining original native brushlands, perhaps a hundred acres or so, lie within the boundaries of the two-thousand-acre Santa Ana Wildlife Refuge. Somewhere to the east, native Texas palms once lined the river so densely that when Alonso Alvarez de Pineda gave it its first Spanish name in 1519, he chose Río de las Palmas. Only two small groves remain, not far from the clay dunes of Boca Chica.

Here in Santa Ana, the allure is the sumptuous assortment of flora: guajillo, huisache, black mimosa, sugar hackberry, anaqua, fragrant coma, cedar elms draped in curtains of Spanish moss, and mesquite. But most special is the tiny-leafed Texas ebony.

These are probably dying. Since the river was dammed upstream, the natural flooding of the Rio Grande that refilled the resacas and fed the ebonies' roots no longer occurs. Refuge managers have con-

sidered irrigating the ebonies, but all the river's waters are allocated.

Along the Rio Grande, 98 percent of the native habitat is lost: cut, burned, and cleared for agriculture. Across the way, Mexico has followed the norteamericano example of turning all the land into fields, even as the United States realizes it shouldn't have.

The Valley's subtropical environment is home to an unusual number of species, like the ocelot, that occur nowhere else in North America. Now their borderlands ecosystem is fragmented into islands. Unable to roam, animals are forced to inbreed and have less genetic diversity for adapting to catastrophes. Development has cut across the migratory patterns of birds like the altamira oriole, to whom subtropics are essential stopovers between summer and winter. Residents of Weslaco and Pharr sometimes swamp the refuge's telephone line, panicked over thousands of Swainson's and broad-winged hawks circling overhead, looking for a place to spend the night. The refuge is overcrowded, sheltering red-lored parrots that should be two hundred miles south. Their tropical river systems have been cleared away by Mexico.

To rescue this delicate riparian centerline of the Valley, the Interior Department proposes a Corridor of Life—an unbroken, 180-mile belt that would be returned to brush, allowing terrestrial creatures movement and survival and birds a place to nest. It will mean purchasing land or arranging easements from farmers. It will mean convincing the Border Patrol, which regards any wilderness as a smuggler's sanctuary.

"It will mean a great deal of beauty," believes Nita Fuller, who manages Santa Ana, "and saving who knows how many ecosystems."

It could also mean income. White-wing doves, which hunters pay millions to massacre every season, thrive in places like Santa Ana. Even more lucrative is birdwatching: Borderlands naturalist Frederick Gehlbach has calculated that a hook-billed kite, nesting in Santa

Ana and seen by numbers of birders, is worth $23,005 of tourist revenue over a single season. The blue-wing teal that only one duck hunter shoots brings in just $3.29.

No one knows how wide the corridor will have to be to sustain the Valley's natural balance. Gehlbach argues for three miles; Fuller, dealing with the reality of budgets, prays for at least 100 meters. But all the naturalists agree on one thing: To maintain wildlife in perpetuity will mean involving Mexico. "And Mexico has trouble feeding its people," says Valley ornithologist Pauline Jones. "And we want them to grow our vegetables. How do we get them to place value on an indigo snake or an ebony tree?"

.   .   .

The Texas Tropical Trail, U.S. 83, rolls upriver through a green and yellow landscape to a remarkable spreading Texas ebony that anchors another waning tradition. The last hand-drawn ferry on the river links the farming villages of Los Ebanos, Texas, and San Miguel, Tamaulipas.

Along the way to Los Ebanos, signs warn of blowing dust. The east wind directs life here, hastening the journey westward. Trees and utility poles lean away from the distant Gulf; houses and silos seem to tilt slightly toward the west, and people even park their vehicles pointing that way.

Alberto Simo, wearing an overly creased, gray felt cowboy hat and a carpenter's pouch he uses for a change purse, collects twenty-five cents a head and $1.00 per vehicle for the ferry. The land here has been in his family since 1750. Ebony pods snap in the wind as cars roll, three at a time, down the dirt bank and onto the flat barge. Pulleys at either end of the craft link it to a steel cable that spans the river; four men with hands like tyrannosaurus rex grasp the stout length of hemp stretched between the banks and pull,

a hundred times a day. For thirty-two years, Carlos Flores has pulled; René García, eighteen years. Their daily salary is $2.00.

Nothing has changed for them, except that all around, land like Simo's rancho has been cleared for growing. Anastasio Solís, grizzled and snag-toothed, either makes $2.00 a day picking on the Mexican side or ten times that on the American. He was headed there to collect his pay for harvesting cucumbers when young Mike Van Hook, just a month out of the Border Patrol Academy, ran into him outside La Grulla.

Mike takes Anastasio down to the ferry, paying his quarter. His Spanish is still hesitant, but he and Anastasio call each other amigo as they shake hands and bid farewell. Carlos Flores slackens a pulley line, letting the boat's stern drift downstream a little so they can tack with the current as they heave.

On the other side, under another ebony, Mario Quito inspects the vehicles that have entered Mexico at this ancient ford, where Coahuiltecan Indians once crossed to collect salt at Salina del Rey, forty miles north. Quito and other customs officers take two-week turns here every seven months; it is not a favorite assignment. During the late sixties, when Gustavo Díaz Ordaz was Mexico's president, San Miguel tried to attract his attention and benevolence by changing its name to Ciudad Díaz Ordaz. But he never bothered to come; burro carts still battle the mud here.

"God himself has never bothered to come here," Quito declares. But the fields of brown-eyed Susans lining the dirt track to town belie his words, and even he softens when he considers them and listens to the thrill of the wind in the carrizo. He picks up a clod and pulverizes it in his hand. "This may be all dust," he tells an American who protests having to empty the contents of his station wagon, "but this dust is Mexico. *That* dust," he says, pointing back to Los Ebanos, "is the United States. This is still ours."

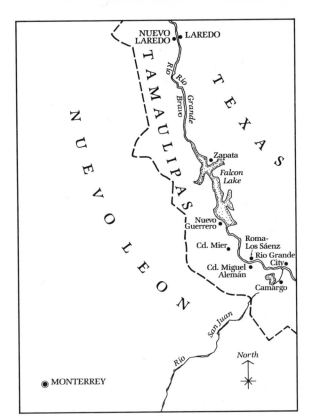

CHAPTER TWO

THE HILLS

In case Starr County, Texas, doesn't know it has a problem, there it is in the papers again. This time it's a series in the *Houston Chronicle* headlined: "Drugs and Murder in Starr County: 'You never know when or where. . . .' "

Which wouldn't be so bad, because the rest of Texas, where no one has ever been known to sin, has been smugly taking potshots at Starr County forever. But the critical blow comes that same week from the *Wall Street Journal*: "Drug Haven—Secluded Texas County Is Smuggler's Paradise."

This couldn't happen at a worse time. With unemployment over 20 percent, Starr County is trying to attract industry. It also needs to sell bonds, quickly, because the attorney general just discovered that the county has been illegally borrowing to meet operating expenses for years. But now, who will want them? And when industry's national house organ convicts them on the front page, who's going to move his factory here?

At LaBorde House, Rio Grande City's stately turn-of-the-century hotel, manager Rosa María Sánchez frets over the cancellations since the articles appeared. Over at old Fort Ringgold, where the Rio Grande City Schools have offices in the garrison Zachary Taylor established during the war with Mexico, administrator R. C. Salinas grows darkly indignant over the latest insult. He drafts a resolution for his Rotary Club condemning the articles. "The *Wall Street Journal*," he states, "drew irresponsible conclusions from facts that have more than one explanation. They say the huge increases in bank deposits here come from Mexican drug money, but we know the bulk of it is really Mexican businessmen exporting their cash to border banks. I challenge them to prove I'm wrong."

The articles advance a vicious kind of hatred, he believes, that distresses him even more than narcotics. "This is the one county where Hispanics are totally in control: politically, economically, and socially. The press in the Valley is always out to get us. Drugs and murder exist, without a doubt, but they kill people in McAllen too."

Rio Grande City, laden with historic architecture, overlooks the river at the beginning of the border's gradual ascent toward distant western mountains. Past Los Ebanos, the semitropics turn to semiarid brush country. A gradual ripple in the landscape becomes a series of long slopes. At Camargo, Tamaulipas, opposite Rio Grande City, the first bona fide hill of the West rises above the confluence of the Ríos Bravo and San Juan. Like a desert acropolis, atop it stand the ghostly structures of Villa Nueva, built of local sandstone by merchants when floods submerged Camargo's commercial district in 1848.

The dry soil has never served well for farming, and cattle provide income for only limited numbers. To the east of Rio Grande City, the Anglo developers who brought the rails to communities like Harlingen and McAllen expanded their vision to create thriving winter tourist and retirement industries. To the west, Zapata County gained Falcon Lake, a reservoir on the Rio Grande built jointly in the 1950s by Mexico and the United States, which attracts pleasure boaters and anglers. Starr County is stuck in the middle with nothing but mesquite thickets. Pete Díaz, Jr., a local citizen whose shopping center developments earned him the billing of "the nation's second most successful Hispanic businessman," owns a nine-hole golf course here along the Rio Grande and dreams of putting in another nine across the river. Golfers would drive over the international bridge, conveniently on his property, and could choose between an American-style clubhouse on the front nine and an after-hours Mexican cantina adjacent to the eighteenth green. Díaz envisions tournaments headlined by the likes of Lee Treviño, but so far he's found no investors willing to risk coming here. With its only asset its proximity to Mexico, Starr County's mainstay historically has been "mercancía noble"—contraband.

In the beginning, goods went in the other direction. Steamboats arrived here for the Confederacy's cotton, and much of it never made it to Bagdad. At Davis Landing, later named Rio Grande City, it was diverted into Mexico. The "Gold Coast"—the stretch between Roma and Rio Grande City where today's drug tycoons build opulent Spanish-style ranch homes—was first described by William Emory, who surveyed the border in the 1850s. He was at a loss to explain how the area's wretched economy could support "such fine residences."

Comparatively little of the alleged narco-emporium's spoils remain in Camargo. Set eight kilometers in from the river, with one of the border's most handsome plazas, Camargo is inordinately peaceful. At night, the white presidencia municipal is bathed softly in the national colors by red, white, and green floodlights. Very little occurs here, policemen insist pointedly. It's quiet. Their presence, they say, and arrangements with contrabandistas to have certain products detour clear of town, keep it tranquil.

For there is tradition to maintain. Camargo is the oldest town on the lower river boundary, founded by New Spain nearly thirty years before the United States declared independence. General José de Escandón was sent to create the new province, two centuries after the shipwrecked explorer Cabeza de Vaca had trudged through these lands and reported their existence to the viceroy. The aridity reminded Escandón of his native provincia of Santander, so Nuevo Santander it became. Its first villas, Camargo, Reynosa, and Laredo, took the names of cities of his homeland. The mouth of the Río Bravo was too swampy to colonize, but years later thirteen Camargo families, sensing its significance, founded the port of Refugio. After independence it became Matamoros.

Escandón issued a call for homesteaders. Seven hundred families responded. Many came from mining cities of the north like Monterrey and Monclova. Often, these frontier people were Spanish Jews who had escaped the Inquisition through conversion, feigned or actual. Tacitly excluded from the inner ranks of Mexico City society, they went north, where they found the ores that eventually established Monterrey as Mexico's financial capital. Among Escandón's families were descendants of Jews named Ben David who became Benavides, or Rodríguez shorted to Ríos, or Treviño or Garza. When they reached the mouth of the San Juan, Don Blas María de la Garza was already there. To him, Escandón bequeathed the official act in the name of the king, and Camargo was born.

Within three generations, the priests of Nuevo Santander had quashed the clandestine Hebrew practices, which they discovered by interrogating children about their home life. But one tradition by which Jews had long survived—marrying among their kind—died slowly. Not until the late 1850s did any mestizaje—breeding with Indians—take place in Escandón's first colony.

During the previous decade, however, an unprecedented matrimony had occurred. An American mercenary named Henry Clay Davis tarried behind while his platoon crossed into Mexico, chasing filibusterers who sometimes raided the newly annexed North American state of Texas. The object of Davis's distraction was Ilania de la Garza, whose father had title to Camargo's opposite bank. He married her and moved onto his father-in-law's land. R. C. Salinas, whose wife is a Garza descendant, notes with pride that Rio Grande City, née Davis Landing, was thus the first community in the nation founded by a binational, bicultural, bilingual couple—the first true border city.

Only it never became a city—at least not for long. Rio Grande City incorporated in 1927 but promptly went bankrupt in the Depression. Since then, voters have rejected incorporation, defeating it seven to one the last time around. Having a city would mean city taxes, which nobody wants to pay. Thus Starr County is in the peculiar position of having a county seat that isn't a legal entity. Instead, it's the largest unincorporated population center in Texas.

No incorporation means no police force and requires the county to provide basic city services. Without much tax base, the judge who administers the county arrived at a simple method: borrow. As a judge, he was supposed to know that Texas law forbids this. This, worries Salinas, only encourages the thinly veiled racism that suggests Hispanics can't run anything right.

The roots of such endemic civic disorder are easily explained by history, he suggests. After centuries, impoverished Mexicans have learned that more government just brings more sorrow. They are more apt to seek support from their relatives than from a bureaucracy. But governance by extended family structure also provides the framework on which Starr County has pilloried itself, because loyalty to kin becomes the highest moral code. Certain activities are justified if there is need. And needs grow. They expand until, at one imperceptible point, they distort into greed. *You either eat or you don't eat. You have a family, man, and like what if there's nothing to eat?*

. . . make megabucks instead of picking cantaloupes.

We go out, you know, I'm sure everybody knows, and have friends whose parents are pushing. Their fathers deal. You go to their uncle's house and you see it there. But you're not going to squeal on your own family members.

Say you're about forty-five and you're unemployed. What can you do? You can't go back to college. You can't get a job here. The odds are against you. And then one of your compadres comes in and offers you to do this or that. You go along with him. Like he says, either eat or don't eat.

The most crucial part of protecting our country is the border. But because we have $35 million worth of trade with Mexico, Washington says be nice to Mexico. Don't waste time, hurry their vegetable trucks through because Mexico feeds us. But Latin perfidy and values, or lack of values, pervade this place.

The voice of the Rattlers. Rio Grande High School is

not a ghetto school. It is nearly new, with carpeted floors, 21,000 volumes in its library, its walls bright with the school colors. There's excitement over football. The Rattlers are undefeated going into a critical game against Brownsville. Several hundred townspeople will accompany the team into the Valley Friday night.

"What are we?"

"Winners!"

Not a pep rally, but a psychology class. The teacher has them shout it out at the beginning of the hour; she doesn't want them to think of themselves as losers, stuck in an immobile life style. But today the class discusses the Journal *and* Chronicle *articles. How does it affect their self-images when this is what the world thinks of them? How do the football players like it when, every time they win, their opponent's rooters jeer that they're all on cocaine?*

Ken Miley worked Starr County from '63 to '70. He came back in '81 and it was worse than ever. Now he is special agent in charge of the Drug Enforcement Agency, housed in a prefab, aluminum-clad building across the street from McAllen's airfield and all the DC-3s. In a blazer, gray slacks, and rep tie, Miley is an impeccable civil servant. His wood-paneled office has law enforcement certificates on the walls and a rack containing antique Winchesters and sawed-off shotguns. The wind pounds the metal roof continually. And every day things seem a little worse.

They make us sound like Russians or something. Stereotyping us. We're all taking the blame for something that only a few . . .

Why get mad? It's the truth.

It can't all be true.

Everything they said about us is true. You say no, no, but deep down you know it's true. They just exaggerated the percent. You know that part where they talk about marijuana growing along the road where seeds drop from the trucks? It's there. You just have to know where to look.

Yeah, just stand on my porch and look.

We see their houses. We have intelligence on all of them, but we don't have manpower for surveillance, and it takes specific information knowing that an event will occur. We bust our asses all year long, pay taxes, live on borrowed money. These people build huge houses and pay no taxes.

You walk into someone's house and it looks real crappy but then you notice all the VCRs, the wide screen TVs . . .

Like where I live there isn't even a paved road, but the neighbors have $95,000 homes and new cars they pay for in cash. I know . . .

My little brother went home and told my mother, he's got boots, and a belt, and a hat, and they all match his car. My grandfather was going to refuse to let me marry him if he found out in any way that they were involved in drugs.

What about your millionaire cousin who's never been caught?

Well, they've covered their eyes to it. They never let the rest of us know that he was involved for the longest time. It wasn't until I was a junior that I figured it out. My grandfather says as long as he doesn't bring it close to him. But he won't accept any money from him. None of us will.

. . . increased enforcement in the Caribbean, so Texas has become the alternate route. The trails have existed here for hundreds of years. The same families are still smuggling. They don't care what the merchandise is. Contraband is contraband.

There's a lag time for enforcement to move here. Planes are flying overhead, and we have no radar. The Department of Defense will tell you that the U.S. is secured from invasion by enemy aircraft. That bill of goods means 500–600 mph at twenty thousand feet. Meanwhile, smugglers in two-engine jobs putt-putt back and forth all day long at 125 mph. We're riding jackasses in a jet age. The traffickers have us outspent, outmanned, outequipped, and outgunned. They can go out tomorrow and buy radar without all the bureaucratic red tape.

What would you think if you were a stranger and

you came on a Saturday and you saw kids cruising in limos? Then you see a Continental. Go out in the parking lot, look at the teachers' cars, look at the students' cars. Teachers with their little Volkswagens. Students with Lincoln town cars. In Roma, a couple of kids in the eighth grade got Cadillacs. And every car in the lot has a pistol, a rifle, a bat.

On Saturday nights, in lots of cars you'll find they have an Uzi, an automatic weapon, magnums. And super-dark-tinted windows. Like if someone is coming to talk to you, you can see him but he cannot see how many you have in the car. You're preparing. In Rio Grande City, tinted windows are a weapon.

Take Rio Grande City. There's a stash on the Mexican side that needs to cross. They'll need mules to cross it, lookouts, skilled people to listen to radio scanners, people to drive trucks. So they find some twenty-year-old kids who're doing nothing Saturday night and who want to make $1,000 driving a truck from the river to town. They're all unemployed, but after two weeks they're buying pickups and ostrich-skin cowboy boots with matching belts. Pretty soon there's money all around town. The car dealers are selling trucks, gas sales go up, so do groceries and clothes. The bank deposits are up—but no one says anything. And no taxes are paid. It creates a false economy. You'd think a community would take a stand, but I don't see it happening. They talk about the problem but don't want to lose the bucks that come from it.

. . . no university, no industry. But you know what? I'll bet twenty years ago our parents said they were leaving too. And only about half of them did. It'll be the same with us. You miss your people, man.

You can't do anything about it. It's like if a brother's going to get his younger brother into it, it just keeps on going. That's the way you're brought up. It just keeps going down the family, and if you ever say anything about it, believe me you won't have breakfast in the morning. You'll be at the funeral home. And nobody will question it.

. . . They make us believe it's our only alternative. Some parents, yeah, but other parents they say it's going to be drugs or you're going to stay here and work carrying out groceries all your life.

. . . get caught they say oh, you'll only serve one-tenth. Behave, we'll get you out. We'll get you out in about seven years, but you'll make a million while you're in.

Everyone who gets out of jail gets back into the business. No one quits. Even the ones out on bail are still in. Law enforcement isn't the answer. Moral fiber of the family is—when that exists we'll see a decrease. People ask if I need more manpower. If they double us, they'll have to double the prosecutors, then double the judges, then build more courthouses. Then build more jails. Right now, judges can't give long sentences because the jails are too full. Mandatory jail would be good. Instead, they hear that pushing gets probation the first time.

. . . cousin shot and stabbed to death. Another one— he got operated on last week. His bladder and I don't know what else. It was drug dealing. And I have an uncle accused of killing another guy near our ranch.

People like it here. They like the way it is, they don't want any industry. That'll ruin everything.

. . . They write their own ten commandments. Like, there's a commandment that says thou shalt not kill? Theirs is 'Thou shalt kill.' Thou shalt not steal? 'I shall steal if I need to.' All the opposite.

"Without citing the county, I can say I know of county commissioners who are narcotic traffickers. Narco-dollars go to run political campaigns—*high* political campaigns. Up to the federal level. When you encounter government corruption, a personal decision has to be made. You stop, back out, don't say anything. I've been faced with it. We're dealing with government priorities. If terrorism is a bigger priority, then narcotics takes a back seat. Narcotics takes a back seat to a lot of U.S. intelligence spook work."

Does this suggest that operations like the CIA are

involved with drug traffickers to get access to other information?

Miley's face reddens with disgust. "The U.S. is powerful and intelligent enough to do whatever it wants about any situation. It puts men on the moon. Looking at the big picture, yes, we can assume that the United States has its reasons for letting these things occur."

The teacher: "We're all involved because we let them get away with it. We close our eyes to it, and because we do, we're to blame too." She stops, looks hard at her desktop. "I mean it, all of us." She stops again. "I mean, in my own family . . ."

The students are quiet, extremely respectful. They know.

The principal: "Good things happen here too. We had a student graduate from Yale in English, who studied summers at Cambridge. The parents don't even speak English. But we lose the upwardly mobile ones to San Antonio, Dallas, McAllen. We don't lose the rural poverty. Rural America has strong religious values, but the spiritual background of rural America isn't found here. The priests have been lackadaisical. Education is the only hope to get out of the poverty cycle and maybe out of drugs. The church isn't doing it. The community isn't doing it. School's the only chance."

.   .   .

The land continues to rise. Fifteen miles west, Roma sits above the river. Until Falcon Dam stopped the flooding, Rio Grande City and Camargo couldn't maintain a bridge. But Roma and its counterpart, Ciudad Miguel Alemán, rest on a fifty-foot sandstone outcrop. A grand suspension bridge, the only one on the border, safely spans the highest flow of the river. For that reason, San Pedro de Roma—now Ciudad Miguel Alemán—became an important customs headquarters, eclipsing Camargo. The merchants of the desert acropolis took their stores upriver.

Ciudad Miguel Alemán adopted its new name to honor the president who constructed highways to the northern border in the late forties. Miguel Alemán had predicted that tourism would be Mexico's postwar bonanza. Besides new roads to entice American motorists, he gambled that a Mexican Riviera would one day outpull Cuba and other Caribbean beach getaways. To show his great faith, he developed his idea on land he purchased himself, risking his own investment with his country's future. He named the bayside resort after the fishing village at its nucleus: Acapulco.

Roma-Los Sáenz: The awkward hyphenation appears on maps but not in the local idiom. Roma is how the town is called, named by missionaries because its surroundings resembled Rome's seven hills. Los Sáenz were ranchers already living on the northern river bluffs when Escandón parceled out the lands here in 1767, and the town's old blood is descended from them. Untouched by the rising river, Roma nevertheless watermarks its history by referring to waves that periodically washed in: European entrepreneurs in 1848, after Roma was forever divided from Mexico; moneyed Mexicans in 1910, escaping the revolution; Mexican peasants in the 1940s, entering as braceros to harvest while American farmers fought abroad; Mexicans again in the 1970s, fleeing poverty.

The waves lapped against, but left intact, Roma's brick Spanish buildings. From their wrought-iron balconies, generations have watched these waves roll across the town and recede, never really increasing the population as people evaporated northward. Heat and isolation preserve the beauty of Roma's plaza from threats of investment and change.

This week, Roma's *South Texas Reporter* analyzes the recent articles that have Starr County residents so irate. The emphasis, the editorial reads, leaves the unfair impression that everyone feasts off drugs. Citizens deny the accusations, deny saying what reporters say they said.

A former civil official shakes his head. He has been privy to certain things on both sides of the line. Despite everything argued to the contrary, he has seen that Mexico is organized to push drugs and the United States is organized to receive them. If it brings money to town, the people concerned don't see anything wrong with it. In Mexico, for a long time it simply happened through the government, everyone up the line taking his cut.

But that has changed. Mexico, he has come to believe, has narcotics enforcement agencies headed by drug kings themselves. And recently, some of the families have gotten too flamboyant. They've had to be wiped out. The status quo has been shaken. When people like Rafael Caro Quintero, assassin of the U.S. drug agent Camarena, tumbled in Guadalajara, everyone else started to tumble too, because everyone is related to everyone else. Currently, there is chaos; people—some his business clients—are hiding right now, their lives in danger. Two weeks before, three thousand federales were combing the countryside between here and Ciudad Mier, looking for certain individuals who hadn't been paying their full quotas.

Outside his office, the incandescence of summer has passed. Today is Halloween; in Ciudad Miguel Alemán, tomorrow is the Day of the Dead. Jack-o'-lanterns replacing candy skulls raise new fears among Mexicans that their culture is being usurped by the greater advertising power to the north. But in these boundary cities, both occasions are observed in both places. In goblin masks from the Roma MiniMax, children from each side trick-or-treat the cars waiting in line at the international bridge, whose back seats overflow with chrysanthemums purchased from Miguel Alemán fruit markets.

On Día de los Muertos, Ovidio Argüello, a squat Mexican customs lieutenant, joins the people arriving at the municipal cemetery with brooms and pails. He hires a boy to scrub the elaborate memorial to his daughter Juanita, who died last year in a Rio Grande City hospital. Not an accident, it grieves him to say, but an overdose. "The accident was mine. She had a boyfriend. I had sent her to school to learn English in Houston, not to have boyfriends. I had prohibited it. She was just fifteen. Now there is nothing to embrace but death."

He is proud of her marble tomb, with its hand-carved image of La Virgen de San Juan del Lago. After the roses and gladiolas are arranged, he fills a glass of water to nourish his daughter's spirit and stoops to place it on the grave.

His niece and mother-in-law accompany him to the cemetery, but his wife cannot. She is recuperating from a highway accident that shattered her legs and killed his brother. They were on their way to the wedding of another brother in Veracruz. "Happiness and sorrow," he murmurs, rubbing his sagging jowl, "are always companions. Here, we celebrate them alike."

It has been a breathless year for him. Following Juanita's tragedy, Sr. Argüello took his señora to Europe. That was a happy time, but then came his brother's death. Now he spends this afternoon in his home in Colonia Argüello, the subdivision he has developed. He looks through a fat scrapbook of pictures from Rome, the Vatican, Capri, Monte Carlo. Here they are in Paris, in front of the gleaming bus in which they rode around the continent with other couples from Latin America. In Scotland, he was photographed wearing a tam o'shanter; at the London Zoo, he hoisted his bulk onto a camel. And this picture is either France or Madrid.

In the living room hangs a painting of Juanita in a folkloric ballet costume, the regional dress of the southern state of Chiapas. Twenty-nine years ago he was transferred to the northern border from their native Chiapas, where his wife grew up two blocks from Guatemala. Immobile in her wheelchair, she recalls Day of the Dead there, when people took picnics of banana-leaf tamales and bread of the dead to the cemetery and then toasted the departed with beer, fireworks, and mariachis. Customs work on the

PLATE 1

Lorenzo Rivera Salazar, Jaime Garza Salinas, and Daniel Maldonado Núñez,
artists, Matamoros, Tamaulipas

PLATE 2
Sebastián Domínguez Sylván, Jorge Luis Pérez, Eusebio Dragustinovis Rodríguez,
and Antonio Lara Verdejas, shrimpers, Brownsville, Texas

PLATE 3
TRIO ASTRAL: ASCENSIÓN RODRÍGUEZ, MIGUEL AVILA, AND JOSÉ LUIS ELIZONDO, PHARR, TEXAS

PLATE 4
SISTER NORMA PIMENTEL, SISTER NINFA GARZA, AND CENTRAL AMERICAN REFUGEE FAMILY,
CASA OSCAR ROMERO, SAN BENITO, TEXAS

PLATE 5
CHURCHES, PLAZA DE ARMAS, REYNOSA, TAMAULIPAS

PLATE 6
RODRÍGUEZ FAMILY, LAS MILPAS, TEXAS

PLATE 7
CALLE HIDALGO, REYNOSA, TAMAULIPAS

PLATE 8
AGENTS LARRY DALTON, ELVIN HARMON, ROGELIO MARTÍNEZ, DOMINGO SÁNCHEZ, AND FABIÁN CASAS,
U.S. BORDER PATROL, RIO GRANDE CITY, TEXAS

PLATE 9
VEGETABLE PICKERS, ESPARZA FARMS, EL RANCHITO, TEXAS

PLATE 10

ROMELIA CHÁVEZ, OVIDIO ARGÜELLO, AND ROSELIA RAMÍREZ AT THE TOMB OF JUANITA ARGÜELLO,
DÍA DE LOS MUERTOS, CIUDAD MIGUEL ALEMÁN, TAMAULIPAS

PLATE 11
CASIMIRO BARRERA, CIUDAD MIER, TAMAULIPAS

PLATE 12

COUNCILMAN JOSÉ VALDEZ AND FAMILY, LAREDO, TEXAS

northern border has been good to them; they have their home, their ranch with cattle and thorough-breds, but she misses the traditions. Here everything is all right, just simpler.

Sr. Argüello understands. When she can get around, he'll take her away for awhile to their house in Puerto Vallarta. That will be better. It's been a very difficult year.

. . .

A buttermilk sky gathers above Ciudad Mier, where there is no bridge, no furious exchange of movement over the mythical line that by distant agreement follows the deepest part of the riverbed. Merely fifteen kilometers from the commercial clutter of Miguel Alemán, Mier's quiet streets receive few touring foreigners. A protective semicircle of agriculture—melons and grains—surrounds Mier, cloaking its changelessness.

It is isolated enough to resemble a pueblo in Mexico's interior. In the afternoon, its sandstone plazas echo with the slap-slap of women making tortillas. Mier's narrow sidewalks barely separate the low, block buildings from the streets, which run like canals through painted stucco neighborhoods.

During the years when the border was taking shape, when Texas had declared independence but the northern and southern United States could not yet agree whether to annex it, an incident here brought shame on both Mexico and the Republic of Texas. For six years the two countries had been in a technical state of war, although few actual skirmishes had occurred. Then, in 1842, each suspected the other of plotting aggression: Mexico to recapture Texas, Texas to claim territory even south of the disputed Rio Grande.

Texas President Sam Houston sent an expeditionary force to the river to assess the Mexican strength. What they saw was sufficient to warrant turning back, but nearly half the troops refused. They had come to fight Mexicans and wouldn't be denied. Under one Colonel William Fisher, they crossed near Roma and marched on Mier. Just as his few hundred men had nearly defeated two thousand Mexican regulars by hacking their way into the homes of the townspeople for cover, Fisher was induced to surrender by a flagrant ruse. A minor wound had dazed his mind and drained his courage, and his men, to their angry bewilderment, found themselves in irons.

They were paraded through the lower river towns on their way to prison. Humiliated, they succeeded in escaping. But the desert slowed them, and they were recaptured on their way north and imprisoned, again in Mier.

This time, Santa Anna decided, Texan marauders would not bother them again. He did not slaughter them all, as he had done to 365 prisoners two weeks after the Alamo at Goliad, Texas. Instead, he ordered a clay jar filled with 159 white beans and 17 black ones. Each captive had to select his fate. White meant life, black meant execution. Tipped by guards, at least one knew to save himself by testing for texture—black was smooth. Chained together in twos, they hobbled up and drew. Seventeen chanced to select death and were slain that afternoon.

On the sidewalk alongside Mier's secondary school, eighty-year-old Casimiro Barrera warms himself in the sunshine, in a straight-backed wooden chair. He is a round man with a belly like a boxer, bald except for a few wisps that stand straight up, and has large, kind ears. Educated through correspondence courses all his life, he is Mier's best-read citizen. To several generations of students who borrow his books, he has indicated where, just down the street, the fateful beans were drawn.

Mier, he tells them, has suffered few traumatic invasions since. In 1882, as the last of the steamboat traffic succumbed to the railroad's arrival upriver at Laredo, something did happen. A boat arrived from Europe carrying—no one recalls what. A stevedore opened a crate, and suddenly "fever spread like an ink stain, from here through Roma and Camargo and beyond. It was bubonic plague, and the dockworker was the first to die. In the cemetery here in Mier is a special section for victims. The doctors say never to open those graves. After a hundred years they could still be contagious."

Thirty years later, the Mexican Revolution touched here briefly. A platoon of the northern general Carranza came for provisions and engaged a force led by town merchants, who feared they would be sacked. The dead, mainly bystanders, included the town's violinist, Casimiro Barrera's father.

"Since then, nothing significant."

The afternoon dims, and Casimiro takes his chair and book indoors. The buttermilk sky has homogenized and emptied. In the approaching twilight, this most beautiful of border towns demonstrates how the pastel tones of a Mexican city truly succeed. The houses, simple block structures, are separated from each other only by color changes. A blue house, a yellow, a green, like paints next to each other in a box of watercolors, balance the sky, which becomes another, greater pastel block superimposed on them. Together they complete an understated spectrum, connecting townscape with land and sky in a way that most architects despair of achieving.

The tranquility of Mier becomes its bridge, spanning the breach between foreignness and fondness. In their mutual rush toward the future, the two societies that encompass it neglect to pass by here. Elsewhere, they bristle with irritation rather than accompany each other as friends. Calm within their winds, Mier's border is with the heavens.

For years, Casimiro Barrera worked as an electrician, and when the United States and Mexico built Falcon Dam, he was there to install the turbines. Zapata, Texas, was moved to make way for the new lake and is now a commercial strip for sportsmen. Equally characterless is Nuevo Guerrero, across the water, lacking both the charm of old Mexico and modern amenities to make up for it. A new resort under construction is intended to fix that. Surrounding its entire forty acres, stonemasons raise a stuccoed wall that contains no stone. The blocks are the casings of auto batteries, junked in the United States and recycled in Mexico.

Along the shore below, cows trail down to the water through stands of thorn acacia, and fishermen set out gill nets for black bass and catfish. Nuevo Guerrero replaces the drowned Viejo Guerrero, which has begun to make a comeback as increased irrigation draws down the lake. First a church spire appeared, then some houses, and finally an entire street. At that point, a few nostalgic squatters returned; their fate depends on melting snows in the distant Rocky Mountains.

On summer evenings, lightning often appears over the lake. The air doesn't cool, but dries as the humidity is sucked into the big, dense, waiting clouds. Moisture rears back, as if to finally crash into the land. The wind builds, and whitecaps and patches of gray appear on the water's surface. But no rain falls; in the morning the clouds disappear, and dampness once again seeps into the leaden air.

After sunset, boats cross the lake, carrying contraband to trucks waiting along its long, unpatrollable shoreline. Men slip past the gate on the unguarded bridge to smuggle racehorses and cattle past checkpoints on the fever tick line. In the Falcon Woodlands, a grove of preserved, upper-Valley native brush, brown jays rustle in their only North American nesting area. Peregrine falcons and Harris hawks stalk pocket mice in the mesquite, and whitetail deer snuggle in the buffelgrass. As much as it ever does, the border settles in for the night.

. . .

Mexico had barely become a nation before it ran into problems in its northern province of Texas. Part of the trouble was geographic: Texas was too far from Mexico City. Part was political: From both the Spaniards and the Aztecs, Mexico inherited an addiction to centralized rule it has yet to shake. Atop both those ancestral hierarchies was God himself, an authority difficult to dispute. Moctezuma ruled from a position of semidivinity, and the dominion of Spanish kings derived, in no small part, from a spiritual and financial agreement with Rome. Mexico eventually loosened its ties to the church, but the custom of deferring authority to the highest possible power continued. Decisions affecting hinterlands like Texas were distorted by the time lag to Mexico City, whose politicians had little sense of what was going on out there.

The third part was racial. The year before Mexico gained independence, Spain had decided that Texas must be populated immediately, lest the aggressive young United States of America press its expansive interests farther westward. The problem was finding inhabitants able to survive the Comanches, who had other ideas about whose land it was. A deal was struck with one Moses Austin of Missouri, who promised, in exchange for land at ten cents an acre, to bring colonists who would swear allegiance to Spain and to the Catholic church.

Before any of this occurred, both Moses Austin and Spanish rule in America were dead. But Austin's son Stephen exacted a similar arrangement with the new Mexican government. By 1830, Anglo colonists in Texas outnumbered native Mexicans four to one, and the alarmed government outlawed further immigration from the United States. Most immigrants were Catholic in name only; few learned Spanish, and they tended to equally despise—indeed, not distinguish between—Mexicans and Indians.

And they were increasingly aggravated with Mexican rule. Texas was appended to the state of Coahuila, so legal matters had to be satisfied hundreds of miles away in Saltillo, the capital. Later that didn't matter anyway, because centralism had nullified states' autonomy. But the most serious irritation for Texans concerned slaves.

Mexico outlawed slavery soon after winning independence in 1822. Texans competed with the American South to produce cotton—how could they do so without slaves? They suspected that Mexico simply wanted to discourage more Americans from coming. Stephen Austin tried to convince Mexico City to exempt Texas from emancipation. Strangely, the opposite occurred: Someone convinced Austin that slavery meant disaster, because Negroes were alleged to reproduce so fast they would one day overrun them.

His fellow colonists were unconcerned about being a racial minority someday. Embittered by President Santa Anna's dictatorship, Austin reverted to agreeing with them. Texas needed to remain Texas, whatever it took: namely, slaves for the economy and rejecting totalitarianism for freedom.

One hundred years later, memorials were unveiled at San Antonio's Alamo, honoring men who died in the "cradle of Texas liberty." It is true that Mexico had no chance of holding a region so physically and culturally distant. But the plaques and legends omit that Texans died partly for the freedom to keep other men in bondage. For eight years, the United States would refuse to annex Texas, because another slave state would upset the North-South deadlock then in effect.

Desire for territory and the prospect of Texan-European alliances eventually subdued that concern. James Knox Polk campaigned for the presidency in 1844 on a platform that included Texas—actually, it included everything to the Pacific. Two years later, he sent Zachary Taylor to the north bank of the Rio Grande, knowing that Mexico still claimed it. His only miscalculation in forcing manifest destiny was that Taylor became so popular that Polk lost his personal mandate and withdrew from the 1848 elections rather than face him. Everything else, he won.

.　　.　　.

From 1836 to 1845, the years between Texas's independence and annexation, its southern border was unclear. Mexico refused to recognize the new republic to the north. For its part, Texas wasn't sure whether it reached to the Rio Grande or the Nueces, which enters the Gulf at Corpus Christi. It kept hoping the United States would annex it and decide the issue. Laredo, Escandón's original community on the Rio Grande's north bank, was so Spanish that it had barely gone along with Mexico's independence. When Texas broke away, Laredo simply didn't.

Texas didn't really notice, either, until 1840 when the states of Tamaulipas, Nuevo León, and Coahuila tried to secede from Mexico. A Republic of the Rio Grande was declared, with Laredo its capital. It lasted just over nine months. The republic's only competent commander, Antonio Zapata, was captured and decapitated, and his head was pickled in brandy and displayed on a spike. At the end of the sad affair, Texas claimed the river and Laredo, and eventually named the territory just east of it Zapata County, for the only hero the Rio Grande Republic had time to produce.

Laredo today is testing a concept that only got it into trouble in the past: representative government. When the United States won the war against Mexico, many Laredoans weren't interested in North American democracy and crossed the river, founding Nuevo Laredo. In the 1880s, the railroad appeared, bringing prosperity, and two political parties formed on the U.S. side, the Botas (boots) and Huaraches (sandals). They used identical tactics to convince voters: booze, prostitutes, and gambling booths erected on San Augustín Plaza, in the shadow of the forlorn adobe capitol of the Republic of the Rio Grande. City council elections in 1886 ended in gunfire, leaving seventeen dead. At that point, an Anglo sheep rancher named Raymond Martin, who had married into a blue-blooded Escandón family, somehow emerged as a voice of reason. Power gravitated toward him; ninety years later, his descendants still held it.

In 1978, Martin's dynastic Independent party finally toppled. Enthroned as mayor for the previous twenty-four years, his grandson J. C. Martin was convicted of a scheme that channeled millions into the Laredo street department while, mysteriously, no streets were ever paved. J. C. liked to dwell publicly on the feudal nature of Laredo politics, about how he could manipulate eight thousand votes here, ten thousand there. His sentence was sixty weekends in prison. Every Friday, a doctor pronounced him dangerously ill, allowing him to serve his time in a suite at Laredo's Mercy Medical Center.

With J. C. gone, there's such democracy now that the town turns out for council meetings, because they're better and cheaper than the movies. Folks cheer the assistant district attorney known as Rambo Ríos—who fancies wearing guns in public—when he tries outshouting the city attorney on a point no one can discern because their microphones are feeding back on each other. The mayor, an Italian sunglasses baron in this 90-percent-plus Hispanic community, mumbles for order into his own mike, but people either don't pay attention or can't understand him. After J. C. Martin, he is regarded with great affection, but the local joke is that he is inarticulate in three languages. He is sometimes heard to declare that international traffic has reached the point that Laredo needs "a t'urd bridge."

Seven Hispanic councilmen try to interpret what the full-blooded Irish city attorney is sputtering, but his brogue thickens when he's riled. Normal citizens address the meeting in either of the most common working languages, Spanish or English, and no translators are required, not even for the press, which is *very* present. Feuds between old Laredo families and new Laredo money escalated into journalism wars to capture public approval. For a city of ninety-eight thousand, Laredo is spectacularly overcovered. Reporters from two daily English-language papers, three network TV stations, and a dial bloated with AM and FM crawl around the meeting's periphery. Tape recorders beep, notebooks drop . . .

". . . all that was missing were the Chinese. But they're coming." Laredo's mayor has just been to Taiwan, as the guest of Nationalist China. Now he has returned the invitation. "They told him that was protocol, and he thought it was a disease, like AIDS."

Councilman José Valdez stayed up until 1:30 A.M., hacking through the agenda. He laughs about the mayor, but he isn't amused about the Chinese. "The Taiwanese intend to set up maquiladoras in Mexico, have their offices on this side and call themselves U.S. companies. Supposedly, that way they're not hurting the U.S. balance of trade. Now why the hell should we be helping them? Ask the mayor."

José Valdez is in his forties. His thick moustache and hair, which reaches to the collar of his denim work shirt, are graying. His eyes are rimmed red from the marathon council session, and his head hurts from pondering how to turn Laredo into a manufacturing center, because hourly peso devaluations have rocked the Mexican trade it once thrived on.

The same keening is heard all along the border, but especially here. Until 1982, when Mexico's borrowing coagulated its oil-based economy, Laredo could make a good claim for being North America's capital of capitalism, regardless of what Wall Street believed. Manhattan, Los Angeles, even Hong Kong, they say— none could touch the sales-per-square-foot of this, Mexico's one-stop appliance center. An upwardly mobile clientele from Monterrey, 150 miles south, routinely drove up to spend a few thousand. Mexico City is close enough that the American Embassy shuttles a truck up here for its mail, and before the crisis wealthy capitalinos often sent their servants with shopping lists. Consumers clogged both Laredo bridges, and fleets of unmarked aircraft shipped its goods south.

Not all the money in Mexico is gone; a few transports still haul digital watches by the metric ton down U.S. 83 each day to McAllen Aviation. But what frustrates Councilman Valdez is that few of the profits reach nine-tenths of Laredo's population, the very Hispanics who founded the place.

Visiting Laredo's commercial district is a little like watching a movie about a Middle Eastern bazaar being filmed in Hollywood, for sole distribution in Latin America. Israel Lewin, a Bolivian whose Laredo stores sell anything from Japan that plays music, tells time, or calculates, has an idea of how Gaul is divided. "Hindus control the gold, which all comes from Italy. Arabs are heavily into textiles. Jews still dominate electronics. Indians sell clothes. Koreans do custom jewelry. All that Mexicans have is perfume and cosmetics, but we all sell those too."

This United Nations garage sale takes place on U.S. soil. The lingua franca is Spanish. The accents in downtown Laredo often defy interpretation. "And while all this goes on," asks José Valdez, "where are my people? Right where I was, and my father before me."

When José was six, the silver mine where his father worked in San Luis Potosí shut down. The family headed north, crossing the river at Laredo on the Day of the Dead, 1943. It was World War II; there was work. By 1950, there was none. "Vámonos," said José's mother. And they departed for what, to young José, was a mystical existence, where geography changed as fast as the seasons turned.

It started with strawberries in Constantine, Michigan. They would buy fresh milk from farmers and walk four miles to town to see a show. Next was Leelanau Lake, near Traverse City. The sun above the strawberry fields had been so hot; here they sat on ladders, in the shade of cherry trees. In the evenings, they watched movies outside, projected on the white wall of a church. The harvest ended. Back to Constantine for the pickles. In neighboring White Pigeon, there was a pickle factory.

Like cattle, they traveled with other families packed into large trucks. The truckers charged them a percentage, and decided where they were going. Their next stop was Lake Odessa, where they strained over short hoes in the sugar beets. There they were hungry. There, and in nearby onion fields, they made a dollar a day. As they moved through the rows, the stems of the cebollas would break, and their clothes reeked of onion juice.

In 1953, a Protestant trucker who accepted no

Catholic nonsense took them out to the Nebraska prairie, again to sugar beets. They'd been classified: Wetbacks were the best at lettuce, getting it out of the ground before it rotted; Jamaicans excelled at sugar cane; and no one could beat a Tex-Mexican at beets. From Nebraska they went to Hart, Michigan, and José saw migrants like he'd never seen before. Thousands in the streets, celebrating the cherry harvest with townspeople in a buenísima fiesta. The truckers took them to Muskegon to see *Rio* with Robert Taylor and Anthony Quinn. José was learning a little English by now.

In Shelby, it was more pickles, and then to a farm so far in the boondocks that the white farmer and his family didn't know not to work right alongside Mexicans. Back to Nebraska for potatoes, which, like sugar beets, was a money crop. Not much in cherries and pickles.

In Gordon, Nebraska, the following year, José met Sioux Indians down from Wounded Knee. Out in the fields, they became friends, sharing water bottles and each other's languages. Their employers added certain functional words in German to their vocabulary, words for *beer* and *friend* and *potato*.

That winter in Laredo, there was no food. Each night, to bed hungry. Today José keeps cans of food all over the house.

That spring, they longed for the road. This time it took them to Colorado. Stranger to the migrants than even those Indians were the local Chicanos. They talked differently. Many were of pure Spanish stock, from families who had never left Mexico because they'd been here for hundreds of years. Mexico had left them. José, nearly a teenager, noticed that the women were very beautiful. They had dances in the evenings. Rock and roll was beginning, and these were the first Mexican Americans he'd ever seen who talked English.

That year, 1954, they bought their first car. José's fourteen-year-old brother George drove it all the way home from Nebraska because their father couldn't or wouldn't. Ay, a carro! The year before they had almost starved in Laredo. Now they had a beautiful 1941 Chevy. At night, José and George would go out and just sit in it, even when it was up on blocks. In it, they'd arrived in style in west Texas for the fall cotton picking, which drew families from all over the state. They lived in big barracks with people from McAllen and La Joya. West Texas was dry, so they smuggled in beer and drank tallboys in the Lubbock heat.

By 1956, his brother was attending seminary in San Antonio. José, driving now, would pick him up and they would go off to Lingle, Wyoming, to the pinto beans. Farmers there taught him to disk and irrigate. He dreamed of having his own farm in these northern states someday. Over in Colorado, they traded the Chevy for a '51 Dodge and bought a used TV, which conked out immediately, so they went a little crazy and bought a new one. In a migrant labor camp in Windsor, Colorado, every day at noon they watched Bob Crosby.

In Windsor, the mayor had a grocery. José would talk to him about politics. At a church that winter in Laredo, he gave his first political speech. "Why do we have to go north to work, while other people here have it made and can stay?" Home in Laredo, there was bitterness and fighting in the barrios. He and other pickers were outcasts at Martin High School. They were embarrassed to say they were migrants— no one used that word—but everyone knew. Why else did they start school late in October or November, never appearing in yearbooks because every fall they missed the school pictures? "Cebolleros. Pinches betabeleros. There's onion and beet stink on your hands. ¿Por qué you don't wash?"

Now that he's a councilman and deputy director of the Texas Migrant Council, with federal money to funnel, some of those same people from high school occasionally appear in his office with outstretched arms, ready to give him a warm abrazo. "Hi," he greets them. "Fuck off."

He passed the balance of his youth in many northern fields. They tried Illinois and tomatoes in '59, and in Chicago Heights he saw black people for the first time, hundreds of them. They made fun of each other's accent; he stayed around for the radishes and onions. The blacks and the Poles in Chicago Heights, José realized, were as poor as he was—poorer, even, because their families weren't as strong.

The army, then back to the fields. One sticky Wyoming afternoon in 1963, his father bent over in the sugar beets and remained down. They brought the body back to Laredo. Like many migrant families, over the years they had invested in a house. Even though they only lived there a few months at a time, Laredo was home.

The army paid for Laredo Junior College. In '65, José got married and was drafted again, this time to serve in Lyndon Johnson's War on Poverty. For $100 a week, he started out teaching appliance repair. Vista volunteers appeared to organize their neighborhoods, teaching odd things like parliamentary procedure. The locals took over, and José became director of a community action agency.

Now he sees that migrant children get what he barely got: schooling. Scattered across Ohio, Indiana, Wisconsin, and Minnesota, Texas Migrant Council workers drive kids to school in vans each morning, and drop them the same afternoon at the asparagus fields. A hundred children leave when the cherries are picked; a hundred more come for the peaches. Council workers reach, and teach, thousands as they pass through. Little border hamlets like La Grulla or Progreso practically close up during the season. Even the schoolteachers go to the fields.

Once, in Wisconsin, their camp was filled with illegals, and José's boss called the INS. "We got crucified for that, but we have a constituency to serve. We sympathize with the illegal aliens, but who sympathizes with the local migrant? He's an American."

Valdez guesses that he supports the Simpson-Rodino-type immigration bills. "How we gonna go on like this? There aren't enough jobs. The employers would rather have Mexicans. Mexicans don't ask questions,

they don't talk about benefits, they just work hard and live under a mesquite tree. We made so many demands on Green Giant that they just said hell and started to bus them in from Mexico. People who've lived here twenty years," he says, looking out at his West Laredo barrio, "want better housing. To the Mexicans, this is a palace."

He envisions Laredo's potential as a golden hub of a wheel with 150-mile spokes, connecting Monterrey, San Antonio, and Corpus Christi. But the hub is crowded; as Valdez sees it, Nuevo Laredo's counterweight upsets the balance. "We came from there, but they're not us. They toss their garbage in the Rio Grande and want us to pay to clean it up. We may share a baseball team and a past, but we aren't one community. Who the hell wants to be part of Mexico?"

Yet, more than any two cities that face each other across the border, the two Laredos are umbilically related. In 1985, they made Latin American sports history when the jointly sponsored Owls—Los Tecolotes de Los Dos Laredos—won the pennant and two games of the Mexican World Series had to be played on U.S. soil. Laredo parents drill children to communicate in correct Spanish and not Tex-Mex. Courtship ignores national sovereignty. After the Mexican-American War, branches of the family trees of old Laredo were transplanted across the river, and cuttings continue to be exchanged in both directions.

For reasons no one recalls, the apex of Laredo's social season is Washington's birthday. Both towns celebrate the event. Nuevo Laredenses explain that it is encouraging to honor the victorious liberator of the original revolution in the Americas. So everybody does, to the same degree of excess that often finds Mexican couples still paying for their weddings years later. Debutantes appear in colonial gowns so prodigiously buoyed by petticoats that they must be transported, standing, in moving vans from ball to ball. The grand marches are apt to be led by George and Martha

Washington portrayed by an elegant Hispanic couple, their olive faces rich and exotic under powdered wigs.

But the politics binding these sibling cities is deeply Latin. The caudillo system, in which a strongman mandates like a feudal lord, continued through Mexico's history long after its liberation. Its own George Washington, Agustín Iturbide, promptly crowned himself emperor. The outrageous Santa Anna ascended to the presidency eleven times, on each occasion alchemizing some previous disgrace into a more insidious dictatorship. He was outdone only by Porfirio Díaz, who simply was Mexico for thirty years. When the revolution that ousted him finally quieted in the 1920s, it was replaced by the only kind of political party that Mexico really understood: a monopoly.

Throughout the country, local bosses known as caciques reflect this pattern in microcosm. Across the line, Laredo, Texas's shameful century under the Martin family's regime is best explained by the city's Mexican heritage. Its sister, Nuevo Laredo, is still ruled by her cacique. Only recently is his grip being loosened by changes seeping into Mexico's bedrock, mainly through fissures exposed along the border itself.

"Like a viceroy," says Eloy Vega, "the cacique gets his control from the federal government. In exchange for votes, it lets him steal federal money destined for the city. It supports him against challenges. The people fear him because he can ostracize them, take away their jobs, see that they get no contracts. So they become apathetic. Complainers are marked men—unless, of course, they are purchased. If someone is a car dealer, the government might buy his cars in gratitude for his loyalty. The cacique can do physical harm or make people disappear. This happens in México. I don't discard the possibility here in Nuevo Laredo. We've had much violence and assassination in the past thirty years."

Eloy Vega, tall, clean-shaven, carefully dressed, is far from being a radical. He is president of Nuevo Laredo's Chamber of Commerce and owns a prominent curio shop on Calle Guerrero. He is nervous about the border's image in the wake of drug-related violence, as demonstrated by his deathly quiet store. Yet his words hardly amount to civic boosterism.

One reason glares at him through his window. Across the street, Plaza Juárez is invisible under a confusion of vendor stalls, covered by a patchwork of awnings, cardboard, and corrugated metal. They have been occupying the square ever since Nuevo Laredo's tourist market burned five years earlier. The vendors' association petitioned the city to rebuild and arranged to purchase a prefabricated metal structure in the United States. But they were refused a building permit on the peculiar grounds that the market, which once injected many dollars into their economy, caused traffic congestion.

They were still puzzling over that when, fairly predictably, construction began. This time, though, the "Profe,"—Profesor Pedro Pérez Ibarra, Nuevo Laredo's cacique—had taken charge. His plan was for individual vendors to pay for the new market. His union would collect the money.

About two-thirds anted up. They knew what it was like to cross the Profe. Complain, and a policeman with a very conspicuous gun would stand in front of your shop, charming tourists in the opposite direction. The others howled that there was no assurance the money would go to the market, or that the best stalls would go to the highest bidders. Would the mayor let the Profe get away with such extortion?

The new market, now completed, stands empty and padlocked, waiting for someone to make a move. The last time a mayor crossed the Profe, he retaliated with a string of crazy strikes. Bus drivers, gas station attendants, garbage collectors, street sweepers, as well as restaurant, hotel, hospital, and maquiladora workers, sat down in unison. Since the Profe runs Nuevo Laredo's labor union, it wasn't hard to figure out what was happening. His strikes were nothing new—he sometimes leveled them against businesses that hadn't even opened yet, just to establish who calls the shots. Still, no one had seen anything like this.

It wasn't entirely unexpected. The graft here had become so flagrant that the PRI, Mexico's ruling party, had allowed the mayor to run independently of the Profe, who was campaigning for congress. This was unprecedented for a party that claims absolute unity, but the Profe was so scandalous that they feared he might lose the whole election for them.

They were correct. Radio tallies of precinct returns showed PRI candidates losing by ten thousand votes to the National Action Party, the PAN—until the broadcasts suddenly stopped. The next morning, as reported by the Profe's own newspaper, *Laredo Ahora*, the results had somehow reversed.

The huge strike was his revenge on the mayor for daring to distance himself. But on February 21, 1984, the day after it began, ten thousand housewives, students, and businessmen and even union members' families massed in Calle Guerrero. They marched from the Plaza Cultural to the international bridge, then turned and went to pay the Profe a call.

First, they set fire to the cars in the driveway. Then they sacked the house and burned it. Next, they marched across town and burned down the *Laredo Ahora* offices. For the next few hours, Nuevo Laredenses, light-headed with self-liberation, went a little berserk. Buses were hijacked and driven crazily around the city. Around nine that evening, somebody spoiled the fun by firing gunshots. Everyone sobered up and went home.

Since the Black Tuesday riots, the Profe has kept a lower profile; aides imply that he is hurt by the public's tantrum, after all he's done for them. At the sweltering little stalls in the makeshift market, vendors don't believe the old tyrant will give up that easily. "He's not even a real professor," protests one, mopping his brow with the tail of his guayabera.

Next to him, the friction of a fan's blades only generates more heat. All around Juárez Plaza, tourists pick though a clutter of Hidalgo ceramics, Saltillo blankets, rebozos and assorted woolens from Oaxaca, guayabera shirts from the Yucatán, sequined sombreros, stuffed armadillos, flour-sack ponchos, straw mobiles from Tzintzuntzán, toy violins, God's eyes, onyx and malachite chess sets, leather vests, goats' milk caramels, vanilla, tooled shotgun cases, rainbow nylon hammocks, whips, and piñatas in the form of dogs, bears, doves, Big Bird, the Playboy rabbit, Batman, children—"I wonder what it's like to hit a child with a pole?" a woman wonders.

"It's a great idea," replies her husband.

With the peso and tourism down, surviving in Nuevo Laredo becomes a challenge. The union leader's hammerlock has even discouraged maquiladoras; many have left for more cooperative places along the border. "It will change," says Eloy Vega. "The crisis is creating brave people. For sixty years, the government has kept the peace by tying our hands, believing that we'd harm ourselves if we were free. They are thieves who justify taking our money so we don't spend it on something stupid. We're supposed to be thankful. But our people have become more informed. Mojados come back from the United States with a car and money to buy things, and their neighbors ask why there is more freedom in the U.S. to earn."

Vega, the Chamber of Commerce president, says these next words in semiwonder: "Our government has caused exponential unhappiness. People who didn't care two years ago are demonstrating now. It is an immature situation still, but when 75 percent of the people admit they are unhappy, we could have an explosion, like in the Porfiriato in 1910. Explosion. A revolution."

• • •

Nuevo Laredo has an urgent feel; its dark sandstone and brick buildings crowd tightly to accommodate the activities required to support 350,000 rushing inhabitants, who fill its streets long into the night. Nuevo Laredo architect Ignacio Quiñones describes them as "different from the rest of Mexico. They are accustomed to hard, heavy work. They tolerate the violent extremes of hot summers and cold winters and land that doesn't produce." With the population rising and the number of maquiladoras dropping, many of these resilient people worry about where they will make their living. In the south of the city is one ancient answer.

On Sunday afternoon at Club Miramar, las chicos lounge in old heels and bathrobes with the newspaper, purging their hangovers with beans and tortillas. Some have long hair; black stubble grows swiftly on their legs. Yawning, they absently rub their jaws and are reminded of needing a shave. In the frankness of daylight, the cabaret shrivels. Like its name, meaning "seaview," Club Miramar is an illusion. What glistened by night is now peeling red foil; the sofa where earlier they drank and conversed under colored spotlights is cheap and frayed and has a wobbly leg. Flies gather around something that spilled and hardened hours ago.

The evening before, everything was primed for fantasy. By night, Club Miramar's girls are among the most striking in the Zona. The weekends are special for them: Crew-cab pickup trucks filled with American college boys and whitewing dove hunters bang up the dirt streets, KC lights flashing and horns a-honk, beer cans and cheers streaming from the windows. For two nights, all is drinks, flutter, and masculine attention. For a little while, disbelief is suspended, and in the dark las chicos are female.

Besides Club Miramar, the Zona—Zona de Tolerancia, also known as Boys' Town—has a few other transvestite houses, such as The Dallas Cowboys just across the way. Most of their clientele are ostensibly robust Texas heterosexuals who are somehow titillated by the idea of a companion hooked on hormone shots and silicone. Elsewhere in the Zona, relative normalcy prevails. Clubs like festive Papagallo and sedate Tamyko, with its neon-rimmed pagodas and tinkling garden, employ biologically guaranteed women. Not unlike the curio market, throughout the Zona merchandise of assorted color, size, and texture presents itself for inspection and sale.

The road to the Zona is unpaved and pitted, to slow anyone trying to escape whatever mayhem the night may inspire. It leads to a walled compound with a guard booth manned by a Nuevo Laredo police officer. Inside awaits a city of women in doorways and men in the streets. Prostitution is legal in Tamaulipas, but the Boys' Towns all along its border have closed in recent years, save this one. A former whore forced the exception.

Martita Cuellar is a madrota—a madam. One of her houses, Martha's, is named for her. She has a round, pretty face with a small mouth and thick black hair. At forty, she is beginning to strain the fabric of her white denims, but her short, ample figure hasn't lost the selling points she now no longer depends on. "I too was once a puta," she admits, gesturing at her girls. Tears appear on her plump cheeks.

When Martita was still attending the rural primary school in Nuevo León, a dove hunter's stray shot pierced her campesino father's shoulder, and he never worked again. To survive, her mother made and sold tortillas. Over the next five years, four of the seven children died for want of medical care—one, the hospital said, because the tortilla oven heated her mother's breast until it could not nourish the suckling infant.

She came to Nuevo Laredo when she was fifteen. "I did not come for this," she says in the dark interior of Martha's. "I was going to work, to earn enough to buy them a house."

It is still early; around the cocktail tables, putas and bartenders converse, largely in insults, and take turns bringing Martita lemonade and cigarettes. A Spanish version of "We Are the World" plays on a chrome jukebox. In Laredo, Texas, Martita Cuellar found work as a maid for a man who distributed Pepsi Cola. But his wife insisted that she did not sew fast enough. When Martita explained that blue jeans are hard to mend, she was fired.

Back in Nuevo Laredo, a girl gave her a place to stay and an address where she could find a job. The bus dropped her at the Zona. When Martita realized where she was, she fled. But her benefactress had disappeared, along with Martita's clothes and savings of $200. She saw no alternative.

She went to church and vowed that although she had entered the life, she would not lose herself to it. "No drinking. I would save the money I made." In just two years, she accumulated enough to buy the Rumba Casino, one of the Zona's less appealing casas. From that time, the life worked for her. Within five years, Martita Cuellar's house was paid for and refurbished, and she was looking around to expand. Five years more, and she owned four cabarets and was president of the owners' association, a post she has never been able to relinquish.

Then a Tamaulipan governor was elected on an antiprostitution platform. "He was a drunk trying to be a saint. They all are." She called a meeting of zona presidents in Matamoras, Reynosa, Mier, Díaz Ordaz, and Miguel Alemán. "If they get rid of the zonas," she told them, "the girls will just end up in the plazas and the hotels. Without sanitary controls there will be problems. Thousands of jobs will be lost—bartenders, shoeshine boys, photographers, tattooists." She proposed they join forces to protest.

"No," they replied, "a little money will fix it." But one day Matamoros closed down. Two weeks later, they bulldozed Reynosa. Then Miguel Alemán and Mier.

"I knew they were coming here next. So I talked to the Profe. He and I went to Ciudad Victoria to see the governor. We told him we were ready to defend the Zona with our lives, that closing meant an increase in delinquency and venereal disease and losing two thousand jobs. Putas aren't in a union, but the Profe likes to help workers. The governor listened, of course. And then Matamoros and Reynosa called and asked us to help. Too late, I told them. Cowards who refuse to fight don't win the war."

Outside, the colored lights filter through the smoke of tacos sizzling in curbside braziers. A vendor garnishes the melody of "Tea for Two" with augmented chords on a guitar warped by grease drippings from his deep-fryer. The crossed legs of prostitutes well beyond ripeness are visible in the portals of low row houses, where they rent one-room cribs and try to continue making a living. They are not banned from places like Martha's, but they can no longer compete with younger, prettier whores. In the cabaret, girls receive $25.00 per half hour, paying $4.00 to the house and another dollar to the towel man, but in the cribs the asking price is $10.00 and they often settle for half or less. Some lie on their narrow beds, glancing without much hope at passersby, or sit in the door, their heads turned to watch a black-and-white television atop a dresser. Hungrier ones clutch at the window shoppers, sometimes scoring, sometimes picking a pocket. During the cold months, they gather in the dirt streets around buckets containing charcoal fires.

Inside, Martita interviews a tiny, weeping woman from El Salvador who has been shut out of the United States. Martita has helped girls return to their families, but lately there are Central Americans who don't dare go home. Migración raids sometimes, and it costs substantial mordida to protect them. When the salvadoreña regains her composure, Martita explains about the weekly checks at the gynecological registry the city maintains inside the compound. She walks her over, loaning her the 700 pesos. Within, male government functionaries sit behind desks piled with forms and carbons; women in Grecian sandals, cowboy boots, mesh socks, slit dresses, microshorts, or just tattoos wait on benches, smoking and gossiping. The girls complain that the exam is too cursory—a cervical mirror for forty-five seconds and a blood test every six months. But when officials in San Antonio started pressuring Mexico because of stubborn gonorrhea strains traced to Nuevo Laredo, doctors were invited down and found the Zona to be clean. Their patients later admtted they had gone with street whores first.

The transvestites are the ones who have Martita worried. VD soared along the border when American soldiers returned from Vietnam, and now the United States is inflicting a new curse known as el Síndrome de Inmuno Deficiencia Adquirida, el SIDA. Mexico is possibly more terrified about AIDS than the U.S. When the conquistadors arrived in 1519, there were twenty-five million Mexicans. Within a century, only a million remained, most succumbing to diseases introduced by the Spaniards, like smallpox and measles. Martita's two male bordellos are disasters waiting to occur.

When she tells them they must shut down, las chicos begin to cry and plead with her. What else can they do? "I never intended to get into this," she worries. She had hired a cashier for the Miramar and he said he could get some girls. The next week he showed up with beautiful women. After four days, she told them they had to register with the doctors to keep working.

"Nena," he said, "I have to tell the truth. They're jotas." She couldn't believe it. The registry said there was no way they could check these girls, because they were guys.

"We agreed it would be okay if they just put on a floor show, which the Americans love. Everyone knows they're really boys. All they basically do is suck."

Martha's begins to fill. Husbandless women, here to feed children, greet their marks at the door and escort them to tables, giggling their few vulgar English phrases. Some of Martita's putas are ex-maquiladora assembly line workers who got bored making $3.00 a day. The loveliest women at Martha's meet Americans here, marry them, and go to the United States. Martita Cuellar turned down that chance, thinking a whore could never fall in love. But she did, with a Nuevo Laredo journalist who insisted they wed. When their daughter turned fifteen, Martita threw a magnificent quinceñera, buying her a Martha Washington gown that cost $7,000.

After the fiesta, she sat with her daughter and explained where the money was coming from. "I know you're ashamed. I also am. We've arranged school for you in Canada. You'll find someone there to marry."

"Mamá," her daughter replied, "I've known since I was thirteen. You did it for us. Just don't send me so far away."

With her daughter now in a Monterrey university, Martita Cuellar considers retirement. She believes she is going to hell. At the same time, she is devoutly grateful for what God has done. Often she has asked him to take all this away from her if he disapproves, but instead she has just made more money. She has helped girls survive, found homes for their abandoned children, and wonders how she landed in a trap where to do good, she has to do bad.

Night arrives; boys from Amarillo and Texas A&M pile out of vehicles, urinate on the bumper, emit war whoops, and stagger off toward Papagallo's. College students, truck drivers passing through Laredo . . . all along the border, even where the Boys' Towns no longer exist, Mexican women are receiving American men and their dollars in their beds. Irresistible Mexico, embodied in her trapped whores, ravished for centuries by aggressive foreigners who lusted after her: At times, she has resigned herself and made the best of it. Hijos de la chingada, children of the violated one. Even at her most powerless, Mexico always has her allure. Like her women, she survives and endures.

•   •   •

Veteran's Day, Laredo, Texas. The peso has been spinning frantically, and customs houses thank God for Visicalc, because otherwise they could never keep up with gyrating exchange rates. Downtown, the air is laden with the lilac scent of perfume, moving by the caseload. In Tepito, an electronics store named for the colonia de contrabando in Mexico City where all this merchandise is going, young mestizo chiveros wearing gold Rolexes and suede jogging shoes haggle over the bulk price of three thousand Casio programmable scientific calculators. The deal expands to include video games, two hundred each of Towering Inferno and Strategy X, along with five hundred Sony VCRs. They reach an agreement; sweaty wads of $100 bills change hands and thousands of individual boxes land on the floor so the calculators can be packed four hundred instead of forty to a crate. Cardboard collectors from Nuevo Laredo gather armloads of discarded wrappings to sell across the bridge for fifteen pesos—about three cents—a kilo. Laredo generates entire forests' worth of jettisoned cardboard, and squadrons of cartoneros peddling three-wheel carts spirit it away to be recycled into Mexican newsprint in Monterrey.

At Seabic, a shop down the street, bearded Sanjive Bhasin, a native of Afghanistan in his twenties who arrived recently, wraps several kilos of fourteen-carat chains, crucifixes, and gold foil faces of the crying Jesus. When the Russians appeared in Kabul, his family moved their currency exchange to India. There they applied to the United States for L-1 visas, which admit foreigners for three years who have at least $40,000 to invest.

Within six months, Sanjive and his seven family members will apply to change their status and get green cards. "It goes to prove," he says, "that all this country wants is money." Yet he notes with interest that none of the lucrative products come from the United States anymore, with one exception:

"Arms. America has only one thing to sell. It has to get its foreign exchange back somehow, so it starts up a war and supplies the equipment. I can understand that."

In Laredo's Jarvis Plaza, two men in caps of the American Legion and the Marine Corps League lay ivy wreaths at a memorial to the American war they fought in Asia. Mike González and Jesse Castañeda have grown a bit stout since then; they are now twice as old as when they went off to battle.

When Castañeda returned, he was greeted by a demonstration informing him that he was a baby killer. On González's first night back in San Francisco, MPs protected him from rock throwers. When they went in, they had anticipated a more auspicious homecoming.

Now the possibility of another unpopular war, in Central America this time, is being discussed. Some have argued that if the United States sends troops to Nicaragua, Mexican American soldiers might refuse to raise arms against their Hispanic brethren. This upsets González and Castañeda. Their people make good soldiers.

"We're ready to go to El Salvador on seventy-two-hour notice if we've got a job to do there," says Mike.

"If we ever have to go to war against Mexico, we will," says Jesse. "Some of the best border patrolmen are Mexican American. You never hear them say they won't arrest somebody because he's Mexican."

Their fathers served in World War II, and their grandfathers fought in World War I. They grew up hearing that Mexican Americans had won more medals as a group than anyone else in the United States. "My family," Jesse says, "is proud of my country, right or wrong. I didn't get to debate like the college students. We didn't have the money for college." He served in the First Marine Division, north of Da Nang. Later, he heard that the majority of Texans lost in Southeast Asia were Mexican Americans.

The polished slab behind them that lists the Laredoans who died in Vietnam includes the name of Fidel Padilla. When Jesse Castañeda returned in 1969, Fidel Padilla's picture was on the visor of the taxi that took him home.

"Are you Mr. Padilla?" he asked the driver.

The man looked at Jesse's uniform and nodded. Jesse told him that he had gone to boot camp with his son, that Fidel had been in the next tent, that they had fought side by side. He saw him picked up by the helicopter.

"Gracias," Mr. Padilla said.

A mile outside Laredo a plaque is unveiled, proclaiming in Spanish and English that U.S. 83 is now the Texas Vietnam Veteran's Memorial Highway. The marker shows the Lone Star flag superimposed on the map of Vietnam.

Up the road, Veteran's Day notwithstanding, two federal employees are at work. Dennis Cogburn and Gerry Tisdale of the U.S. Border Patrol, riding a bay quarterhorse and a sorrel Appaloosa, cut for sign along an alkaline trail. In their forties, both men are lean and youthful; by working in the patrol they have maintained the physical conditioning that got them through Vietnam.

Much of the horseback work here is in the railyards, chasing wets between lines of cars. Days like this, spent out in the whitebrush and prickly pear, are much more enjoyable. They can use their skills to determine the freshness of a wavy-soled footprint by the insect or lizard tracks running across it. Catching a group with a five-hour head start is an interesting challenge.

The numbers of wets surge with every new devaluation. Tisdale's wife has taken to packing him an extra lunch, because he usually gives his to someone he's apprehended. More juveniles are working as coyotes too, which is irritating because the United States doesn't like to prosecute minors. Lately, they've resorted to turning them over to Mexican authorities, who sometimes use cattle prods to persuade them not to return.

The prospect isn't pleasant, but neither was the episode of the young pollero who thought he could avoid spending money on heavy duty shock absorbers. The next time he took a load of aliens across in his trunk, he wedged a pair of two-by-fours under the springs. Rough ride, but it worked—until a half hour later when the boards caught fire.

The driver ran. Two illegals in the back seat tried to free their companions from the trunk. Unfortunately, it was locked. The coyote had the keys. The aliens finally had to back away before the gas tank exploded. "It would have been nice to think," Tisdale reported, "that they died of smoke inhalation, but the position of their bodies indicated that they burned to death trying to claw their way out."

High overhead, a caracara soars. The desert smells like fresh-cut herbs. The ground isn't yielding much sign today, but Cogburn finds some Coahuiltecan atlatl points and worked bits of Archaic stone dating back ten thousand years. He does not dwell much on the fact that the aliens they arrest for trespassing descend from people who lived here first, whose artifacts he collects.

If he were in their place, Tisdale supposes, the Border Patrol would be throwing him back every day too. The trick is to not focus on personal feelings for these people. His brother once was interested in joining the patrol, so Gerry brought him along. He showed him how to feel the crust around a track to know within an hour or two when the alien passed by. But his brother couldn't handle dealing with other people's misery nor forget that the ones they were sending back had people depending on them.

But the line has to be drawn somewhere, Tisdale believes. Only so many spoons fit in the soupbowl before someone goes hungry. He and Cogburn concentrate on doing their job professionally. Charged with a mission they are too undermanned and underbudgeted to fulfill, border patrolmen sometimes compare their jobs to the futile war in Vietnam. Yet apart from the drugs and the smuggled M-16s and the coyotes, this can be pleasant work, not unlike sport bass fishing. Catch them after an interesting pursuit, toss them back, and catch them again the next day. Keep your tracking skills sharp; spend time in the clean desert aboard a horse. There are worse ways to make a living.

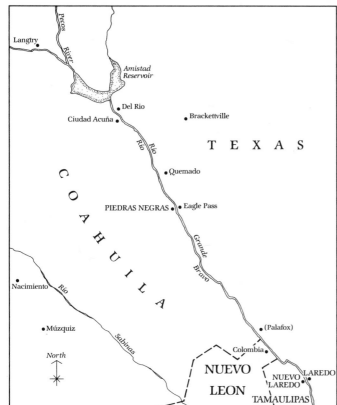

CHAPTER THREE
THE EAGLES

Texas Farm Road 472 crosses a western landscape in miniature, with eroded, mesalike bluffs and outcroppings that imitate mountains. Streams trickle to the Rio Grande through patches of carrizo, watering pastures fenced with deer mesh. Like the Mexicans, who have lately let grains go to seed to attract ducks, ranchers here have begun catering to hunters. In south Texas, white-tailed deer have become an encouraging cash crop.

The road is mostly deserted, except for coveys of darting bobwhites and an occasional lumbering tortoise. Shadows of kestrels click over the purple sage and the reflecting pads of the prickly pear. The border opens up and breathes; for many miles the only human sign is an infrequent windmill, slowly mixing the horizon. Nothing hints at the former presence of Palafox, obliterated in 1818 by Comanches.

Across from where its murdered settlers once ran their cattle, the pueblo of Colombia lives for an empty dream. It is the state of Nuevo León's only border town. Eighty years ago, Colombia was part of an American coal-mining operation: Coal cars would descend in the United States through a tunnel under the river and emerge in Mexico. Then one day the shafts flooded, and there was no more work in the mines.

But the defunct economy here could revive if only the bridge would come. Eighty-one-year-old María de Jesús Rodríguez has been waiting for it all her life, as has all Nuevo León. After years of appeals, the landlocked state was granted a twenty-kilometer fragment of border, sliced from neighboring Coahuila. A skiff crossed here, but Nuevo León wanted a bridge so all the customs taxes wouldn't accrue to Nuevo Laredo.

It made sense: Colombia was the nearest entry point to Monterrey. Yet regardless of what Monterrey might like, Laredo, Texas, didn't want any rival bridge just upstream. Today, Colombianos gaze at an empty bank across the way, choked with reeds, and wonder what prosperity would be like. A few new houses are going up, but María de Jesús has seen that before. "Gossip birds are twittering about the bridge again. The young people don't know any better. They will learn. The United States decides what is best."

Long before anyone cared whose country this was, it was covered by a tropical swamp. Blackened and compressed, it now lies beneath the dry hills that rise in these borderlands. West of Colombia, veins of carbon known as the Olmos Formation deepen and widen until they crop out near the river. Following long-disappeared drainages, these veins interbed with shales, fireclay, and rippled layers of sandstones throughout much of the state of Coahuila and south Texas. The native Coahuiltecans called the soft formations that break the surface *tetelezco*. The Spanish who built missions nearby translated this as piedras negras—black rocks.

A pleasant Mexican city by that name rests atop these layers. Piedras Negras's long blocks are lined with sunny limestone buildings that lend a protective feeling in this open region. Its two main plazas enclose its tourist and business district. With 150,000 inhabitants to neighboring Eagle Pass's 23,000, Piedras Negras demonstrates less of an inferiority complex with respect to its counterpart than other Mexican border communities.

In December 1984, it showed both sides of the border one aspect of its independence when its citizens burned down the town hall. Then they freed the prisoners, torched the jail, and smashed the offices of *El Zócalo*, the town's leading newspaper.

Police started firing, killing two and wounding at least forty. By then the news from Piedras Negras was all over both countries, and historians speculated whether December 29 would someday join the ranks of other memorable dates for which streets are named all over Mexico.

The occasion was an election. Mexico's ruling Institutional Revolutionary Party chooses not to lose them. When the PRI's mayoral candidate in Piedras Negras apparently did so, the Coahuila legislature felt obliged to disqualify enough ballots (entire ballot boxes, actually) to turn the results in the party's favor. This was nothing particularly new. The difference was that the resulting violence seemed to echo the commotion that once led the PRI itself to power.

As in Laredo, the opposition was the PAN—the right-of-center Partido de Acción Nacional. It is accused of being the party of the rich, with unpatriotic ties to the United States, but its free enterprise rhetoric attracts many border residents who daily compare their lives with life across the line. The PAN suggests that monopoly politics have corrupted the country. Many who otherwise would reject its rosy capitalistic visions support the PAN as the only alternative solvent enough to mount a serious challenge to the PRI.

Back in 1910, the challenger of the status quo was Francisco Madero. Scion of a wealthy Coahuila ranching family, he was hardly a revolutionary. Causes like land reform, espoused by inveterate strugglers like Emiliano Zapata, left him somewhat glazed. But he wrote an awkward treatise suggesting that after thirty years, Presidente Porfirio Díaz may have been in office long enough. Somewhat to his surprise, Madero's less-than-strident call for real elections resulted in his own candidacy. The Porfiriato government's almost automatic response was to jail him. The ensuing explosion—the Mexican Revolution—reverberated for a decade. When it calmed, it was only because a president who'd seen nearly all his immediate predecessors assassinated knew that Mexico needed a strong, central, stabilizing force. The PRI was born.

Madero originally hoped to begin his revolution symbolically, in a border city whose name had been changed to honor the dictator. This plan was thwarted. Yet in 1984, when the first significant violence connected to the PAN occurred in Piedras Negras (née Ciudad Porfirio Díaz), it revived the old omen. These portents frighten but don't surprise Eleazar Cobos, who was the PAN's mayoral candidate. "People will meet violence with violence. Hunger and corruption are like two halves of a bomb. Together they can achieve critical mass."

Like many PAN candidates, a year before his campaign he'd never considered politics. Trimly built, with thick hair and a fondness for red neckties, Cobos is an endocrinologist. At his peach-colored, neo-Renaissance clinic, he had noticed that people lately can't afford essential medical care. His friends persuaded him to run for office—not to start a revolution, but to try to prevent one.

In his study, Cobos ticks off the evidence on his fingers: "No liquidity in the country. Debt. Scarcity of food. Tourism down. Oil price down. Unemployment up. Corruption up. Money fleeing. It all points to an eruption. In 1910, when it last happened, a million people ran to the United States for cover. The U.S. won't permit that today. So what happens?"

When the PRI was forming back in the 1920s, President Plutarco Elias Calles often consulted with U.S. Ambassador Dwight Morrow, Charles Lindbergh's father-in-law. Morrow is credited with helping to end the Cristero Rebellion, a murderous power struggle between the new, anticlerical revolutionary government and the Catholic church.

"The PRI claims that we're supported by the U.S.," said Cobos in his campaign, "but they were first. Dwight Morrow told Plutarco Calles that México needed a strong central party to establish calm. Like in Russia, the revolution became doctrine. México supports socialism for Cuba and Nicaragua, but here we lack enough potable water, clinics, school breakfasts—things that taxes provide for the poor in the United States. Here, los pobres are stealing, eating road-killed animals. Instead of public works, the PRI gives us cantinas, contraband, and corruption."

Cobos accuses Mexico of beaming television up from the capital to distract viewers from U.S. channels. In every border city, new monuments to Mexican heroes are appearing. "Nacionalismo," he says, "is a way of maintaining power, as long as the nation and the PRI are synonymous." Control of news media especially aggravates the PAN. The Mexican government subsidizes newsprint and has been known to make it scarce when displeased. Similarly, radio stations fear for their licenses.

Which made Dean Cary's contribution all the more compelling. Cary, host of a bilingual radio bulletin board in Eagle Pass, invited Cobos on his show after the tainted election. Radio waves don't stop at the border, so for weeks afterward Piedras Negras citizens took advantage of the U.S. First Amendment to air local grievances. This unprecedented exposure, the PRI charges, was ultimately responsible for the riots that burned city hall and blockaded the international bridge. Those incidents have not warmed the relations between the two cities. American journalists now enter Piedras Negras with some difficulty, and rumors hint of a price on Cary's scalp.

Next to the bridge on the U.S. side, six hundred Kickapoo Indians ignore all this. They are also indifferent to Eagle Pass's plan to relocate their cardboard wickiup village four miles east of town. The public explanation for the move is to give them sanitation and other good things they now lack. Also, the wickiups will no longer catch fire from cigarettes tossed from cars passing overhead.

A few citizens believe this is just a way to remove an eyesore; that somebody is making out like a bandit on worthless land that well-meaning benefactors are pitching in to buy for the Indians; that it's inconvenient to transportation; that the Kickapoos never asked for land in the first place. What they'd like is to be left alone to follow a pattern that, for them, has always existed.

On either side of this stretch of river, where eagles cross freely between bluffs redolent of wild oregano, middens dating back to 8000 B.C. indicate that humans once did so too. These Paleo people, and the

Archaic people and Coahuiltecans after them, were not the Kickapoo's direct ancestors; their descendants have interbred with Mexicans and North Americans. It has fallen on the transplanted Kickapoo to unknowingly preserve an ancient rhythm in this landscape.

Their name is Algonquin for nomad, suggesting they came from the east. They had followed game routes to the Great Lakes, but French settlements drove them south to Missouri. Around 1805, the Spanish invited the Kickapoo to Texas, because they were willing to stand against the Comanches and Lipan Apaches. But still they wandered, so Mexico encouraged them to settle at Nacimiento, near Múzquiz, Coahuila, 130 kilometers below the Río Bravo, to serve as a buffer against the hostiles.

The Kickapoos were pleased with the juniper hills of Nacimiento, but their nomadic nature didn't accommodate to staying put. Incurable hunters and gatherers, their blood surged with the seasons. From Múzquiz they began a cyclical migration north to Oklahoma, using Texas as a way station. They have yet to stop doing this.

Today they travel, not after deer herds, but to gather in the spirit of the cash economy to which they've adapted. In April, they migrate to sugar beet fields in Montana and Wyoming, and then work their way to Kickapoo reservation land in Oklahoma to pick cherries and peaches. After a while, they return to Eagle Pass. When they're ready, they cross the border with unconscious impunity, driving vehicles with Oklahoma license plates into the interior of Mexico and home to Múzquiz. No one tells them they need a car permit; no one checks them coming or going. In Mexico, they are ejidatarios, giving them citizens' rights to the use of designated rural lands. Recently they've been officially declared U.S. citizens, members of the Texas band of the Oklahoma Kickapoo. If this puts them in violation of both country's laws, they are the last to know about it.

Their settlement under the Eagle Pass bridge began in 1974, for no more mystical a reason than to qualify for food stamps in Texas while waiting for the harvests to commence. It consists of temporary dwellings; there is no ritual menstrual hut as in Múzquiz, and the traditional paneling of woven tule is unavailable along the Rio Grande. The exterior carrizo walls are an aesthetic concession to the city, which deemed 100 percent cardboard unattractive.

The quadrangular wickiups have turtle-backed roofs clad with flattened packing crates, fastened to frameworks of river willow. The tie straps are ends of denim bolts, gleaned from Eagle Pass's Williamson-Dickey work clothes plant. Their interiors stay comfortable during the summer, as the weather-whitened cardboard deflects the worst of the sun. Outside, open ramadas shade platforms used for sleeping.

On one of these sits Nanate, a thin man with long hair and skin the color of cedar bark, dressed in a plaid cowboy shirt. He shakes his head with wonder over Eagle Pass's plan to put them in mobile homes in "Nuevo Nacimiento." The expense doesn't take into account that few individuals stay here very long. "We go home to Nacimiento. And we go up to Oklahoma. And we come here. And go home."

So simple. But they roam a landscape ruled by two very distinct bureaucracies, and they are relevant to neither. Texas has now intervened, and Mexico could be next. Much of the Kickapoo's prime Múzquiz ejido lies fallow or is rented to neighboring oat farmers. According to the agrarian reform laws, ejidatarios have to cultivate. But except for casual attempts at squash patches, the Kickapoos have no tradition of agriculture; the land means something different to them.

"In Nacimiento we store our customs." Nanate searches for words to explain what, to Kickapoos, is beyond explanation. "We offer deer meat in prayer. We cook deer when our young get their names. When someone dies, one or two years later we have a fiesta so the spirit goes to God. When women die, women dance. When men die, men dance."

But when Coahuila informs them that they have let their deer permit expire, they must go to Mexico City to request a new one. In Texas, the Bureau of Indian Affairs is putting showers in the mobile homes so they won't bathe in the river and instructing mothers that letting their babies sniff the spray paint bought at Riverside Auto Parts is an improper method of sedation. The bureau has found them jobs with the city, but employers can't comprehend why the Kickapoo periodically have to go down to Múzquiz.

Nanate knows the reason, and knows that it is good, whether anyone else understands or not. In February, they go for the new year. Alongside a foothill stream, the clear Sabinas, they dance their rituals in the sotol and sumac flats. Behind them rise limestone mountains of virgin juniper and piñon. They sing their puberty masses and honor the religious guide Manaqua with hours of hop-step dancing accompanied by deerskin drums. Their wickiups are not made from materials that once packaged commodes or kitchen appliances, but of tules woven to air-tightness, in rows so neat they resemble a thatched military compound in a meadow.

Nacimiento reminds them that in the dim beginnings, God promised them he will come back. Only if they do not leave their traditions will he recognize them and lead them to paradise. "So," says Nanate, watching the arc of vehicular energy connecting Piedras Negras and Eagle Pass, "we must follow a pattern made up of days and seasons. This is just one station along our way."

"If the Indians had had tighter immigration laws," John Stockley observes, "we'd still be in England."

Stockley lives twelve miles upriver in Quemado, where groves of pecans burnish the Rio Grande bottomlands to deep gold in autumn. A ruddy man in his fifties, Stockley is a Maverick County drug and alcohol abuse counselor who often visits the Kickapoo, including in Múzquiz. In his office, he guards documents pertaining to Kickapoo lands in Mexico, which they trust no one else to keep. Stockley's family has ranched on both sides of the river around Eagle Pass for generations. During the fifties, he worked as a bagman in the bracero program, paying off Mexican inspectors so ranchers got the men they wanted. Today there's talk of guest worker plans similar to the braceros, but Stockley has his doubts, because machines have cut the demand for agricultural labor. "Eighty percent of the aliens are in restaurants and working construction. An urban bracero program would be pretty expensive to police."

Eagle Pass still has its spinach fields and feedlots, but its citizens wonder what else it has to look forward to. A jarring monument to the trauma of currency devaluations is its shiny, empty Mall de las Aguilas, a shopping complex that opened the same month in 1982 that the peso started its bottomless bellyflop. The town began as a way station for fortyniners, and Fort Duncan was added as a link in the chain of frontier posts the United States erected along its new border after 1848. Coal mining built the gracious, columned homes along Ceylon Street, but trains switched to oil burners, sealing the mining shafts.

Eagle Pass's crenelated Victorian courthouse, flanked by tropical palms that Victoria would not have recognized, has a startling mural painted across its white facade, incongruous with its design but corresponding to its locality. The irresistible Mexican temptation to decorate public buildings in ways architects never intend has crept across the river. The images are stalwartly American: Abe Lincoln superimposed on the Declaration of Independence, Neil Armstrong disembarking on the surface of the moon. Lincoln is special here; alone in Texas, Eagle Pass rejected the Confederacy by an 80-3 vote, and Union loyalists waited out the war in Piedras Negras. They nearly starved, but lived to jeer in 1865 as Confederate General Joseph

O. Shelby wrapped the Stars and Bars around a stone and dropped it into the Rio Grande on his way south. He was leading his unsurrendered brigade away from Lee's disgrace, into Mexico to serve the French emperor Maximilian. It was yet another lost cause.

.   .   .

The men know each other mainly by nicknames—Gato, Brujo—because they only see one another in the dark. At the top of an inclined tunnel, they catch a descending chairlift. Halfway down, the earth absorbs all sound except for the soft click of pulleys.

One hundred and twenty meters below the surface, the miners begin their nightly journey into the very black rock itself. Since 1981, they have carved fifty kilometers of tunnels underneath the municipios of Nava and Piedras Negras. They walk underground for several of those kilometers to reach the face they are digging; as they do, the air distributes itself through the branching corridors, dividing and growing thinner, and the temperature rises.

They are passing through a seam of brownish-black, bituminous coal that parallels the Rio Grande, beginning ten kilometers north of Piedras Negras and reaching nearly to Nuevo Laredo. One of Coahuila's two great coal fields, it contains known deposits of 600 million tons. Its rock is soft, with many subcubical cleavages. Such coal will not form coke, the potent fuel needed to transform iron ore into steel. But it will fire turbines, and thirteen kilometers away, the largest coal-fired electrical generator in Latin America consumes twelve thousand metric tons per day of the substance they tear from the earth. Two more such units are planned.

The Minera Carbonífera Río Escondido and its accompanying Proyecto Carboeléctrico represent Mexico's hope of selling a product, rather than raw materials, as it does with its oil. It sees the United States as a logical customer for its excess power. At the same time, population and demand for energy in its northern borderlands have increased in ways Mexico City never anticipated. Since the mine began to operate, Piedras Negras alone has added thirty thousand inhabitants.

The only lights in the tunnels are the lamps bobbing on the miners' helmets, connected to twelve-hour battery packs. The tunnels, shored with wide-flange beams on posts of thick pine, are sprayed with a ghostly coat of inert white powder to lessen the chance of fires. The area is known for bursts of methane; at night, colored balls of flame sometimes rise like gaseous spirits over Piedras Negras and Eagle Pass. Nine hundred miners work under the earth continuously, in three eight-hour shifts. Only one has died; every day, the miners pass the cross that marks where the overhead viga fell.

At Frente C-3, a rotating diamond-tipped mace sweeps over a lustrous shelf of exposed coal, spewing black clouds and chunks of pure carbon as it consumes the earth from within. A spray of water cuts the dust and kills sparks; miners stand in black pools, their faces anonymous under the soot and dim lamplight. A howling ventilator duct emits a strange, mechanical breeze, cooling the buried air, but men still work shirtless, with bandanna filters covering their noses and mouths.

Fifteen of them shovel, guiding the clawing machine, heaping the crushed coal onto a moving belt that shrieks in half-second pulses. It disappears behind them, to the main conveyor far in the underground distance. The conveyor carries the black matter out of the mine and into the night, continuing for thirteen kilometers to the ovens of the generating plant.

The machine reaches higher, explores, almost caresses, and then savages the wall, scouring a tubular swath two feet in diameter from the ceiling as the spray follows it, depositing black sludge over the newly revealed tunnel floor. For forty-five minutes, it convulses until the passage has lengthened by seventy centimeters. During the next hour, the men shore up the tunnel. They lug, then hoist another eighteen-foot steel beam into position. With sledgehammers, they drive in the supports on either end of the viga, which is all that holds 375 vertical feet of planetary crust from collapsing on them.

The manpower, the banging machine, the timber, steel, and miles of underground track and conveyors belie the conclusion that coal is a cheap source of electricity. Yet eight hours later, the men return along the dark passages and ascend into a city lighted by their efforts. Most of them come from mining families, from the zona carbonífera in the Sabinas basin south toward Múzquiz. Their fathers dug a harder, less oxygenated coal with fewer machines, less ventilation, and more black lung. Some of these men commute back to their villages nightly, two hours each way. The border is where the work is now, work that pays an average of 1,500 pesos—$3.10—a day, but pays steadily.

Some have had illusions about going to the United States, but there the migra pursues them. When they apply for a mica just to cross and shop, they have to tell how much money they have, which is an embarrassment. Besides, their salaries have turned to dust with the devaluation. Here, as long as they can survive breathing the tiny particles of piedras negras into their lungs, they will have something to do. And Mexico will have power to sell and burn.

.   .   .

Up at Amistad Dam, nobody notices the dozens of pink scissor-tail flycatchers resembling airborne swizzle sticks that settle onto the power lines leading from the generators. The attention is focused instead around the bronze, identical twin eagles in the middle of the highway that crosses the dam. On the left, the more interesting one holds a writhing serpent in its mouth and perches on a prickly pear cactus. A few feet to the north, its companion clasps an olive branch in one talon, but the usual cluster of arrows has been tactfully omitted from the other.

The occasion is Fiesta Amistad. Specifically, this is El Abrazo, when the mayors of Ciudad Acuña and Del Rio share an embrace of good will at the Coahuila-Texas border. It's a tradition lifted from the George Washington pageant in the Laredos, but Fiesta Amistad has two original touches: the only parade and ten-kilometer race to start in one nation and end in another. "Actually," admits the festival's chairman, "in Europe, they're common. But those countries are pretty much alike; this is Mexico!"

All pertinent dignitaries are present, along with Miss Del Rio and Señorita Ciudad Acuña. The United States's color guard is in place, but everyone is waiting for Mexico's. Back in Acuña, fifteen miles away, their vehicle has broken down. Meanwhile, the bands of Del Rio High School and Colegio de Las Américas— the former a brass squadron of blue and white peacocks, the latter a kind of nine-piece conjunto—alternate with selections from their very distinct repertoires. The captain of the junior ROTC uses the delay to explain a problem to the INS director. His unit has been invited up to Houston, but several cadets are Mexican nationals who only have border micas. Can something be arranged?

Miss Del Rio reaches over the border, a strip of brushed aluminum embedded in the pavement, to loan Señorita Acuña a stick of gum; they're classmates at Del Rio High. Two hundred and fifty feet below, water-skiers slalom from country to country. Amistad (Friendship) Reservoir was completed in 1969. The first abrazo here was a handshake between presidents Richard Nixon and Gustavo Díaz Ordaz. The preceding October, Díaz Ordaz had found it necessary to silence, permanently, hundeds of protesters who might have conveyed a bad impression of Mexico to journalists covering the 1968 Olympics. Nixon was employing similar persuasion to make a point on a grander scale throughout much of Southeast Asia. Dedicating a new lake allowed them a tranquil, even reflective interlude. For a moment, the confluence of their two nations must have seemed among the world's more benign geographical encounters.

The reservoir stores up to five million acre-feet of

the Rio Grande's runoff. With increasing irrigation demands, especially in Mexico, it lately contains just half that. It is not one of the world's prettier lakes. During the fall, purple cenizo covers nearly everything in the vicinity, but most of the year Amistad's shores are low and barren. Still, in an area with relatively little standing water, striped bass fishermen consider it an international miracle.

The Mexican tricolor appears, guarded by panting, double-timing soldiers carrying automatic weapons. They march to the boundary and face the contingent from Laughlin Air Force Base. A century earlier, someone might have fired. Now they stare straight ahead while blushing preschoolers dressed as Uncle Sam, a pioneer woman, a miniature charro, and a folkloric bailarina are led to each other's countries to exchange little hugs. Next come the mayors, one wearing a serge suit, the other in a guayabera. Then, even colonels and comandantes are at it, embracing in the sculpted bronze gaze of their two national eagles.

The reception that follows is on the American side, a relief to the Mexicans because their money buys only one-third of what it did last year when it was their turn. At Amistad Lodge, contingents from each side munch picante hors d'oeuvres and drink a frozen punch called border buttermilk, made from tequila and pink lemonade. Throughout the room, crêpe-paper sombreros hang from red, white, and blue bunting. Del Rio's Anglo mayor translates his own speech as he goes, saying that Washington and Mexico City really don't understand what the border represents. "Here we are blessed every day to be international ambassadors. The river doesn't divide us, it joins us."

Afterward, he recounts how he sent over city equipment to help unclog Acuña's sewers in response to his counterpart's call, implying that had they followed protocol and gone through their respective state departments, they'd all have been buried in shit. His

Spanish is colloquially Mexican, his abrazos are unabashed American back thumps.

"These cities," he declares, "have a history of helping each other," although no example of how Ciudad Acuña comes to Del Rio's aid immediately leaps to mind. He accepts a glass of border buttermilk and huddles with a Mexican general, a consul, a rancher, and two customs officers. Arms draped around each other's shoulders, they toast various mutual interests in both languages.

Two hundred million years or so earlier, owing to some molten event in the continent's mantle, part of Texas heaved while the other side slipped. Hundreds of feet of limestone cracked in half, and through that crack issued a spring, seven miles above the present course of the Rio Grande. Its human discoverers, twelve thousand years back, had neither the means nor any reason to measure its flow. If they had, they would have arrived at the considerable figure of sixty-five million gallons a day. So awesome was the quantity that this was the one of the last places in Texas that their descendants, the Apaches and Comanches, yielded to the white intruders.

Once those enterprising folks took over, they immediately set about making improvements. A well-traveled road connecting San Antonio and distant San Diego already passed by here, so teamsters could replenish their water in what Franciscan missionaries had named San Felipe Spring. With the addition of an eighteen-mile irrigation network in 1868, the stage stop became a town.

It was a town that looked like no other in dry Texas. Flowing canals created a lushness more reminiscent of Biloxi, Mississippi, than Eagle Pass, fifty miles distant and fifty times drier. (Years later, the weight of Lake Amistad would press so hard on the aquifer that San Felipe Spring's flow would increase by another fifteen million daily gallons.) Spanish architecture vied with pure antebellum for honors along willow-shaded Hudson Drive and Griner Street. A Mexican village called Paso de Las Vacas materialized across the Rio Grande, but there the geology had not been as kind. The gushing artesian rift uncovered by the Balcones Fault closed by the time it reached the river. The Mexican side would forever look like the desert it was.

San Felipe del Río, later simply Del Río, grew around a life source that was only coincidentally near the border. The spring was its heart, and its orientation was east to west along a trade route, not north to south across a river. In a sense, Del Rio has always had its back to Mexico; as it spread, it approached but never quite reached the Rio Grande. When Mexicans fleeing the revolution arrived here in 1910, they found Anglos. The influx of refugees changed everyone's life, but no one would know how profoundly until the 1971 school year.

"Let's put it this way," says Nick Chávez, a local ranger with Texas Parks and Wildlife, "I would never send my kids to Del Rio schools." Instead, they go to a private colegio over in Cuidad Acuña. Many Anglos similarly enroll their children in parochial schools, whose founding coincided with what Del Rioans darkly refer to as "the consolidation." After fifteen years, many others who can't afford such alternatives wish they could. "That," Chávez says, "is because San Felipe still lives."

The San Felipe he means was a school district, not the sort of entity that normally inspires undying loyalty. As far away as California, San Felipe ex-student associations keep a ghost alive. The "exes," as they are known, have even built a San Felipe School District Museum.

In the 1920s, the stream that flowed from the spring to the Rio Grande was Del Rio's social as well as topographic watershed. With few exceptions, San Felipe Creek divided Anglos from Mexicans. San Felipe community, as the barrio was known, had elementary schools, but the Hispanic children attended Del Rio High School with the whites. It was an experience that none relished and few completed.

When Del Rio formed a school district separate from the county's in 1928, San Felipe's citizens went to court to do the same. To their surprise, they succeeded. Now they could have their own high school, free from Caucasian intimidation. So they did, and for forty years this community of less than twenty thousand maintained two separate, largely segregated school districts, as everybody preferred. The football rivalries that resulted were spirited, and a little lethal.

The decision to turn Laughlin Field into a Strategic Air Command base in the 1950s meant a windfall for Del Rio. Air Force families moved in, and Del Rio's school district received federal impact money for two new schools. Then housing was completed on the base, and technically the newcomers were now living in the San Felipe school district. San Felipe's modest system couldn't accommodate them, so by arrangement base kids were bused to school in Del Rio. But a decade later, San Felipe got into budget and accreditation trouble, and somebody figured that if they rightfully demanded to keep the Air Force kids, the federal government would have to bail them out.

The notion brought shudders to Del Rio. A federal court decision stating that children cannot transfer school districts supported San Felipe's claim. But an education adviser from the Pentagon said that another law prohibited the military from duplicating money already spent on the extra Del Rio schools. San Felipe proposed half-day sessions, and an unpleasant rumor circulated, warning that the Air Force would leave Del Rio if their kids had to be taught by a bunch of beaners.

"Why not," suggested the Pentagon, "solve everything by consolidating the two districts?" Nobody liked that idea. But Del Rio's businessmen liked the thought of losing Laughlin's payroll even less.

Then Justice stepped in. The great school consolidation issue ended up in the courtroom of District Judge William Justice in Tyler, Texas, who is regarded in Texas as having written more law than the legislature. Some Texans hold him responsible for prison killings that have occurred since he supposedly lost control of the inmates. In Del Rio he turned the school issue into the most radical desegregation plan in the United States, "more so than Little Rock or Boston," residents recall, not altogether happily. No phasing in—it had to be done in three months.

During the late sixties, Governor Preston Smith's decision to remove Vista volunteers from south Texas prompted civil rights activists to announce, from Ted Kennedy's office, that Del Rio would become the Chicano version of Selma, Alabama. The next day, Del Rio stores sold out of ammunition. On the day of the official withdrawal, marchers arrived in buses from as far as Houston and Laredo.

The sheriff had taken thoughtful precautions. First, he shut every bar and liquor store in town. Next, he instructed Del Rio rednecks to arm themselves and report to the jail, where they would be sworn in as vigilantes. Informing them they'd be on standby until they were needed, he locked them inside. The FBI men with violin cases who'd rented apartments all over town he could do nothing about, but the troops the DPS flew in were kept hidden in a barn out on U.S. 90. By the time the militant priests were saying Mass in front of the courthouse under César Chávez's brown-beret Raza Unida flag, a riot had been averted. Del Rio's mayor stood impassively by in a steel police helmet, his family safely out of town, and wondered where Del Rio was headed.

Diana Abrego, her hair pulled back over silver drop earrings, wearing an embroidered Mexican dress and a look both weary and worried, remembers what consolidation was like. "Students hated each other. The judge outlawed the traditions of both districts. They had to give up their mascots, songs, colors—the blue and white rams meant nothing to the old

grads. I have nothing against the consolidation; I wish we could put our grudges behind us. Parents still tell their kids that Del Rio sucks. Dropouts who come here say they'd still be in if San Felipe still existed."

"Here" is the headquarters of El Comité Cultural del Pueblo. Diana is the volunteer director. It is a combined arts workshop and counseling center, run out of a former San Felipe mortuary with a water-stained ceiling and a floor full of signs and murals-in-progress. Diana is preoccupied over a funding cut that eliminates federal matching grants that have been keeping the place open. "How do you tell that to two hundred kids? When I sit them down and say we may have to close, they get hate inside them. Then they're told they're illegally in this country. The paper runs articles saying stop the flow into the U.S., keep America clean. They quote generals who call illegals a disease in this country."

Most of her kids are legal residents. But during the Depression, the United States rounded up thousands of Hispanics, many with documents, and "repatriated" them to Mexico. Diana Abrego's mother, born in Del Rio, was one of the repatriados. Diana and many Mexican Americans simply assume it could happen again. The Border Patrol has come by the center, and once even tried to take her away.

As a girl picking cotton in west Texas, being sprayed in the face with insecticide for seventy-five cents an hour, she watched the Border Patrol drag women from the fields. "You grow up hating a little when you see your mother hauled away screaming." She holds up a sign that reads ¡Ya basta con la migra! "A nine-year-old thought up this slogan. You'd have enough of the migra too if you saw them pull your parents out of a car and punch your brother, like he did."

World War II changed the lives of Mexican Americans. Men went off to Europe and the South Pacific and returned with incredulous stories of another world out there. They also returned with the GI Bill. For the first time, significant numbers of them enrolled in

PLATE 13

María de Jesús Rodríguez vd. de Martínez, Colombia, Nuevo León

PLATE 14

SCHOOLGIRLS, SECUNDARIA TÉCNICA NO. 32, LIC. ADOLFO LÓPEZ MATEOS, NUEVO LAREDO, TAMAULIPAS

PLATE 15
TRANSVESTITE PROSTITUTES, CLUB MIRAMAR, NUEVO LAREDO, TAMAULIPAS

PLATE 16
MAVERICK COUNTY COURTHOUSE, EAGLE PASS, TEXAS

PLATE 17
KICKAPOO VILLAGE
TERESA GONZÁLEZ, CAROLINA GARZA, AND ELISEO VALDEZ, EAGLE PASS, TEXAS

PLATE 18
COAL MINERS, PIEDRAS NEGRAS, COAHUILA

PLATE 19
WILLIAM WARRIOR, DEL RIO, TEXAS

PLATE 20

RIO GRANDE BELOW BOQUILLAS CANYON, COAHUILA/TEXAS

PLATE 21

ENRIQUE, RUBY, AND LUCÍA REDE MADRID, REDFORD, TEXAS

PLATE 22
PABLO ACOSTA, NARCOTRAFICANTE, OJINAGA, CHIHUAHUA

PLATE 23

Doña Crispina Gonzales vd. de Martínez, curandera, Ojinaga, Chihuahua

PLATE 24
BOQUILLAS CANYON OF THE RÍO BRAVO, COAHUILA

college. The border had no institutions of higher learning, so young men and women from San Felipe community hopped freights to universities in San Antonio and Austin. Many returned as teachers. Since the consolidation, Hispanics have made it to the school board, and voter drives in San Felipe ensure they'll stay there.

"Townspeople call it racist. They sure didn't say that when the whites were in power. If you live in Del Rio, you naturally become racist. If you're brown in this border town, you're seen as a little Pepito or Juanita, just good for sweeping floors or making tortillas. At school, San Felipe kids get shunted into development and vocational classes. The whites go to college prep."

Teenagers arrive on bicycles to work on a backdrop for a play about a giant spray can in a death mask that haunts a family. They retouch where water has leaked onto the scenery. Rock music fills the old, pewless chapel. Diana Abrego takes pride in the doctors and attorneys that have come from San Felipe, but she thinks many forget they were once poor like these kids. She is disgusted that Reagan takes their money away but gives the Del Rio sector of the migra a 36 percent budget increase. She is disgusted that 67 percent of Chicanos voted for him.

"People like him make me think this society is run by rich whites. I organized voters for the election. The mayor handed out free tamales and beer, and now he ignores us. The roof leaks, the artwork gets wet, there's cockroaches but no air conditioning, and now they want to take our building."

Three boys enter, hesitating in the doorway. Diana waves them in. They are from illegal families, just over from Acuña. "Things aren't changing fast enough in society to keep up with this border," she says. "This will be a battleground someday. Brown trying to get in, white trying to keep them out."

.   .   .

For one day in 1908, it *was* a battleground. Insurrectionists crossed the river from Del Rio into Las Vacas and attacked the federales. They were annihilated in the process, but this was the first blood shed in the anti-Porfirist cause. Four years later, with Madero's revolution a temporary success, Coahuila's Maderist Governor Venustiano Carranza felt that event should not go unremembered. He decided to rename the village, but not for the heroes of the battle. Carranza envisioned a Mexico now destined for beauty and peace, so he commemorated Manuel Acuña, a nineteenth-century Coahuilan poet who died in 1873 at age twenty-four.

Villa Acuña became Mexico's only city named, not for a war hero, but for a poet who could produce such verses as:

> *. . . Círculo es la existencia, y mal hacemos*
> *cuando al querer medirla le asignamos*
> *la cuna y el sepulcro por extremos . . .*

> (Existence is a circle; we err, it seems
> when to measure it we assign
> cradle and tomb as its extremes)

> *Que al fin de esta existencia transitoria,*
> *a la que tanto nuestro afán se adhiere,*
> *la materia, inmortal como la gloria,*
> *cambia de forma pero nunca muere.*

> (At the end of this life transitory
> to which our desire clings forever
> our matter, immortal as glory,
> changes in form, but dies never.)

A year later the revolutionary president, Madero, was dead, betrayed by General Victoriano Huerta, who then assumed the presidency. Among Huerta's accomplices was U.S. Ambassador Henry Lane Wilson. Wilson, a solid dollar diplomat, had decided that the United States' business interests had fared better under the comfortably stable dictatorship of Porfirio Díaz. He arranged an alliance between Díaz's nephew and Huerta; all three apparently knew that the coup would end with assassination of Madero and his vice president.

In Coahuila, Governor Carranza raised arms against the new reactionary government and called on other northern revolutionaries like Francisco "Pancho" Villa to join him. Eventually, he was victorious and also became president for a while; eventually, he was also assassinated. Mexico resumed naming towns and cities for its dead warriors. Except for Acuña, Mexico's poets must continue to wait for beauty and peace.

.   .   .

When Juan Raul Rodríguez was a boy living in Ciudad Acuña, he would stay awake at night to hear the music coming from the sky. His family had a ranchito on the outskirts of the city, where they raised a few hogs and goats. After dark, he and his brothers would lie outside on blankets, listening and watching the show in the heavens. Above them rose three metal towers. Huge iridescent sparks flew between them, sparks of surprising colors that intensified with the music. Once, Juan Raul's father held an electric light fixture under the towers and it too began to glow. On another occasion, they realized that the reason their pigs never escaped was because the fence had somehow become electrified.

His father showed the neighbors; it was the towers, they agreed. They ran lines from the guy cables to their houses, grounding them on automobile flotsam, and enjoyed the free energy that the towers shed each night like excess cells.

The towers belonged to an americano named Dr. Brinkley. Sometimes he would appear in one of his Fords along the road he'd built—Acuña's only paved surface—which led from the border bridge through the city to his white building. He would wave, and Juan Raul and his friends would follow him inside. Like one of the bearded Three Kings, each Christmas

their beloved, goateed Dr. Brinkley brought a truck loaded with candy and clothes. Reverently, they watched for hours as he recorded in his glass booth. Later he'd give them used aluminum master disks, which they skimmed through the sky at night to reflect the sparks. All the adjacent houses were shingled with those disks.

John R. Brinkley came to Acuña in 1931, after being kicked out of Kansas. He had the first radio station in that state, from which he broadcast advertisements for his medical treatments. Brinkley offered many sure cures, but the most popular was his surgical solution for impotence. The operation involved inserting goat glands into the scrotums of dysfunctional human males.

For this controversial approach, and for his habit of diagnosing and prescribing treatments over the air, Brinkley lost both his medical and broadcasting licenses during one discouraging year. But later he surfaced in Mexico, with permission to transmit from a Coahuila hamlet then known as Villa Acuña. Its attraction, of course, was its proximity to the United States, combined with the fact that radio waves are oblivious to borders. To ensure that he would reach his audience, Brinkley pumped forth his propaganda at 500,000 watts. His station, XER, was one of the world's most potent radio transmitters, its signals often clearly reaching France and Argentina. The Federal Radio Commission (later the FCC) was powerless to stop him.

Thousands of men traveled thousands of miles and spent thousands of dollars at Brinkley's Del Rio clinic. By this time he had refined his technique, sometimes employing glands mined from the corpses of freshly executed criminals. Besides his personal highway in Mexico, Brinkley built Del Rio's Roswell Hotel, the site of his clinic, and a mansion for himself inlaid with Spanish tiles, surrounded by grounds stocked with peacocks and flamingos.

Malpractice suits and the IRS eventually overtook him, and he died bankrupt in 1941. But during his tenure on the border, he was a beloved man. A 1984 article in the *Del Rio Guide* credited Brinkley with paving the way for today's transplant operations. It stated that many patients actually recovered their sexual capacities from, at the very least, the psychological comfort of the gland implants, and went on to father offspring. A short civic history published by Del Rio's Whitehead Museum features Brinkley's hospital, radio station, and the "international notice" he brought to the city, without alluding to his delusions. Estela Carvajal, the museum's director, becomes impatient when she detects hints of derision in inquiries about him.

"Dr. Brinkley meant a lot to Del Rio. Both banks were folding when he came, and he made deposits in each to keep them going through the Depression. He brought money, dignitaries, jobs, and he played Santa Claus to the kids. He was just too advanced for his time—how many people would've thought we'd ever be putting plastic hearts into humans?"

Brinkley's lasting contribution wasn't his manipulation of gonads, but of U.S. federal communication laws. Supercharged radio stations soon appeared in Mexican cities all along the boundary. Haranguing preachers jammed frequencies with blanket transmissions of their version of the Word and accompanying pitches for donations, a tradition honored by today's television ministries. Clear-channel country-western music reached the entire continent, expanding its formerly regional appeal. Mellifluous-voiced Paul Kallinger, the most famous postwar country DJ, broadcast from Ciudad Acuña. A pilgrimage to Kallinger's studio "in beautiful Ciudad Acuña, 1570 on your dial, alongside the silvery Rio Grande where the sun spends the winter," was a crucial opportunity for hopeful young country stars like Porter Wagoner, Maybelle Carter, Johnny Cash, and Webb Pierce.

Kallinger, who still lives in Del Rio, swears that the Russians learned English from listening to him. Later, a new kind of sound beamed across the United States out of Ciudad Acuña, and a Mexican-based disk jockey changed North American culture forever. The music was called rock and roll, and the disk jockey was Wolfman Jack.

Since the sixties, Mexican law has increasingly required Spanish-language programming. Station owners have generally complied, in part because the Spanish-speaking consumer audience in the United States has grown so large that advertising revenues remain steady. Ciudad Juárez's XEROK, the last of the huge clear-channel rock stations, changed to all Spanish in the early eighties. XEROK's request shows have received frequent calls from undocumented workers all over the United States. The song titles they dedicate are prearranged codes for families listening down in Guadalajara or Michoacán, to let them know they've arrived safely.

. . .

In 1950, a paved Mexican highway reached Villa Acuña for the first time, ending the pueblo's nearly total isolation from the rest of the republic. Servicemen from Laughlin were coming over to spend money, and people from Mexico's interior responded by moving to the border. Acuña's population pushed beyond 20,000, and the villa became a ciudad. In 1960, the railroad came, and the seventies brought maquiladoras to manufacture Johnson & Johnson Pampers and other North American products. Then, like a single, unexpected raindrop, a devaluation fell from the clear blue; then another, and then they seemed to pour down in torrents.

Acuña remains lovely, with horse-drawn taxis and hotels with Spanish stucco courtyards, iron window grillwork, tiled exterior staircases, and ceramic fountains shaded by spreading laurels. But it is growing. Its housing projects fill long before they are completed, and the federal government threatens to relocate earthquake disaster victims up to the more prosperous border. The town swells and groans; the hum from the radio towers is joined by maquila whistles, the motors of circulating automobiles, televisions, crying infants, fans, trains, electricity, machinery, crickets, footsteps, wind, whispers. Acuña's sounds never cease. Like the woolen summer heat, sound is a blanket that everyone sleeps with in this city.

Del Rio's sound is the cicada. The large, beautiful insects with filigreed wings throb in the spring-fed foliage. They vibrate in pastures of silky angora goats that produce Del Rio mohair. Past Brinkley Estates, the subdivision just south of Dr. Brinkley's exfoliating old mansion, cicadas gather in the pecan and persimmon trees shading the entry to the Val Verde Winery, the oldest in Texas. Lenoir grapes, later joined by Herbemonts and Rieslings, have grown plump here to the cicada's drone for more than one hundred years.

Frank Qualia, Val Verde's founder, left northern Italy in 1881 with a group of fruit growers and viticulturists to found a colony in Chihuahua. Many Europeans were then on their way to Mexico at the open invitation of Porfirio Díaz. The dictator wanted the progressive, cultured heritage of the continent to mix with his own people's and bring sophistication to Mexico.

Troubles with land allocation and the sheer danger of the Mexican frontier led Qualia's group to scout possibilities in Texas. At a hacienda in Del Rio, they saw big grapes growing in an arbor. The Mediterranean climate would be good for year-round fruit, and their countrymen were there. The U.S. Army had imported Italian stonemasons to build Fort Clark, thirty miles away at Brackettville, and the master builders were now quarrying the limestone for Del Rio's courthouse.

The grapes Qualia found here were brought to Mexico by European missionaries. Grafting them onto native Del Rio stock, he began the winery now run by his grandson Thomas. The heat is too intense to produce delicate cabernets, but the vintage reds and tawny ports from Val Verde's exotic Lenoir grapes have become regionally famous over the past century. Inspired by Val Verde's success, vineyards of many distinct varietals are appearing across Texas.

Just down the road from the winery is the Border Patrol's headquarters, and within a mile is Mexico. No wine industry has yet begun around Acuña, although Thomas Qualia has sold some cuttings for table grapes. He would like to see vineyards there, because he would like to see anything that might help Mexico's frightening economic plight. A legalized Mexican hires his pickers, and Thomas looks the other way rather than check their papers. "But in eighteen or twenty days, my harvest is over. These poor, honest people in sandals from Zacatecas arrive constantly. They come up right behind the Border Patrol. Many of them are desperate. They'll knock on doors, ask for yard work, and if there's nobody home they sometimes kick in a window and look for jewelry."

Qualia's voice is as complex as his port: Italian inflections underlie a Texas English scented by his second native language, Spanish. He has grayed and prospered among these green and golden vines, and now the future brings him concern. The efforts in Congress to control immigration worry him especially.

"Will the farmer get squeezed out if his labor goes? Will we cause a revolution in Mexico if there's no one to send home money? What will that do to us here on the border? We're America's front line of defense. We'll need ten-foot walls with broken glass embedded on top, like in Mexico."

He runs his hand over the darkened wood of his grandfather's original wine press. "That's not the kind of life we want. Will they send the National Guard to help preserve this?"

The Qualia family's product graces the wine lists of Del Rio restaurants; limestone civic buildings attest to the contribution of Italians who helped settle the border. Like other immigrant Europeans, they assimilated quickly because an ocean lay between them and the country of their origin. By contrast, Mexicans who can often be in their homeland in less than a day have mixed less easily, like lumps that refuse to dissolve completely in the melting pot. Their distinct bronze color is another factor that impedes their absorption, although they have not suffered the degree of racial isolation that America's blacks have endured.

When Judge Justice ruled that the composition of faculties in Del Rio schools must reflect their biracial student bodies, the committees appointed to enforce the law were confronted with the dilemma of Willie Warrior's people. Because they were a minority, they could not be counted with the Hispanics, who now constituted a majority. The system demanded they be classified somewhere, but the only remaining choice was with the Anglos. Willie Warrior grins delightedly at the stunning evolutionary pace of border social dynamics that no longer distinguishes his kind from whitey.

East of town, in a cemetery surrounded by a glade of cloakfern just outside Brackettville, is his proof that such equality is fitting and earned. Here lie more than a hundred American and Mexican war heroes. Willie, a black man whose boyish appearance contradicts his fifty-eight years, is related to at least half of them. Many fought for both countries. Four received the American Congressional Medal of Honor—despite the fact that their immediate forebears had to fight against the United States.

They were runaway slaves who joined forces with the Seminole Indians in the Florida wilderness. An odd relationship ensued. Technically, they became property of the Seminoles, who coveted the prestige white men derived from owning slaves. Yet they were the Seminoles' most expert farmers and warriors. Andrew Jackson's Seminole Wars were waged more to stem the growing power of Florida Negroes than to pacify Indians. Those wars proved to be the young nation's most costly military endeavors.

Black Seminoles battled so successfully that the original idea of returning them to slavery was rejected as suicidal. Since many were the indispensable advisers to Seminole chiefs, the United States bargained for their voluntary surrender by treating them as Indians. They would go to Indian territory in east Oklahoma with the tribe and there be free.

Indian territory proved less idyllic than the United States had promised. Some Seminoles, out of sorts in the arid country, attempted to enslave their black allies again. When the government failed to interfere, a group of Seminole Negroes ran for Mexico. Coahuila allowed them to settle in exchange for periodic duty against the Comanches and Apaches. They were superbly proficient, tracking the marauders in terrain that Mexican dragoons never dreamed of entering. Gratefully, Mexico offered them a permanent arrangement in the form of eleven square miles of land at Nacimiento, next to the Kickapoos.

Seminole Negroes intermarried with Mexicans, tracked Indians, and raised the stolen cattle they retrieved from the Apaches. More runaways joined them, and in 1855 a troop of Texas Rangers decided to end their affront to the American tradition of slavery. Ignoring the new treaty with Mexico, they invaded Nacimiento. After the battle, the Seminole Negroes charitably allowed the surviving rangers to crawl back to Texas.

Following the Civil War, the U.S. Cavalry invited them back. The Seminole Negro Scouts became a brilliant Indian fighting force out of Fort Clark in Brackettville. But they kept their land in Mexico, and like the Kickapoo, floated between southern Texas and Múzquiz, Coahuila.

In the Brackettville cemetery, horned toads and armadillos scuffle through the tall grass as local blacks chat in Spanish with families up for the day from Nacimiento. Willie Warrior, still in his grandfather's cavalry outfit that he wore that morning in the Fiesta Amistad parade, comes to inspect gravesites that need repair. Since tick eradication laws forbid bringing a horse back into the United States from Mexico, he couldn't ride into Acuña. Instead, he came to Brackettville to check on his ancestors.

"Every time it rains, graves begin to sink. I can see

some new ones starting to cave in. We had to pull my Uncle John Daniels's headstone out with a truck. It had sunk right into the ground, it was so soft with rain." Daniels was killed by Texas Rangers at the still he ran during Prohibition, a few yards from where he is now buried. "They ambushed him. He was going through the fence, and they had a Gatling gun set up. Pumped him so full they even shot his teeth out."

Willie, a reserve deputy sheriff in Del Rio, grew up in Brackettville. Blacks attended one school; whites and Mexicans went to another. He has a natural daughter who speaks fluent Spanish and an adopted teenage Mexican son who does not. He finds none of this confusing; after eight generations as blacks who are also Indians and who live in both Mexico and the United States, the Seminole Negroes are accustomed to every conceivable border ambiguity.

Under a fine old mesquite are four official Medal of Honor headstones that Willie requested from the Defense Department. Beneath one lies Adam Paine, one of MacKenzie's Raiders. The other three, John Ward, Isaac Payne, and Pompey Factor, performed an impossible rescue of a cavalry lieutenant, horseless and surrounded by Indians, in a border canyon near the Pecos River. Around them rest buffalo soldiers, veterans of Negro platoons ravaged by malaria in the Philippines, and Seminole Negro descendants who fell in Vietnam. Many wooden crosses mark Depression graves, when sometimes there was only armadillo to eat. Some of the deceased fought against Pancho Villa. Others fought for him.

Nick Chávez sees his daughter off to school at the colegio in Ciudad Acuña, then heads to his job twenty minutes up the road at Seminole Canyon State Park. The name honors the black men who saved their white colonel from red men who claimed both Mexico and the United States for their own. Nick knows this, but what means the most to him in this limestone canyon are the red, ochre, and black pictographs. In shelter caves, forms of human beings, millipedes, atlatls, deer, and insects fill the walls until, at one point, they merge into a multilayered palimpsest, with images superimposed on each other for the entire length of the rockface. It is a mural created by many generations.

Nick, whose family has been here as long as anyone remembers, guesses he is one of the generations, as is his child. The pictographs record something to which the current inheritors of these riverine borderlands must now add.

What, he sometimes wonders, will that be?

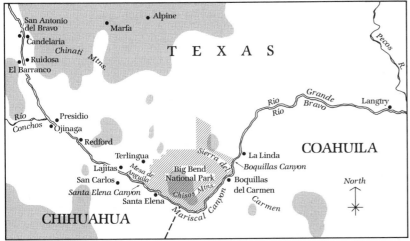

CHAPTER FOUR

THE BIG BEND

In 1882, the tracks of the Southern Pacific Railroad, progressing from both directions, converged three miles west of Seminole Canyon. Separating them was a long gorge, 270 feet deep. Below the laborers—Chinese on the west bank; Mexican, Irish, and German on the east—black vultures circled between perpendicular cliffs that contained the broad Pecos River. For a year, the men tunneled through Cretaceous bedrock on either side, until they could construct a water-level bridge.

With the Pecos spanned, a silver spike was driven to connect the Southwest. The development of the borderlands commenced. Towns named for Southern Pacific Railway officials appeared at thirty-mile intervals, to fuel and water the steam engines. The first of these, Langtry, was situated on a bluff above the Rio Grande fifteen miles west of the Pecos. An itinerant who had sold whiskey to railroad workers from a movable tent buffaloed the Texas Rangers into appointing him as Langtry's first justice of the peace.

Roy Bean, the self-proclaimed law west of the Pecos, fancied that the town was really named for his obsession, actress Lillie Langtry, whose portrait hung in his combination courtroom and tavern named The Jersey Lilly. He wrote to her repeatedly, including an invitation to the heavyweight championship bout between Bob Fitzsimmons and Peter Maher that he staged on a sandbar in the Rio Grande when each country banned it. Lillie Langtry never replied, but in 1904 she came through in a private parlor car en route to the coast. By then, Bean was dead and buried in Del Rio.

Langtry today is little more than a tourist stop at the old saloon. Below its bluff, hunters poach deer, javelina, and wild turkey in tamarisk thickets along the Rio Grande, and trap raccoons and ringtails. Sheep ranchers hire toothless

Amador Cantú, a bounty hunter for sixty years, to lure pumas into sprays of cyanide pellets.

Across the way, the wildlife is a little safer. No Mexican town faces Langtry from the steep opposite banks. Carretera 2, the frontera highway, has stopped back at Acuña. Farther upriver, the Coahuilan villages of Portales, Parrita, and Juzgado wait in rustic isolation for long-proposed paved connections to the interior and to each other.

Both the Southern Pacific tracks and U.S. 90 also leave the river after Langtry. For the next 150 westward miles, the border can only be followed closely on foot, horse, or mule. The river itself has struggled to force a route through this country, encountering uplifted beds of marl and chert and massive layers of yellowish-gray limestone, maroon clay, and dark, flaking shales. Compressed at times between unyielding strata, the Rio Grande gains speed and cuts deeper, leaving long, narrow chasms. The edges of the two countries grow vertical and sheer, poised across frothing rapids.

On the Mexican side, this region became known for a mountain range, the Sierra del Carmen. In the United States, it takes its name from the twist of the river itself: Big Bend.

Marco Antonio Girón of SEDUE, Mexico's Ministry of Ecology and Urban Development, cannot stay away from the Sierra del Carmen. The dark-haired young biologist leaves his office in Saltillo, the capital of Coahuila, and drives north for hours, through Monclova and Múzquiz, until he runs out of pavement. Past the Sierra de La Encantada, he crosses an expanse of Chihuahuan Desert covered with lechugilla, Spanish dagger and creosote bush. A northeast jog takes him onto a rut of a road that scrambles upward. Where the thorns turn to evergreens, he stops his pickup and sits motionless. Otro mundo, he tell himself. Truly another world.

The ascending forest of drooping juniper, encino, piñon, ponderosa pine, and Douglas fir is the Maderas del Carmen, a woodland that fills Girón with a kind of desperation. Where but here can he still watch the black bears chomp prickly pear and then retreat to green canopies where lions stalk mule deer? Where else in these overgrazed Tex-Coahuilan highlands does the grama grass still grow thick as a savanna and Montezuma quail hide among the bluebonnets? Where else do del Carmen whitetail, desert sheep, wild Mexican turkey . . .

. . . yet, for how much longer? If he hikes to the 9,000-foot hogback ridge of the del Carmens, he can see where they become the Dead Horse range. Directly west, the Chisos Mountains fill the horizon, a view that thrills and frustrates. Somewhere between here and there, in a narrow drainage imperceptible from the faulted outcropping where he perches, everything that matters to him changes. The Dead Horse, the Chisos, and their surrounding aprons of desert have been granted an indulgence, an immunity from dangers that once threatened them from their pine tops down to the bedrock. Yet his cherished del Carmens, even more pristine than the mountains across the way, are as vulnerable as they are lovely. Why must the blessing be withheld here, since the land is continuous?

The nature-defying reason is a distinction dreamed up thousands of miles away, superseding the reality of one of the world's most blessed ecosystems. The southern end of that myth, his country, has no money these days for luxuries such as environmental preservation.

Marcos Antonio Girón doesn't accept that. La crisis already existed when the current president, Miguel de la Madrid, took office. It was de la Madrid who elevated the ecology ministry to cabinet level. Back in Saltillo, he writes a proposal, listing every area he can think of in the Maderas del Carmen that must be protected from poachers, cattle ranchers, and the lumber industry. He mentions the income that a national park could accrue. And he closes by suggesting that in some not-too-distant future, the new park could be "a Mexican counterpart to Big Bend National Park in the United States, so as to share and work in harmony, with both parks benefiting the region."

Gil Lusk, the superintendent of Big Bend National Park, often has the del Carmens on his mind. When viewed from his side of the Rio Grande, which forms the park's southern boundary, the Sierra del Carmen presents a formidable escarpment, with white limestone bands alternating with strips of darker shale. The uplift forms the south wall of Boquillas Canyon, the longest in the park.

Sometimes he watches that wall in the afternoon, until the setting sun turns the limestone layers so orange they nearly melt the intervening shales. It is too fine a resource, Gil Lusk has concluded. There are too few reasons why the good people on both sides shouldn't have this together. So he plans for what he has decided they must do.

Until he begins to speak, tall, clean-shaven, sandy-haired Gil Lusk seems too young to run a national park. He has a soft, even voice that compels attention, lest something crucial be missed. Like most Park Service veterans, he has rotated through the system—Valley Forge, Utah's Canyonlands, the Blue Ridge—before arriving here. The idea of directing a park that shared an international resource intrigued him. In the early thirties, when a national park at Big Bend was first considered, an international peace park with Mexico was included in the recommendation. A similar idea was proposed for Canada, which resulted in Waterton-Glacier International Peace Park. The Mexican counterpart never resulted at all.

At Big Bend headquarters in Panther Junction at the foot of the Chisos, Lusk did some research to find out why. "The archives show that we've never taken the time to understand Mexico," he says. "We'd meet in the U.S. and talk about an international park. Being very polite, the Mexicans would say it was a marvelous idea. Then they'd go back to Mexico, and we'd be shocked when no park materialized. We never thought

to ask what they needed. It's like Lake Amistad—Mexico has no use for it. Officials in their hydraulic resources ministry come right out and say that the Americans gave it to them, but they can't control it. They don't have people to put in marinas to attract gringos, and no one in Acuña has big cabin cruisers."

He shakes his head. "Yet the U.S. still can't understand why Mexico doesn't do anything. They're just having a hard enough time keeping the trees up in the mountains. They consider that a higher priority than developing recreational facilities for wealthy people."

He figured he had to establish a demand for an international park, something more pertinent than some gringo thinking it was a good idea. He began getting to know his neighbors better. His first move was to change the policy on confiscated cattle. At any time, about fifty cows that have waded over from Mexico are grazing in the protected foliage of Big Bend Park. Each seized animal used to be taken 100 miles upriver to Presidio, Texas, where ranchers had to pay U.S. Customs a $250 fine per head plus the mordida when they crossed back into Mexico. In essence, they lost the cow.

Lusk began penalizing them on the spot, $25 for first offense, up to $75 thereafter. It was stiff enough to discourage trespassing, but retrieving their animals was affordable. The Mexican ranchers allowed that this was fair.

Then he instituted an October fiesta with beer, food, games, and piñatas, and invited all the Mexican villages for fifty miles. Before long, people were bringing their relatives up to Big Bend from as far as Chihuahua City, and it had become an established event for hundreds of area residents. For Santa Elena and Boquillas, the pueblos directly across the river, he appointed good-will ambassadors to visit frequently and be available for emergencies.

Next he went to Saltillo and Monterrey, and started knocking on doors. The idea was to avoid trying to do business with Mexico in the United States this time.

What he wanted was simply a meeting where parks and wildlife managers from both sides could convene to share data. Contiguous regions do that all the time in the United States, but it had never happened between neighboring border states. The trick, he knew, would be to keep the national governments out of it.

The U.S. State Department and Mexico's Relaciones Exteriores view encounters between officials from different countries as diplomatic affairs, requiring their knowledgeable interference. Lusk and his Mexican colleagues agreed that informality rather than diplomacy would best encourage an exchange of ideas. So they didn't tell any feds and planned a Laredo conference for November 1985.

Two days before, Relaciones Exteriores figured things out. Mexican officials, they decreed, could not represent their ministries in a foreign country without proper sanction. After some pleading and shuffling, a compromise emerged. Mexicans could attend as private persons. The papers they presented would represent their private opinions, not their government's. Biologists like Marco Antonio Girón, already aware that their opinions were not necessarily shared by distant Mexico City, exhaled with relief and headed to Laredo.

"I had no idea how well trained, professional, and advanced the Mexican scientists are," Lusk kept hearing. By the end of the meeting, North Americans and Mexicans were sitting together at lunch, starting to communicate.

There were no great accomplishments, but more joint conferences were planned. "Probably nothing too productive will happen for the first four meetings. It'll take that long for the attitudinal change to set in."

And once it does, Lusk knows what he's after. From his park headquarters he drives over to Rio Grande Village and walks through a mesquite glen down to the river. A boy poles a chalupa, an aluminum rowboat, across to pick him up. On the other side, a saddled donkey waits to take him up the road into the earthen pueblo of Boquillas del Carmen. At José Falcón's, a restaurant built from slabs of del Carmen flagstone, he has bean burritos for lunch and leans back to admire the incredible Mexican sierra.

"There are fifty thousand acres in the Maderas del Carmen that are as near to Colorado as anything I've ever seen," he says dreamily. "Right now, the forests are being selectively cut. The owners are losing money on the logging, but they like to keep their assets working. So we will propose a way to do that." The owners, a Coahuila family that includes a former mayor of Múzquiz, want at least $1 million, which Mexico doesn't have to spare. Lusk isn't sure that buying is necessary. "It just won't be the U.S. concept of a park."

José Falcón, confined to a wheelchair from an auto accident, rolls over to listen. Lusk recommends that park visitors eat here, and José is grateful. Once, fluorocarbons from local mines crossed from Boquillas to waiting transport trucks in the United States, but the traffic was curtailed when the park was established. If this park superintendent has an idea that will mean some money here, people will be most interested.

Lusk explains. "In Europe and Japan, many parks are working landscapes. The luxury that we have in the U.S. of dealing with massive spaces just doesn't apply. It doesn't matter whether Mexico calls it a park or a protected zone or whatever. Recreationists could pay the owners a fee. People from the area could be trained as guides and rangers. They hardly make anything from cattle, and their only alternative is dealing drugs, stealing cactus, or trapping furs—we've intercepted whole pack trains in the park with thousands of pelts. Our deer and birds depend on the del Carmens habitat—they don't just stop at the border. If the Maderas were ever denuded by logging, it would have an awful impact on both countries."

With an adjacent Wild and Scenic section of the Rio Grande, Big Bend National Park manages 13 percent of the U.S. boundary with Mexico. Together with Organ Pipe Cactus National Monument and the Amistad

National Recreation Area, the National Park Service controls nearly one-fifth of the entire border. The service has an international office, but, as Lusk points out, "we have agreements with countries in the Middle East. We send people to Africa. With Mexico, we have nothing. No agreements, only a shared birthright. The river resource won't wait if we play word games until the year 2020. We have to begin together now."

Recognizing Gil Lusk's talents for international relations, three months after the Laredo conference the National Park Service named him the new superintendent of the U.S. portion of Waterton-Glacier International Peace Park.

.   .   .

Outward Bound instructor Robin Kelly has run rivers all over North America, but only in Big Bend can her oars sometimes touch two different countries simultaneously. From Redford, fifty miles west of the park, to Langtry, the border is a bright liquid chain with priceless canyons for links. So clean and severe are the region's geologic faults that the river can pass in seconds from open desert into shadowy crevices between two-thousand-foot blocks of petrified earth.

After a few false starts, the first joint U.S.-Mexican boundary survey was completed in the early 1850s. The line was redrawn and corrected in 1882. But the topographers did not dare enter most of these canyons; not until 1899 did white men finally see them all. As Robin waves to the chalupero on her way into Boquillas Canyon one February afternoon, she is rowing into the last one the surveyors explored. This is a reconnaissance run for a course she will lead in the spring for university students, but it's also a chance to get on the river and think. Lately, her life has crowded into a pass with a distinct choice of egresses. It seems fitting to analyze her alternatives while traveling along a current enclosed by two distinct worlds.

There are rapids here, but no real danger for an experienced boat handler. The major trauma for commercial river runners on the Rio Grande has been gunfire emanating from somewhere on Little Switzerland, a midstream island where drug exchanges are usually more discreet. Recently, a bullet passed through the front pontoon of an inflatable raft; the matter was brought to the attention of the military comandante in Ojinaga, Chihuahua, who apparently decreed that it never happen again. Authorities suggested that river trips avoid the Mexican shore, but in canyons reminiscent of cathedrals, the politics that distinguish one wall of rock from another lose substance.

Two bends beyond the village, rising steam reveals a hot springs on the Mexican side, and Robin can't resist. One-hundred-and-five-degree water has dissolved a shower stall in the limestone bank, but she finds it occupied by a shampooing cowboy, his buckskin mare tethered to a honey mesquite. "Ahorita," he calls to her, but she shakes her head, making it understood that she doesn't want him to hurry. Three miles later she encounters more heated currents joining the river, their source a geologic mystery, the delight they offer her back muscles indescribable. She strips off her woolens and sprawls naked in eight inches of hot, transparent rushing water, her long brown hair extending downstream.

Robin Kelly is a college graduate who spurned better-paying options to sleep two-thirds of every year outdoors. As a course director for programs like Minnesota's Voyageur Outward Bound, which sensibly winters in south Texas, she earns $10,000 a year and respect from her peers for her wilderness skills. Her executive father pressures her to join the real world, but she considers these environs more real than the Chicago Loop where he is. Only, something about the Rio Grande is nagging her. Although it's as stunning as the Grand Canyon, she can't surrender to it the same way, knowing that it's a river divided. The landscape feels simultaneously privileged and burdened.

The canyon's air warms only slightly during the sun's brief appearance across the tight gap of sky.

The silence is remarkable. The water's caramel color confirms that the river is noiselessly loosening the clastic bonds of this former seabed, returning the limestone to the sea itself. A cycle that took 100 million years can now begin all over. What else does the water have to do?

For a day, a pair of great blue herons flap along about two hundred feet ahead of her. Their ungainly, outsized wings recall the giant pteranodons that once flailed awkwardly over the Big Bend, when the limestone was still clamshells. They lead her into one of the canyon's few straightaways, which siphons enough wind down from the rim to nearly neutralize the current, and she must row in earnest to make headway. Within a mile, the flow resumes its switchbacks. Her Redshank raft passes through slots and corners that never appear on conventional maps—the jagged, pinked edges of the border, the tongue-and-groove, intractably jointed union of two countries that dovetail more tightly than they often care to think.

A professor once told Robin that had it not been for World War II, there might not be much river here to run. Mexico threatened to impound the major tributaries of the lower Río Bravo, because the United States wanted to use all of the Colorado River's water before it reached Baja California. "The war convinced Franklin Roosevelt that we wanted friends on our southern flank," he said, "so he implemented his Good Neighbor Policy and came up with a water treaty."

She recalls that lecture as the castellated Boquillas walls rise a thousand feet around her. From this perspective, with Texas and Coahuila equally exquisite and overwhelming, the international boundary is pure fiction. The idea that some human being's whim in Washington or Mexico City could steal the river that carved all this astounds her. To think that the water could drain away during a tug of war between governments reduces the glory of wilderness to the level of a functionary's warped vision. Robin bends to her oars and tries to forget where such speculation leads.

The carrizo along the narrow banks rustles and sways as the wind rises. Strawberry cactus and false agave grow out of bare rock above the high water mark. Robin beaches the Redshank and walks a little way up a Mexican side canyon, polished white by alternating flash floods and desiccation. She builds a mesquite fire and opens a can of smoked oysters. At the sound of hooves, she turns; three young burros have wandered down the wash. Somehow, they remind her of her class a month hence.

She senses a responsibility here beyond teaching whitewater skills and identifying canyon wrens and whiptail lizards. This riparian border is the connective tissue of a continent straining under the double weight of both the First and Third Worlds. How can she convey to students from the Midwest an image of nature fracturing under social pressure?

After three days, her journey ends with an unexpected treat: the Arroyo del Veinte rapids turn out to be more absorbing than the river guidebook described. Exhilarated and renewed, Robin lands at the bridge leading to the fluorspar mine near the Coahuilan village of La Linda. A bit later a friend picks her up at the Mexican gatehouse, where the customs official shared his coffee with her while she waited.

Earlier that morning, for several miles she watched a Mexican boy on horseback following cattle on trails that paralleled the river. It occurred to her that despite the Rio Grande's jointly shared status, Mexicans never run the river—they ride or walk alongside it. Americans recreate by devising rigorous tasks like scaling mountains or defying turbulent streams. Residents of the Third World don't need to invent struggles.

The customs man watches them deflate the Redshank and disassemble the oar frame. "Do you want to come with us sometime?" she asks on an impulse.

"Señorita," he replies gravely. "Who has the time?"

From an against-the-flow perspective, the Rio Grande emerges abruptly from Santa Elena Canyon at the western extreme of Big Bend. Like a movie run backward, the cliffs of Texas's Mesa de Anguila and Chihuahua's Sierra Ponce drop away from the taut chasm and flatten into desert. The river backs out of Big Bend's trenches and suns itself along the surface.

Where the National Park ends, the village of Lajitas begins. The wood frame Lajitas trading post, circa 1900, sells supplies and foodstuffs and features gentle peculiarities like baby javelinas and a one-horned goat that guzzles beer straight from bottles. Around it, an inauthentic, authentic western town is under development, to attract filmmakers from the coast and rhinestone tourists from urban Texas. Week nights, the project's mojado construction crew settles around the trading post's wood stove with $3.50 six-packs of Budweiser. On Fridays, they return to their village of San Carlos, Chihuahua, eighteen kilometers south.

The trading post belongs to Rex Ivey and his son Bill. The Iveys aren't directly involved in the development of Lajitas. But the beginnings of this boom have given them some ideas and the capital to pursue them, and they have purchased the nearby ghost town of Terlingua, with intentions of resurrecting its spirit.

Terlingua (tres lenguas, three languages: English, Spanish, and Comanche) was once known for cinnabar mines employing seven thousand workers in the production of mercury. The introduction of labor and safety laws during the 1930s made digging too expensive. The mine reopened during World War II, but workers hit an underground river, floating the operation out of business for good. By 1946, Terlingua was a memory resting atop miles of waterlogged tunnels.

Terlingua's renaissance began in 1967 with its Chili Cook-Off, an event attracting berserk hordes each November from as far as Dallas to brave Texas's most torrid culinary conditions. Locals have retaliated by holding a Cookie Chill-Off in January, enjoying home-baked folklore and confections, free from imported hype. But the future here is set. A stucco gateway to an empty clearing that will develop into "Terlingua Springs" already interrupts the view along Highway 170. Land speculators with names like Big Bend Realty are busy establishing beachheads in the west Texas desert sand.

"No way to stop it," says Bill Ivey, who now carries Lajitas Trading Post t-shirts along with his line of basics. "People who have been coming here for years complain that it's being turned into a Houston, that it's losing its attraction, that the place is being ruined. But when I ask them where they're staying, they're in the new hotel, eating in the restaurant and playing the nine-hole golf course."

The Iveys also have a stake in another venerable Big Bend business: candelilla, a pencil-thin desert plant with a high natural wax content. It grows on both sides of the river, but collecting it is a labor-intensive business more suited to the economics of Mexico. For a century, Mexicans have harvested the wild plant and smuggled it across the river on pack burros. Mexican law prohibits exporting candelilla without paying duties, but Mexico can't extradite hot wax once it's in the United States. The Iveys avoid the tariffs and bribes involved in importing it legally by purchasing wetback candelilla in Lajitas and clearing it through U.S. Customs in Presidio on the way to the wax-rendering plant in Alpine, Texas.

Twelve to fourteen metric tons of candelilla enter Lajitas two times each month, eventually ending up in products like Merle Norman cosmetics and Wrigley's chewing gum. The Iveys pay just over the official rate of their competition, the Mexican government. The recent devaluations have yielded more raw wax for fewer dollars.

Tall, fair-haired Bill Ivey grew up in Lajitas when the population was only nine—four of them his own family. His friends lived across the river, and when they had to flee during Border Patrol raids, Bill often ran with them. Early on, he sensed a stronger force on his side of the Rio Grande. He knew that his friends' fathers worked for his father, that patrón and peón roles prevailed. "It was a tradition. Sometimes to deviate from a tradition is not healthy."

The deviations Bill Ivey sees today include once-unheard-of transriver marriages. When he attended Central High School up in Alpine, ninety-five miles away, it was Anglo only, the Mexicans all going to Centennial. Things have changed. The river is not as mean as it was—the locals attend dances on both banks—but it is still a barrier. The Mexican workers know that, but Lajitas is their lifeline of construction and cattle. This is the Border Patrol's Alpine immigration district, and Alpine is too far away for them to be seriously hassled.

A chalupa connects Lajitas with the agricultural ejidos across the river. On Fridays, the construction workers from San Carlos sometimes have the boat detour to a long sandbar known locally as Mischer's Island, named for Lajitas's Houston-based owner. Mischer's Island is tierra de nadie, no man's land, and people from San Carlos often go there for cockfights or horse races. Afterward, with water pouring over the hoods of their pickups, they drive over to Mexico along an underwater road that parallels the south bank for some distance before surfacing.

They pass through an eroded Chihuahuan terrain of olive-brown clay, covered with creosote bush, stiletto lechugilla, ocotillo, and candelilla. Mighty blocks of limestone crop out in the washes like exposed tectonic plates. Pinkish flagstone lajas cleave in large sheets and shatter into smaller lajitas. The torturous road, once a branch of the Comanche Trail, hugs the haunch of a ridge that climbs the volcanic Montañas de San Carlos. When it begins to descend, the men stand in the pickup beds and look over the cab at el cielo—heaven in Mexico.

What they see are springs gushing from two vertical, hairline canyons in a spectacular uplift. At its base, a cottonwood halo crowns the village of San Carlos. Beyond it, the springs flow to an alluvial plain where Lipan Apaches once dwelt and where the people of San Carlos now raise pecans and corn.

The pickups roll to a stop on the cobbles; Ramiro Morales, one of the carpinteros from Lajitas, looks around with satisfaction. Quiet and clean, San Carlos is reputed to have the most divine women in Mexico—because of the water, they say. The flagstone and adobe pueblo is lovely in its own right. Ramiro allows that the new structures in Lajitas are comfortable and impressive. But their Disneyish presence bewilders him.

"When I work in Lajitas," he says, "I use lumber and blocks that arrive in a truck—from where, I can't imagine. The building that results is beautiful, but it is a foreigner. Here, if I build a house, I make the adobe from the very earth the house will stand on. The rock is from here. We are so much closer to the land. We comprehend nature. The Americans don't."

· · ·

The Camino del Rio, a Möbius strip of a highway, begins on the American side west of Lajitas. Suddenly, vehicles must negotiate fifteen-degree grades and vertiginous passes, while the Rio Grande churns menacingly below. Hoodoos, ghostly wind-cut formations in the white volcanic tuff, hover along the Camino's writhing path. There is no nearby alternative route on the Mexican side, which is simply perpendicular.

Between two of the most stalwart Camino del Rio ridges lies a jarring sight—concrete Indian teepees decorated with an unintelligible fusion of American Indian symbology: buffaloes, New Mexico suns, snakes, thunderbirds. These anomalies were erected in 1964, for Lady Bird Johnson when she rafted downriver to visit Big Bend National Park. Beyond, the Camino relaxes a little. Land and river meet and expand; strings of adobe Mexican villages come into view on the southern horizon beyond broad, river-irrigated fields. On the U.S. side, the terrain is less benevolent. Piles of boulders add character but interfere with notions of extensive cultivation, and attempts at crops like melons have produced varying results over the years.

The Camino becomes simply Texas Farm Road 170. It arrives at a town, a collection of colorless structures spread one-deep along the highway. On its western extreme, a few aged adobes and a former church drop back from the road and extend thinly a half mile to the riverbank. Cavalrymen stationed here during 1916 noted that the red sandstone banks formed a shallow place to ford the Rio Grande, and began to call it Redford. The name stuck and appears on maps today. Where it doesn't appear is in the vocabulary of the primarily Spanish-speaking inhabitants, who use the old name: El Polvo, meaning dust. Dust, Texas.

El Polvo has just 125 inhabitants, but Redford's post office serves at least 500 people. Tall poplar obelisks filled with fat sparrows line the short walk that leads to the mail room, which is located in the front of postmistress Lucía Morales's house. Several generations of Moraleses have lived here, often concurrently. As the family increased, so did the house's adobe appendages, anticipating the concept of modular homes by nearly a century.

Behind a caged window next to wooden PO boxes, Lucía bends her diminutive bulk to the task of packing a shipment of rolls of stamps that came by mistake—people only buy singles here. A glassed-in diorama against one wall contains a three-dimensional Morales family saga, portrayed by painted sycamore figures carved by her great-uncle Benito. Generations of little wooden men and women drive a wooden oxcart across a river, break ground, plant cotton, build ocotillo huts, and fire up tiny diesel engines. On an adjacent wall hangs a complicated, spreading family tree.

Outside, the women who sit and converse under the portico come to attention when a blue Chevy van rattles up and Faustino Pineda gets out. For thirty-eight years, he has brought the morning mail down from Marfa, the county seat. He also brings medicines, food, and dry cleaning, and takes more orders back.

It doesn't take Lucy long to sort the mail, most of which she tosses into a cardboard box. These are for people in the pueblos across the river, who use Gen-eral Delivery, Redford, as their mailing address. The closest Mexican maildrop for them is in Ojinaga, two hours away over discouraging roads. Postal inspectors figured this out a few years ago and wanted to close Lucy's operation. But someone pointed out that stamp sales were repatriating dollars, so they stopped inspecting. The notion of Mexicans sending letters destined for someone in Mexico via the United States seems circuitous and possibly illegal, but practically all the mail in the cardboard box originates in the United States. "Everyone they know is working over here," Lucy explains.

A man in his sixties enters, wearing a flannel shirt, a corduroy coat, and scuffed wingtips. Eleuterio Salazar is a predicador from across the river, a preacher of God who has found, he tells everyone, perfect peace. His mission in life is to describe that peace to all he meets. Lucy hands him the cardboard box. Eleuterio lives by doing double duty, delivering the mail as he passes among the river pueblos on his evangelical wanderings. His card states that he represents the Church of Christ of Amarillo, Texas.

At the edge of town, Eleuterio heads south along a dirt road. Near the river, Redford is virtually Mexico. The houses are long, one-story adobes. At one of these, Eleuterio parks the car he borrows from his immigrant sister and follows a worn path to the Rio Grande. A red-faced, grizzled man in a stocking cap rows over in a chalupa with pieces of board bolted to aluminum tubes for oars. He charges 100 pesos to paddle Eleuterio to Mexico, where his red Ford pickup awaits. Behind the fringed windshield, a vinyl-covered Bible rests on the sun-cracked dashboard.

For the next four hours, Eleuterio travels in second gear through irrigation ditches and over roads soft with dust. He drives as if by Braille, feeling the way, wondering when the missionaries in Amarillo will send him money for new tires. He visits border towns that don't appear on maps. Palomas. El Salitre. Loma de Juárez. Labor de Abajo. The villages are indistinguishable, blinding reflections of each other in the bright, early winter light. The roads intertwine and turn back on themselves, meandering down gulches and rolling up hillocks. His route's circuitry has no internal logic, except that Eleuterio knows it. After generations, knowledge of local trails becomes part of the genetic imprint in rural Latin America.

Except for his truck, the village streets are empty of vehicles. The pueblos seem nearly deserted, as though people were driven away by the implacable sun. Only women and very old men emerge from the mud brick interiors to meet the postman. The able-bodied are all in the United States.

For each delivery, Eleuterio receives payment, sometimes in the form of a bottle of milk, a kilo of eggs, or fresh asadero cheese. Otherwise, he charges 100 pesos per letter. But sometimes the price goes up to 200 or even 300. As he bumps into Loma de Juárez, he fishes out one of the expensive kind. The green computer card showing through the manila envelope's window is a U.S. Treasury check. The grateful anciano who hands over 300 pesos is one of sixty thousand residents of Mexico who receive monthly U.S. Social Security payments.

"Gracias a Dios y a Tío Sam," he gums fervently.

Other envelopes are fat with cash, sent home by men working the oil fields or citrus orchards. In his sermonettes, Eleuterio preens a bit, reminding that "for nineteen years, people have trusted me to deliver their mail because they know I'm a preacher of the Lord and would never steal." When he retires, he doesn't know what they're going to do.

He has more than a hundred families on his route, and, like Faustino Pineda, he also handles other services. Women do piecework sewing and tailoring for customers as far away as Marfa, using the postman for pickups and deliveries. He also takes orders for candy and cosmetics. Sometimes he slips Bible tracts into the packages he brings. "How many customers have you actually converted?" someone asks.

"Eight."

"Only eight?"

"Most people reject me. They just want their letters. I don't get disappointed. My faith is in God, not people." He reaches for the Bible and turns to Juan 14:6. "Yo soy el camino . . ." he reads.*

The way he knows this unchartable camino, it's possibly true.

In El Salitre, he delivers a Sears catalog to his daughter. Her husband, who works on oil rigs near Odessa, languishes in a Texas jail for being repeatedly apprehended as an illegal. "They should arrest men for being drunks, not for doing honest work," Eleuterio tells her.

From a hilltop, the view of the aquamarine river and adjacent fields refreshes his senses after the glare of the shadeless pueblos. Columns of Villistas, Pancho Villa's followers, once descended this same hill in pursuit of Federalist troops, driving them across the river and into the United States. Today, the only pursuit is of drug traffickers, and rarely at that. Little Switzerland, the island just below that neither country claims, ripples with marijuana.

The road approaches the fields, passing an incongruous mansion of brick and stained wood. The mafioso who owns it lives in the States, but likes having a little cottage on his home tierra. Eleuterio won't deliver mail there. A little farther along is Eleuterio's own adobe house. He has a hectare planted in wheat and corn, a few pear and apple trees, and his church. "Here," he tells his eight converts, "I work both heaven and earth." The wooden chapel has gas lamps and two pews apiece for each of his parishioners. It was built years ago by the Amarillo mission; the missionaries haven't returned since. The following day in Redford, Eleuterio dictates a letter to them, which Lucía Morales translates into English.

"Dear brothers," he says, "can you please send money for shock absorbers?"

· · ·

―――――
*"I am the way . . ."

Doña Crispina Gonzales, in her blue nightgown with a pink scarf wrapping her silken white hair like a babushka, concentrates on a clear, sunlit gallon jug of water in the stillness of her unpainted room. On the table in front of her are three similar jars, a few smaller vessels of tinted glass, and several crumpled paper sacks. Behind the table is a wall of saints. Outside, the clucking chickens grow silent. Fingering the white plastic cross at the end of her rosary, Doña Crispina shakes her head and mutters her prayer.

She turns in her homemade wooden chair. Her visitors, a farmer and his wife, are perched on the edge of Doña Crispina's small spring mattress. They straighten. "All I can tell you," she says in a voice clear as a viola, "is that they have taken it very far. I see them rounding a curve. Far from here." She names another curandera they can see for more specific information. "I'm not the person qualified to tell. I'm sorry."

They all stand; Doña Crispina is less than five feet tall. She raises her hands and blesses them. They thank her and with bowed heads depart through the screen door.

Crispina returns to the jar of water. It appears crystalline and still, but to her it swirls darkly. In it she can plainly see the two men, one short and stout, the other tall, who stole the farmer's tractor here in Ojinaga and are headed with it into the Sierra Santa Cruz. Others may give out that kind of information, but Crispina knows what will happen if she does. Guns will be pulled, revenge will be sought. It would end up in a blood battle, and the sin would be partly her responsibility.

In two weeks she will be one hundred years old. In her time she has served as an instrument of God's remedios; her hands have delivered thousands of his newborns, including six of her own daughters. It's one thing to tell people if the migra is waiting at the checkpoints; it's another to lead them to where harm will surely result. She has no intention of staining her soul at this point.

She glances into the other jars and her mood softens, because she sees visitors coming whom she likes. Lupita Ramírez up in Odessa wants another healing for her back; already she is better and has stopped going for her useless injections. And the yellow car means her lawyer friend from Chihuahua City will be here tomorrow.

She inventories her vials. For rheumatism and varicose veins, she will need coyote and rattlesnake lard. Pink palo de rosa flowers and flor de tila . . . ay, Dios nos vigila. Since the earthquake in Mexico City disrupted delivery of so many vital herbs, it has been impossible to find flor de tila.

The door opens; her one-eyed son Martín announces that Enrique—

"I know."

Doña Crispina loves Enrique and Ruby Madrid, who have brought a gift of Hostess Twinkies from across the river. "Have you been doing what I told you?" she asks.

They have. Two months earlier, Crispina informed them that their store had been bewitched and that they had to undo the hex. She prepared them an exorcist's kit that included incense, herbal water, some crushed leaves, and mustard seed. The water had to be sprayed in every corner, the smoking incense carried throughout the premises. For seven weeks, they sprinkled crushed herbs around the place and threw mustard seed on the roof, as Crispina had instructed them.

"Good," she says. "The spell will be broken."

They have not come for a specific cure, but for her general blessing. She has them stand side by side, and then rises from her chair. Enrique, a giant of a man, looms over her. Although bent by age and responsibilities, Doña Crispina's grasp is still firm as she takes their wrists. She starts to inquire about Ruby's allergies, but suddenly senses that Enrique is having trouble swallowing. On the way here, he tells her, a bee stung him, and his throat feels like it's starting to swell.

"*...el mundo vino del Padre Nuestro; se lo dió a doce apóstoles que comieron el pan cada día de los cuatro evangelios....*" For ten minutes she moans prayers and incantations, casting out toxins with deft healing motions, her strong fingers milking their forearms. She lays transparent hands on Enrique's massive head and Ruby's blonde hair. "*...Virgen de la soledad, del refugio, del planeta, del socorro...lo pido de corazón, amén.*" Doña Crispina hands them a bottle of scented water and instructs them to sprinkle their clothing. She spins them around and annoints their heads and shoulders.

Afterward, they sit and talk. Doña Crispina has noticed that Halley's comet is accompanied this time by chariots in the sky. When she last saw it, she remembers, it had come alone. When they leave, Enrique gives her some wadded cash, and she blesses him again. "Now we can pay the light bill." Most people pay her with beans or cheese these days. There is very little money.

"The next time I go to Boquillas," says Father Melvin LaFollette, "I have to bless a house and cleanse it with incense and holy water. They tell me a Baptist who doesn't want our mission there hired a witch to put a curse on it."

In the Madrid Store in Redford, wearing a Chili Cook-Off shirt and rubber thongs and with stringy gray hair and mustache, LaFollette looks more like a ravaged poet than an Episcopal priest. In fact, the Madrid's grocery-gas station-lending library includes a collection of poems he penned during an earlier career. "People here believe witches can put a spell on you." Enrique Madrid looks at the floor. "I mean, would a Baptist hire a witch?"

LaFollette has been serving congregations from Presidio to Boquillas for two years. His ministry is on both sides of the river, but anywhere below Highway 90, which is one hundred miles to the north, it's all one underdeveloped country to him. LaFollette thinks

his church should establish an official international parish. Both sides, he says, suffer from spiritual, cultural, and literal malnourishment.

Enrique Madrid, who at last count owns nine thousand books, does not entirely agree. That is not something he would come right out and say. Instead, his tendency is to continue gazing humbly downward, his intelligent, doleful eyes magnified by black-rimmed glasses, while his mind photographically scans the contents of his library. Eventually, in his exquisitely gentle voice, he offers a synthesis that goes something like:

"Well, you know, with 12 percent of the people, the United States uses one-third of the world's resources to maintain its standard of living. That means the entire earth can only support three Americas. Therefore, there's no way for Mexicans to become Americans, because there's too little earth for them. So we'll never have a developed world, not in the American sense, because there's not enough wealth for every country. Given today's technology and availability of resources, we can't raise the poor to the level of the rich. Maybe the rich will end up at the level of the poor."

Enrique Madrid sees a chronic sense of inferiority permeating his people's history, brown people first wishing to be white, civilized Spaniards and then blond Americans. "Hispanics have been misled to want what Americans have. Many are coming to get it. It should mean an end to the American dream, because if they all achieve it, America as we know it won't exist. The influx of migrants will change what America wants."

People of Mexican heritage in the United States usually migrated northward or were already living here when the land under them changed sovereignty, but Enrique Madrid's family came by request. In 1870, Governor Richard Coke recruited Mexican desert farmers to settle west Texas, then inhabited mainly by Apaches. It was the exact reverse of Mexico's invitation to Moses Austin's Anglo colonists fifty years earlier in east Texas, although so far the Mexicans have failed to wrest Texas away from the United States. Enrique's great-grandfather Secundino Luján was one of five to bring his family from Ojinaga, Chihuahua, to farm the area they soon referred to as El Polvo.

They cleared the land, breathed the dust, dug irrigation canals with picks and shovels, and planted beans, chiles, and grains. Indians kept raiding until 1927. Enrique's mother, Lucía Rede Madrid, tells of her grandfather, on horseback, racing before several Apaches to the river with the hammer of his pistol cocked, ready to kill his wife and child if they were caught. Her own mother, the first person in El Polvo to learn English, had eight children, seven of whom became teachers. Lucía Rede Madrid calculates that, collectively, they have taught 190 years of classes. Among her siblings and their offspring, family members have earned 155 college degrees.

Enrique does not number among the graduates. He began studying philosophy at St. Mary's, a Catholic university in San Antonio largely attended by Mexican Americans. In 1965, ROTC was compulsory. After two years of drilling under Chicano officers who'd fought in Vietnam, Enrique transferred to the University of Texas.

"All my friends were dying. The casualty ratios for Mexicans were absurd. Vietnam really hit the Chicano community—the military is a ticket out of the barrio. I talk to white people who know no one who went to Vietnam. Every Chicano knows too many."

The antiwar movement was barely visible at the University of Texas in 1967. A rural Mexican American like Enrique Madrid already felt isolated and anonymous. Nineteen years old, he decided not to participate in what he saw as madness.

"It was so easy to go along with it. It was America's social reality at the time. To me, it made no sense. If you've seen an auto accident or hunted animals," says Enrique, a hunter and a member of the National Rifle Association, "you've seen the ease of killing and the ease of joining in a cooperative venture to create pain and suffering. So you say no. And you get arrested. For trying not to cause pain."

He was the first University of Texas student to return his draft card. It was not a popular stand—potentially a dangerous one for a border Chicano in a white, urban university. His application for conscientious objector's status was refused, because he based it on moral principles rather than religious beliefs. In the process, he lost his student deferment. But instead of going to war, he went to court.

There, he argued that the war in Vietnam was unconstitutional, because Congress had never declared it as the Constitution explicitly requires. To fight in it was therefore against the law, and he would be knowingly committing a crime if he obeyed the order to participate. Furthermore, the press had presented almost nightly evidence that U.S. troops were routinely violating several laws of international warfare, including torture and bombardment of civilian villages. As a soldier, he could likely be placed in the double bind of being a felon if he followed orders or facing court-martial if he didn't. The Nuremberg trials had eliminated "following orders" as a defense.

He concluded by invoking the Thirteenth Amendment, which outlaws slavery. To force someone to fight and to kill against his conscience constituted involuntary servitude in the extreme.

Enrique Madrid had chosen a defense that if successful would influence a nation, because to find in his favor a judge would have to rule the war in Vietnam illegal. The district court sidestepped the issue. After three years of motions and litigation, his induction was thrown out on a due process violation—his draft board, not taking his CO application seriously, had not bothered to give him the obligatory hearing. "Another time, another place than Texas, another person than a Mexican, it all might have helped." By winning on a technicality, he had ultimately proved nothing.

With Ruby, the wife he met at college, he returned to Redford, disillusioned, broke, and a few credits short of a degree. His family had supported him through the fruitless moral battle, and he owed them a lot.

No other town in the forty-eight contiguous states is as far from a metropolitan area or a major airport as Enrique Madrid's west Texas border village. Until she learned the language, for Ruby, a Caucasian from Houston, living in Redford meant plenty of time to read. Enrique's schoolteacher mother had begun the library in their store for the people of El Polvo, and Enrique and Ruby added to it relentlessly.

Enrique became known in the trans-Pecos borderlands as a steward of knowledge. His locality concerned him, not as an isolated curiosity, but as part of a greater truth. The Madrid household, an appendage to the store, became like a museum, containing stone weapons, whale vertebrae, fossils—and the books to interpret them. Enrique learned the natural taxonomy of the land. He sorrowed over the trucks that passed by, carrying away one of the last remaining North American wildernesses in cardboard boxes— piles of smuggled cacti that evolved here over a million years, headed to nurseries in Europe to die in six months.

The preservation of archeological sites particularly impassioned him, because the Indians weren't merely ancient people, but his ancestors. At the rate of five thousand sites a year, pottery hunters and developers in Texas violate or discard the history that his people have been too busy surviving to preserve. The endangered species he defends, like the Conchos pupfish and the rough-footed mud turtle, can always be bred, but archeological sites are irreplaceable.

To the west, where Mexico's Río Conchos merges with the Río Bravo del Norte, the Presidio-Ojinaga area was once known as La Junta, the junction. Above Presidio, the Rio Grande is an intermittent stream, but at La Junta it is perpetually replenished. The Conchos prob-

ably formed the Rio Grande's canyons; it carries so much Sierra Madre runoff that Ojinaga is the only district in Mexico without irrigation limits. Here, the Jumanos Indians lived in long adobes similar to the Pueblo Indians of New Mexico. Despite the transcendental heat—Presidio's temperature frequently leads the nation—the area has been continuously inhabited for at least twelve thousand years.

On bluffs yellow with wild desert dahlias, which overlook oxbows that confuse the issue of what is Mexico and what is the United States, Enrique Madrid sifts through pit ovens surrounded by middens of exploded river rock, once used for baking sotol hearts. He is in his ancestors' kitchen, enjoying the same bel canto of mockingbirds that entertained his grandmothers a hundred times removed. Centuries of female human hands hollowed the deep circular metates in the nearby exposed Boquillas limestone as they crushed seeds with their basalt manos.

When he finds evidence of ancient warfare, Enrique wonders about the heritage of killing. Had prehistoric population pressures driven his own forebears to violent defense of these sites? During his draft resister days, he noticed that he received little support from his own culture. The Latino psyche, he decided, has had few qualms about warring. Machismo has fathered cultures leading to Latin American military dictatorships. He sometimes envisions an apocalyptic future of a United States a half-century hence, when 200 million desperate Mexicans show up. He is aware of American history, how people have responded whenever they perceived a threat from another race.

Someone—was it a joke?—has sent their library a subscription to *Ultra*, a Texas coffee table magazine replete with color evocations of Houston and Dallas overindulgence. It depicts a society where wealth is accumulated mainly to be displayed. He has no doubts about the extremes to which such people will go to avoid sharing what they have.

In Mexico, a commonly expressed fear is that the United States will someday try to push the border farther south, as it has done before. North Americans are less concerned about their frontier being usurped militarily; a demographic shift is the threat they worry about. With half of Mexico's eighty-five million people under age sixteen and yet to enter their breeding years, Enrique Madrid guesses this shift is inevitable. Mexico must create more new jobs each year, and each year it falls short. Last year, it needed 800,000 jobs. This year, a million. So far, the United States has been a safety valve for Mexican unemployment, but the boiler has barely begun to heat.

He regards the barrier between the two countries. Even with the added flow of the nearby Conchos, the sluggish Rio Grande is a fordable stream. "Nowhere else on the planet," he notes, "is migration more likely to occur than here. The U.S. and Mexico form one of the world's only topographic North-South corridors. Indonesia is separated from Asia. India abuts China, but there's the Himalayas. Sea and desert divide Africa from Europe. Russia and Iran—well, the Russians have already become a minority in their own land."

In the summers here, even the stars radiate heat. The nearby Sierra Rica, a large collapsed volcano near Ojinaga, ripples in the atmospheric distortions as though it were under water. Across the river, the pagodas of the Sierra de Bufecillos are suspended on a hidden hydrofoil, levitated by the mirages that re-arrange reality in the Chihuahuan Desert.

Presidio, Texas, exists mainly to offer Ojinaga the minimum of U.S. services that enhance border life for Mexicans. It is a random clutch of concrete block structures, including a bank whose flashing thermometer seems stuck in triple figures, the Border Patrol, and uninviting migrant housing units for onion harvesters. Against that competition, Ojinaga is practically charming. There is even a hint of prosperity in its hillside neighborhoods, as newer homes of brick join the durable stuccoed adobes.

Like elsewhere on the border, Ojinaga feels unnat-urally feminized, its streets filled in the evenings with girls and women. On graduation from secundaria, the young men ritually head to the United States. "It would be nice," says pharmacist Pedro Madrid, "if we could offer them a dream here. The greatest ambitions even of the smartest ones are to become mojados, cultivate a taste for Budweiser, and buy a car and cowboy boots."

There seems to be little else. Ojinaga's well-watered agriculture ends at the volcanic landforms that crowd the river bottom. Few maquiladoras or tourists venture this far from airports and dial telephones. A local tradition exists of returning after six-month tours of the U.S. circuit and marrying into one of the families that have long been exchanging offspring, but that doesn't account for all the new brick façades in town.

Victor Pantoja, a secundaria teacher with a professorial gray mustache and haggard eyes, knows the explanation, and it chills him.

Pantoja is not new to disappointment. For twenty years, he has tried to interest his government in preserving a splendid Chihuahuan Desert site south of Ojinaga as a national park, before someone discovers it. With great difficulty, he arranged a VIP slide show of the area, but the governor of Chihuahua never removed his sunglasses and departed at the end without comment. In Mexico City, Pantoja was refused a permit to start an Ojinaga museum to exhibit fossils because, he was told, antiquities are property of the national government. On the way home, he noticed fossils being sold in the Chihuahua City airport.

But teaching has been his love, ever since his own days in this same school thirty years earlier, when a history professor became his model. He has similarly tried to provide a moral, inquisitive example to his students, but it's become impossible.

"Narcotics changed everything. Pushers respect no authority. We have shootouts at any hour on our major streets. The villians sponsor fiestas with horse races, cockfights, and mariachis. No one touches them. The police and army are all involved. At the fair this summer, the soldiers were taking people's jackknives. But the pushers arrive with their guns, and no one says anything."

Not long after the U.S. drug agent Camarena was assassinated in Guadalajara, the Mexican army announced the capture of a vast marijuana plantation near Coyame, due west of Ojinaga. They freed ten thousand slave workers living in concentration camps, and burned forty tons of seedless, hybrid mota. "All they burned was the soil. The plants had already been harvested. Bales sat along the highway with soldiers guarding them. Students from this school helped load their trucks."

Pantoja sinks into an empty desk in his salón. His angry face weakens. Once, when rural schools had just begun in Mexico, students sat on the ground and the teacher was an apostle, a doctor, a spiritual guide. It was rustic but beautiful. "Now, what kind of values can we instill? I try to be an example, but students tell me, 'Perdone, Profesor, but you are a pendejo. I make more in one night carrying a plastic bag across the Río Bravo than you make all year. My último modelo pickup has doble tracción. You'll drive that broken cucaracha until you die.' What can I tell them?"

Not only them. Nobody wants to hear. "I go collecting in the desert and I come across a hidden airstrip. If I report this to the police or the general, I won't wake up the next morning. People shut up here out of fear. If I tell my pupils that drugs are evil, they tell their parents that I'm making accusations. Someday I'll wake up dead, my trunk stuffed with mota, and the police will say I was a pusher."

His classroom door fastens with a piece of wire. The school has no money for locks or books, although money is evident all over town. "This is now part of our corrupt culture. Responsibility is in the dirt. Our values have been junked. Our children imitate swaggering criminals. On the radio they sing corridos about them, like they were heroes. So much for Emiliano Zapata."

·   ·   ·

Para cantarles primero	To sing for you first
voy a afinar mi guitarra,	I will tune mi guitarra,
para cantarles, señores	so I can tell you, sirs
las tragedias de Ojinaga.	the tragedies of Ojinaga.
Siendo pueblito tan serio	A town once so sober
por toditos sus lugares,	wherever you'd go,
todo se ha vuelto un infierno	now all's gone to hell
por do'quiera corre sangre.	and blood it does flow.
Todo se debe a La Mafia	All due to the Mafia
que ha invadido estos lugares	an invasion malicious
para traficar la hierba	selling its pot
y el polvo que tanto vale.	and a powder so precious.

It began in silence. A man's burned body was found in the Río Conchos. Apparently, he had also been hung. No one could identify him, and it was assumed he was from out of town. No one knew who killed him or why. But the rumors began.

Dr. Artemio Gallegos began to understand better one afternoon in 1977 when a large stranger with a bullet in his foot barged past his waiting room and flopped onto the table. The examination was interrupted by the simultaneous arrival of the police and a prominent local hoodlum, both looking for his patient. Gallegos and his nurse dived under the furniture and didn't surface until eighteen rounds later. One policeman had been hit in the spine by his own men. The patient, named Heraclio Rodríguez, had been hit nearly everywhere.

Rodríguez, Gallegos learned, was from Culiacán, Sonora, northern Mexico's narcotics hub. He had arrived to take control of a developing situation, but found out a little too late that the Ojinaguenses were not interested in being controlled. His death was a signal triumph; inexplicable wealth suddenly became apparent all over Ojinaga. Men who once worked like everyone else were now staying home, lounging in fine new clothes, driving 2 million-peso Ford pickups and traveling regularly up to Odessa on no clear business.

Gallegos, a candidate for mayor, vowed to investigate. "Don't," he was told in the governor's office upon his election.

"¿Por qué? It's a free municipality."

"Not so free. And we can investigate you too," he was warned. The message was repeated to make certain he got it straight: "Don't get involved. It's not your business. Leave it to others. It's not your department."

Fermín su nombre de pila,	He was christened
Arévalo su apellido	Fermín,
en el norte de Chihuahua	Arévalo, his last name,
por todo muy conocido.	in northern Chihuahua
	All knew of his fame.

The corrido celebrates how Fermín Arévalo ended up in Islas Marías, Mexico's Alcatraz, for helping himself to millions of pesos one day in an Ojinaga bank. His career was already distinguished by cattle rustling and candelilla smuggling. After his release, he became a gentleman farmer, growing marijuana at El Mulato, just up the road from Eleuterio Salazar. He acquired the obligatory four-wheel-drive pickup, a bigger plantation with more dope acreage, and an airplane. The word was that Fermín Arévalo was now a very big man.

The same was said about Pablo Acosta, who had a ranch near San Carlos. Acosta's and Fermín Arévalo's operations were expanding like two dirigibles being inflated in a hangar built for one. Outside of Cuidad Juárez, they were reputed to be bigger than anyone else in Chihuahua, with diversified investments in marijuana, cocaine, and Mexican brown heroin.

Fleets of matching new pickups began zooming around Ojinaga. The Acosta family became one of the city's more prominent employers. Pablo Acosta's army was drafting willing cadets from the ranks of the secundaria. Teachers were already accustomed to students leaving because their mojado parents took them to the States, but now dropouts were staying in town, flashing money and spoon-shaped silver jewelry.

One Sunday in June 1982, Fermín Arévalo's son Lilí stood at an ice cream stand on Calle Translinea, drinking lemonade. A Ford Bronco passed by: A window rolled down and twenty-one M-16 rounds took care of Lilí. His cousin Lupe, not quite dead, was rushed to the hospital and then rushed right out again, because Acosta soldiers were spotted on the way. Two days later, he underwent surgery, surrounded by armed guards.

After that, things in Ojinaga deteriorated. People disappeared, and unidentifiable bodies appeared in their place. Cars careened down city streets, firing at each other. When Pablo Acosta's brother Juan was added to the list of casualties, gunned down at a dance in San Carlos, Fermín Arévalo stopped going to town. His mother told her neighbors that she had raised her children to know right from wrong. If they chose the latter, they were responsible for paying for their actions.

Members of both families agree that Pablo Acosta, his little brother Héctor, and their bodyguards went to Fermín Arévalo's ranch with the intention of discussing peace. Fermín was away, his wife apologized. Only the maid was around. Would they like to wait? Pablo and his men declined. As they slowed for a cattleguard on the way out, they were ambushed by Fermín and the maid's husband. Automatic weapon fire shattered the windshield of their Bronco.

Somehow, no one within was wounded fatally. Their attackers were less fortunate. After carefully running over Fermín's body until no bones remained unbroken, one of the Acosta delegation performed a ritual mutilation, stuffing the results into Fermín's gaping mouth. Then, perhaps feeling that a pious gesture was in order, he slit the corpse lengthwise and again across the breast to form a cross. They took the women hostage, and kept them until the perforated but still operable Bronco got them safely past any traps. "Spread the news," Acosta told Arévalo's wife, dumping her in an arroyo.

Héctor Acosta pulls up alongside the light-skinned woman. He is slender, with slick black hair, and wears a blue-striped cowboy shirt and fancy leather boots. A small automatic rifle points muzzle down into the floorboards. From his neck hangs a square gold pendant. His silver rodeo buckle has a gold armadillo in its center.

Héctor is considerate of the woman. Her husband used to package for Pablo, but he became addicted to the gummy brown heroin that he scraped from under his fingernails after work every day. Pablo felt badly—the husband was good neither as a worker nor as a husband anymore—and he has since helped her secure permits so she can have a business. She is grateful, and sometimes Pablo's daughter stays with her. What was she doing in Ojinaga? She explains. "I'll tell Pablo," Héctor says.

Waiting for Pablo in the Ojinaga military comandante's office, Comandante Malaquías Flores is all solicitousness, offering her and her companions beer from his refrigerator or Chivas Regal from the credenza behind his wide desk. In the office are two television sets, a large yellow safe, a couch, and some plush chairs. He excuses himself briefly and goes across the hall to the dispatch radio, which he uses to reach Pablo's mobile unit. "He'll be here shortly," Flores says, smiling. "He's on his way into town. There was a little trouble last night. Pablo took care of it."

Malaquías Flores wears a powder blue cowboy shirt, partially unbuttoned, and gray gabardine Levi's. The butt of an automatic pistol protrudes from his belt. His hair is thinning, but he maintains a luxurious mustache, its ends carefully turned down. Two grams of Credit Suisse gold and an Italian crucifix dangle on his chest. A diamond-inlaid gold horseshoe wraps

around his ring finger, and the hammered gold watchband of a black jeweled Rolex encircles his wrist.

He is afraid these days, he says. Before he was named military comandante, he served as Ojinaga's chief of police under Dr. Artemio Gallegos. "Everything was under control then. Now there are so many different police. Every little while another special force shows up, all wanting money and cars and television sets. Each one says it's here to enforce some new law. You'd think the authorities would tell us. You don't know whether to pay attention or not. In the U.S. you can ask. Here, you just don't know."

He checks his watch; Pablo should be here any time now. Maybe someone would like another beer.

The woman asks what was the trouble that Pablo had taken care of. Not long before, after kids showing off their semiautomatics accidentally killed a tamale seller's son, she had gone to Pablo and told him, "Look what's happening. It's because you guys are all caught up in this macho stuff." Pablo had liked her saying that, and the mafiosi stopped displaying Uzis and AR-15s on the street. Then a punk from Odessa took a shot at him in front of the Motel Ojinaga. Pablo was carrying a small piece in his bulletproof vest and he killed the dumb culero himself and took $3,000 off the body, so people were nervous again.

The comandante says nobody died this time. Pablo is a decent person, he believes. All mafiosi should be like him, though he admits things were frightening when he and Fermín were after each other. Flores's superiors in Mexico City would like him to inform on Pablo. "As if they don't already know. They've even asked me to arrest him. I tell them: You want him, you come and arrest him. You don't know him; he's my friend. He buys radios from my stores, I get him gas for his plane and his cars. How can I go after him? I don't mind informing, but I've got my family to consider."

The government's whole attitude is so hypocritical, he continues. They're in on the Mafia—they'd be coming for them otherwise. "We steal a little, they steal

PLATE 25
MERCADO CUAUHTÉMOC, CIUDAD JUÁREZ, CHIHUAHUA

PLATE 26
René and Carmen Mascareñas, Ciudad Juárez, Chihuahua

PLATE 27

FERNANDO NÁJERA, JUÁREZ EXPORT, CIUDAD JUÁREZ, CHIHUAHUA

PLATE 28
PANORAMA: EL PASO AND CIUDAD JUÁREZ
INDOCUMENTADOS, EL PASO, TEXAS

PLATE 29

JESÚS PERES RÍOS AND ANTONIA CABALLERO, COLONIA 16 DE SEPTIEMBRE, CIUDAD JUÁREZ, CHIHUAHUA

PLATE 30
RICHARD SALAZAR WITH LOW RIDER, EL PASO, TEXAS

PLATE 31
DR. OSCAR MARTÍNEZ, DIRECTOR, CENTER FOR INTER-AMERICAN AND BORDER STUDIES,
UNIVERSITY OF TEXAS AT EL PASO

PLATE 32
Cajón Bonito, Sonora

a lot more, and so on up the line." The gringos too. "They come over and say they want to end el narcotráfico. I tell them if that were true, they'd lock people up for one hundred years instead of letting them out on bail. Or just kill them. CIA guys tell me that México allows drugs to flourish, but I tell them that they do too. Who are they kidding? They know what's coming over and when. México grows the stuff because it sells. The U.S. makes a big noise about it, but they make big money too. The CIA knew all about the Coyame plantation. So did I. If Caro Quintero hadn't shot the U.S. agent, everything would've been left as it was."

He pours more scotch, and gets philosophical. He's the military comandante of the city. He owns two record stores, an electronics store, a brick factory, a company that makes cement drains, and a tortillería. He's trying to put in a drive-in movie, but it's a long, expensive process, because the government is in on movies. "You know," he says, "the system is so rotten that it's what lets us live in peace. It's so bad, it's good. The law doesn't let you do anything. It encourages you to be crooked. You are guaranteed much more that way."

He rambles on, about how no one likes to work anymore, how everyone lies around while one person goes off to the States and sends back money, how a revolution won't happen in spite of the suffering because there are no leaders like Villa. All the smart leaders go into the Mafia instead of politics, he explains, and at that moment the door opens. Comandante Flores ushers Pablo Acosta into the room, into his own chair. He sets the Chivas bottle in front of him. Discreetly, he departs.

Pablo Acosta is sweaty and dusty, dressed in a blue western shirt, fading gringo Levi's and a worn straw Resistol. On his right hip, a chrome-plated .45 automatic rides high in a holster clip under his flower-tooled belt, hammer cocked, safety on.

He is in his mid-forties, of medium build, with black hair waved over his ears and a mustache that droops below dilated nostrils. When Acosta was younger, rude dentistry outlined his incisors with a cheap compound matrix, which has now been replaced with gold. His face looks more sandpapered than shaved. His heavy hands are encumbered by a ring made from a $10 gold piece. His eyes do not trust.

It is ten in the morning. Acosta pours a tumbler of scotch. Extracting a filtered Marlboro from his pocket, he begins to roll it between his thumb and middle finger, removing most of the tobacco. All the while, he is watching. Like a wild animal on display, he acts both trapped and in command. "¿Qué pasó?" he asks the woman. She introduces him to the people she's brought. For some time, Pablo has been telling her he should do this. She produces the tape recorder. His handshake offers no warmth. But he feels that finally he ought to talk. He realizes people don't understand him. And they should.

Pablo Acosta was born in Santa Elena. His family ranched on federal land along the Río Bravo across from Big Bend. In 1948, hoof-and-mouth disease reached the borderlands; across the river, the United States was destroying thousands of cattle. The Acostas' own cows were not affected, but Mexico made his father sell them anyway. As compensation, the land was granted to them as an ejido.

They tried raising beans and wheat as they were told. But to survive, they crossed into Texas without papers to pick cotton. "I was twelve years old," Acosta whispers in a voice like poured sand. "I continued following the harvests for twenty years. I was not allowed an education."

He excuses himself for a few moments. When he returns, his Marlboro resembles a digesting boa constrictor. He burns it away in three sustained inhalations. His close-set eyes widen and separate, and he pours himself another double. "In 1968, my father was dead. I had to support my mother and my family. I decided to try contraband." His neck veins bulge, and he speaks louder. "I chose la droga. Drugs were easiest. I was working construction in Odessa and knew many people bringing heroin up from here." He was carrying his first ounce when a roadblock stopped him at Marfa. Someone informed.

Pablo Acosta's attorney advised him to plead not guilty. He now believes this was an intentional maneuver to set him up, because he was sentenced to eight years in prison. A guilty plea would've meant five, with parole in three. His lawyer was intelligent and well known, so Pablo decided that his misleading counsel was part of a greater system in which everyone cooperates. Whoever informed on him had power. He remembered the lesson.

In Fort Leavenworth, he made paint brushes and attended night school. After five years, he was released for good behavior. He had paid for his mistake and learned how to avoid repeating it. "The same authorities that jailed me, taught me. There is more drug business inside Leavenworth than outside. In jail, I realized that contraband would be around forever—that the U.S. government approves."

When he left, he knew how and what to do. He offered his services to people he'd met through the penitentiary, leading him to his Guadalajara contacts. "My investment was the risk, and I was paid well for it. I wanted the money to educate my children, the way I was never educated." For instance, he says, he regularly donates necessities like sports equipment to Ojinaga schools.

In northern Chihuahua, corridos are sung to the Robin Hood-like virtues of Shorty Martínez, a drug thug who paid for poor peoples' operations and financed ranches for his neighbors. Shorty's philanthropy ended in a pyrotechnic farewell party one evening in Santa Elena, arranged by federales whom he'd refused to pay off. On his way into local history, he managed to bring four of them with him. Nobody in Ojinaga seriously ranks Pablo Acosta's charitable urges with San Shorty's, but no one disputes that he came to power by knowing just when someone needed a favor.

"It is so simple," Pablo says, "in a world where people must be protected from their own government. Now the police can't touch me. I stand on their shadow. They try to control people by force. I do it with assistance."

The comandante leans into the room. Pablo is wanted on the radio. He excuses himself, snatching from the ashtray the cigarette he's been emptying. When he returns, it is full again.

He has not, he resumes, neglected to use force when needed. "I have never intended to hurt or offend anyone. I've never fired first. When Fermín's son died, I wasn't even in town. Of course, it was easy to blame me. And of course, I defended myself. I feel no guilt over that. Everyone has to defend themselves. People wanted me dead and paid money. I was stupid enough to go to a place unfamiliar to me, where I talked sincerely with his wife for an hour while they prepared an ambush. My brother and cousin were already dead. Now Fermín is too."

Ten bullets hit Pablo Acosta that day in 1984. He emerged, bloodied but alive, a lord of northern Chihuahuan narcotics. With coca fanning his ego, his eyes like ball bearings glinting through dirty lubricant, he describes his survival as a sort of resurrection. He is inspired by accomplishments that his people would have never imagined back on their stony ejido. And no one challenges him now. "The law has no charge against me. I've never fought with the law or with honest people. What I do is wrong, but I do it to remedy many things, like education for young people who lack resources. I put on benefit horse races and cockfights. It's for them. The government never gives them anything. I buy them sports equipment," he repeats.

This raises the question of how he can justify paying for their basketballs with the profits derived from addicting other young people. That, Pablo argues, wasn't his fault.

"It all began when the U.S. treated soldiers returning from World War II with heroin. They knew it was dangerous, but they permitted it. And the young people developed a taste. Besides," he adds, "I only traffic marijuana. Not heroin." He nearly smiles, revealing a glimmer of his gilt-edged teeth. On the couch, the woman stares at her feet.

"People think I'm a rich man. That I make my money lying down. They are mistaken. Mistaken. I don't even have a carport. I sacrifice myself. Someone has to. I work harder than anybody, harder than any teacher or politician. And I don't do it just for myself." Two weeks ago, he mentions, he gave $2,000 to a policeman to take his polio-stricken daughter to El Paso. "I do one bad thing so I can do 100 good things."

He admires the United States government because it helps people. But he is no fool. "The same governors and mayors in the U.S. are in the Mafia. If they wanted to stop drugs, they could do it in a day." The fact that they don't is another reason he admires the United States, because its officials profit splendidly in private from what they publicly oppose.

"I learned from them. I have done much wrong, but the U.S. is my accomplice. In the United States, whether a person turns out bad or good, they make money from him. Look at me. You don't think the United States could control me if they wanted to? How can that rich country say that I am smarter than they are?"

The phone rings. Pablo listens, murmurs tersely, and grunts with satisfaction. He stands. "You know," he says, "the U.S. can't keep money in its pocket. It has to keep circulating it. The drug money goes to México, to South America. Then those countries buy Caterpillar tractors from the U.S. They put narco-dollars back into americano banks. The banks loan it back to Latin America and earn more interest. Then Latin America can't pay it all back, so U.S. companies arrange to come in and manufacture cheaply. The money is always building. Drugs will never go, because they're too important to that spiral. What does the U.S. care if drug money leaves the country? It comes back tripled."

Pablo Acosta drives his fortified Ford Explorer pickup, its chrome rollbar studded with KC lights, to an ironworker's shop. Outside, the shell of his bullet-riddled Bronco, souvenir of Fermín Arévalo's bon voyage, stands rusting on blocks. He shows where volleys of gunfire penetrated its skin, points out a grisly crease in its upholstered roof, and tells who bled and suffered. The experience confirmed his resolve to continue. "I want them to respect me. I am always on the side of good."

The system is so bad, it's good, says the comandante. The law corrupts and the criminals keep order. Pablo Acosta's hubris gleams darkly back when society is held up to his malevolent light. He struts through a taut borderline region that causes some to turn out like him. His need for justification lies mainly in the awful isolation he's purchased, with only bodyguards and potential traitors for companions. But he fulfills a demand that he did not create, one both loudly denounced and quietly encouraged.

The boundary between morality and depravity intersects la frontera. At their junction, narcotics and weapons pour between the Americas. The political division itself adds to their value. Danger heightens and profits increase. As they do, hopes decline and drag the future along with them.

.   .   .

Less than a kilometer past the Ojinaga customs kiosk stands a monument on a traffic island. Several white block buildings behind it form the headquarters of an army garrison. Here, Mexico is transmitting a symbolic message across the border, one that is largely lost on its uncomprehending North American neighbor.

The monument is a smaller replica of the six-columned, white marble homage to Los Niños Héroes at the entrance to Mexico City's Chapultepec Park. Since 1984, other copies of it have appeared in Nuevo Laredo, Ciudad Acuña, and Nogales. The heroic children it honors were cadets of the National Military College, then housed in Chapultepec Castle, who defended it to their death in the final battle of the Mexican-American War in 1847. In a capital known for sparing no expense on its statuary, the Niños Héroes monument is one of Mexico City's most lavish public tributes. American tourists walk by it daily without realizing that it bitterly memorializes the beginning of Yankee aggression in Latin America.

Shabby by comparison, the miniature columns of Ojinaga's version are reinforced concrete covered with quasi-marble tiles. On the same day that Pablo Acosta justifies his twisted defiance for the record, two Mexican soldiers emerge from the cuartel, crossing in front of the monument on their way into town. One is mestizo. The other is also of mixed heritage, but one tributary that contributed to his bloodline is revealed by his orange-red hair and freckles.

Here in the north, his lineage probably extends from the Irish railroad builders imported during Porfirio Díaz's dictatorship. But it is just possible that he has an ancestor whose fate was sealed by that of the young cadets whose memorial he has just passed.

The Mexican-American War coincided with the arrival in the United States of refugees escaping Ireland's potato famine. Mostly Catholic, they were welcomed to their new land by businesses that posted signs reading "I.N.N.A."—Irish Need Not Apply.

Many took the only job available: the army. Often they ended up in poorly equipped, all-Irish platoons under brutish Protestant sergeants. When they marched into Mexico, some began to wonder why they were fighting for a country that hated and abused them, against gentle people who were Roman Catholics like themselves. Eventually, many deserted and joined the Mexican army. When Winfield Scott and Zachary Taylor entered Mexico City, among its defenders was a contingent known as los San Patricios—the St. Patrick's Brigade.

The Mexicans and the San Patricios engaged Scott at Churubusco in their finest stand of the war. When the Americans prevailed, they took as prisoners twenty-seven Irish deserters. A week later, when the last Mexican stronghold fell—the Military College, defended by the heroic cadets—the Irishmen stood on a gallows in Mixcoac, facing Chapultepec Hill. Mexican schoolchildren learn that the last surviving cadet wrapped himself in their flag and jumped to his death rather than surrender to the Yankee invaders. As the Stars and Stripes went up over Chapultepec Castle, an American colonel gave the order to release the trapdoors.

Monuments to Los Niños Héroes, streets named for los mártires irlandeses—the Irish martyrs—and $18 million in reparations are what Mexico came away with from the war with the United States. Lost was its entire North. The border was falling into place.

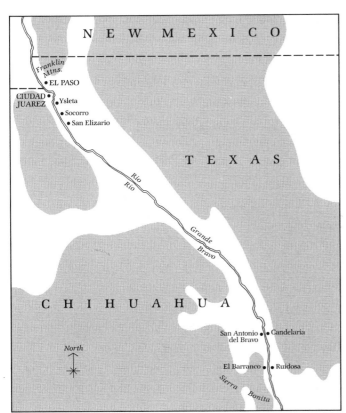

CHAPTER FIVE

EL PASO

DEL NORTE

amarisk was introduced into North America from the Middle East in the nineteenth century to control erosion. It soon became a plague. Also known as salt cedar, it colonizes wildly down watercourses and chokes off side canyons. Since the 1930s, when floods containing tamarisk seeds overflowed Elephant Butte Dam north of El Paso, the slender-branched exotic has steadily moved down the Rio Grande. At Candelaria, Texas, fifty miles above Presidio, grayish tamarisk foliage has replaced the bright green cottonwoods along the river. Even when cleared, the salt accumulation from tamarisk's needlelike leaves ruins the soil for anything else.

Both Candelaria and Ruidosa, twelve miles away, once had cotton fields, but upstream damming on the Rio Grande ended that. Ruidosa's adobes are cracking and dissolving, and someday the tamarisks will have the place to themselves. Both towns now exist mainly to sell package goods to Mexicans from the villages of El Barranco and San Antonio del Bravo who cross the río on footbridges. The children in Candelaria's one-room white schoolhouse are mainly from over the river, but the law requires them to live in the United States at least Monday through Friday. Schoolmarm Johnnie Chambers dutifully checks their shoes for riverbottom mud—she could lose her job for teaching the wrong children.

Most of her pupils will only hear the English language in two places all their lives: her school and the Candelaria store run by two sisters, Marion Walker and Frances Howard. But Mrs. Chambers tells them they are Americans: that their Spanish-Indian blood is purer than her own, an indecipherable mixture of so many Old World strains. Some of them will partake of her education and move on to the Texas cities. The river is a lovely place to grow up, but there's nothing on the American side except food stamps and yearly visits from missionaries. The alternative is the rancherías in Mexico. Several former students, their brush with North America and English a brief interlude left behind with childhood, send her their own children, hoping that maybe this is the generation that makes it—whatever it is.

Five miles above Candelaria, a rockslide has obliterated the lava border road. To continue up the Chihuahua side, locals drive across the river, knowing just where to veer away from a dropoff that swallows pickup trucks whole. The Rio Grande is protected here by Mexico's Sierra Bonita and the U.S.'s Sierra Chinati, gorgeous ranges that fracture into buttes and pinnacles. Gambel's quail, roadrunners, and jackrabbits the size of coyotes share this land with the rattlesnakes. Tiny Mexican outposts of whitewashed adobe like El Comedor and Los Fresnos huddle below natural stone bridges and blue mountains, surviving on candelilla and bony cattle that forage on tobosa grass amid the catclaw.

The river can be forded at Los Fresnos and again at Pilares. On the Texas side, the road is a dinosaur hide, filled with primeval cracks. Blood veins descend the mountain faces, widening into bleached yellow alluvial fans. Rimrock crops out in organic waves. Above the narrow valley, the wind and runoff carve hoodoo canyons of red and gray clay, filled with cathedrals, minarets, hourglasses, and torsos. Few North Americans ever see this country. They generally avoid these forbidding roads that connect distant segments of nowhere familiar, but Mexicans cherish them as lifelines into regions where no one bothers to come look for them.

The procession of the sierras, one after another, continues along the river. Explorers half a millenium ago despaired of crossing them. But in 1536, Indians showed the shipwrecked explorer Alvar Núñez Cabeza de Vaca a place where the Rockies briefly parted, and he told others. It became *the* pass, El Paso del Norte. Through it, Spain poured into the north, and Mexico after her.

Mexico is still there, meshing metropolises with the United States. Nowhere else but Los Angeles is there

such an international city. Nowhere else but Berlin are so many souls skewered by a line drawn on a map.

•   •   •

"There is a theory of real estate," El Paso developer Michael Ridley explains, "which says that—barring geographic barriers—cities will grow, and grow affluent, toward the northwest. A town begins along a main street. A residential district forms next, usually to the southwest, and gradually circles to the right."

Like the Coriolis Effect, which causes water to swirl clockwise or counterclockwise depending on which side of the equator it drains, cities in the Southern Hemisphere seem to do just the opposite. "One explanation is that most rivers in this hemisphere run northwest to southeast, carrying effluent away. Whether or not that's the case, in most cities a line does divide north from south. The least affluent usually live to the southeast."

In El Paso, that line is Interstate 10. Property to its south is worth approximately half the value of real estate to the north. Although El Paso's Mexican Americans outnumber its Anglos nearly two to one, most of them are crowded into the smaller south side.

El Paso has yet another east-west line, the U.S.-Mexican border, and Michael Ridley wonders if it doesn't operate in much the same way. "It seems to be a completely human trait to seek this division."

If anyone tried to prove the existence of a biological inclination to impose boundaries, isolated El Paso–Ciudad Juárez could provide the laboratory. In any direction, its nearest major metropolitan neighbor—Tucson, Albuquerque, Chihuahua City, Lubbock—is 300 miles away. At least 1,500,000 people live in EPJAZ, as planners refer to it, making it one of the world's largest desert cities. Its north and south sections are among the fastest-growing urban areas of their respective countries. After 140 years, the parts have diverged yet coils of history and topography keep yanking them together. Although both try to ignore or deny it, their futures are as inseparable as their common origins.

In Mesa Hills, his northwest El Paso subdivision, husky, dark-haired Michael Ridley is building contemporary homes set within two degrees of perfect solar orientation. By adding proper insulation and overhangs, his houses require no air conditioning in a city where temperatures reach one hundred degrees thirty days a year. He does not rely on new technology so much as old traditions. Ridley has discovered perfect solar haciendas in Chihuahua, where centuries ago men jammed sticks into the ground and watched their shadows to determine how dwellings should be situated.

He takes pains not to violate limits that arid lands impose. El Paso ordinances require that houses be set back twenty-five feet on their lots, which creates a city of thirsty front lawns. Ridley uses the space instead for off-street parking and landscapes the rest with indigenous Chihuahuan foliage. In a subdivision he will only build on half the acreage, leaving a survival margin for the desert itself.

Progressive developers like Ridley have ideas about how to get along with the desert. What is anybody's guess is how they will contend with the other prominent factor in their environment, Ciudad Juárez. Ridley has been in urban planning seminars at the University of Juárez, but at this point he's stumped. "Juárez gets edicts from Mexico City for housing projects with sixty units—about 360 people per acre. That's real density. When they're built, they're already slums."

Ridley's own home has one of the few views in El Paso that doesn't overlook Mexico. He never forgets, though, what is growing just behind him. His live-in maid violates immigration laws every Monday morning. Despite El Paso's distinction of having the lowest per capita income among large U.S. cities, everybody here seems to have a Juárez maid, and nearly everyone's maid supports a large family. A few years ago, the Carter administration erected an expanded-metal

Tortilla Curtain along the U.S. side of the river to keep the Mexicans out. Within a week, most of the fencing had been transformed into chicken pens in Juárez backyards. The ballyhooed curtain, conceived in the distant cortex of Washington, D.C., did not turn out to be appropriate urban planning.

But how can an urban entity so capitally divided plan for anything? With 3 percent of its streets paved, Juárez's infrastructure lags so far behind its needs that hardly anyone dares make an attempt. One idea, widely cherished along the border, interests Michael Ridley. "If the two cities were one big free trade zone, a lot of capital would flow into Juárez. The border is unenforceable anyway, so why not push it back a few miles in each direction and let the economy flourish?"

The free zone: It is a border promise that never dies, although it also never satisfies. The latest bill before Congress suggests a two-hundred mile strip on either side of the line, which would include Phoenix, Los Angeles, San Antonio, and Monterrey in one fabulous, two-thousand-mile Hong Kong. El Pasoans like Ridley suspect that's impossible, given the international police force probably required to manage it. But why not here in the border's urban fulcrum, where the river gives way to the fence and where North and South have been horsetrading for centuries?

Oscar Martínez has often considered that. His view is a little different from Ridley's, since his second-floor offices in the University of Texas at El Paso literally look out a window on Latin America, a thousand yards away. From it, Juárez resembles a wound in the earth. The desert has been scraped and peeled back, exposing lifeless white soil. Shadeless, unpaved colonias stare in turn at the mysterious architecture of the university. The sloped-wall design of the hilltop structures is Bhutanese, chosen by a college president's wife after a journey to the Himalayas. From the colonias, it resembles a monastery suspended just beyond the reach of mortals.

"I don't think," Martínez says, turning from the fascination of his windows, "that either government is ready for a free exchange zone here. The U.S. doesn't want anything that might promote immigration by attracting more Mexican people to the border. And Mexico is concerned about increased U.S. economic influence on its side. It worries about northern Mexico drifting away from the rest of the country."

Martínez directs UTEP's Center for Inter-American and Border Studies, and is president of the binational Association of Borderland Scholars. Once the border was a culturally contaminated strip that academics leapfrogged on their way south to study the authentic and exotic; now colleges regard the clash and blend of disparate civilizations as the stuff dissertations are made from. Centers like the one Martínez heads have become standard in southwestern U.S. universities. Tijuana's border think tank, El Colegio de La Frontera Norte, has branches in nearly every city along the boundary, but not even these are quite so fortuitously situated as UTEP. Border studies classes here can sit on a knoll and watch indocumentados hop from rock to rock into North America without wetting their feet, then cut through campus on the way to work. Many graciously pause for interviews, although uncompassionate campus police sometimes snitch to the Border Patrol.

Martínez himself used to enter the United States without permission. He was less than a year old when he came to Ciudad Juárez from southern Chihuahua, after the American company where his father labored shut its mines. From Juárez, Bernardo Martínez roamed without documents across the border, working mines and railroads from Texas to California. At his mother's behest and sacrificial expense, Oscar crossed the river to attend a barrio Catholic school near the international bridge. He never stopped. One of a growing number of UTEP Ph.D.s from Ciudad Juárez, his scholarship has led him back to the very place he once had to escape to get an education.

The Ciudad Juárez he describes has felt the shocks of great alternating currents of prosperity and depression. Many times Mexico City granted it a zona libre,

a free trade zone, only to have second thoughts. The schizophrenia began in 1859. Only eleven years earlier, Paso del Norte was one city. After the Mexican-American War, the northern section was connected to the United States, whereas the southern half was far enough from Mexico City to not feel much connected to anything. Its people suddenly had to pay high tariffs for goods from just over the river. For many, the solution was to move there. Mexico had to establish a twenty-kilometer-deep-duty-free zone before it lost its entire border population.

It worked—a little too well. People could now buy what they wanted without paying import taxes. Soon, American companies opened in Mexico, circulating money and jobs. Mexicans from the interior complained that the competition threatened national industries. And Texas storekeepers weren't pleased that customers from Mexico were now staying home.

Feeling pressure from both sides, Mexico City rescinded the zona libre. Mexicans shifted north again to avoid tariffs and customs searches, and commerce in the United States rejuvenated. So, after a while, the zona returned. Each time it did, Mexican population along the border rose, U.S. business along the border stagnated, Mexico City industry protested, and the federal government spun with a confusion that has never totally abated.

In the 1880s, with the new railroads streamlining the Santa Fe-Chihuahua Trail, trading through the Pass intensified. For a golden half-decade, Juárez blossomed with an unrestricted commerce zone that included grand North American and European merchant houses. Manufacturing in Mexico's interior was overwhelmed by foreign goods until a stiff duty barrier could be erected at the end of the free zone. Smuggling stepped into the breach and has yet to diminish. Only its point of departure has shifted with the ebb and flow of the trade zones.

They still come and go. For several years, Mexico has tried a limited approach, using artículos ganchos—"hook items"—a selected few U.S. imports sold on the Mexican side to quench consumers' lust for American products. Toward the exhausted end of the revolution, the border got a break when the Volstead Act prohibited liquor in the United States. Ciudad Juárez had already gotten the idea of making a living from entertaining gringos, but the income from bullfights and gaming was nothing like the windfall of Prohibition. More than anything in the first half of the twentieth century, booze built the Mexican border. The haute monde of Hollywood turned a ranchería of a thousand farmers into Tijuana. Juárez's growth wasn't quite so dramatic, but its reputation was as sordid and its bonanza equally impressive.

Which is why repeal of Prohibition in 1933 staggered both cities so badly. Tijuana immediately demanded a free zone, and soon all Baja California followed. It was a time when Mexico was intent on populating its far western peninsula to counter suspected U.S. interest in its most remote province, so Baja got its zone. But Ciudad Juárez, considered nearer to the center of things, never did.

It was also the Depression and the United States added to Juárez's difficulties by "repatriating" thousands of Hispanics across the border. The town that celebrated in the twenties with new streetlights and bistros now saw its newly paved streets lined with beggars. Like the rest of the continent, it would take World War II to resuscitate Ciudad Juárez. Playgrounds for soldiers from El Paso's Fort Bliss and gimmicks like quickie divorces contributed to its survival. But in what Oscar Martínez refers to as Mexico's "border boom town," the loudest noise was yet to come.

The house was nearly in the country, on the principal road that connected farms and ranches to the Juárez market. It was Spanish, yet even more Romanesque, with a turret containing a curving stair tower rising alongside columnar poplars. Churrigueresque flourishes were applied to its white stucco until it resembled an emperor's birthday cake.

As Ciudad Juárez grew, streets began to intersect the market road, which was named Avenida 16 de Septiembre to commemorate Mexico's independence. The city pushed south, until it met the Sierra Juárez and climbed its slope. It pressed north against the border and spread west and east, filling the Paso del Norte. It grew because the country to the north offered jobs for bracero farmworkers, expelled them, and then accepted even more illegally. During all that equivocating, it became convenient for Mexicans from the interior to base their families in Juárez. In the 1960s, it began to grow again for a different reason. The man responsible was the owner of the mansion on Avenida 16 de Septiembre.

"Don Antonio J. Bermúdez. My brother-in-law. My second father."

René Mascareñas keeps only two photographs in his den: one of Bermúdez and the other of his friend Gustavo Díaz Ordaz, president of Mexico from 1964 to 1970. The room also holds one of the Americas' most unique armament collections. From a wall adorned with a fan-shaped spray of battleaxes and pikes hang war banners: Napoleon's, Joan of Arc's, León de Castillo's, five different Mexican eagles, and the Mascareñas family coat of arms. A rack is filled with antique flintlocks and percussions, and two massive 1800s swivel guns, as formidable as howitzers, occupy the expansive area near Mascareñas's broad hardwood desk. Other walls display iron stirrups used by Arabs when they conquered Spain before the discovery of America, brought to the New World by Cortés to be melted down for mission bells. Italian bronze gladiators stand on shelves with engraved sword handles decorated with fleurs-de-lis and sets of Smith & Wesson double-actions.

The Mascareñas home, all sixteen thousand square feet of it, is in Colonia Campestre, several miles east of Bermúdez's house. In either country, Campestre may be the border's most exclusive neighborhood. It exists because of what Bermúdez and Mascareñas dreamed up just down the road. "It's not that I was an enemy of bars and cabarets. But Juárez had gone overboard. In 1954, I was selected to represent five northern Mexican states in a meeting in New York City. My job was to persuade the U.S. to invest in the border."

Which he did. At the time, René Mascareñas was president of the Juárez Chamber of Commerce, and would soon be the city's mayor. He offered the Americans land and ten-year, tax-free subsidies in Ciudad Juárez. His in-law Bermúdez already had the site. They were ready to bring industries other than gambling and prostitution to their town.

Antonio J. Bermúdez was then the director of Petroleos Mexicanos, the national oil company. He had served previously as mayor of Ciudad Juárez at the request of President Manuel Avila Camacho. Later, he was a senator and ambassador-at-large in the Middle East, but his most memorable challenge was to develop the border.

At the time, Juárez was so squalid that civic officials kept their families in El Paso or Chihuahua City. Bermúdez brought his along, including his young brother-in-law, then a Mexico City accountant with the American firm Price Waterhouse. René was to manage the family's banking and real estate investments while Bermúdez figured how to change the border's vice capital image.

Mascareñas was then thirty, the California-born son of a Sonora rancher who sent his family to Los Angeles during the revolution. His father eventually served as governor of both Sonora and Chihuahua, but René did not leave Los Angeles until he was twenty-one. Years later, when he was accused during his mayoral election of being a gringo, he could state honestly that, unlike his opponent, he had chosen his country, voluntarily renouncing his U.S. citizenship.

At seventy-two, René Mascareñas still looks youthful in his corduroy slacks, a tweed jacket worn over a knit shirt, and Italian shoes. He is bald and powerfully built, with thick eyebrows. "This is one of the unique places in the world," he contends. "Three thousand kilometers long and undefended, with no rifles or bazookas between the world leader of democracy and—I begin to hesitate here—the leader of the Third World. Of course, we Mexicans also call ourselves a democracy, but we're quite different. America was formed by a melting pot of different nationalities, all seeking liberty, happiness, and religious freedom. Mexico, on the other hand, is the result of a conquest."

His voice, warm but commanding, polishes the Spanish language as if it were fine mahogany. "The effects of that conquest aren't over. Where North America eliminated the Indians, we kept them and began a mixed-breed nationality. Later, North Americans brought colored slaves. Time will tell if the U.S. would have done better to keep the Indians and not import blacks. Or if we were right not to have made a European nation here."

The one thing the two countries had in common was their neglect of their mutual border. This led to the strong independence of pioneer border dwellers. It also led Mascareñas and Bermúdez to believe that their idea to attract U.S. investment would work.

That idea was BIP, the Border Industrialization Program that created the maquiladoras. In Spanish, *maquila* refers to the portion of cornmeal a miller retains as payment for grinding a farmer's grains. In this instance, Mexico would allow American companies to assemble premanufactured parts, using inexpensive labor on the Mexican side. Completed items would return to the United States, which charged duty only on the value added in the assembly process. Mexico's share would be critically needed jobs and industrialization. Although American companies have always operated in Mexico, since the 1930s at least 51 percent of any foreign business had to be Mexican owned. But maquiladoras were exempted.

Five minutes from Campestre, Parque Industrial Antonio J. Bermúdez is the border's most famous center of maquila activity and home to many of Ciudad Juárez's 150 twin plants, as they are sometimes called in English. The term reflects the original assurance that companies would construct finishing plants on the U.S. side, creating prosperity in both halves of paired border cities. That largely hasn't happened. In 1983, El Paso had only thirteen corresponding installations, and smaller border cities had proportionately fewer. One of El Paso's biggest employers, Farah Manufacturing, opened a maquiladora and exported 5,000 jobs to Juárez.

Parque Bermúdez is an American industrial park freed from the usual zoning restrictions. Low, modern, windowless buildings, some with Spanish tile, crowd tightly into a tended enclosure. The density is somewhat alleviated by pastel exteriors, narrow lawns, and imported shrubbery. Corporate logos identify companies like AMF, Westinghouse, Ampex, and Marsh Instruments. Usually, the only sound outside comes from automatic sprinkler systems maintaining the token landscape. The silence is interrupted three times a day, when the parque flushes out a large percentage of Ciudad Juárez's fifty-five thousand maquila workers and refills itself with the incoming shift.

RCA has been building its color TV chassis here since 1968, a noteworthy example of longevity. The comparative investment in a maquiladora is low enough that several companies have simply left if something lowers their profit margin. In 1975, when workers demanded some basic benefits, Mattel abandoned a plant and eliminated three thousand jobs in Mexicali on its way to more obedient labor in South Korea. Working on a maquiladora assembly line can be a combination of job insecurity, mind-numbing boredom, eyestrain, and absurd minimum wages, but in Juárez, some derive prestige from a job at relatively venerable RCA.

RCA, in turn, acknowledges its gratitude. "We saved a business by operating in Mexico," insists Ron Seidner, director of RCA's industrial relations in Juárez. "With Asian competition, we wouldn't have been able to stay in this. Some see it as a loss of American jobs,

but they were never really there. Who's in consumer electronics in the U.S. these days?"

Seidner is from Indianapolis, a tall, carefully spoken man who did the same work for RCA in Taiwan. His problems there were similar to here: communication and heavy turnover. Taiwanese tended to disappear around the lunar new year and also award themselves a summer vacation. "With Mexicans, it's constant. Mexicans are very creative people and not as taken to—I don't like to use this word—regimentation. Taiwanese get regimented early in school. They're generally better educated and have higher standards. It's an easier place to work."

But Taiwan is across an ocean, while Mexico couldn't be more handy to the world's biggest consumer market. There are other advantages. Like most maquila executives, Seidner works in a foreign country but gets to live in his own. That fact, maquila boosters like to point out, plus the estimated 30–80 percent of their salaries that maquila workers spend across the line, represents a considerable boon to El Paso's economy. And whenever the peso devalues, the cost of operating a business in Mexico drops. The government, strapped for cash, makes further concessions to attract more U.S. companies. Once restricted to the border strip, maquiladoras are now allowed in the interior, where the minimum wage is even lower. Seidner is confident that Mexican school systems will respond to the needs of arriving technology to ensure an increasingly prepared work force.

The Mexican minimum wages that assembly workers earn once hovered about $4.00 for an eight-hour day. Companies point out that their worker costs were actually higher, about ninety cents per hour, figuring in Christmas bonuses, six days' vacation pay, and miscellaneous taxes for housing and day care. By autumn of 1985, the 1,250 pesos each worker made per day were worth only $2.50. Subtracting a couple of hundred pesos for bus fare, this is not very much money.

Nearly 90 percent of maquila workers are women.

The reasons for this, and the repercussions, are the stuff of sociologists' dreams, and graduate students often are found waiting across the street from assembly plants with their questionnaires poised. After generations of submitting to machismo, the reasoning goes, Mexican women are docile enough not to protest the tedium of winding the same armature 9,800 times a day. Their small, dexterous fingers and traditional passiveness fit the profile of ideal assembly line drones. Critics suggest that the maquiladoras have failed to alleviate unemployment, because they have not hired traditional male workers. Moreover, they have disrupted family patterns by taking women away from their kitchens.

After talking it over with twenty thousand of them, Guillermina Valdés-Villalva, director of Ciudad Juárez's Women Workers' Orientation Center (Centro de Orientación para la Mujer Obrera), discounts much of this. For one thing, any model that doesn't include women in the border's work force was created from some male's delusions. "If it were true that enough masculine breadwinners existed, there would never have been prostitution here. El Paso wouldn't have maids." She agrees that feminization of Mexico's border is an increased reality, although cycles of male migration have often left women in charge at home. The difference now is that more families are educating daughters first, because the maquilas require a secundaria education, which means a serious investment in tuition.

"Now we must consider how being more educated than most men affects their love lives and marriages. Many are choosing to remain single, even to be single parents. Many have fantasies about their supervisor, the only man they can relate to." Guillermina sees things in Juárez now that never existed when she was growing up, like happy hours for women and discotheques featuring girls' nights. Feminization this may be, but women's liberation it isn't. "The ultimate measure of that is decison-making. Women don't."

What bothers Valdés-Villalva is a curious statistic showing that a worker's average duration in a maquiladora is 2.8 years. "That is hardly a career. During the late seventies a maquila salary might have been a family's principal income. Not any more. This is just one of several things they try." Many things drive them out of the maquilas: the pay, the gradual realization that there is hardly any advancement, the maddeningly repetitive work, health hazards, the physical toll. "And we do nothing to absorb the workers who leave, who are now supposedly trained for technology."

The truth is that they're not. The machinery twin plants employ is often outmoded, still in use because Mexican wages extend its cost-effectiveness, or so specific that an operator can't apply her knowledge elsewhere. Although maquiladoras now bring in more cash than tourism, Mexico has long since awakened from the fantasy of technology transfusions and solving its unemployment with twin plants. At any given moment, a few hundred thousand women are working in maquiladoras, but they wear out quickly and new human parts cycle through. Or they hear, "Oye, pendeja, I make more in one hour across the line than you make in a day," and they think about that. And they go.

After his term as mayor, René Mascareñas settled into an engrossing life of banking, investment, real estate, and construction. He now spends his time training his sons to take over these businesses and wandering through his vast house, filled with French engravings, champagne crystal, and imperial furniture inlaid with bronze by Mexico City craftsmen. His biggest satisfaction is that BIP now brings $1 billion into Mexico each year. His country can no longer regard Juárez as a sleazy little border town.

Yet sometimes he sits in his downstairs library, papered with his diplomas and honors and containing seventy-two leather-bound volumes documenting his political career, and considers whether what he and Antonio Bermúdez did turned out for the best.

Ciudad Júarez's population has quadrupled since his term in office, an unpleasant side effect of employment promised by the maquiladoras. Crime is up, and housing and schools are in critical supply. Water is so scarce that many people die of dysentery and dehydration each summer. Women have pushed men aside in the new factories, causing divorce and separation. Yet the maquiladoras created hundreds of thousands of jobs. "That's the way dreams come out. Some glitter, some are dark. Juárez has progressed. But on the way it has become a big, poor metropolis."

On this day in November 1985, he is feeling a bit more hopeful, because Mexico has finally agreed to join GATT, the General Agreement on Tariffs and Trade, which will mean more foreign investment and capital and a chance to pay the crushing debt. American enterprises will operate more freely in Mexico, and maybe that will mean real opportunities for a labor pool already trained in the maquiladoras. He knows that no one can live on 1,250 pesos a day, even by Mexican standards.

But recently he heard an American banker, who made a fortune in this country, say that El Paso should forget about Mexico, that doing business there made sense when there was economic stability, but now El Paso should think of itself. Mascareñas was angered. The United States neglects them, takes for granted the solid vote Mexico has always provided in the United Nations, and does more for Europe and Asia and the Middle East than for its nearest neighbor. He sees that the rapport between the two cities has deteriorated since his term in office. Back then, he was awarded crossing card No. 00001 and made an admiral in the Texas navy. But at that time each city had 250,000 people. Now Juárez is more than twice as big as El Paso, has a birthrate that frightens him, and more keep arriving from the desperate south.

Nine million people now live along the border, and relations, like the economy, are growing strained. René Mascareñas has made his copious living in a land of extreme wealth and poverty, and has always believed

that the rich will have and the poor will be subsidized. It's the middle that's suffering now, though, and he considers a country without a middle class condemned. For two-and-a-half administrations, traitors have hurled mud on the letters PRI, the party whose ideals he believed would eventually lead Mexico to social justice. That justice would include a competitive, two-party system, but many must be educated before they are ready for such an arrangement.

Yet the savage frustration of his city caused the unthinkable to occur in 1983: So many people voted against the establishment that Ciudad Juárez got a PAN mayor. It was heralded as a victory for democracy, but René Mascareñas only worries more. "We are not ready for that."

· · ·

Who can tell how big Juárez really is? Maps, ostensibly current, define its edge, but the neighborhoods along it are already surrounded by even more cinder block, cardboard, adobe, and scrap wood colonias. By night, Ciudad Juárez shimmers under its corona of suspended dust. René Mascareñas's big, poor metropolis has its lovely plaza, baroque mansions, and its magnificent PRONAF tourist complex, but more of this city resembles a slum than any other in northern Mexico. Dirt streets point in all directions, following the unexpected number of possible routes human beings can carve into hillsides.

There is much poverty, but the torpor of the destitute tropics is not evident here. Juárez's treeless, stony colonias are in constant motion. People hustle on nutritional allotments so meager that their energy levels defy normal physics. The ravines are full of children playing with milk cartons, banging on trampolines of rusted sheet metal, setting fire to tumbleweeds. Horse carts, pushcarts, bicycles, pedestrians, automobiles, motorbikes, and dogs navigate the uneven terrain. Amid cacophony and chaos, the one semblance of order is established by the ruteras, brave little machines that are the transporation marvels of Juárez.

They penetrate everywhere. Wherever colonos gain new pick-and-shovel headway on the slope of the Sierra Juárez, the nine-passenger Chevy vans, bearing signs announcing that their occupancy is eighteen people, bump along closely behind. Overloaded, frequently fender deep in road muck, the ruteras do not make up a streamlined fleet. But women who start out at 3:00 A.M. to make the necessary transfers so they arrive at their maquiladoras on time depend on this intrepid mass transit system.

The most important artery of rutera traffic, El Viaducto, is both roadway and drainage canal. A steeply banked, concrete channel, the Viaducto connects a series of indistinguishable colonias and carries away their debris. Even in the dead of drought, it is constantly wet, filled with weaving ruteras using their windshield wipers to fend off the spray of sewage. The garbage washing down the causeway has created a small riparian system complete with oxbows, as residue accumulates first on one bank and then the other.

There are no real markets, only spontaneous bazaars where colonos spread sheets of plastic and display vegetables and utensils. Used clothing, purchased by the bale in El Paso for twenty-nine cents a pound, retails here at 100–300 pesos per article. Inventories of coffeepots, velvet paintings, aguardiente, and herbs spring from the mud. Vehicles collapse and expire, and traffic reroutes around them. Local ditch-digging crews excavate and abandon unexplained holes. Roosters announce the dawn regardless of the hour. And from every rise can be seen the tall glass banks and offices of downtown El Paso looking reluctantly back at the Juárez rubble.

Historically, there is no justice in this. The Pass was originally settled on the south bank of the river. From the first Spanish colony in 1598 until the Mexican-American War ended in 1848, few lived in what is now El Paso, Texas. Paso del Norte, site of present-day Ciudad Juárez, coalesced around a mission; its priests were known throughout New Spain for the wines and brandies they produced from irrigated grapes on the desert's edge.

Just downriver were three other agricultural missions: Ysleta, Soccoro, and San Elizario. Only the last of these was north of the Rio Grande, but in the 1830s an act of nature proved a weird portent of the misfortunes to follow. Awakening with the spring floods, the river tossed in its bed and ended up outside its own banks. Ysleta and Socorro were stranded on an island; inexorably, the Rio Grande cut its new channel below them, nudging them farther north. By the next decade, when the two countries divided their territory according to the course of the river, the two Mexican mission villages found themselves geographically appended to the United States, severed forever from their homeland by a trick of erosion.

They were far more populous than the ranch pueblo Franklin Coons purchased on the U.S. side of the Pass and named for himself. But with two countries now represented in the only viable North-South passage in the Rockies, Franklin, Texas had a reason to exist, if for nothing more than to entice El Paso del Norte from across the new tariff barrier. So many frustrated Mexicans switched sides from El Paso del Norte that the name began to apply to both towns.

And Mexico lost still more. Within a year of surrendering its northern territories to the United States, gold was discovered in California. What, Mexicans wonder, might have occurred had that happened ten years before? Instead of coming up from Mexico City to reach California, fortune seekers headed across the United States, stopping over and establishing El Paso del Norte as an east-west as well as a transborder connection. When the railroads appeared from all directions in the 1880s, it made no sense for them to go anywhere but through the Pass itself. Compared with its Mexican counterpart and the mission villages, El Paso began the 1850s as an unintegrated hamlet, but finished that decade as the United States's most prominent gateway to markets south.

Once the boundary was established, the twin cities of El Paso de Norte leaped into Mexican history, leaving no doubt that the border would be critical to Mexico's destiny. While the French ruled Mexico during the 1860s, deposed Mexican president Benito Juárez took refuge in the Pass. Abraham Lincoln, who as a congressman unsuccessfully opposed the U.S. war with Mexico, bestowed recognition on Juárez's government-in-exile. When Lee surrendered, Union veterans and captured Confederate arms poured through El Paso to reassert the Monroe Doctrine by assuring Juárez's overthrow of Emperor Maximilian.

Benito Juárez resumed the presidency and became regarded as Mexico's Lincoln. Following his death, thousands of memorials were dedicated to him, and Paso del Norte was renamed Ciudad Juárez. After years of sustained corruption culminating with the loss to the United States, Mexico needed an honorable hero. The irony that his triumph depended on the cooperation of the United States was excluded from his public image. But that fact has not been lost on Mexican politicians since.

Juárez was followed by the dictator Porfirio Díaz, who modernized Mexico at any human cost and brought in foreigners to oversee the job. Díaz pushed the railroads to the border. He rebuilt Mexico City in the image of Paris, with Avenida de la Reforma as its Champs Élysées. He traded for power with landowners who soon ruled haciendas the length of Connecticut. Under the Porfiriato, only 3 percent of the people owned land. When Francisco Madero's revolution upended Díaz, many of the wealthiest ones ended up in El Paso. They settled near what is now UTEP on a gracious avenue they named Porfirio Díaz Street, overlooking Ciudad Juárez.

Madero had been convinced by two military allies from Chihuahua that the most crucial target for his assault on the dictatorship was on the northern bor-

der: Ciudad Juárez. When he hesitated, they went ahead and attacked anyway. On May 8, 1911, the citizens of El Paso climbed onto their roofs to watch an effulgent spectacle of artillery and cannonades as the two impatient revolutionaries, Pascual Orozco and Pancho Villa, took Ciudad Juárez and handed it over to an astonished Madero. It turned out they were right about the momentous symbolism of capturing the keystone border city, as Díaz resigned two weeks later. Within days, he sailed for France and never returned.

The revolution pitched back and forth among would-be saviors and dictators for the next ten years. Ciudad Juárez was seized repeatedly. The protagonists frequently relaxed and plotted in El Paso, especially Pancho Villa, who was all but lionized. Reporters often located him in an El Paso ice cream parlor, his burly face dipping into dairy confections. The rooftop battle matinees played all decade long—sometimes too realistically, as the border was no barrier to stray bullets. El Paso's old Indian post, Fort Bliss, was garrisoned and ready for the day when Mexico's bloody woes would spill into the American city. They never did, but its commanding general, John J. Pershing, stayed busy patrolling the bordering hinterlands.

As years passed without making much difference, El Paso wearied of the war next door. Throughout the country, a reaction grew to Mexico's instability, which was especially irritating after the iron rule of Porfirio Díaz that the United States found so reassuring. In El Paso, that backlash rarely discriminated between Mexicans and Mexican Americans. White vigilantes descended on the barrios. El Paso had grown for Anglo reasons—rails, smelting, and manufacturing—that took priority over Hispanic agriculture. A white minority consolidated power, fixing elections and buying influence. In the 1920s, the Ku Klux Klan ran El Paso's school board and nearly ruled the city.

Despite El Paso's low economic ranking, its Anglos are as prosperous as their compatriots in Dayton or Portland—and in those places, skilled Mexican barbers don't make house calls. Ever since Caucasian-controlled El Paso managed to steal the county seat from larger Ysleta in 1883, the whites have been buoyed from below by an abused subculture. First the northeast, and now the northwest arms of El Paso that encircle the Franklin Mountains have become theirs, segregating the community and its schools. Its elected officals have been embarrassingly white, except nobody's been too embarrassed.

Next door in Ciudad Juárez live thousands of resident alien green carders who work in El Paso. At least 300,000 more Juárez citizens illegally use shopping micas as work passports. Their willingness to accept low wages hasn't helped El Paso's Chicanos. Besides creating stereotyped Anglo assumptions about Mexicans, the result is blood resentment among Hispanics. The privileged minority status of Caucasians in El Paso may not be so entrenched as in the past, but lighter colors still rise to the top, and most of the money rises with them.

.   .   .

In the Chew & Chat Cafe, behind the Texas Department of Health Resources where he is El Paso's chief of communicable diseases, Dr. Earl Gorby resorts to a bowl of menudo. Anyone who knows Mexico knows that menudo—tripe soup—is the world's only reliable hangover cure. Gorby doesn't have a hangover, although that would have been nice, considering how he acquired his current headache.

That state of mental affairs came about earlier in the day, when two staggering, coughing Mexicans slogged across the Rio Grande, holding each other up. It took the combined strength of both to heave a rock through a jeweler's plate glass window on Stanton Street. Instead of stealing some rings and running, they stood there, waiting to be arrested. "Maybe," they wheezed when the cop arrived, "you could get us a little something for this tuberculosis."

They were rushed to Gorby's clinic, where they will stay until they're no longer contagious. Later, jail will include nine months of continued TB treatment, costing Texas $100 a month apiece. The alternative is to throw them back over the border and let Juárez worry about them, but it's hard to treat communicable diseases by ignoring what happens thirty feet across a river.

At one time, Juárez residents who wanted a crossing card had to submit to X-ray screening. There was some diplomatic discomfiture when Mexico discovered that Canadians weren't subject to the same scrutiny, and the practice was discontinued. But while it went on, one of every thousand applicants was found with active tuberculosis. An INS medical survey of alien detainees in El Paso's detention center turned up similar percentages, although its results could be skewed since indocumentados with TB don't run too fast from the migra. But given Juárez's population, a fair assumption is that at least one thousand of its residents have contagious tuberculosis.

What worries Earl Gorby is that he can only account for 150 of them.

At least half of the others, he knows, will enter the United States. They rarely announce their presence as dramatically as the two rock throwers. Instead, they look for work, maybe even in restaurants, and infect a lot of people in the process. It would be lovely if the Border Patrol could stop them, but Gorby has long assumed that situation to be hopelessly out of control. He doesn't ask TB cases where they're from anymore, knowing that if he turned people over to the INS, they wouldn't come to him. "Texicans," he instructs his staff to call patients. Since germs don't make political distinctions, medics can't either if they want to prevent disease.

Tuberculosis raises little concern throughout most of the United States, but most of the United States doesn't have an underdeveloped nation down the street. Besides TB, border cities see some rather medieval diseases, like whooping cough and leprosy, as well as standbys like measles, pinkeye, and dysentery. "The difference between a developed and a developing country," Gorby likes to chuckle, "is that one's billboards hype remedies for constipation and the other for diarrhea."

Gorby, smooth skulled and gray bearded, is a retired colonel from Fort Bliss who took this job after twenty-six years in the army. His office is papered with maps of Vietnam, and his conversation is filled with jocular observations about the little border war he fights against pestilence. He chairs the El Paso-Ciudad Juárez Binational Health Council, and respects his colleagues across the river. But tuberculosis in Juárez is no small threat.

He pulls out a chest X-ray that resembles a blizzard inside a cave. The snow is TB. X-rays are expensive and not widely obtainable in Mexico, but although TB is a disease of the poor, money isn't the only problem. He sees Mexican politics standing in the way of its prevention. Every year, both sides get together with the Pan American Health Organization to discuss it. Nothing happens.

Sometime between birth and age fifteen, Mexican children are inoculated with a vaccine called BCG. "The army goes out, corrals kids, and shoots them up. Some get it two or three times. Some get missed completely." BCG had been around for eighty years, and conflicting studies indicate it is anywhere from useless to 80 percent effective. Americans no longer use it, preferring skin test screenings, sputum cultures, and treatment of infected patients with a drug called INH.

Because BCG is derived from a TB germ, anyone who's had it reacts positively to a skin test. For the same reason, it is sensitive to INH. "So we wipe out their BCG program and they screw up our skin tests." What American doctors like Gorby want is for the Mexicans to switch to their system. "Right now, they diagnose more cases of TB in autopsies than in the clinic. Even their health officials admit that their whole TB control has self-destructed."

Gorby tries to help, smuggling over sputum samples from Juárez's Centro de Salud's TB unit. But fewer than 40 percent of the highly infectious cases ever return for treatment. "The medical agencies themselves don't know what they've got," he has concluded. "They literally don't talk to each other. Figures get manipulated for political purposes. If your party wants to be elected, it's nice to show a drop in contagious diseases. Mexican doctors are always aspiring to political office. Heads of Centros de Salud want to be mayor, and if a restaurateur isn't in compliance, he can always slip the doc a campaign contribution."

In his office at El Paso's Thomason General Hospital, Dr Paul Casner has a growing collection of boxes and bottles. An assistant professor of internal medicine at Texas Tech University, Casner has been getting educated along with his residents since coming to El Paso. At New York Medical College, he wasn't prepared to encounter the contents of those containers in the course of a normal medical practice.

They hold pills like phenformin, a diabetes drug that sometimes kills the patient. Or several varieties of addictive analgesics known as pyrazolones, whose side effects include kidney damage and suppression of bone marrow. Then there's lincomycin, sold under the trade name Lincocin by Upjohn, a powerful antibiotic that doctors usually avoid because it can attack stomach and intestinal linings. Whatever infection the patient originally had becomes irrelevant after he or she's been slain by Lincocin-induced colitis.

What Casner finds most bizarre are the combination drugs—miscegenetic couplings of, for instance, a potent antiinflammatory like phenylbutazone with a steroid. Because of its array of alarming side effects, phenylbutazone alone is rarely prescribed. To Casner, lumping it in with a steroid seems rather reckless, but there it is, manufactured by Riker, a division of 3M.

Another combo medication is Redotex, a diet pill that touches off a small war inside the body as its components struggle to counteract each other. Redotex contains an appetite suppressant, a tranquilizer similar to Valium to relieve the jitters it causes, a thyroid hormone, a powerful laxative, and an anti-diuretic. A vaginal suppository made by Merck Sharp & Dohme called Decadron, recommended for minor problems like yeast infections, mixes an antifungal, an antiamoebic compound, and dexamethasone. The latter is an especially powerful steroid, which, if taken over a period of time, can redistribute a woman's body fat from her limbs to her face.

All these drugs are sold, without prescription, over Juárez pharmacy counters. Prompted by advice from relatives who once took a given remedy or simply by inability to afford a doctor, Mexicans have been self-medicating since drugstores were invented. All over the Third World, companies like Upjohn and Squibb sell pills either banned or seldom used in the United States. They also know that their sales depend heavily on self-prescriptions, and some have lobbied and even sued to protect their lucrative share of these markets.

In Mexican farmacias, a customer can browse through the thick physician's desk reference manual until he finds something that seems appropriate, and purchase it on the spot. Many drugs in the Mexican version of the directory are listed without the warnings found in the book's U.S. edition. Pharmacists often suggest favorites, sell syringes if the occasion calls for it, and sometimes do the injecting. Casner came to his clinic one day to find one of his nurse's aides swollen with a body rash from a penicillin overdose. She had self-diagnosed her cold virus as an infection, and her husband shot her up with eight million units.

Like many El Paso residents, she had bought the antibiotic in Juárez. Although Casner sees mainly indigent Mexican American patients in his clinic, after a series of articles in the *El Paso Times,* he fielded enough inquiries to realize that no sector of society could resist the urge to try healing themselves. Part of the attraction is price. Doctors frequently let patients know how much cheaper tetracycline is over the bridge. Sheer availability is also a factor. In El

Paso, pyrazolone wrappers accumulate in street gutters. Maquiladora management people bring all kinds of things back with them, Casner had discovered. In Juárez, stressed maquiladora employees spend much of their meager salaries in farmacias.

"I've wondered," he muses, "why some companies keep making questionable drugs and why they keep selling them in other countries when they can't sell them here." Since not a day goes by without some patient bringing in something from Juárez, Casner also understandably wonders what kind of black market might be spreading cut-rate prescription pharmaceuticals around the United States. Like DDT, which is banned but still produced in the United States for sales in the Third World (which uses it on coffee and fruit that are sold to North America), some things just seem to return forever.

．　．　．

The rate of exchange, dollar to peso, accelerates and ebbs, but the exchange of everything else only increases between these two cities. Mojados make plasma deposits in blood banks situated conveniently adjacent to El Paso's border bridges and return to Juárez with ten easy U.S. dollars. An X-ray machine, obsolete in the United States, is sold to a Juárez hospital and eventually stored when parts are no longer available. A colono salvages its metal, unknowingly spilling radioactive cobalt-60 pellets around his neighborhood on the way to one of the junkyards encircling the city.

The remaining pellets silently contaminate tons of scrap iron. The metal is forged into reinforcing rods and table legs and shipped to markets in nearly every state in North America. All this is discovered months later when a driver makes a wrong turn and passes through a Geiger counter check in Los Alamos, New Mexico. Far from the border, houses braced with hot rebar have to be razed. Juárez colonos retch from radiation sickness, their sperm and white blood cells devastated.

In nearby Carlsbad, New Mexico, the Department

of Energy excavates a cemetery for the military's atomic wastes. The plan is to bury them in salt domes. Geologists in both the United States and Mexico argue that the layers between the dump and south-flowing aquifers are so cracked and dissolved that water hot with plutonium could reach the Pecos River in a matter of months. As construction workers stand knee-deep in seepage inside the vault, the DOE contends that the formation is stable, and continues on.

At the edge of a mesa that Ciudad Juárez has engulfed, orthopedist Jim Boone spends his Saturdays trying to save lives and his own soul in a clinic operated by Our Lady's Youth Center from El Paso. The colonia is all weeds and stubble, with no wooden structures to absorb the noise from radios and hammers on bare metal. Even bicycle tires shriek. Nasal passages grow irritated from a dry, fecal wind blown up from a thousand privies.

Dr. Boone has long, sensitive fingers, wavy salt-and-pepper hair, and brilliant blue eyes. All day he tends babies with diarrhea and tapeworm, women with extraordinary levels of hypertension, men with advanced congestive heart failure. Recently, he converted from nothing to Catholicism, and tries to see the face of Christ in the little dying babies or the old men contorted with arthritis. He thinks that without religion, a volunteer here would quickly become disillusioned and see them as just a bunch of smelly Mexicans. It is hard enough for him. He just put a $70,000 addition onto his house and works in a prestigious medical group with luxury trimmings. His partners have told him they feel no particular responsibility to these people.

Someone brings a crate of grapes, and purple juice stains the mouths and fingers of the waiting patients. There are not enough grapes in the world for all of them. "Either we are facing a disaster of huge proportions," Boone says, "or . . ." He doesn't know. "We've been pretty much told that what humans try will fail. No social, economic, or political structure we can put together can cure this. It's been tried for five thousand years. You convert to Christianity when you see that nothing else works."

· · ·

At all hours, but especially in the mornings, people from Juárez pour across the trickle of river. Using closed-circuit televison, horses, vans, and plainclothes agents, the Border Patrol tries to turn them back. They grab them reroofing the gabled officers' quarters at Fort Bliss. They catch women trying to find husbands with green cards who have another family on the Texas side. They endure the wrath of horse trainers and owners when they sweep mojado handlers out of Sunland Park Racetrack. They patrol twenty-two miles of river and feel sometimes like they might as well try to stop the wind.

Youths in running shoes dash through the tattered remains of the Tortilla Curtain and blend into the swarm of students headed to Bowie High School. Men in undershorts known as mules give $1.00 piggyback rides across the channelized riverbed to women in dresses and heels. To the amazement of a group of utility commissioners emerging from a meeting, five mojados pop out of a manhole in the city hall parking lot. Three hundred of them wait impatiently on the U.S. side while border patrolman Joe Estrada interviews some who've been preyed on that morning by thieves.

"Vámonos, José, we're all going to be late," they complain. Estrada knows nearly all of them. Via loudspeakers, he and Juárez police on the opposite side confer back and forth. The ratón is identified and caught. While everybody is congratulating and thanking Joe, a mojado on a bicycle makes a successful run for it. Estrada has to move farther up; three hundred undocumented Mexicans follow in his rearview mirror, strolling briskly to awaiting employment.

Some make it past the plainclothes units, and some don't. A half-hour later, the Paso del Norte Processing Center is as hectic as a Mexico City subway station.

Six Border Patrol agents type furiously as lines in front of them keep getting longer. People enter carrying suitcases, carrying babies, carrying their lunch. The atmosphere is nearly festive. Inside the black mesh cage, everyone knows each other, knows the plain-clothesmen with their crackling walkie-talkies, knows that today is just not their day but chances are tomorrow will be, so they accept this as an unscheduled holiday from work. Nobody acts desperate; nearly everyone smiles and cheers when more come strutting in.

The cities exchange their difficulties and vitalities. Radios the size of valises in Ciudad Juárez reproduce the FM transmissions of a Los Angeles mariachi group playing on El Paso Public Radio. When the music ends and Garrison Keillor interviews them, the clear reception of "A Prairie Home Companion" in a Third World dirt colonia elevates the nonsense of the border to sublime levels. In the evening, Juarenses find their way across to the El Paso Civic Center where el rey of borderland beat, Little Joe and his Familia, mixes up both languages in a bola of ranchera music, scat singing, black blues wrenched from Houston ghettos, hill country swing, and el inmortal Pedro Infante, and gets the whole thing exactly right.

In the opposite direction, UTEP fraternity boys escort gum-chewing freshmen girls in 100 percent cotton outfits into Ciudad Juárez to get drunk at the Kentucky Club. Lines of Texas cars head for Mexican dining and the Juárez dog track. A Shriner waits at the end of the bridge to guide fellow conventioneers back into the United States after they've visited the dollies. Underneath, five homeless niños who survive by washing windshields at border crossings are asleep. Their bellies are filled with hotdogs and they have fresh haircuts, gifts bestowed on them by border patrolmen who at other times are employed in chasing them back into Mexico.

———

Unbeknownst to most of these border citizens, the continued sharing of the Pass of the North by El Paso and Ciudad Juárez is quickly approaching its limits. Stranded together in the desert, they are running out of something to drink. The maddening part of it is that plenty of water is in easy reach, but so far, neither can have any.

To this day, how El Paso ended up on Texas soil while surrounded by both New and Old Mexico puzzles historians. Inaccurate maps, a suspect municipal election, and threats of war that rumbled from Austin in the direction of Albuquerque had something to do with it. After more than a century of neglect, six hundred miles from its state capital, El Paso would probably like to reconsider the results of that mysterious election. In every sense but one, it belongs to New Mexico, and a foreigner unfamiliar with Texan hegemony might conclude that even a claim by Chihuahua would make more sense. But the issue of water now makes this more serious than a mere geographic blooper.

Beneath El Paso lies an aquifer known as the Hueco Bolsón—part of it, anyhow. It provides most of the city's water, since by agreement with Mexico, the Rio Grande is reserved mainly for agriculture. As aquifers go, the Hueco Bolsón isn't particularly generous. A thin, potable layer floats atop mostly brackish water, and in 1973 El Paso figured it had perhaps a sixty-year supply left. But it had forgotten that Ciudad Juárez, whose numbers have tripled since 1960, has its straw stuck in the same bolsón.

No one knows for certain how many people in Juárez have access to running water. It has worked hard to extend water delivery systems through the city, bringing even nearer the day when both city's straws will be sucking up salt water. 1995 is when the cities of the Pass expect to run dry.

El Paso thinks it has an alternative, though. Just northwest lies the deep, relatively untouched Mesilla Bolsón. The catch is that it lies underneath New Mexico. Since 1980, Texas and New Mexico have been taking each other to court over who has right to that water. The essence of Texas's argument is that hundreds of thousands of urban dwellers are more important than a few New Mexico farmers. Agriculture, which uses far more water than cities, isn't appropriate for deserts. The state boundary is an artificial line that threatens Texas's livelihood.

New Mexico replies that it deserves some protection against foreign invaders. How can it plan its own development if other states can help themselves to its resources?

The real problem is that groundwater policy is anybody's guess when state and international borders are involved. After years of threatening to cut each other off from the Colorado River and lower Rio Grande, respectively, the United States and Mexico satisfactorily divided their rivers—but that agreement only applied to water flowing along the surface, not buried underground.

And while Texas and New Mexico sue and countersue, Ciudad Juárez and its water needs keep growing. In 1983, a rare PAN victory bestowed the city's leadership on a group of young businessmen headed by a thirty-three-year-old mayor. Francisco Barrios Terrazas's election was the result of unusual preparation, and helped by a spectacular scandal involving the PRIista chief of Mexico City's police, whose hobby—collecting palaces—outraged the nation.

The city he inherited has little opportunity to plan its future while it struggles to survive the present. The PRIista state and federal governments, contemptuous of Ciudad Juárez's maverick PANismo, do not help matters. A left-wing movement, El Comité de Defensa Popular, boasts of pirating electricity and water for desperate Juaranses while the parties in power waste time and money arguing among themselves.

Their tactics are popular, but only as long as there's a resource to pirate. Because this is a separate country, Juárez hasn't any chance for New Mexico's reservoir.

But if Ciudad Juárez's expected two million residents find themselves without water in the coming decade, the border may turn out to be immaterial. The cities that share the Pass's watershed will probably share the consequences of its depletion.

And as the bowl beneath them empties, the bubble above them fills. Atmospheric pollution can turn the Paso del Norte's air almost opaque during a winter inversion. After $90 million worth of controls, El Paso's big ASARCO smelter now complies with federal lead emission standards, but levels are still high from the exhaust of thousands of automobiles whose catalytic converters have been bypassed by Juárez mechanics. The border itself is an air quality problem. Cars wait an average of twenty minutes to cross, during which time idling engines expel enough carbon monoxide to fuddle many a customs official's mind.

Evidence suggests that one reason women leave their jobs in electronics maquiladoras after just 2.8 years is neurological damage due to cadmium poisoning. After breathing soldering fumes for a while, they can't reach their quotas. Jesús Reynosa, El Paso's air pollution program supervisor, is even more concerned about the use of asbestos thread in Juárez maquiladoras. "We don't know what's going on over there. Emissions just go out the window, uncontrolled. Heaven knows what kinds of exotic solvents GM, RCA, and Sylvania use in Juárez. The Mexican government doesn't care, as long as they get the dollars. But we all end up with the air toxins."

At night, colonos contribute their share of inky hydrocarbons as they warm themselves around burning automobile tires. Many of these are salvaged from the dump, where a union of garbage pickers has formed, paying its members more than maquiladora workers make. Seen through the oily haze, El Paso seems bathed in a rose mist drifting down from the seven blinking radio towers atop the Franklin Mountains. Over Fort Bliss, more lights wink from the training aircraft of eighteen allied nations—including the entire German Luftwaffe—but no Latin American country. Juárez residents always know when the United States has a fresh new international crisis because the light show intensifies.

"If there is a nuclear war," says Antonia Caballero, who has never set foot in the American city she sees every day, "it will kill more mexicanos here than americanos. We can't afford the bomb shelters."

·   ·   ·

In 1864, the Rio Grande again jumped its banks. Six hundred acres of Ciudad Juárez known as El Chamizal ended up in El Paso. Mexico asked the United States to give it back, but was reminded that the river was the boundary they'd agreed on. As this windfall of real estate seemed a bit extreme, Mexico continued to protest until, in 1911, the United States agreed to international arbitration. To its unpleasant surprise, a Canadian tribunal awarded two-thirds of the shifted land back to Mexico. The United States ignored the decision.

The issue was forgotten in El Paso. Neighborhoods went up in the Chamizal; railroad tracks ran across it. Mexico seethed for decades, until 1962, when John Kennedy was courting Latin support during his escalating confrontation with Cuba. Informed of the lingering blot on relations between the two countries, Kennedy agreed to settle. More than three thousand people and some large bridges had to be relocated, and the river itself was entombed in a concrete channel to dissuade it from further meandering. Mexico gained 437 acres and regarded the affair as a national triumph against imperialism. It never did denounce Castro, either.

A park was built on the American side to commemorate this diplomatic achievement, and Bowie High School—La Bowie, the barrio alma mater—moved over here. El Paso's Chicanos still attend the school, but don't use the park very much. A preferred Sunday gathering spot is Ascarate Lake. Ascarate is surrounded by grass and softball fields and a sinuous park boulevard where, around dusk, the lowriders cruise in.

Anglo teenagers go for fast cars, but lowriding is a reaction against high-velocity American culture. The traffic here slows to near stasis as jeeps, converted pickups, candy-apple red Suzuki motorcycles, and the bajitos themselves make the long circuit. The radios of two hundred parked cars and trucks, their hoods and tailgates laden with perspiring coolers filled with Coors, emit the same salsa. Music, motors, and sensuality are the only concerns; this is a peaceful pageant, and the cops stay out of it. Their main beef with lowriders is when they drop their scrape plates to send up a rooster tail of sparks, but the slow majesty of the cruise through Ascarate eliminates that problem.

Richard Salazar, president of the Undertakers Car Club, has spent three years on his best bajito, a chulísimo honey gold '76 Chevy Caprice, and he's still not satisfied. Right now it flaunts a chocolate-brown, crushed velour interior, including its upholstered engine compartment. It has a double gull-wing sunroof; its air cleaner is chromed; and the plush back seat comes complete with a silver champagne bucket. Of the $9,000 he's invested in improvements, $1,500 went for the mural on the hood depicting the face of Christ hovering over a space ship platform on Mount Franklin, where an angel guides a futuristic ark to rescue El Paso and Juárez from nuclear destruction. The total does not count the $2,000 check won for Best Lowrider in Texas, which Richard and his brothers decided to frame rather than cash.

Salazar is El Paso's más firme designer, winner of thirty trophies and twenty plaques for best-in-show, best interior, best trick painting, wickedest side-to-side hydraulic lifts, and—twice—the Low Rider Magazine Editor's Award. His dad, Jorge, started as a mechanic in a Mexico City Packard agency at age twelve. A decade later, when his earnings had risen to the peso equivalent of $13 a week, he had mastered bodywork and upholstery. He followed a sister to Ciudad Juárez, fell in love with an El Paso citizen before the migra tossed him across the river, and moved over for good when he married her.

Señor Salazar, a dash of mustache poised just above his upper lip, is a smaller version of his six stocky sons. He is proud that they have grown healthy on the American food he was able to afford after God and the government gave him the opportunity to work here. For fifteen years he's had his own shop, George and Sons, where his boys now work their automotive artistry. The sculpted Pontiacs and Chevys are the family pride, and as a family they go to Houston or Phoenix or Del Rio or wherever Richard and his brothers are showing. Over in Juárez, his sister's kids are working in the maquiladoras for RCA, and he knows how tough things are getting. If the crisis ever explodes, he'll take them all in a minute.

George Junior, the eldest and part owner of the champion Caprice, can't get greasy as much anymore since he became an attorney for the Department of Justice. But he comes by the shop after work, in a leather sportcoat and two-tone wingtip cowboy boots, and checks out the gold-leaf pinstriping Richard is applying.

George doesn't consider lowriders a puerile ethnic extravagance. "The Latin can express his flair for the romantic almost anywhere, even taking a product off a General Motors assembly line and giving it an identity." Maybe, he implies, as more Mexican Americans like himself enter the governing institutions of our country, the same warmth will infect the system. "Why not? If we can make something as American as a car reflect our culture, we can probably do it to anything."

On Calle Constitución in Ciudad Juárez, Fernando Nájera studies the border's reflections through a different mirror. At thirty, he is part owner of Juárez Exports, the world's largest dealer of black velvet paintings. About fifty thousand of the tacky oils move through his warehouse every year, mostly headed to wholesalers in the eastern United States. Nájera has no idea why that might be. He has simply touched a nerve.

It is a populist kind of art that he truly believes in. Several—depicting landscapes, flowers, and a still life of fruit—hang in his own home.

Yes, he knows that critics consider them the aesthetic nadir of the century. Yes, he understands that artists who churn out twenty-five originals a day, ranging from Jesus to Elvis to Rambo, are hard to take with a straight face. But some painters who started in velvet, like Manuel Espinosa in Mexico City, are now making names for themselves in galleries, albeit on canvas. And Julian Schnabel in New York has gone the other direction, treating the inexpensive black cloth as a serious medium.

Nájera understands something else as well about the respective cultures that produce and buy these things. "For two years now, the unicorn has been our number one seller. Pegasus is also very big. Why are American people in such need of fantasies? The U.S. is crazy for landscapes, but the trees have to be gold. Or frosty blues. They won't buy a natural green landscape, but México will."

Stars like Springsteen and Michael Jackson come and go, and with the exception of the durable Presley, their day-glow popularity doesn't say much that isn't already known about the fleeting allure of fads. But Nájera is intrigued by the recent demise of one of the industry's mainstays.

"Nudes are dead. They never sold in México, but the United States was a huge market for them." The shift signifies something, but he's not sure what it is.

"Now everyone's asking for religious. Jesús. The Virgin Mary. The Last Supper. I wonder, sometimes, if people are getting a little scared."

From a jagged peak of the Sierra Cristo Rey, at the confluence of Texas, Chihuahua, and New Mexico, Christ the King gazes down on the smoke and dust and multitudes of the Paso del Norte. Each October, thousands of barefoot pilgrims climb the four-mile trail to reach the limestone statue. At the edge of the river below them, another monument—a white obelisk—marks where the border leaves the Rio Grande and becomes a fence. On the far bank rise the tall stacks of the American Smelting and Refining Company. A nearby neighborhood known as Smeltertown had to be abandoned owing to extraordinary levels of lead in children's blood.

A plaque on the monument explains that Francisco Madero himself camped at this spot in May 1911, with the batallions that began the Mexican Revolution. On either side, a block factory stands where the soldiers once slept, reducing the surrounding hills of Old and New Mexico to rubble and forming it into masonry units.

The famed border fence itself starts out as a low cable a foot from the ground. It leaps twenty near-vertical yards up an incline, and then quits. For a while, only mountains and brush form the westward boundary. Back in Washington, it is assumed that there's at least barbed wire here, but when this terrain is seen up close, it's obvious that it would be pointless. After following one thousand miles of squirming, uncooperative river, the border is now on firm footing. In this desert sierra, it seems to make even less sense.

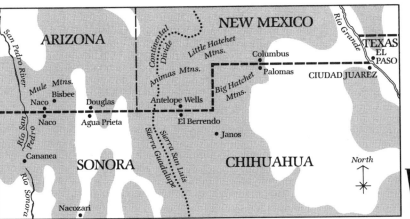

C H A P T E R S I X

T H E

G R E A T D I V I D E

West of the Rio Grande, the border ignores nature. Except for one short jog at the Colorado River, a series of straight lines adhering to treaty, not topography, define the boundary. As a result, the terrain along these political extremities often refuses to cooperate. Water flows where we don't want it; the land tilts unfavorably in one direction or another; and much of the frontier discourages access, even by the Border Patrol. The logic of the natural boundary as seen in the glories of the Big Bend gorges is absent. Like retribution for imposing distinctions where none should exist, the faint delineation between Old and New Mexico beyond Juárez and El Paso is one of the border's more violent excesses.

Sixty miles of sand begin the land border. The Chihuahuan desert dwindles to bleak expanses of stunted mesquite, creosote, and spiny yucca. Except for stands of yellow broomweed, the runtish vegetation is the uniform dullness of faded khaki. Beyond the rustling of a badger and an owl's shadow, nothing seems to move.

A few isolated lava flows and scattered craters interrupt the void surrounding the hardbacked, cinder road that hugs the invisible border. Once it bore the tracks of the El Paso and Southwestern Railroad, which carried copper from Arizona to be smelted in Texas. Now the road is seldom traveled, except by a few ranchers and eighteen-wheel smuggling rigs that run the flat stretch at night, sans headlights, leaving jackrabbit carcasses in their wake.

South of the line, the desert is even more featureless. Burnt sticks and windborne grit provide the only variety against colorless sand and sky. Of the four U.S. border states, New Mexico shares the least appealing common boundary with Mexico. Columbus, its only border town that isn't an El Paso suburb, is a nearly vacant counterweight to its desiccated neighbor, Palomas, Chihuahua.

By night, the green fluorescence of Columbus and Palomas's dim amber are visible for miles across the flats. A three-mile gap separates them, but the towns have edged nearer over the years. Palomas was once eight kilometers south, the headquarters of an immense, American-owned hacienda. After the revolution, there was no more hacienda, and the town moved up to the border to take advantage of Prohibition. When that also ended, its once-proud casino, eighty feet from the United States, relinquished its former hilarity to bureaucracy and became a customs house.

Only a few farmers, retirees, and welfare recipients live in obscure Columbus, its silence preserved save for the overhead squawk of migrating sandhill cranes. Heaps of old John Deere combine parts destined for Mexico, along with stacks of even older wringer washing machines, are the only signs of enterprise. But ghosts are the residents' neighbors. At one time, Columbus swelled to twenty thousand inhabitants and toppled into American history.

It was here in 1916 that the continental United States was invaded, the only time during this century. Why the Mexican revolutionary general Pancho Villa led his troops northward was never clear, though an explanation may exist in German military archives.

Between 1914 and 1917, Germany plotted relentlessly to distract the United States from entering World War I. The kaiser's strategists proposed and financed a racial uprising in which Mexican Americans, Indians, and blacks would seize territory Mexico lost in 1848 to found an independent nation of color along the border. Sporadic raids occurred in Texas, with the instigators suffering the greatest losses. On another front, the Germans apparently managed to plant an agent, Dr. Lyman Rauschbaum, on Pancho Villa's staff. Rauschbaum became the general's secretary and bookkeeper, and convinced Villa that the state bank in Columbus had cheated them out of an account bearing $10,000.

During the subsequent raid, the Mexican rebels robbed the bank, killed seventeen Americans, and lost nearly one hundred of their own troops. Woodrow Wilson set General John "Black Jack" Pershing after them. Pershing and ten thousand men floundered around northern Mexico for eleven months, trailed by huge supply lines of covered wagons. They never laid eyes on Villa. The expedition distinguished itself mainly as the first to use mechanized equipment and airplanes, with pack animals supplying fuel to trucks and biplanes that ventured far into the desert. Columbus's one great affair with prosperity was its brief tenure as the first U.S. Army air base.

The following year, an intercepted telegram revealed Germany's proposed war pact to help Mexico regain its former territories in exchange for keeping the United States militarily occupied. Shortly thereafter, Pershing and American troops entered the Great War.

With the United States right down the street, mostly adobe Palomas is a border town that still looks the way border towns used to look. Barely four blocks long, its traditional industry is revealed by counting the bars. Except to leave town, nobody drives anywhere. Horses graze in an abandoned schoolyard; a few structures with yellow and green patches are evidence of some forgotten, mild attempts at painting, but everything else is the color of the earth. Outside doorways lining the dirt streets hang ristras of long red chiles. The only building rising above one story is a little double-steepled stone church with blue domes.

But change is about. Nine years ago, Palomas, Chihuahua, was officially renamed Rodrigo Quevedo, after a local general. This has served to create extra work for the postmaster and customs chief, who must use the longer name in their paperwork, even though no one else does. And Palomas now has its first maquiladora, an El Paso firm that makes picture frames, where just about everyone in town is employed. Before, they went to the United States.

MCG Frames came to Palomas instead of Juárez because of competition for employees and a myriad of regulations that don't exist here yet. Two more steel buildings are going up, with the intention of renting to other maquilas. As they spread to smaller towns, the sleepy image of the border passes into mythology.

In Tillie's, a restaurant that has an AT&T line to its pay phone even though the United States is at least twenty yards away, diners watch five young couples march around the wooden plank dance floor to the strains of *Aïda*. The room is hung with purple, magenta, and white crêpe-paper streamers. On a bandstand at one end, an old man runs a disco machine.

The occasion is a wedding rehearsal. Verdi segues to *Tales of the Vienna Woods*, and the couples form a circle. Dora Martínez, the bride-to-be, wears heels, red slacks, and a blue sweater, and has long, braided hair. Her novio, Cirilio Otoño, is in a leather jacket, black bell bottoms, and cream-colored cowboy boots. He has a thick mustache, black hair, and a very lovely fiancée. In the center of the ring, they shuffle through a Mexican polka slowed to waltz time, both chewing bubble gum, their eyes locked and dreamy.

On the wall, a heart surrounded by paper carnations entwines the names of José Isabel and Yolanda, the subjects of last Saturday's wedding. Like them, Dora and Cirilio will be joined in matrimonio in the little stone Iglesia de Nuestra Señora de Guadalupe. Dora is local; Cirilio, who works in an upholstery shop, came to the border from the city of Durango to find his fortune. "Y ya la encontré," he declares happily, holding on to Dora's hand—"and I have found her."

Except for the bleaching asphalt leading down to Columbus and the seedy RV drive-through known as Pancho Villa State Park, the nearest paved American road approaching this desolate expanse is Interstate 10, forty miles north of the border. New Mexico's only other international gate, Antelope Wells, is a simple customs station deep in a grassy valley in the state's southwestern panhandle. The route to Antelope Wells cuts between the Big and Little Hatchet mountains, and is better suited for cattle than cars, cattle being the reason a border crossing exists here at all.

Across the fence, El Berrendo, Chihuahua, is not a town but a shipping terminus for steers. Carlos Johnson, the Mexican customs agent here for thirty years, may have seen more pronghorn antelope than people in his life. His father, a Canadian who owned a coffee plantation in Chiapas, went off to World War II and never returned. When this post opened, Carlos seized the chance to go north. In his mind was the thought of discovering his father's fate, but he hasn't gotten beyond El Berrendo.

The road that most nearly parallels the border is a newly completed segment of Mexico Carretera 2, the first reasonably negotiable route connecting northern municipalities in the states of Chihuahua and Sonora. Construction on this highway began in 1977, a year after it was scheduled to open. Road crews from both directions, working in atrocious heat, sweated to link up in the San Luis Mountains rising midway between the towns of Janos and Agua Prieta. Well before the final kilometers were finished, the first buses began running. Passengers were informed that they would have to transfer at the state line, but not that they would have to hike over the Continental Divide to do so. Accommodating equipment operators for Mexico's highway department provided shuttle rides, packing six travelers at a time into an earthmover's bucket.

The thin black highway leads beyond the alkaline desert into nominal plains, then abruptly begins traversing switchbacks into the Sierra San Luis. Just below the frontier, the mountains form the Great Divide itself, partitioning Mexico's runoff waters west to the Pacific and east to the Gulf. Here, in scattered deposits of soil among ragged outcroppings, the bare Chihuahuan sticks become century plants, chaparral, and palo blanco, with an occasional piñon tree shading a patch of snow.

Carretera 2 approaches the top and pauses. The wind claws at North America's spine. As if delighted over the vista, the road improvises a fandango around the summit, descends a little way, and does it again. As a consequence, the view that fills the west repeats itself, and repeats itself.

Below lies the beginning of the Sonoran Desert, varied and generous in comparison to the next desert over. Grasses named tobosa, blue grama, Indian wheat, and sacaton grow here along with its famed cacti and succulents. During spring thaws and the summer monsoon, water cuts channels through the two valleys visible from the divide: the high Animas and, beyond, the lower San Bernardino. In the winter, many of the washes freeze, and snow fills them waist-deep.

Cinder cones and old pocked flows of lava jut from the plains. The purple and gray Guadalupe Mountains, a puzzle of rooster-comb buttes, rimrocks, and Byzantine canyons, hunker midway to the horizon. To the northwest broods the Chiricahua range. Below these mountains, the land gentles, rolling back on itself to form creased bajadas covered with whitethorn and mesquite. This is aromatic country, pungent with flora that have achieved equilibrium with the desert's dryness. Kangaroo rats, bobcats, jackrabbits, coyotes—resilient animals who extract a living from a minimum of moisture—abound here in the creosote flats.

This was once the home of the last unsubdued American Indians; the Chiricahua Apaches. Just a century ago, Apachería scorned whatever claims Mexico or the United States made to this portion of the borderlands, and the ferocity with which they patrolled their territory kept the two countries apart more effectively than any political boundary since. Today, several armies later, the Apaches are gone. Cowboys now wax sentimental over this country, composing songs about it like Stan Jones's "Ghost Riders in the Sky," finding here the quintessential West of their dreams.

The border itself, composed of seven endless barbed-wire strands of five-foot-high cattle fence, is sharply visible from the top of the divide. Different rhythms of bovine grazing on either side vary the texture of their respective ranges, making the boundary resemble a colossal seam joining separate national fabrics clear to the horizon. Long before the Herefords arrived, bison filled these plains and Apaches picked them off at their leisure. In the place of both buffalo and Indian, many cattle ranches now share this big, useful landscape.

. . .

Carretera 2, the lightly tarred trail, slithers into the valley, straightening out to parallel the border. As it flattens, a spur to the right leads to a small cow camp named El Valle set among trees half a kilometer from the main road, its headquarters a shabby, two-room, whitewashed adobe. Inside, on a stove fueled with bottled gas, vaqueros brew coffee in the can it came in, using a pair of pliers to lift and pour. After breakfast they stroll out back, where a picket corral stands less than a hundred yards behind the house, next to a stone watering tank. A saddle-horse gate with a looped-wire latch opens to a second corral, which has its own stock tank—this one of galvanized steel.

Although practically adjacent, the tanks have separate wells, each topped with identical windmills built in Chicago in the 1890s. The common fence running between the two corrals continues forever in either direction. The little wooden gate connecting them leads, in fact, from Latin America into North America.

And where is the protocol of customs, and what of the sovereign laws of two jealous countries that supposedly govern all such traffic and movement? The vaqueros shrug. The gate has always been there. "Este alambre"—this fence, explains the one called

El Pelón, indicating the entire Fence—"is just another one cattle go through. Or crawl under, when the washes are dry. We go get them, and we bring them back. So do they," he adds, waving his straw cowboy hat at the vast nation looming just beyond. The vaqueros, who have paused at the fence, nod, puff Delicados, unbutton, and relieve themselves through the wire into the United States.

Farther down the highway, where the landscape to the north imperceptibly changes from New Mexico to Arizona, a dirt cutoff to the south drops quickly into a box canyon. Vertical bluffs and porphyry outcroppings pile up haphazardly into uneven walls and ledges that mountain lions favor as habitat. Clear, drinkable water appears, snowmelt streamlets called Agua Blanca and Arroyo de las Muchachas. Where the canyon deepens, sycamores, enormous Fremont cottonwoods, massive downed oaks, velvet ash, willow, and black walnut trees line the water's path for several shaded miles.

Between narrowing and widening walls, rare Mexican black hawks float and plunge on changing microthermals. The flags of small Sonoran whitetail deer flash and disappear into undetected places. Leaves stir overhead and collect underfoot, pooling on the bedrock, laying mulched bedding for soft grass and mosses. Threading among the granite protrusions and patches of watercress, the water multiplies the sunlight. Hot springs release evanescent vapors.

This is Cajón Bonito. It is not merely pretty. Many of the lucky few who have seen it contend this is the most beautiful place on earth.

Toward the end of the Apache Wars in 1886, sixty U.S. Cavalry troops waited here nervously while their compatriots pursued Geronimo south into Sonora. They were sitting ducks, and knew it, but a general who was new to this country had bivouacked troops at every watering place along the line from Nogales to El Paso, even to the point of ignorantly trapping his men in box canyons. As it happened, this particular regiment was lucky, because Geronimo surrendered, for the fourth and final time, after reaching an agreement with U.S. forces on the Río Bavispe thirty miles below the border.

The army had entered Mexico under an agreement that marked a diplomatic breakthrough. The impunity of Texas Rangers, who frequently violated the river border, had further degraded relations between the two countries since the war. But Mexico, which felt the United States had usurped its territory, had no hesitation about doing the same to the Apaches. In the Indians, the countries had found something they agreed on: a common enemy in their midst. The decision to allow each other's troops to cross the boundary in pursuit of hostiles was the first cooperation between the two nations along the border since it had been fixed by survey. That it was done at the expense of a third nation was not considered ironic, but opportune.

Today, in more peaceful endeavors, cows and their calves forage along the lush bottom of Cajón Bonito. Just beyond where the box widens as the various rivulets intersect lies the headquarters of Rancho Nuevo. The ranch, which includes El Valle, belongs to Juan "Chapo" Varela. Once this was the Varela family's home. Now complexities of the modern ranching business and his wife's concern about decent schools for their children require Chapo to live in Agua Prieta, an hour farther up the road. He and his brother Armando ("Fupau"—nicknamed after a local Chinese grocer) own a changing checkerboard of cattle land scattered between the Chihuahua line and Cananea, one hundred miles to the west. They are seasoned ranchers, and the unstable character of their ownership derives not from a lack of business acumen but from the continuous need to stay ahead of another endless series of blind decisions being made 2,400 kilometers away.

———

One day in 1982, Fupau Varela's daughter Melinda, married and living in Mexico City, noticed her family's name in the newspaper. Fupau's home ranch at Cananea was listed with property the Mexican government would expropriate during the coming year, in the revolutionary spirit of agrarian reform. Legal notice of the seizure had appeared in the press—but, conveniently, only in the Mexico City papers.

Land reform—La Reforma—has been sacred to Mexican politics since Mexico declared itself independent in 1810 and its people rose up against the Spanish colonial estates. A century later, a peasant named Emiliano Zapata from the agricultural state of Morelos was still fighting the same battle. He, Pancho Villa, and others sought to free the land, this time from 800 wealthy squires who owned nine-tenths of rural Mexico. They included John D. Rockefeller, who controlled major Yucatán oilfields, and William Randolph Hearst, who owned seven million acres of Chihuahua.

Eventually, the survivors forged the broad coalition party that became the PRI. Its virtual monopoly has spawned prodigious corruption, but dominance also gave it stability. In 1938, this enabled Mexican president Lázaro Cárdenas to nationalize the foreigners' oil industries and distribute their vast holdings to the people. The Hearst newspapers demanded that the U.S. invade and complete the unfinished business of manifest destiny. However, noting the ominous events in Europe, Franklin Roosevelt preferred to have a friend rather than an extra conflict immediately to the south. For once, Mexico was left to control its own resources.

Cárdenas became the first Mexican leader to truly enact land reform, and his resulting near-deification encouraged the PRI, at least symbolically, to continue doing so ever since. Accordingly, each new president has expropriated private property and converted it to government-owned cooperative ejidos for peasants to occupy.

But after decades of this institutionalized reforma,

only so much available real estate remains. Border ranchland is doubly attractive, being both sizable and too remote to defend easily against the machinations of the distant capital. Cattlemen in Sonora, Mexico's top beef-producing state, now find themselves paying off federal agrarian agents to keep confiscation at bay. Just a year earlier, Fupau Varela had grown tired of fighting and relinquished several hundred hectares to the government in the belief that they'd now leave him alone. Apparently, he just gave them an opening. Thanks to his daughter, he learned that everything else he owned was going next.

It took thousands of pesos, but Varela fought the expropriation all the way to Mexico's supreme court. His action was unexpected, and owing to government clumsiness, the justices ruled in his favor. Back in Agua Prieta, however, his brother wasn't satisfied.

The name Agua Prieta, meaning murky water, derives from a nearby muddy hole that nevertheless supplied enough moisture in this dry country to make a settlement worthwhile. (Directly across the line, Douglas, Arizona, was once known as Black Water.) Agua Prieta's Calle Uno—First Street—is an alley running alongside the international fence; from there, street numbers progressively increase as the boundary recedes. Chapo Varela lives on affluent Second Street. Only heavy doses of wrought iron and Spanish masonry distinguish it from a suburban neighborhood in the United States. Many homes have satellite dishes in their backyards, positioned to tap cable transmissions from across the border. A block away, Third Street is more middle class, and Fourth Street goes yet a rung lower, and so on, until within six blocks of Second Street, pavement disappears and neighborhoods become dust-entombed streets lined with unpainted cinder-block dwellings. Where the numbers run out, a shantytown of no streets in particular continues on.

In his home on Calle 2, Chapo Varela sits on the

edge of a leather recliner by a fireplace, talking on a cordless phone. He is tall, well-built, with a square jaw and cleft chin, dressed in western clothing. His skin is tanned rather than dark. The phone rings often and he frequently switches languages. His English is more than flawless; after years of doing border cattle business, Chapo Varela sounds and looks a great deal like a Texan. Texans would understand his meaning.

"Land up here," he intones, "serves for one thing: grazing cattle, which can't be done on forty-hectare parcels. Look at these ejidos, trying to grow vegetables on sparse range, spraying irrigation water around that evaporates before it hits the ground." Grimacing, Chapo blames John F. Kennedy's well-meaning but uninformed interference with perpetuating this. Kennedy, adored in Mexico for kneeling at the image of the Virgin of Guadalupe in the national basílica, endorsed land reform in his 1960s vision for Latin America, the Alliance for Progress. "If only his Harvard advisers could've distinguished ranchland from farmland."

So new ejidos keep appearing, often furnished with government technicians and fancy sprinkler equipment. Ranchers fret not only over their land but also about peasant hordes they imagine arriving from the crowded south to occupy new grants. Lately, a criminal element has appeared, attracted to the marijuana everyone assumes the ejidatarios are growing. To protect themselves and to get around the limits on individually owned property (that if observed would make ranching impossible), cattlemen like Chapo and Fupau play a real estate shell game, putting land into each other's names and the names of their children and relatives.

During the peso devaluations of the early 1980s, several Sonoran businessmen were rumored to have contacted American congressmen over the possibility of two or three border states seceding from Mexico and annexing themselves to the United States. Although Chapo was not one of them, at times he re-flects on how much simpler things might be if the border were, say, a thousand miles farther south.

"Mexico," he believes, "is trying to bring the affluent down to the level of the poor, instead of vice versa. This is a rich country. We have minerals, oil, forests, farmland—the farmers of Sonora and Sinaloa are the best in the world, but they're not being allowed to produce. The government takes land out of production and gives it to campesinos who lack the knowhow." Mexico's protectionist policies especially rankle him. He is now forbidden to purchase barbed wire from the United States because a factory in Monterrey has begun manufacturing it. "Unfortunately, they produce only about 2 percent of the country's needs." He stands, paces, sits again. "The damn law is forcing us to be smugglers in order to keep our cows fenced."

Chapo's alternative is Mexico's conservative National Action Party, the PAN. But conservative versus liberal, he insists, is not the issue. "Competition is. Even my maid, who ought to be a communist, is voting PAN. Anything is better than one-party domination."

Agua Prieta is, in fact, one of only three border cities that has ever managed to elect a PAN mayor. That is not enough for Chapo. He and several other Sonorans are set on nothing less than electing a PAN governor. But the PRI will not easily give up a state—especially a state as wealthy, by Mexican standards, as Sonora. Preparing for the 1985 elections, Chapo knew full well the PAN's claim, acknowledged by some PRIistas, that in 1983 the PRI stole the governorship of Baja California.

"We'll have to contend with that here too," Chapo said at the time. "But we're going to win. We represent the only chance for a real choice in Mexico." Chapo's public stance had made enemies and possibly jeopardized his business. He didn't care. His son José, bred to the cattle business, was attending the University of Arizona like his father before him. But he chose engineering rather than agriculture, because he doesn't know if there will be any ranch when he's through. "If I don't buck the system," said Chapo, "I know my boy will never be a rancher. Their so-called 'reform' will keep chipping away at my land until there's nothing left."

In 1985, the PAN gubernatorial candidate, Adalberto Rosas, charmed Sonora with an animated campaign, during which he walked the length of the state. His PRI opponent, Rodolfo Félix Valdés, had a reputation for relative honesty, but was a Mexico City functionary who hadn't lived in Sonora for thirty years. Many believed the PAN would actually win.

After the polls had been open for two hours, so much fraud was alleged that several PAN candidates withdrew in protest. Hundreds of registered PANistas claimed they weren't allowed to vote. Ballot boxes were discovered already filled with PRI votes before voting even began. In Agua Prieta, after PAN observers were denied access to the polls, frustrated crowds blockaded the border crossing. The PRI announced a lopsided victory.

Their opponents concluded that the PRI had chosen a brazen show of force as the best strategy to discourage further competition. On inauguration day in Agua Prieta, a mob responded with what was becoming a new border tradition by burning down city hall. A year later, the Chihuahuan state elections went much the same way. Protesters blocked the international bridges, PRI buses were burned, and army troops occupied Juárez to preserve the peace. And Chapo Varela continues to brood over the future of his business and his country.

. . .

Saturday evening in Agua Prieta: two of Chapo's cowpunchers from Rancho Nuevo, Tirso Amaya and Rubén Contreras, bring their families to town for dinner. They go to the Club Santa Fe on dusty Calle Cinco. The Club Santa Fe stands in a dirt field, a low, windowless rectangle painted institutional green. If its exterior is unimpressive, within it is a kind of architectural miracle.

Except for the kitchen and a narrow, partitioned bar on one end, the Club Santa Fe consists entirely of a single room, wallpapered in flocked red and approaching the dimensions of a football field. Yet somehow, just one central pillar of concrete supports its vast, glittery ceiling. Strategically spaced red lightbulbs provide the only illumination. During the rainy season, even this obscure radiance often fails, as one of northern Mexico's habitual outages leaves Agua Prieta in darkness. Then, by the dim glow entering the doorway from a lighted softball field over in Douglas, the Santa Fe's cooks haul out butane lanterns and camping stoves and resume their fiery alchemy.

The Club Santa Fe is so spacious that families can eat, drunks can brawl, children play, couples dance, and waiters serve without anyone disturbing each other. When the power does give out, patrons exchange friendly screams through the blackness until bartenders appear bearing trays of beer and candles. The chiles rellenos and steak tampiqueño and other fine things arrive next—begun over a restaurant range and finished on Coleman two-burners. The food is extravagantly good.

The downed electricity silences the norteño band's guitars, but music continues. Young boys with repertoires acquired in the streets of Agua Prieta peddle their clear, strong vibratos from table to table. Tirso Amaya and Rubén Contreras purchase a ballad for fifty pesos. Pleased, they do so again; they and their wives join, with considerable northern pride, in a song of the revolution:

Me fuí para el Agua Prieta   I went to Agua Prieta
a ver quien me conocía   to see who I might
y a las once de la noche   know
me aprehendió la policía   but an hour before midnight
the police had laid me low.

*Me aprehendieron los
 gendarmes
al estilo americano
como era hombre de
 delito
todos con pistola en mano*

They had me appre-
 hended
the way the Americans
 will
as if I'd committed evil
their pistols ready to
 kill.

*La cárcel de Cananea
se edificó en una mesa
y en ella fuí procesado
por causa de mi
 torpeza. . . .*

The jailhouse at Cana-
 nea
is built on a high pla-
 teau
in it I was processed
for my ignorance, I
 know. . . .

. . .

A museum now occupies the jailhouse at Cananea, commemorating events that gave this town the title of "Cradle of the Mexican Revolution." Its displays emphasize that it was no accident that the first major people's revolt of this century began just twenty miles from the United States, on Friday, June 1, 1906.

A quarter-century earlier, an itinerant miner named William Greene arrived in southern Arizona. By the time he was thirty-five, Greene had hunted Apaches, shot a justice of the peace, and in several other ways ingratiated himself with his fellow frontierspeople. In Tombstone, he prospected and gambled, then married a divorcée and parlayed her ample dowry into a cattle herd and a homestead. He was then able to convince investors to follow him to where he was sure he would become seriously rich.

That place was Mexico. The Treaty of Guadalupe Hidalgo that ended the Mexican-American War had established the border between Arizona and Sonora at the Gila River. The mission pueblo of Tucson remained in Mexico; had Phoenix then existed, its outskirts would have lain along the border. Within five years, the U.S. minister to Mexico, James Gadsden, pressured the defeated nation to sell what is now southern New Mexico and Arizona for $10 million, to provide a route around the mountains for the transcontinental railroad. At the time, few understood that the United States incidentally had acquired several of the world's finest copper deposits.

Forty years later, everyone knew. Southern Arizona shuddered continually with dynamite blasts, and fledgling companies like Phelps Dodge, Anaconda, and ASARCO were suddenly wealthy. Across the line in Mexico, still more lodes were discovered. But this was during Porfirio Díaz's dictatorship, when the border could turn to elastic under the steady pressure of American money.

Like other foreign investors, William C. Greene was virtually welcomed into Mexico as a benefactor. He came with a plan. When mines in the Sierra Cananea had been worked earlier for gold and silver, no one had known that Thomas Edison was about to invent lightbulbs. Greene guessed that amidst the slag from previous operations, he would find plenty of discarded copper. He not only did so but he also uncovered an entire mountain of blue copper ore, which he proceeded to move to one side over the course of a decade as he extracted hundreds of millions of dollars from it.

The expansive Colonel Greene (the title was self-bestowed and never disputed) became Wall Street's favorite turn-of-the-century sideshow. He would arrive in his private railroad car, ensconce himself in the Waldorf, pull $1,000 bills from his vest, and hypnotize investors. Bankers and senators accompanied him on bacchanalian sportsmen's business trips, over Mexican railroads he built and owned, through his prodigious cattle and lumber holdings and into the town he created. Cananea, Sonora, swarmed with American mining experts and machinery and English-language signs and newspapers. Nearby, but rather apart from the general bonanza, its native laborers dwelt in a shantytown called Ronquillo.

These Mexican workers received part of their wages in scrip, redeemable at the Cananea Consolidated

Copper Company Store. They earned three pesos—$1.50— for a ten-hour day, somewhat less than the $5.00 paid to American miners who worked with them. On June 1, 1906, they struck for two more pesos and advancement opportunities. They demanded to know why Americans should receive more for the same work and why no foremen were Mexicans.

The night before, an alerted Greene had taken his train up to nearby Bisbee, Arizona, and stocked up on munitions. Thus fortified, he faced the strikers. His hands, he explained, were tied by Mexico. Already, the government had complained that his wages, the highest of any Mexican mine, were causing unrest among workers elsewhere. Greene argued that he had to pay U.S. wages to attract needed, skilled American miners, but failed to explain why he had never trained Mexicans to do their jobs. They were unconvinced.

That afternoon, a company supply manager turned a fire hose on the still peaceful demonstrators. Grabbing iron mining tools, they charged. Shots were fired, and Americans and Mexicans alike died. Greene phoned Bisbee for reinforcements and then called Hermosillo, the capital of Sonora. To his eternal disgrace in Mexican history, Governor Rafael Izábal of Sonora invited two hundred Bisbee volunteers to invade Mexico and protect the American industrialist Greene from his Mexican labor force.

The North American troops, hastily sworn into the Mexican army as they crossed the border, stayed until a column of rurales arrested the strike leaders and locked them into the Cananea jail. There the incident ended, and the legend began. Porfirio Díaz had underestimated his people's antipathy toward the Americans who profited at their expense—and toward the Mexican government that was the gringos' accomplice. Canenea ignited a revolution that, at least officially, still continues.

.   .   .

Lavender Pit, purpler even than it sounds, bottoms out after several hundred excavated feet into a tur-quoise pool. Were the steep, surrounding brown hills suddenly to shake off their incrustation of structures, all of Bisbee, Arizona, could tumble down Mule Gulch and neatly fit in this tiered abyss. Bisbee's old queen—the Copper Queen Mine—rests now, the once humming pit her open-air tomb. Crammed around and above it, devoid of level surfaces, the town exists today for intrinsic reasons, sustained by sightseers who come to admire the jumbled beauty of its boomtown architecture.

Just below the mesa of tailings that took nearly a century to haul out of Lavender Pit, Cathé ("The Flying") Fish crawls aboard her weathered Cessna 182 at the Bisbee, Arizona, airfield. Her passengers are two U.S. Forest Service rangers. A good-spirited, blond woman in her mid-thirties, Cathé trains flight instructors throughout the United States. Lately, she's been taking people on a little tour of this section of the border. Bisbee is her home, and something here is making her angry.

On rising warm air currents, they ride the twenty miles east past the Mule Mountains to Douglas, Arizona, and Agua Prieta, Sonora. Unlike most U.S. border cities, Douglas has never depended symbiotically on its Mexican neighbor. Named for William Douglas, who discovered a cheap way of freeing copper from the local chlorides, Douglas developed and prospered as a company town while, across the line, Agua Prieta lived off its pickings. Since 1906, when fat ore deposits at Bisbee led to the construction of a smelter, the Phelps Dodge Corporation has been *the* employer in Douglas. Its citizens have worked at the Phelps Dodge smelter or up at Phelps Dodge's Copper Queen Mine, lived in company housing, and shopped at the Phelps Dodge Mercantile.

The Cessna passes over the Gadsden Hotel, Douglas's jewel. Built in the early part of the century, the ceiling of its gilded rococo lobby rests on columns of rich French marble. Opposite the walnut registry is a grand staircase, slightly chipped from when Pancho Villa once ascended it on his horse. It leads to a mezzanine whose wall is a Tiffany stained-glass desert mural, spanning the hotel's façade. During its distinguished history, the Gadsden has hosted balls, weddings, inaugurations, and the great banquet meetings of a proud American industry. Millions exchanged hands in its lobby. The Gadsden Hotel is a palace that mining built.

A mile or so away, looking like the twin exhaust pipes of hell, looms the Phelps Dodge smelter. "You'll never understand unless you get on the top to see it," Cathé tells her passengers. Unrenovated since 1913, the Douglas smelter is a dinosaur, the acknowledged dirtiest industrial plant in the United States. Its murky plume fans across the landscape, obliterating the Continental Divide forty miles away and filling the broad valleys in between.

"I don't even bother to paint my plane anymore— the sulfur starts to eat it inside of a week," The Flying Fish shouts over the engine whine. She holds the Cessna steady, but the fumes are making her guests nauseous anyway. Great smoky tendrils encircle the mountains and snake upward. To the northeast, the College Peaks appear hung with huge, broken spiderwebs. Across the line, dust devils swirl through Agua Prieta's streets.

During the next hour, she takes them over the mining complex at Cananea, now owned by Mexico's government. Smaller than Douglas, its smelter too remains essentially as Colonel Greene built it, back when spewing chimneys were considered bright symbols of progress. Curiously, Mexico has built an astronomical observatory on a nearby peak, directly in the path of Cananea's smoke. Apparently, no one in Mexico City bothered to first make a site visit. Its telescopes have sat for two years on pallets in front of the now state-owned Greene mansion while the government tries to decide if it's worth proceeding, given the perpetual smog.

Cathé points out a bright orange drainage pouring off Cananea's tailings. Jobless men eke their survival by tossing beer cans attached to fishing lines into this frightening stream and selling the resulting copper-coated containers to the smelter. At different times, the runoff has flowed into both the San Pedro and Sonora rivers, poisoning bottomland in two countries. "It hurts to watch all this," she says, hovering on the hot updraft. "If they open Nacozari, I'm moving. Period."

Fifty miles south of Agua Prieta, she shows them what she means. Below sprouts a gigantic smokestack, 400 feet higher than Phelps Dodge-Douglas, taller than anything around except the mountains themselves. Here, Mexico is building one of the world's most modern copper refineries, except for one small detail: To save money, pollution controls have been omitted. "They also plan to expand Cananea and double its chimney height," Cathé adds.

When Nacozari starts melting rocks, its unchecked emissions will blend with Cananea's and Douglas's to form what locals have dubbed the Gray Triangle, the most dreaded violator of air standards in the West. "I've followed the Douglas plume into northern Utah," Cathé Fish swears. "Acid rain from here to Idaho is going to double because of this. You people should ask Dick Kamp."

As they reenter U.S. airspace, she points to an odd structure about a mile from the border, below Bisbee. "He lives there," she says, dipping a wing.

·   ·   ·

Dick Kamp follows the phone wire through a pile of domestic wreckage so he can hang up the receiver. The State Department official he has been speaking to has just inelegantly, but succinctly, characterized the Gray Triangle as "a regular Mexican standoff." Considering the surroundings, it is hard to know how Foggy Bottom would characterize Dick Kamp, clad in boxer shorts and remnants of a shirt.

Dick Kamp has done many things in his life, but currently his sole mission is to explain, and maybe solve, the standoff:

"It would cost more than a brand-new refinery to retrofit Douglas with pollution devices. Claiming abject poverty, Phelps Dodge refuses, so Arizona congressmen bailed out local jobs by finagling Douglas an exemption from the Clean Air Act, good through the late eighties. Meanwhile, Mexico is trying to lower its debt by exploiting its resources. To save about 100 million bucks, it leaves controls off Nacozari and Cananea. Instead, both smelters will use tall smokestacks to carry away emissions." Kamp has this scenario synopsized and down pat, but occasionally, such as here, he has to stop for breath.

"Prevailing winds blow north by day, so their smoke will pour into the United States. We've appealed to both federal governments to halt a potential disaster. Nacozari will be using compressed oxygen, which triples the sulfur dioxide. No one, not here, not in Japan, has ever ignited an oxygen-enriched smelter without controls.

"We'll be gassed by something worse than anyone's ever seen. But when we try reasoning with Mexico, they point out that for eighty years Douglas has turned up its big converters by night, when the winds reverse and blow south. Mexicans show me the stink over Agua Prieta and ask me why they should spend fantastic amounts of money they don't have when the U.S. does this to them. 'Control Douglas first,' they tell me, 'and then we'll talk.' But Phelps Dodge has no intention of doing that. They aim to extend their Clean Air exemption instead. Control-free smelting is cheaper. How else can they compete with Chile, Peru— or Mexico?"

Again, the phone: it's the Arizona Air Quality Board. Kamp makes notes on a corner ripped from a Safeway bag, gives a rapid, detailed response, and hangs up. Immediately, there's another call: San Francisco office of the EPA. Before the phone can ring again, Kamp dials it himself, calling Dr. Alberto Durazo in Cananea. Durazo, whose father was once paymaster for the Cananea mine, is a pediatrician and a founder of the Cananea Jail Museum. He has been charting his patients' pulmonary disorders, trying to prove a connection to smelter smoke. In Douglas, Kamp and oth-

ers charge that the company has routinely concealed medical records. For years, farmers in both countries have watched the leaves of their tomato plants shrivel when inversions force the smoke down to ground level.

Kamp and Durazo discuss trips they've made to Mexico City, to New York, to Albuquerque, to wherever, to further their international assault on air pollution. Kamp has just returned from Amsterdam. He is amazed at what has happened to his life.

Years before, Dick Kamp and his girlfriend, Mimi, dropped out of Grinnell College in Iowa and headed west. Their search for a place to hang out ended between Bisbee and the border town of Naco, Arizona, where land was cheap and the mountains pretty, if a little foggy. They bought ten acres and got married. Gradually, the truth penetrated about the nearby Douglas smelter. When their baby daughter died of pneumonia that may or may not have been complicated by its proximity, Kamp's grief drove him to confrontations that have spread to both sides of the line.

From his hand-built adobe hogan-in-progress, he founded the international Smelter Crisis Education Project. Amidst potted herbs and the clucking of pet hens, Kamp holds long-distance court with governors, ambassadors, and a variety of other feds from two nations. A wealthy supporter has purchased Phelps Dodge stock in his name, so he can introduce motions at shareholders' meetings to either clean up or close down Douglas.

"Which, sooner or later, we will do. The question is if we can do it before Nacozari opens." He's been trying to convince Mexico that controls could be affordable if sulfuric acid produced from captured smelter smoke were used for products like fertilizer or wallboard. If financing the acid plants and developing markets were beyond Mexico's means, American companies could even be invited as partners and perhaps receive tax breaks from both countries for helping to solve a mutual problem. But so far, no progress. And since the Camarena killing, the spirit of cooperation seems to have chilled. Still, Kamp maintains his grim struggle, having taken on American industry, a southwestern mining tradition of folkloric proportions, the self-destructing Mexican economy, and the deteriorating state of diplomacy. The outcome may determine who's really winning the West these days.

He wanders outside, crossing a sandy draw via a footbridge he built from the undercarriages of two former schoolbuses. He piles his family into a Volvo assembled from several defunct specimens he's acquired over the years, and drives to the twin hamlets known collectively as Naco. Naco, Arizona, is a level mile away. Naco, Sonora, elevated just enough for its sewage to drain in the direction of Bisbee's water supply, is just past it.

Both Nacos exist because Colonel Greene needed a railhead at the border for his Mexican cattle and copper. As that era passed, the American side faded to little more than a bar and a couple of groceries to serve neighboring Mexicans. Naco, Arizona's only subsequent thrill occurred in 1929. To quell a Sonoran revolt against the PRI's emerging monopoly, Mexico outfitted tractors with machine guns and drafted bombardiers to root the insurrectionists out of the countryside. One pilot, aiming for a rebel nest in Naco, Sonora, mistakenly targeted the wrong side of the line, blowing up an empty boxcar.

In the years that followed, Naco, Sonora, grew so neglected and pitiful that one night in 1971, its mayor crashed a banquet that Mexican president Luis Echeverría was attending two hours away in Nogales. He begged his excellency to do something for his pueblo. Echeverría was so moved, perhaps by the evening's wine, that he organized an expedition on the spot. At 3:00 A.M. a presidential caravan rolled into muddy, woebegone Naco.

True to the dramatic words Echeverría spoke that night, Naco today has some of the border's widest asphalt streets. A government-sponsored shoe cooperative failed to catch on, but a commercial renaissance owing to drugs and other smuggled goods has kept Naco reasonably alive. Not long ago, an ex-mayor and police chief were nabbed with 160 contraband parrots; soldiers from Fort Huachuca, Arizona, still arrive in search of El Rainbow Club, notorious for its racially eclectic mix of prostitutes.

As a result of the U.S. government's reaction to the Camarena slaying, the Naco border gate now closes at 8:00 P.M. Two blocks down, a hole has been peeled in the chain link, big enough to admit a vehicle bearing refrigerators, small arms, or bales of dope. Kamp drives through, down dark streets of low buildings, to a house where a huge woman named Esperanza chases her kids from the sagging table and then serves beans and fat chiles rellenos.

Dick Kamp watches his little girls, who are sopping up tomato salsa with flour tortillas. "I'm taking everybody in for chest X-rays," he tells Mimi. They've had a lung thing this year that won't go away. "When they start up Nacozari . . ." She agrees. They've talked about what they will do. But the time is coming closer, and nothing's happened. The town of Nacozari itself is built in a canyon. Kamp worries that come the first inversion, people there will start keeling over. Several scientists in both countries agree with him. But politicians are the ones who count.

"No one's ever died fast from a smelter so far," he tells congressional subcommittees. "We can't ask Mexico not to try to make money, not to mess up our air, especially if we ignore Canada when they ask the same thing of us. But someday this will all reach some kind of limit, and we'll feel it when it comes." He can take his family and move, go to work for an environmental group somewhere. "But"—he says to his wife now, gesturing at Esperanza, visible through a pantry leading to the kitchen—"what about these people? They're stuck." He shakes his head. "We're all stuck, aren't we?"

———

This is a border that marks the limits of two countries, one that sometimes delineates the good and bad caused by their respective governments. Often, one side benefits while the other suffers. If one profits at the expense of its neighbor, it does so at the risk that the balance may someday swing in the neighbor's favor. Douglas mayor Ben Williams, campaigning in the lobby of the Gadsden Hotel, doesn't want Nacozari's and Cananea's exhaust. But he wins the applause and votes of his constitutents by agreeing with Phelps Dodge's intransigent position. They can't imagine their town without the copper industry.

But there are others who point north, to the lovely Sulphur Springs Valley, where farmers would like to grow vegetables and apples without losing their crops to airborne arsenic and sulfates. They note the splendid landscape and the inviting, high desert climate and imagine a smoke-free Douglas enjoying a retirement industry like the rest of Arizona. Or Douglas and Agua Prieta attracting some of the twin assembly plants that have gone elsewhere on the border, because Douglas often seems like Pittsburgh in the twenties.

Nobody alive remembers this land before the smoke. But everyone recalls 1981, when a strike closed the smelter for three months and the air turned to crystal. Snow fell and melted again, leaving everything startlingly clean. The haze over the Chiricahuas dissolved, and the freshened valleys bordered not only on Mexico but also on the sublime. It was obvious why Geronimo and Cochise fought to keep this land. It was also understandable why generals Crook and Miles and the United States of America wanted it too.

· · ·

Douglas, with its neat houses of gypsum block, and Agua Prieta, with its layer of imported soot, share a history of strained relations. Intercity exchange is less cordial and frequent here than elsewhere along la frontera. Recently, a Douglas youth was found hanged in the jail across the way. Two pathologists who ex-amined the body came to conflicting conclusions. One pronounced it an obvious suicide. The other said torture by electrocution, noting cattle prod burns and indications that mineral water laced with chili had been forced up the victim's nose.

The story did not surprise the locals. Among residents of Douglas, Agua Prieta's police have a reputation for mayhem and extortion. Mexican officials respond to such accusations in wounded, bewildered tones. "There are always a few bad apples," they observe regretfully.

But on this particular night, Agua Prietans in a festive mood are pouring into Douglas. Tony Aguilar and Flor Silvestre—Mexico's Roy Rogers and Dale Evans—are playing the Cochise County Fairgrounds. The event is held on the U.S. side, partly because the facilities are larger and partly because there they can get away with charging ten bucks a head.

Aguilar has made scores of movies, and one of the most famous is based on a ballad, a corrido, entitled "El Moro de Cumpas"—"The Dappled Colt of Cumpas"—by the musical laureate of Agua Prieta, Leonardo "El Nano" Yáñez. Mounted on silk-maned, white Andalusians that prance to the accompaniment of mariachis, with remote microphones hidden in their charro suits, Tony, Flor, and son José have the crowd delirious as they honor the beloved folk poet in trio harmony.

But the pride of Agua Prieta, it happens, now lives in Douglas. "Every time I'd get invited to perform someplace that pays, like Phoenix or San José," Yáñez apologizes, "it meant weeks of trying to get a new visa. Finally I had to immigrate just so I can travel where I want."

Yáñez's copper skin has been tarnished by seventy-eight burdensome years, many of them spent as a miner in Cananea and Nacozari. A plastic left eye is a memento from digging ditches as a bracero in Superior, Arizona. Somehow, these travails soften into harmony and pleasure in the corridos he writes. His classics, like "El Moro de Cumpas" and "El Tío Juan," have been heard from Madrid nightclubs to Vietnam foxholes. But their composer, who began as a Cananea miner, survives on a U.S. Social Security check and by teaching music in an Agua Prieta secundaria. "Mexico pays very badly. You sell a million records, and they claim it was only a hundred. You end up making thirty-one centavos. Groups pay to get recorded. The only reason I'm composing is to provide a cultural legacy for my children."

Tony Aguilar, he says with pride but not overwhelming enthusiasm, has just agreed to record Yáñez's latest creation, about a race between a palomino and his spotted challenger, sons of two proud studs at Chapo Varela's ranch in Cajón Bonito. Serious money and machismo were on the line to determine which animal was swifter:

Era su primera carrera	It was their very first race
La cosa estaba difícil	And it was hard to
De atinar una quiniela;	Pick a winner;
Los dos fueron compañeros	On Chapo Varela's ranch
Criados en la misma tierra	These two comrades
Rancho de Chapo Varela.	Had been raised together.
El contrato fue firmado	Their bet was sealed,
Interviniendo Varela	Varela held the
Sin mencionar retrocesos	Agreed-upon purse
Dentro de trescientos metros	For three hundred meters
Los potrillos correrían	The colts would run for
Por dos millones de pesos.	Two million pesos' worth.

In the days preceding Mexico's elections, many people pass through Yáñez's narrow clapboard bungalow in the Douglas barrio. Their discussions continue long into the night. Yáñez's son, Leonardo Junior is Agua

Prieta's outgoing PAN mayor. By law, he cannot succeed himself, but he has been lumped into a smear campaign that has the city even more tense than usual. On the sofa in his straw cowboy hat, El Nano is sickened and angered by groundless innuendos suggesting that his son molests young boys.

To dispel the growing anxieties, he picks out melodies on a cracked Aria guitar. Some beer appears, and voices blend with his mossy tenor. "¿Por qué es," someone asks after awhile, "that songs are always about desperate love, getting drunk, or horses?"

Yáñez grins. He wrote a happy love song on the occasion of his own fiftieth wedding anniversary, but romance often fills hearts until they break. As for las borracheras: "We Mexicans drink for happiness, relaxation, for celebration, for . . ." he pauses, glancing at his wife, Socorro. She goes to the kitchen and returns with more bottles of Miller's. ". . . for friendship," he concludes. "Except, of course, when we get violent." The bottles clack together in a toast. The room is so small that no one has to rise.

His obsession with horses carries over to his political convictions. "If México knew anything, it would legalize racing and pay off half its debt," he grumbles, and no one chooses to disagree. "Horses are a spectator sport, not just gambling—I mean, who goes to watch poker games?" Mexicans wouldn't run a dozen horses all owned by big syndicates nobody cares about, like Americans do. "The Mexican way is for two men to prove who has the finest."

But Mexico's government is too fregado to do anything right anymore, he thinks. A few years ago, three members of a Douglas ranching family, the Hanigans, were accused of capturing and torturing three illegal aliens. The case went to trial three times before one was convicted; it became a cause célèbre for Hispanics. People wanted Yáñez to write a corrido about the Hanigans, but he refused. "I didn't," he recalls, "because I would have written the truth, and nobody would have liked that. The truth is that the Mexican government was as much to blame as the gringo ranchers. If it took better care of its people, they wouldn't have to be crossing the border all the time."

Again, a toast. "You should be president, Nano," they tell him. "Songs instead of speeches. ¡Viva tu música!"

Yáñez agrees. The country may explode, but its music will remain intact. Last year, he even saw a touring group of mariachis from Japan. He picks at the label of his American beer for a moment, and says, "It's funny, though. I went to Tucson to play a mariachi festival, and the only musicians who could read the arrangements I brought along were Americans. There are more mariachi groups in the U.S. today than in México. Sometimes I wonder if we're going to have to depend on foreigners to carry on our own traditions."

. . .

Twenty years ago, Drummond Hadley hoisted a saddle and bedroll across the international fence, snagged his Levi's climbing into Mexico, reverse-wetbacked down to the headquarters of Rancho San Bernardino, and signed on. They took him to Los Chirriones, a cow camp, and kept him there two years. As his compañero Porfirio Somoza puts it:

El 28 de noviembre   The 28th of November
Presente lo tengo yo,   It's my remembrance,
En el Rancho Los Chirriones   That in Rancho Los
La corrida comenzó.   Chirriones
                              His run it did
                                commence.

Hadley nods. Two decades later, Somoza's still around—outside just now, distributing alfalfa hay to two grays, a palomino, some sorrels, and a zebra dun. "No one ever knows how they have come to a place or why they are there. That lays the mystery where it ought to be."

The mystery of Drummond Hadley leads over the faintest, farthest of back roads, to this working hideout of an American poet who forsook literary circles for the ones men make astride equines while tending bovines—specifically, circles tangential to, and even overlapping, Mexico. Some of his lyric contemporaries, like Allen Ginsberg, Robert Creeley, and Gary Snyder, follow the trail to Hadley's from time to time, curious and respectful of the power of the place and the poetry it spawns. "Like time and death," Ginsberg opines.

During his teens, Missouri-born Drum Hadley cowboyed for his uncles in Wyoming. At the University of Arizona, he kept riding but studied literature and composition. He published his first poems in his twenties, met Charles Olson (who included Hadley's words in his own works), and for a while traveled the literary landscape with Snyder. He ended up both in anthologies and on the border, making cattle drives to Agua Prieta and riding his horse into bars.

Over tequila in the kitchen of his ranch house, Hadley expounds between agave-rich pauses. "I had an idea that if anyone was carrying knowledges that resulted from man existing in frontiers and large spaces, it would have been the cowboy culture. I set about to record those knowledges."

In the kerosene light, Hadley's bespectacled eyes are wild but learned; his roping hand is calloused. Shocks of thick, dark hair fall in two directions across his forehead. A few inches into the smooth, diabolical Sauza, his conversation casts a loop around the Brahma-Hereford cross, the Psyche myth, alleged truths of Tarahumara Indians, Mexican women, and his drinking companions. Taking his lyric dallies around the saddle horn of his imagination, he draws this loop snug. The legs of his wooden stool scrape the brick floor; reaching across the oak kitchen table, he gathers an idle guitar and, half saying, half singing, settles into a mournful A minor—and Mexico.

There's old Juan walking along the ridgeline
from Mexico Route 2 through the border fence,
then down the rough side of the canyon to the
   Escondida Camp

where he hoped his friend Walterio would be
waiting.

Tortillas in a sack, a half-filled bottle of tequila.
Old heart walking, centuries singing,
dry times, the rangelands and wetback trails,
his own people, Sonora, Mexico.

Night draws them outside, where earlier a warm rain briefly fell. Under diffusing starlight, the land rises prominently on either side of Hadley's ranch headquarters. Just over the ridge to the south is Mexico. Hadley and the friends who are here to help with tomorrow's roundup amble down a canyon that a few miles away drops into Arizona, and then continues under the barbed-wire into Sonora.

"Pure horseback societies still exist in the Sierra Madres," he says. "They carry something that we may have lost." The sides of the canyon play catch with his round tones, juggling them with the trill of nighthawks. "In Mexico there are fine cowboys who in our country would have been lawyers, bankers, carpenters, accountants, poets, singers. In America there is so much opportunity for someone to become something other than what he was born into. Mexicans have fewer options—but then, you don't find their kind of diversity anymore among American cowboys."

"Where are you headed Juan?"
"Where there's work to do," he'd say.
Mexican vaquero following traces of cattle trails
drifting through the Peloncillo Mountains to find
work in America.

Humming of flies along that winding path,
trembling side-oats seeds.

Cowboying itself, synonymous with the United States anywhere movies have penetrated, truly originated in Mexico. The traditions and the knowledges crossed the border to get here, and still do. Hadley needs a crew this week because his late calves have to be branded. Mysteriously, the Mexican cowboys have appeared from the hills, up out of Cajón Bonito, down into his corrals, up onto his horses. They range from graying Porfirio to eight-year-old Betito who's here with his father—generations of cowboys, connecting lineally back to Coronado's men who drove the first cattle across what are now the western borderlands.

Different stars have arranged themselves in the canyon's narrow canopy. The stream, switching along the bouldered floor, has to be forded repeatedly. They cross a cattleguard, signifying the state line. Hadley sits on a flood-smoothed outcropping. Water from New Mexico sluices around his boots into Arizona. A little rain means so much here; even the rocks smell fertile. Clouds in the form of question marks drift across the gap above. They are practically in three states, one Mexican, two North American, but the place feels only like itself, not like any overseeing sovereign entity.

His ranch is so landlocked in New Mexico that it can only be reached by vehicle over a washboard road leading up Guadalupe Canyon from Arizona. Here, the Drummond Hadley of poetry journals has achieved formidable intellectual isolation. The voices of the border now fill his writings. Spanish creeps in melodically. Mexican time draws out his poetic lines, loosening the joinings between words.

"Mira, there," says Roberto, "look past those
mesquite leaves."
Faded levis, tan shirt, sombrero by the cliff-rock.
"Where the trail climbs the ridge, do you see him?"
A hawk goes gliding low over Juan's bones.

Sunlight and the rains, summertime, the worms,
odor like a cow dead about four weeks.

Grease from his body turning the side-oats grasses
  brown.
Grease, coyotes, lightning, who knows?

"Their knowledges are a consciousness of land,
weather, and animals. This doesn't mean any kind
of ecological consciousness, but a consciousness of
what their value imposes on human beings."

Someone has thoughtfully toted the tequila along.
This far into the night, one theory is to still be drunk
in the morning, so the hangover can come later when
all are exhausted anyway from the roping and branding. But Hadley sounds sober as hell.

"In an environment of land, events take on a hor-
izontal quality of continuance; in a town, there's much
more verticality. Our attention is constantly drawn
to flashing lights, to advertising—millions are spent
on irresistible duck calls to attract us. Stop signs,
passing cars—not only are we bombarded by them
physically upon entering a city, but they impose themselves in people's perceptions and in their very voices."

But he could escape that on a Dakota farm or a
ranch in Oregon. Why the border?

"Because Mexico provides the continuum of the traditions created in the image of the earth, in the image
of weather and land patterns. Because Mexicans also
have the knowledge of waiting."

Dawn. Knowledge of Drummond Hadley comes from
the opposite side of the wall, thrashing his cells back
to consciousness in a bathtub filled with ice water.

A poultice of eggs, jalapeños, and black coffee is
applied to the wounds of the evening. Drummond
Hadley chooses the zebra dun, mounts his guests on
a gray and a veteran Appaloosa. The Mexican cowboys set out to roam the upper pastures. The rest
head down canyon, then split up and enter tangled
barrancas of mesquite, manzanita, and redberry juniper. Like fragments of the sun, bright vermilion
flycatchers hunt on the wing, at eye level. Undulating

rimrock, petrified manifestations of the aurora bo-
realis, cap the surrounding buttes. The horses listen
for bawling baby calves.

The riders locate them in the thickets, flush out
their mothers, head them toward the draw, and join
up. Everyone keeps pushing into the opening terrain
and morning, up canyon to the headquarters where
the boys have another bunch in a small holding pasture. There the dance begins.

Cowboys on savvy horses cut through a confusion
of milling, distressed ruminants, pairing separated
calves with their mommas, then driving them back
across the stream to the big corrals. They jostle past
the pen where Porfirio has kindled a mesquite fire,
which heats the long-handled branding irons. The
horseback cowboys flow in after them; when the tremendous dust finally calms, the cows are somehow
in one picket corral, and the calves, alone and nervous, in another.

Early fall clouds rolling over the ridgelines.
Bodies, clouds, dry falling seeds,
pretty quick men disappear in the winds
and the creeks and the mountain sand.

Hadley rides up. Although a coiled lazo hangs from
every cowboy's saddle, throughout the morning no
one relies on anything other than horsemanship to
control a cow brute. But now it is time to rope. Porfirio nudges Israel, who's never cowboyed here before,
and points at his patrón. "Mira su reata." Cheaper,
more durable nylon has long since replaced cowboys'
grass ropes, but in Mexico the old vaqueros bestowed
upon Hadley the equipment and knowledge of a far
richer tradition. La reata—lariat—is sixty feet of hand-
braided rawhide. Stiff nylon ropes practically form
themselves into nice loops; reata men, who can silently set a trap of pliable leather cord in front of a
calf's heels, are now rare and respected. The Mexican
cowboys are clearly admiring and proud of their boss.

Laying soft, unerring loops, Hadley necks 'em, aiming for the meaner crossbreds first, dallying his rawhide line twice around his saddle horn, and pulling them to the fire. Israel and Agustín patrol the sides of the gate, lest the calf hang himself up. As each animal rushes by, Justin flanks him, grabbing reata and midsection and landing him on his side. Hands and bootheels immobilize the hind legs; a knee pins down the neck. Beto's jacknife slices off half an ear, so later on riders will know from a distance that this one's been branded. Little Betito grabs the other ear and pours in tick powder, while his father cuts away a furry sac that exposes the veined gray testicles, pulling them free and slicing through their pink cords. At the same time, someone has jabbed a stubby needle into an exposed foreleg pit and injected two milky cubic centimeters of blackleg vaccine.

Except for a protesting bleat when he was wrestled to the dirt, the helpless baby has endured this series of indignities in silence, including his dramatic transformation from bull to steer. But now, even as men flail about in close quarters at their different tasks, here's Porfirio, finding an opening with mere millimeters to spare and inserting the incandescent metal. As the forked-W and then the bar are seared into his hide, the calf's exposed eye rolls all the way around, and he bellows. From the next pen, his frantic momma answers; they continue this line of dialogue as hot irons on either side of the head cauterize the horn-buds. The cowpunchers jump back; the calf is free and runs under the bars tied across the opening between the corrals, back to her side.

The whole operation has taken less than forty seconds, and as morning draws toward noon a rhythm develops and the branding quickens. They trade positions; Hadley, who hasn't missed once, observes proper ranch etiquette by inviting Justin, who's visiting from northern Arizona, to join in the roping. Unlimbering his nylon, Justin turns it into an international exposition with some North American heel-in' and draggin'. Hadley responds by switching to their hind legs too, showing a dazzling, immobilizing figure-eight loop they used on bigger, less cooperative critters back at Los Chirriones.

After all the calves are worked, the crew is dusty, bloody, exhilarated, and hungry. Any hangover has passed unnoticed. Calves, having already forgotten the whole thing, nurse peacefully. Later, the vaqueros will drive them and the relieved mothers back out to the range and the ridges.

The following day, Hadley and Beto ride up a long side canyon. Some slopes are badly eroded from a time when a previous owner's stock heavily overgrazed the land, but Drummond has been careful to limit the number of cattle he runs and now the native grama grasses are coming back. They stop to rope a brood cow to milk out a dangerously enlarged teat, then continue up into the high Animas Valley. After checking a pasture and a cattle tank belonging to Hadley, they turn back west.

Before them lies the infinite texture of the canyon, whose setting, people, and the two countries they live in have become Drummond Hadley's source of inspiration. "The border," Hadley has said, "is where hard gringo practicality has blended with a more romantic, older, nonmechanistic view of how men should live."

So be it. Hadley's border is far from the colonias of Juárez, deep in a landscape whose spirit drives men and women to song, which they pay for with age and sweat. The nations embrace here, simply for the joy of this beauty and because no diplomats are looking. Somewhere beyond either horizon, romance along the border withers, and the fence still remains.

But then again, so does all this.

Old dust in the wind drifting on the Guadalupe
   Canyon trail,
"Where are you headed Juan?"

"Siempre tengo mi camino en la punta de los pies. Always my way is before me," he said,

"Only the tips of my feet know where I will go."*

• • •

Twenty miles east of Douglas, across the Perilla Mountains, a dirt road known as the Geronimo Trail runs on the U.S. side, past the old San Bernardino grant. Here, a Mexican hacendado named Ignacio Pérez once ran more than 100,000 head of cattle. During the Apache Wars of the past century, the San Bernardino lay abandoned. But when mining activity created a premium local market for beef, a Texas cowman named John Horton Slaughter arrived here. Bribing the Indians from time to time with a few steers, he established one of the West's most re-knowned ranches.

Today, the headquarters of the Slaughter Ranch is a preserved historic shrine adjacent to a wildlife ref-uge, protecting the likes of the Yaqui topminnow and the Mexican stoneroller. The surrounding land is all working cattle range. Malpai Ranch, a cow-and-calf outfit run by Warner and Wendy Glenn, was once

___

*"Juan's Last Trail," by Drummond Hadley

part of the original Slaughter empire. The Glenns were born to this country: Warner's parents have a ranch in the Chiricahuas, and Wendy's grandfather surveyed the original townsite of Douglas. Their ties to Mexico are strong: Both grew up speaking Spanish, and Warner's sister Janet, wed to Fupau Varela, lives in Cananea. Malpai Ranch runs along the Mexican border, and illegals frequently cross their land on the way to some vague promise to the north.

Riding their range, Warner and Wendy Glenn find relics such as old broken Chihuahua spurs or last century's wagon hubs—remembrances of times be-fore the Gadsden Purchase, when all this land was Mexico. And further back: The clink of a horseshoe against metal has occasionally turned up tarnished coins bearing the likeness of a Spanish king of the colonial era. And even further: pottery sherds and stone axes from when the Apaches were young. And further still: fossils, remnants of camel and masto-don, from the age when only animals dwelt here. The seven-strand barbed-wire fence was still ore locked in the earth then. No border: Only rivers and moun-tains crossed this country—and then, as now, the lay of the terrain and the flow of the water was north and south. No line running east to west. The land here was inseparably one.

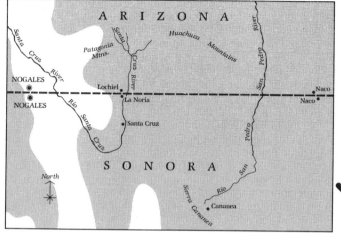

CHAPTER SEVEN

AMBOS NOGALES

"De la Osa," reads the first gravestone, and so does the second and several after that, until gradually the spelling changes: "de la Ossa." The stonecutters must have been confused, because all around the cemetery de la Osas alternated with de la Ossas well into the twentieth century. The epitaphs too reveal an inconclusive sense of identity: Some are in Spanish, some in English.

The hilltop where generations of de la Os(s)as lay sleeping is forty miles due west of the two Nacos, across the southeastern haunch of the Huachuca Mountains. One hundred yards below, a cluster of five buildings sits squarely on the line between the developed and the developing worlds. Except for the wisp of a fence trailing off to the east, that line is pretty negligible here. Ranchers and miners entered this place, Lochiel—also known as La Noria, The Well—during the 1880s as Apache territory receded toward the Chiricahuas and finally disappeared altogether. When the boundary was resurveyed a decade later, they learned that the settlement actually straddled the international line, with the well in Mexico. Today, two-fifths of the village is comprised of back-to-back customs houses of the respective nations.

A dark cottonwood grove shades the silent buildings, paralleling the dirt road that runs to the border gate. A line of low power poles arriving from the north doesn't stop at the fence but continues on through, disappearing into Mexico. Beyond is the San Rafael Valley. The first white cattlemen here, Colin and Brewster Cameron from Pennsylvania, were so taken by its loveliness that they named their settlement Lochiel after an ancestral Scottish home they'd never seen. Colonel William Greene himself homesteaded in the San Rafael. So great was his love for the place that years later, when he learned he had inadvertently claimed land owned by the Camerons, he plunged deep into his

fortune and bought the entire valley.

Any argument that the San Rafael is not the perfect American West has been settled by this century's peculiar standard of quintessence: It is repeatedly the location for commercials and cowboy movies. To the distress of the Sooner State, even *Oklahoma!* was filmed here.

Looming like a citadel on the plain, Colonel Greene's homestead is still occupied by his daughter Bebe. The large, square headquarters, one of the most famous pieces of architecture in the West, was built of bricks fired on the premises. Its roof, dormers, and beams were cut from California redwood logs floated down the Colorado River. Completely encircled by a wide veranda, it overlooks the surrounding hills where descendants of Greene's blooded cattle and fine quarterhorses graze.

Inside, a light fixture made of copper hangs from the tall living room ceiling. A Miró lithograph is situated aside a mantel. A glass bookcase holds rows of leather-bound volumes, which contain the breeding histories of the thoroughbred Herefords run by the Greene Cattle Company. A study has artifacts from Japan, to where the colonel escaped the year he lost his copper empire to Anaconda.

Florence "Bebe" Sharp, née Greene, thin, aging but attractive, with cropped, gray-streaked hair, takes coffee at a five-leaf oak table in a sunny breakfast parlor. On either side of the doorway leading to the wood-paneled kitchen hang framed prints of fighting cocks. Another door enters the cowboy's dining room, where Greene loved to eat with his men. Mrs. Sharp is tired—tired of smugglers coming across her land, tired of the coyotes going after her sheep, tired of a cattle business that now means competing against tax shelter interests that profit more by losing than by making money.

On the porch, barn swallows crowd around a bird feeder. She walks out and looks down into Mexico. A large oak stands just over the line, marking where drug runners like to come through, where she will again have to repair the fence torn away in the process. Border economics are now fueled with rolls of $100 bills, about which people prudently have learned not to inquire. She doesn't like to think about it. About her girlhood in Cananea, she thinks hardly at all. She imagines a life much simpler than the one the United States and Mexico have wrought in this land, and muses sometimes about selling her cattle and returning her ranch to its original state, with large cats prowling its grassy ridges for pronghorn antelope.

A trapper arrives to see about the coyotes. They walk out by the big, tin-roofed barn to discuss. The gossip lately is that things are getting better here, that patrols on both sides have somewhat neutralized the violent aspects of the drug traffic. Neutralization seems to characterize the better interactions of the two neighboring countries on the border.

"Oh, the U.S. and Mexico will manage together," she sighs. "Bad-tempered men and good-natured women have been getting married forever."

Semana Santa—the Holy Week that precedes Easter—is when Mexicans, especially those in the United States, yearn for their patria chica, their home pueblo. And so they go. In states like Hidalgo or Tlaxcala, so cruelly impoverished that the populations of entire villages must migrate, deserted towns emulate the Resurrection by miraculously returning to life. For a few divine days, Mexicans are home, and they can even pretend that the money in their pockets wasn't earned in a distant, sometimes hostile land.

All along the 1,936-mile border, the crossings jam during Semana Santa. But the port of entry at Lochiel is an exception. A chrome padlock the size of a small anvil clenches the ends of a chain passing through the bars of the gate into Mexico and back into the United States. The U.S. Customs house is tightly shuttered. Across the fence, Ricardo Méndez, the stringy Mexican gatekeeper, informs travelers that the United States closed Lochiel's gate in 1983 to save money. "El Presidente Reagan decided that the richest nation

on earth couldn't afford the salaries of a couple of customs officials."

His own peso wages add up to about $66 per week. Mexican customs officers are sometimes likened to American waitresses, in that their real living comes from tips, but with the border crossing officially closed, Méndez doesn't get many customers. And the big opportunities don't really exist here. "Why would a pusher come through here, when they can cross anywhere?" he asks, gesturing east and west. "There's a road, and there's a road. They can choose any one they want, so why go through customs? I never get to see those cabrones, except from a distance."

His uniform has buttons missing, and he longs to be transferred to someplace profitable. But he is here because people still pass, to and from the village of Santa Cruz, six miles below the line. Because la garita is locked, Méndez has to direct them east along the fence to a stucco ranch house about a quarter mile away, where the de la Ossas have a gate and sometimes grant permission to cross.

In 1880, Antonio de la Osa was overcome with an urge for something new. More than a century before, his parents had emigrated to California from Spain. Now he wanted to see, and be, something different. He packed his family, added an "s" to the spelling of their name, and led them east on foot, following a team and wagon headed for Chihuahua. After eight hundred miles, his wife announced that she was tired of walking. They were at Lochiel.

Admiring this splendid country from the kitchen window where he warms himself, Rosamel de la Ossa figures that his mother probably feigned fatigue. Now in his eighties, his skin rubbed nearly transparent by wind and sun, Rosamel has lived his entire life within a hundred yards of Mexico. His only language is Spanish. Isolated from the rest of the United States by land and language, he nonetheless feels loyally American.

When the Mexican Revolution periodically veered across the line between 1910 and 1920, his mother kept an accounting of the number of cows and horses stolen, and billed the United States for their losses. "And our government made Mexico pay. You don't see Mexico getting its people reimbursed for what the Americans have stolen from them," Rosamel points out.

A clutch of de la Ossa children direct travelers in two languages to a barbed wire cattle gate, held in place by a bent coat hanger. On the other side, the terraced velour hills are Mexico. The unpaved road follows a vanished railroad line that once led from mines above Lochiel to a spur near Santa Cruz. Instead of ore cars, meadowlarks accompany the pickups that bounce along.

The Arizona county to the north is also called Santa Cruz. The name derives from the indefatigable Jesuit founder of missions, Padre Eusebio Kino, whose footsteps crossed and recrossed the borderlands from here to California. Kino came this way in the late 1690s, but he was not the region's first white man. The plaque on a monumental cement cross at Lochiel proclaims that Fray Marcos de Niza, the first European to enter what is now the United States west of the Rockies, did so right here. That was in 1539; he was journeying for the viceroy of Mexico to find the seven golden cities. A few months later, out of exhaustion, delirium, or simply from the amber reflections of the honey-colored landforms, de Niza gazed at tiers of Zuñi dwellings in New Mexico and believed he'd discovered Cíbola.

When he came through here, he was following the course of the Santa Cruz River. Beginning as runoff in the Patagonia and Huachuca mountains above Lochiel, it flows into Mexico, then curves along topography that capriciously tips it back into the United States. Just outside its namesake village, the river's bottomland is planted entirely in orchards. In Santa Cruz, which means Holy Cross, Easter arrives perfumed with apple blossoms.

Because the priest who travels up from Hermosillo must be in the next village downriver the following morning, Saturday evening's vigil is Santa Cruz's only Easter service. In the municipal square, a small boy dressed in jeans and a white shirt pulls a bell rope leading to the white church tower. Gray pigeons explode from the belfry; as the tolling abates, they settle back within.

The women of Santa Cruz—mothers in skirts, girls in bright slacks—filter into the plaza. They gather in front of the church, where an unlit bonfire awaits. An hour passes, and men start to arrive, fussing with unfamiliar neckties. The white stucco Santa Cruz buildings mellow in the dusk. Six miles below the border, a peaceful town of neatly swept streets and uniform, whitewashed architecture readies to celebrate the season.

A few years earlier, Mexico's government restored Santa Cruz's church, built a municipal palace, installed a concrete water tower, and placed ornamental streetlamps in the square. The electricity was brought from the United States, over a line from Tucson that once serviced now depleted mines above Lochiel. The utility company realized it was cheaper to extend it a few miles farther and sell electricity to Mexico than to tear it down. With considerable fanfare, power was inaugurated at the stroke of midnight on New Year's Eve, 1968. As the newly electrified pueblo gleamed with light, everyone cheered and policemen fired their pistols into the air. A bullet struck the new transformer and the celebration climaxed in a nova of dazzling blue sparks—which blazed, died, and left the town again in darkness.

For Easter, the lights are out once more. The evening has cooled; stars appear and a young blond priest arrives to kindle the fire. The crowd forms a circle. "This flame," he intones, "represents the Life that illuminated the darkness. This is the night when all who believe can sever the chains of death." Two hundred people draw nearer. Altar boys light candles; they and the priest lead the congregants inside. The church's pink interior turns to rose in the candlelight.

Women and children fill the pews, men stand in back. The fragrance of incense and scented wax mingle as Mass begins.

After a while, the crowd seems to swell from within, pushing back toward the door. Pressure on the rear gradually expands the standing congregation, like some sort of human balloon, until some are actually out on the steps. Within, the service languishes as the priest calls on students to read from the Gospels. When there are no volunteers, he waits serenely. Eventually, to the turgid pace of the melting candles, he begins to drone his homily. But the bubble in back has already burst. Men are trickling away silently, escaping to lights that shine beyond the plaza . . . to music that leaks into the holy Saturday night from a bar named Mi Oficina—my office, old joke. Inside, its walls are pink, green, and unwashed. The wine list is straightforward enough: Tecate, tequila, or both. Mounted behind the bar, a painting of a corpse being carried off by gleeful, horned demons bears the caption: "He died before paying his bill."

The backsliders concentrate guiltily on their beers. The rest of the clientele, mostly vaqueros, scream to make themselves understood over dueling speakers connected to two trunk-sized cassette players on either side of the cash register. At top volume and out of sync, each plays a different arrangement of "Mexicali Rose"—one for clarinet, one for accordion and tuba.

A cowboy in precarious, slant-heeled boots buys another round. The fallen angels drink up and creep back to the temple, only to find there was no great rush: They haven't gotten to communion yet. "It's always like this," one comrade complains. "The padres think that if they come all the way from the capital, a one-hour Mass isn't good enough."

They stand around the still-blazing Light of Christ, warming their hands. A farmer with a fine white goatee remarks, "I get so hungry in there I always think I'm going to pass out. I can't remember how long it's been since I've made it to communion." Mur-

PLATE 33
LEONARDO "EL NANO" YÁÑEZ ROMO, COMPOSER, DOUGLAS, ARIZONA

PLATE 34
CANANEA, SONORA

PLATE 35

MICAELA, MIMI, SERI, AND DICK KAMP, BISBEE JUNCTION, ARIZONA

PLATE 36
DRUMMOND HADLEY AND VAQUEROS, GUADALUPE CANYON RANCH, NEW MEXICO

PLATE 37
ROSAMEL AND RAMÓN DE LA OSSA, R BAR 9 RANCH, LOCHIEL, ARIZONA

PLATE 38
TERESA LEAL AND FAMILY, NOGALES, SONORA

PLATE 39
FATHER TONY CLARK AND LOS GUADALUPANOS BOXING TEAM,
SACRED HEART CHURCH, NOGALES, ARIZONA

PLATE 40
MAQUILADORA
MAQUILADORA WORKER AND FAMILY, NOGALES, SONORA

PLATE 41
COLONIA NUEVA, NOGALES, SONORA

PLATE 42
CALLE PIERSON, NOGALES, SONORA

PLATE 43

AURORA, MARTHA DELFINA, AND ERNESTINA NORIEGA, KI:TOWAK (QUITOVAC), SONORA

PLATE 44
AJO MOUNTAINS, ORGAN PIPE CACTUS NATIONAL MONUMENT, ARIZONA

murs of assent arise from the dozen or so at the fire, and someone proposes fetching a grill and hamburgers. A railroad whistle momentarily overpowers the conversation and the service within, resounding off the hills, as the Cananea freight rolls by.

Talk turns to Santa Cruz's most important subject, the weather. For more than thirty years, apple growing has been the region's mainstay, and each spring suspense grips the town when the fragile blossoms appear. In most years, including this one, late frost suddenly strips the branches bare. This is the second bloom; one more freeze and they can forget it until next year. Inevitably, 1979 is mentioned, the year when one-hundred-year-old oaks froze to their core. Reflexively, the men make the sign of the cross and draw nearer to the fire.

A newer chronic worry is the border closing. Santa Cruz residents once relied on Arizona for farm machinery parts, medical care, and several basics. But passing through Lochiel was also the route of least resistance to the rest of Mexico. To reach Nogales, the nearest city, meant either two-and-a-half hours over Sonoran outback or forty-five minutes via U.S. Forest Service roads. Several arroyos intersect the Mexican route, including the Santa Cruz River itself. With the border gate closed, whenever the washes flood the town is stranded. Rain as well as frost now threatens their livelihood: They can end up marooned with several hundred tons of Red and Golden Delicious apples that can't reach market.

The governor of Sonora protested to Washington, claiming it was a violation of international treaty. Although no one bothers vehicles from the United States that use de la Ossa's gate to enter Mexico, the Border Patrol confiscates the cars of Santa Cruz residents who try that in the other direction.

"It insults history," the goateed farmer declares. Founded by Padre Kino, Santa Cruz was one of the first settlements along the entire border. From here, Kino entered what is now Arizona many times, on his way to his San Xavier mission near the Papago village of Tuqui Son. "And before Kino, Marcos de Niza. This is the oldest crossing route along the whole frontera. What gives Americans the right to close it?"

The famished congregation stumbles from the three-hour Mass. The men subtly merge with the crowd. "Mañana at the fiesta," they say to each other. The party is a celebration for Rubén Peralta, who has just been named the PRI's mayoral candidate, tantamount here to election. The opposition PANista stronghold is two valleys back, at Agua Prieta.

On Easter morning, eighty-three-year-old José Lorta sits in the shelter of his 1,200-tree orchard, just smelling the perfume. Nearly half his trees died in the killing winter of '79. This is the dangerous month; the climate is a wild woman, and it could happen again. But that seems unlikely. Acorn woodpeckers sun and peck at sap-gorged ants on the warm, peeling apple bark. Occasional gentle zephyrs loosen fragrant, snowy showers of apple blossoms. Every succulent flower holds a delirious honeybee; their glad humming and a transcendental aroma pervade the orchard. A purer idea of spring than this morning in Santa Cruz is inconceivable.

"God willing," prays Lorta. "Si Dios permite." His face reveals an Apache heritage, rare for these parts where Apaches were pariahs. In a year without frost, his trees can produce four hundred kilos of export-quality fruit apiece. He has seen apples that weighed more than a pound. The fall harvest is a happy thing, working in the pleasant shade. People don't think about politics. Just the apples. That is, of course, if the weather doesn't do something mysterious.

While the whole town, even the PAN's candidate, is eating tacos of pit-roasted barbecue that afternoon at the ranch of the PRI's Rubén Peralta, the mysterious occurs. With no discernible warning, dark moisture coalesces in a hitherto unclouded sky. Abruptly, spring collapses, dragging the temperature with it. Projectile raindrops whip by on a wind that tears live branches from two-hundred-year-old cottonwoods. Serving tables upend, scattering the styrofoam underpinnings of lunch.

The chubasco lasts just four minutes. Then the sun reappears, the air calms, the warmth returns. Everyone sighs. Already knowing, they step to the edge of the river plain to gaze at their orchards. Boughs that earlier had been heavy with blooms are now exposed and naked. Mounds of shriveling blossoms lie like popcorn dregs against the banked irrigation ditches.

"Así es," they tell each other. So it goes. New paper cups appear. They pour more beer.

The road from Santa Cruz to Nogales on the Mexican side follows the river until it curves northward again into Nogales Pass. This is the route that washes out half the time, the one Mexico has promised for years to improve by placing bridges over the twisting river and its tributaries.

The *cucuchea* of whippoorwills accompanies the twilight in the quiet glades of the Río Santa Cruz. Coatimundis forage in soft undergrowth, and silent raptors glide overhead. Huge, perfect Emory oaks grow from lawnlike wild pastures, and cottonwood canopies shelter the tributary washes. Children from a series of doleful new ejidos, established on land that once belonged to René Mascareñas's father, jump from fallen sycamore logs and splash about in the shallow riverbed. In arid country, the enormous white trunk of a standing sycamore is a startling thing; every bend of the Santa Cruz is worthy of a gasp. The river continues, cutting through deep green fields where Hereford and Charolais cattle and horses graze, until it flows through a set of water gaps in a barbed wire fence and reenters the United States.

.   .   .

A border joke goes as follows:

Question: What are the first four words a Mexican learns in the United States?

Answer: "Attention, K Mart shoppers."

Nogales has a K Mart too, and although it does plenty of business, it doesn't have what La Morley has.

Mention La Morley almost anywhere in northwestern Mexico and people know exactly what you mean. The phrase refers to Morley Avenue, across the international line in Nogales, Arizona. The street dead-ends at a border exclusive: a special international pedestrian gate, far removed from the vehicle entry. Here, citizens from Culiacan stroll into the United States and routinely run into friends from Hermosillo, cousins from Navojoa, compadres from Arizpe. For many, it's the place they most often get to see each other.

For a century, La Morley has been the favored shopping ground for Sonora, Sinaloa, and several points beyond. There's the usual border fare of Japanese electronics and Woolworth's potpourri, but the real lure is style.

Though Morley Street is a bit remote from the epicenters of high fashion, Parisian haute couture, Oriental silks, the sleek Italian cut—whatever ultimate in sophistication the Scottsdale boutiques are showing is also here. Mexicans who can afford quality and garment business pros take Nogales seriously.

In 1880, Jacob Isaacson, a Russian Jewish peddler, built the first trading post in then-uninhabited Nogales Pass, named for a pair of resident walnut trees. A few months later, Juan José Vásquez opened a nearby roadhouse. They shared a hunch that the pass would someday become a natural traffic funnel between cities of the American and Mexican West.

When topographers later determined that Isaacson

was on one side of the line and Vásquez on the other, they were so isolated it made little difference. But in 1882, surveyor William Morley of the Atchison, Topeka, Santa Fe, and Sonora Railway decided that the track connecting Tucson and Guaymas should cross the border right here. In the West, wherever two lines intersect, things start developing. Isaacson named the street that materialized around his trading post in honor of the surveyor. He also appointed himself postmaster of the burgeoning new town, modestly called Isaacson.

Neither the name nor the man stuck for long, but the immigrant tradition he'd begun did. Rochlins, Puchis, Brackers, Epsteins, Piersóns, Prestinis, Capins, Kyriakises, Karams—families of risk takers who left difficulties in foreign lands—sensed an opportunity here. The Jews, Greeks, Lebanese, and other Mediterranean refugees in Nogales were soon joined by the Anglos and Hispanics more commonly associated with the border. Polyglot entrepreneurs began importing goods from Asia and California up through the harbor at Guaymas, Sonora, and introducing vegetables from fertile Sinaloa into the United States. In return, they shipped everything from flivvers to boxcars filled with toothpicks to Mexico.

Those who got along with customers and associates of all flavors tended to thrive; prosperity softened the ethnic collision. Born at the international junction of two growing states, what citizens from both sides referred to as Ambos (Both) Nogales developed into one of the West's most tolerant communities.

The open ambience eased the reality of the dividing line. During the 1890s, John Brickwood, who prospected with William Greene before anyone suspected that the latter would one day own half these borderlands, plunked down a saloon here right astride the boundary. The establishment confounded any serious attempts to enforce customs laws, until Washington finally ordered a fence erected down the middle of International Street in 1916. The boundary is now

formally observed, but two former mayors of the respective towns live on that street, on either side of three meters of chain link, and if necessary could discuss twin city policy simply by leaning out their windows.

Probably nowhere else do U.S. Department of Agriculture agents go to work in Mexico every morning. At shipping docks in Nogales, Sonora, they inspect tomatoes and peppers coming from Sinaloa. Except for lettuce, 50 percent of the vegetables eaten in the United States from November through May are grown in Mexico and enter at Nogales—a fact that Florida's vegetable industry finds unpatriotic. The Nogales, Arizona-based West Mexico Vegetable Growers' Association responds that, much to the United States's advantage, Mexican produce keeps down the price of vegetables.

"Without Mexico, the U.S. would have starved during World War II," says George Uribe, its executive director and chief Washington lobbyist. "Don't forget: We used to depend on Cuba for much of our winter vegetables. Shouldn't we be grateful that we're maintaining such a nice relationship here at Nogales?"

Then too, many of the huge vegetable growers in northern Mexico are really North Americans. Over the years they have avoided expropriation by keeping their lands in the names of prestanombres, some of whom are the infant children of trusted employees. Their financing is through American banks and supermarket chains like Safeway, and much of their seed, fertilizer, and pesticides come from the United States. Americans needn't worry too much about disloyalty for eating a Mexican cucumber—unless, of course, their concern is over disloyalty to Mexico.

The decision to temporarily close several crossings, including the Morley Avenue pedestrian gate, in response to the Camarena killing drove everybody here crazy.

"One hundred and fifty million dollars worth of

tax-paying business a year on this street and our government thinks it's done the American public some great favor by cutting it off. All they proved is how powerful the terrorists are." Bobby Bracker, an exasperated, hefty man in an open-necked knit shirt and a gray poplin suit, is the proprietor of a Morley Avenue clothiery. "Mexico is laughing. They don't want their people spending all their money over here anyway. Some punishment."

Bracker, whose father began the store in 1924, called Washington. He explained things carefully to a senator. The senator suggested reopening the border, but also calling for immediate payment of Mexico's debt or refusing to buy their oil or both. Now Bracker laughed. He knows something about dealing with debts here: He used to travel the coastal states of northwestern Mexico to collect overdue accounts. "If Mexicans have money, they pay. They regard obligations as matters of personal honor. Mexico doesn't have any money to pay its debt, and the only way it ever might is by selling us the oil we need. Is our only foreign policy to cut off our nose to spite our face?"

If the United States ever had a good reason to put pressure on Mexico, which he's not sure it does, the simple way, Bracker believes, would be to suspend all commercial airline traffic to Mexico for one week. "Cut travel off to Acapulco and watch how fast things mess up. Diverting American vacationers to the Caribbean would bring Mexico to its knees."

What he would like most, however, is a respite from the devaluations and a nice, stable relationship between the two countries, so he can enjoy the border business to which he was born. In 1982, after the peso sunk and sales dropped by 75 percent, Bobby Bracker gambled by going to the New York fall market to maintain his "fashion-forward" merchandising appeal, and saved his store. "My clientele here sees all the catalogs. I told my buyers that we could only go for 25 percent of normal and that they'd better choose right."

That time his risk seemed to pay off—three years later, out of great confidence or greater recklessness, he is installing new wall-to-wall carpet throughout the store's upper level. As the peso plumbs new depths, he can only pray it's not a mistake.

"Pretty smart," says fellow Morley merchant Dick Capin, dropping by to inspect the carpeting job. "You created more retail floor space." Capin's family owns several border dry goods establishments; their private, antishoplifting police force at one time outnumbered that of the city. "Doing business on the border," Capin says, "is kids pissing in my elevators. Shitting in my dressing rooms."

"Same as selling schmatahs anywhere else," Bracker reminds him. "¿Verdad, mensch?"

.   .   .

The Sonoran press calls the problem "Nogalitis," suggesting that with the coming of the maquiladora twin plant industry a virus of sorts has settled over Nogales Pass. Like gout, the disease is one of overindulgence.

Twenty-five thousand people live in Nogales, Arizona; during the past decade, its hyperthyroid Mexican twin has sprouted to 150,000. Housing is the critical issue for maquiladora workers and their considerable families. The tax the companies pay for this is far from sufficient, but Mexico won't press the Americans for fear they will leave if expenses become too great. What government housing that does result usually goes to supervisors, not to assemblers. And even they have to enter a lottery to be eligible: Entering is often a euphemism for bribing their way in.

Consuelo Alaniz has sewn paper surgical gowns for Disposable Products, brassieres for Bali Company, and ready-to-wear dresses for West Coast Industries. Lately, she's been at Samsonite. Consuelo's family is one of 1,200 living in the colonia known as Pueblo Nuevo, where automobile carcasses line gullied roads and dwellings are buttressed by retaining walls of embedded automobile tires. Consuelo, her six children, her sister, and her sister's baby live in a two-room pastiche construction of sheetrock, recycled plywood, and wood pallets discarded by the maquiladoras. Her husband, who is not really her husband, sometimes joins her here too.

Consuelo is in her early thirties. Her brown hair curls at her neck, and she is still thin enough to look good in jeans. She lives in one of the few dirt colonias with electricity and water. "It was not luck. The city had no intention of giving us anything. We painted protest banners and camped in front of the palacio municipal. There were so many of us we finally embarrassed them into giving in. Of course, they now take all the credit."

The hardscrabble soil of Pueblo Nuevo erodes rather than percolates. Next to the colonia is the municipal dump, where the street department tosses dead dogs and where the flies take over during the hot months. The sole relief is that the city has begun to bury its garbage. Before, it was burned nightly; the people of Pueblo Nuevo did not breathe so much as choke. Consuelo thinks switching to a landfill implies ulterior motives. To make room, they will probably subdivide the dump. "Already they are pushing the garbage back and putting people there."

Her treeless colonia is toned a light sepia from the tan powder that billows from under passing automobiles. Water from a broken pipe etches feathery rivulets in the road until it saturates with dust, turns sluggish, and evaporates. Ubiquitous children take brief turns on two worn, communal bicycles. There is a tiny store, a Conasupo—the government grocery chain that purports to buy from small farmers and provide inexpensive food to the public. However, Conasupo is frequently undersold by private supermarkets. A sign reads, "Supply Center for the Marginal Classes." Its owner is the PRI's precinct leader for Pueblo Nuevo. "The prices are all right," Consuelo says. "The quality isn't. We get whatever the government can't sell to the U.S."

The gulch dead-ends where two perspiring men with hammers labor at a mountain of wooden pallets,

dismantling them for building materials. "I stopped listening to the PRI's promises when I realized that life kept getting worse instead of better," says Consuelo, watching. Instead, she joined the PRT—el Partido Revolucionario de Trabajadores, the Revolutionary Workers' Party.

Mexico's socialist movement is infamous for splintering into warring factions and creating more ineffectual minority parties. Consuelo knows this, but she won't support the PAN, even though it has the greatest chance of cracking the PRI's dominance.

"We workers need a change. The PAN would give the power to even richer people."

She tries to organize women, believing they are the principal workers and the foundation of her society. Very few men live in Pueblo Nuevo; they are off in the United States or have abandoned the women they impregnated. And their children—the Nogales maquilas jointly maintain a day-care center, with a capacity of 265 for the 5,000 women with children who work in Nogales assembly plants.

Consuelo's sister works the night shift at General Instruments, leaving the baby with her. At 4:30 A.M., Consuelo is up to get to Samsonite by 6:15, a trip requiring two bus transfers, so she turns the infant over to her own eldest daughter.

At 4:30 P.M., she returns, begins cooking, and relieves her daughter who has been watching the kids. "I want to go out and talk to women. But I'm tired. So I save it for the weekend. I invite twenty women to meet, and maybe five show up. All of them are tired. We are all so tired."

The PRT has been helping her and other colonos gain title to their land. Now that they have light and water, a Nogales businessman holding an obscure land grant is trying to evict them. "We won't permit it," Consuelo vows. "We're also helping people in other new colonias to organize and fight for their right to live here."

She does not tell them instead to go back where they came from, that the right to live this way isn't worth struggling for, because they wouldn't pay any attention. "It would be harder to go back than to stay, and it's no worse here than wherever they left. So we try to help."

Consuelo's efforts have produced at least one result. The ruling PRI, observing a tradition of seducing its critics, offered her a job with just enough pay to be tempting. She refused. "I couldn't face my children, after what I've tried to teach them."

Yet it's more important to be able to feed them, so about every six months she goes wet, up to Phoenix, to work as a domestic and make enough money to tide them over here. "It's not bad," she says. She has met a lot of people that way, Salvadorans and Nicaraguans, who are finding a life for themselves up there.

The paradox intrigues: a Mexican socialist using the United States, the arch perpetrator of capitalism's excesses, as a means to avoid being co-opted by her own country. Consuelo's dark green eyes reveal the bitterness of living a forced contradiction. "At least the U.S. helps women. If a señora has babies and no job, they help her. If they take too much for taxes, they give some back. She can get food. Not like here. Here life crushes a woman."

Is it just corruption, then, that's the enemy, and not capitalism? If Mexico were capitalistic like the U.S., would it be better for the people?

She regards the wretched hillsides of her pueblo for a long, troubled moment. Finally, she murmurs, "¿Ay, quién sabe?"

Who knows.

The maquiladora is not a dank sweatshop; banks of fluorescence and pale yellow walls combine in a synthetic pastel gleam. Seventy-two operators, mostly female, sit twelve to a bench, forty-eight hours a week. Each turns a screw, sets a rivet, adds a gasket, punches a hole. At the end, small carburetors pop out, the kind used in lawnmowers and chainsaws.

A shrill buzzer overwhelms assembly line chatter and the paroxysms of compressed air tools, signaling the first of three thirty-minute lunch shifts. A third of the workers head for the cafeteria or outside to the concrete patio. Help-wanted signs adorn the slump block exterior. Turnover is about 90 percent each year. Leo Pérez, an engineer from Spain who is plant technical manager, knows that paying higher wages would avoid the expense of absenteeism and training new workers. "At these salaries, Nogales attracts about half the labor its maquiladoras need. If we raised them," he explains, echoing Col. William Greene eighty years earlier, "Mexico would throw us out. If American factories start offering more than the minimum wage here, it will begin a revolution."

One result is pervasive dishonesty. "It's understandable. If my baby were hungry, I'd steal anything I could from the boss. That still doesn't make me respect these qualities in my employees."

Paul Bond's custom boot factory in Nogales, Arizona, produces some of the world's best, most expensive cowboy boots. Bond runs what could be considered one of the first maquiladoras. For thirty years, he has maintained about fifteen employees on each side, measuring and cutting in the U.S. plant, stitching and attaching in Nogales, Sonora. Some of his Mexican employees have stayed with him more than twenty years. The difference is one of scale.

"I'd lose quality if I made more than ten pairs a day, so we keep our business small and family-like. In Mexico, I can only pay my workers the legally allowed wage. But nothing can stop me from handing them a little bonus when they come over here to visit me. Which," he adds, "they do every week."

When employees number in the hundreds and the goal is quantity, those bonuses would add up. Leo Pérez has awarded some when the budget permitted—"if for no other reason than it makes you feel better about something crummy you're doing." When he married an American woman and came to the

United States, this job was what was available. It depresses him to work with people in a system designed so they can never advance.

"If you know that you will die at the same level you're at now, how could you care about anything? We have managerial meetings to discuss motivating the employees. We bring in social workers. Absenteeism is still absurd. Defects still run over 15 percent. The companies would like Mexicans to work like Americans, but this requires a future view, being able to project one's self. These people think at most one week into the future. The present is more important—it's been this way since colonial rule."

Leo chews on his mustache, reflecting on what his ancestors wrought in the New World. After three years, he has decided, he doesn't know anything about Mexicans. "If I ask Mexicans how their people think, they don't know either. Too many passions in their decisions. If I could predict how they react, I'd make millions." He points to some inked posters taped to the wall. "The company tried improving workers' output by appealing to their pride—the Mexican thing about saving face in front of others. So now we have flowcharts in front of each machine showing everybody's production."

The flowcharts are in English.

"It doesn't matter. The majority of these people aren't competitive anyway. They don't want to be last—but they don't want to be first, either. They only want to do the necessary work and remain unnoticed."

Their swift brown fingers flick like the hands of Navajo weavers, picking up tiny washers with one tool and fitting them into orifices with another, five thousand times and it's only noon. The monotony, some say, is better than being at home and getting no salary.

Leo Pérez passes among the rows of workers, his tall, continental good looks attracting obvious attention from female assemblers. Many of them in turn are very attractive. For a married man, this could be like supervising inside Pandora's box. The border seethes with innuendos about maquiladora managers who fornicate their way down assembly lines or companies that provide stud services as incentives. Leo discounts the rumors, but not the underlying passions. They are real.

"For most of these women, the only fun they ever have is love. Last month 10 percent of them were pregnant—imagine if we could harness sexual energy. When someone here has sex, the news travels up the table, down the other side, and around the room like electricity through a printed circuit. The whole plant not only knows who did what with whom, but how many times, the duration, and the pertinent dimensions."

Leo and his wife, artist Theresa Brutcher Pérez, rent a home in Rio Rico, a Spanish-tiled subdivision nine miles north of Nogales. Its residents are mainly maquiladora executives who commute daily to Mexico. Leo and Theresa, who also teaches English to supervisors at Leo's plant, are tired of being here; they have not established close ties in Nogales and the work is joyless. Theresa reads histories of the coup in Guatemala orchestrated by the CIA to protect the United Fruit Company, and wonders if, either subtly or overtly, it could come to that on the border.

"If Mexico ever insisted that U.S. companies do more for Mexicans than they're willing to, it's possible," she believes. "I don't like the fact that we're a part of this. But if you stretch it a little, we're all a part of it—anyone who has anything to do with Ford, GM, GE, or if you own anything electronic that's not Asian. Anyone in Wisconsin or Michigan working for these firms or using their products does so at the expense of Latin America."

In 1963, Sherman Montgomery came to Nogales from Tucson to manage the Southern Arizona Bank and then fought not to be transferred back. With mainly

Mexican customers, he had the lowest loss ratio on loans in eleven western states. "They valued their credit ratings because U.S. banks offer better services." Even liquidations were friendlier: Borrowers invited him to their homes for dinner and drinks on the night of a foreclosure.

Retired from banking, he now deals in real estate. An engaging man with a thick, gray crew-cut, Montgomery laughs easily, but the subject of maquiladoras raises a frown.

"The twin plants provide income, but their people haven't been taken into the town social set as such. That's why they live up at Rio Rico." He says the name with condescension, pointedly omitting to roll the *r*'s. "A lot of them just don't understand Nogales, the way it's developed over the years. Nogales once was a real man's town, and I hate to see that change."

He tilts back in his black upholstered swivel chair, and explains what the man's town used to be like. "Sexual interchange is an easy thing on the border. Women used to tolerate that, and everyone got along fine." An example is a development he is currently marketing. It was once the property of a family that owned a farm, which for years sold produce to both Nogaleses. According to the sales brochure, during the Depression they "made sure that any family in the Valley with small children received fresh milk, whether they could pay for it or not."

Actually, Sherman explains, the son in charge got paid for the milk in interesting ways. "He once confessed that he'd probably screwed between five and six hundred women. He had a generous love of people, and they needed the milk. Many of them paid him the only way they knew how." He smiles.

"Today you get some maquiladora managers with haranguing wives, and suddenly they meet women who really know how to please a man. As a result, some of their marriages suffer. A lot of these guys come out of the Midwest, or were raised in a puritan culture, and they may not be able to handle the exposure to friendly sex. These dark-eyed little Mexican girls are all cute and they're all flirts. They really know how to work you over, and the guy may not be prepared for all this."

He leans forward, placing his elbows on the desk blotter.

"Some of the smarter managers develop relationships their wives can tolerate, once they accept it. Women who don't complain, who involve themselves in community affairs, get along fine. In the produce business, some of the men who travel down south even have second families. But with the maquiladoras, most of these guys aren't prepared for having a kept woman." He looks disconcerted. "I don't know why they think they have to marry them, but your average midwesterner in his forties believes you don't sleep with someone without marrying them." He shakes his head. "It's tough on their wives."

.   .   .

On November 8, 1907, the phone rang in the office of James Douglas at the Copper Queen Mine in Bisbee—the same line over which, one year earlier, Col. William Greene had summoned American troops to quell rising strikers in Cananea. This call was also from Mexico. The news Douglas heard became one of Mexico's legends; he and his thirteen-year-old son Lewis were the first Americans to know.

Fifty miles below the border, in the mining town of Nacozari, a train filled with dynamite had ignited. People saw the flames and panicked. An explosion within Nacozari's tight canyon would annihilate them. But a young engineer named Jesús García jumped aboard and drove the train out of town where, seconds later, it detonated. Both the train and García were obliterated, but Nacozari was safe. Young Lewis Douglas, raised in Nacozari where his father directed the Montezuma Mine, wept in wonder over this act of heroism. García had been his riding instructor.

For the rest of his life, Lewis was obsessed with Jesús García's sacrifice. He went on to become a congressman, director of the federal budget, and ambassador to Great Britain. To everyone—to his brother trustees of the Rockefeller Foundation and his fellow directors of General Motors—he recounted the story of Jesús García's martyrdom. A portrait of García decorated his office at the Southern Arizona Bank and Trust in Tucson where he was chairman of the board; a copy hung in his bedroom.

He also told the story of Jesús García repeatedly to a young Mexican girl named Teresa Leal. "Heroes are brave just a few seconds longer than you or I," he would tell her. "Will you be able to be brave that long someday?"

It was a strange question to ask the daughter of his cook. But her presence in his house was already unusual. She had come with her mother from Sonora to live with the Douglases after her uncle's assassination. Her father and his two brothers were agitators for agrarian reform, and now one was dead. Convinced that her husband was endangering them all, Teresa's mother took the child and left him. Teresa's godfather, a Sonoran aristocrat, arranged for her mother to cook for Lewis Douglas.

Teresa Leal grew up at the Douglas family homes in upstate New York and near Patagonia, Arizona, an hour from Nogales. Her playmates were Douglas's grandchildren, but she rarely had time for playing. Lewis Douglas oversaw her education, assigning her books from his library and teaching her about politics. Douglas was excited about Mexico's future. He told her that Mexico should be a different kind of country, a country of honor embodying the spirit of men like Jesús García. Under Lázaro Cárdenas, he said, Mexico had begun to come of age. American capital had been necessary for its development, but now it could start getting along on its own.

During her years in the Douglas home, Teresa's father and surviving uncle, lawyers during the Cárdenas era, continued the ideas Cárdenas promoted. As founding members of Mexico's Popular Socialist Party, they targeted the enormous Sonoran landholdings of the Greene Cattle Company for expropriation.

They brought in squatters, including women and children, who occupied Greene's land and dared their government that preached la reforma to incite an uprising by removing them. By 1957, the final dismantling of the Greene family's Mexican holdings was complete; the efforts of Teresa Leal's father and uncle are commemorated in the Cananea Jail Museum.

About that time, Mexico's population started to suffer under its own weight. Growing protests over the skewed distribution of the nation's wealth climaxed in 1968, the year Mexico became the first developing nation to host the Olympics. Thousands marched in the Federal District, objecting to the millions spent to beautify Mexico City for the event. Threatening to disrupt the Olympics so the whole world could view their struggle, they asked why wasn't such money available to feed the people?

The demonstrations ceased abruptly when government troops gunned down hundreds of citizens during a peaceable gathering in Tlaltelolco, Mexico City's Plaza of the Three Cultures. "I had hoped," a depressed Douglas told Teresa, now married and living in the border city of Nogales, Sonora, "that your generation could administer an ideology. But now you'll have to recreate one. I pray you'll be strong."

Teresa Leal was too busy having children to think about ideology. By the time she was thirty, she had borne her husband, a Nogales customs broker, six daughters and two sons. "I wanted a dozen," she reflects, "and I would have had them if I could have stood him any longer."

Bilingual, educated on both sides of the border, Teresa Leal insisted on working despite household duties and her husband's objections. Her marriage, arranged by her mother years earlier, cooled early. Her husband called her a pocha, deriding her independent gringa attitude and the New York inflection in her voice. Determined, she went to work, purifying her accent and eventually becoming director of DIF, Nogales's family and child development agency.

She began occupational workshops for Nogales women who came to her, unable to support families on maquiladora wages. They began confiding in her, stories about brutality inflicted by husbands and lovers.

After years in the United States, she knew what battered women should do. "These are assaults. Report them to the police," she said. They were timid. Would she accompany them? She did, and sent several men to prison.

The same women would then cry that they wanted their husbands out of jail. Now she was a villain and a home-wrecker.

A thirteen-year-old girl confessed that her father was raping her. Teresa confronted the mother, who already knew but let it continue because she couldn't bear the thought of him leaving. Teresa had him jailed. The wife got him out. Each time he'd return home and would molest and beat his daughter. Once she had to be hospitalized; enraged, Teresa had him locked up within hours. But when the girl was released three days later, he was home, waiting.

That night she hung herself. An autopsy showed that she'd had intercourse only minutes earlier. Crazed with anguish, Teresa Leal appealed to every authority she could find. The man stayed out of jail and attended the funeral with his wife.

Resigning in protest over the empty response in her own agency, Teresa Leal did not so much join a political movement as become one. Her husband forbade her growing radicalism. She then realized that she was living a victim's life herself.

Mexican women don't often get divorced, especially with eight children. Teresa did, continuing to raise them even as she slept fewer hours and took on more causes. She began a hotline and a center for abused women. She became the Nogales representative for a Central American information network, showing films about El Salvador to Rotary and Lions clubs. She wrote columns for *La Voz del Norte* in Sonora and sometimes for the *Nogales International* in Arizona and newspapers in Mexico City. She organized for CIDAL, a Mexican feminist group, counseled street gangs, tutored, and taught: advanced English in a private preparatory, free classes to maquila workers at Preparatoria de la Solidaridad, pedagogy at a teachers college, and Mexican-American relations through the University of Arizona's Elderhostel program.

She is also a scout leader.

Teresa Leal lives above a Nogales street that Spain might have deposited on the edge of the United States, all walls and staircases rising from a narrow concrete passageway. Her house is simple inside, partly painted and with a wood stove. Somehow fresh after three hours of rest, Teresa sits on a kitchen stool, preparing her children's breakfast. She is making tortillas, a humbling activity that, like Gandhi at his spinning wheel, she undertakes daily. At thirty-six she looks both tired and new, pixielike but powerful.

She is worried over a speech she has to give in Los Angeles to the National Organization of Women. Mexican feminists are so far behind the Americans— what can she tell them? She has been invited to Cuba. Three weeks earlier, she brought Joan Baez to sing at the Nogales prison. Today the telephone began ringing at 7:30 A.M., and had rung well after midnight the night before.

If ever anyone was impaled on the boundary fence, it is surely Teresa, with her Mexican socialist father and American industrialist guardian. Her almond-eyed daughter, Isabel, testifies to more borderlands history: Teresa's Spanish-blooded grandfather married a Chinese woman at a time when Mexico and the United States both were trying to eject encroaching Chinese farmers, sometimes into each other's country. Mexico finally deported her back to Shanghai.

At night, Teresa attends a planning session of the Revolutionary Workers' Party. She is not a member, but her friend Salvador Flores is the PRT candidate for mayor, and his platform contains a notion critical to her: unionizing maquiladora employees. In some border cities, twin plant laborers belong to Mexico's huge umbrella union, the CTM, the Confederation of Mexican Workers. But the CTM is part of the ruling PRI, and its participation only enforces the government's arrangement with the American management. Its members receive no more than maquila workers in Nogales, which has no unions.

Again, the pervasive fixation with maquiladoras: Nothing save hunger itself has riveted Mexico's attention like the return, en masse, of gringos and their coolly efficient industries. Not that American names weren't already affixed to half of Mexico's groceries and dry goods, but the maquilas have meant 100 percent, openly owned gabacho businesses here for the first time since the Porfiriato. Mexico started by saying they were for the border, but now they're below the border; that their products would not stay in the country to compete with domestic goods, but now "limited" exceptions are appearing; that they would assemble, not manufacture, but suddenly Ford has a wholly owned plant in Hermosillo and IBM is building in Guadalajara, and these aren't even maquilas, but full factories.

Is this, many ask, the maturing of Mexico, its leap out of the deserts and jungles into civilized economics, eligible finally for a place among signatories to trade and tariff agreements? Accepting a junior executive multinational position, contributing to the gross planetary product at a level beyond merely squandering its raw resources?

Or is this the resurrection of Don Porfirio, who is enjoying a recent, unscheduled comeback among Mexican revisionist historians who acknowledge that, despite the unpleasantness of Yaqui enslavement for the benefit of various Rockefellers, if it weren't for Presidente Días, Mexico would still be like Honduras?

Teresa's socialist acquaintances are deeply worried. Mexican intellectuals, preoccupied with the huge foreign debt, have lately muted their criticism of the maquilas, forgetting their effect on people. Incredibly, the hyperconservative PAN has portrayed itself as the voice of the oppressed, and they're getting away with that. Someone has to be the nation's conscience.

So five Nogales socialists plus Teresa gather around a kitchen table in a government housing development—a schoolteacher, a student, a truck driver, a maquila drill press operator, a scion of curio shop impresarios. They review what they know: that maquila workers get fired if caught talking to union people, that companies threaten to pull out of Mexico if unions come in, that maquila managers throw drunken pachangas for employees for not voting for the unions, that asbestos plants banned in Colorado have been reincarnated as maquilas in Mexicali, and that the government protects the companies instead of the workers.

Salvador, the bearded, soft-spoken mayoral candidate, leans against the wall and listens. Like a benediction, he contributes the last word. "The United States has unions. It honors the Polish people for demanding the right to unionize in defiance of their government. Why not us, then, in American plants here?"

Teresa Leal takes an American writer to the Instituto Tecnológico de Nogales, a handsome campus of low, glass-and-brick buildings arranged on landscaped terraces. Its professors are in the third day of what began as a one-day work stoppage to protest their salaries. Most make less than $250 per month. With the deepening crisis, this is scheduled to worsen.

They sit with an economist, a sociologist, and a poet. Talk shifts from the strike to the border's tenacious influence on academic thought. They discuss whether it's true that the Aztecs may have been even more capitalistic than the Americans, whether Mexico's corruption is too intrinsic to ever be eradicated. The huge debt Mexico owes the United States, the sociologist says, is integrally related to this strike. "There's no money to run the country. Getting us in their debt was just to keep us under their control, to give the U.S. a prextext for invasion if necessary."

The economist disagrees. "The banks didn't do it deliberately. The oil market was saturated. Production dropped, profits dropped, and investors had to speculate to earn anything. Profits are no longer the world's economic motor: interest is. Powerful nations will fight out the solutions in the marketplace, while poor countries suffer and watch. It's an opportunity for socialists to take advantage of a historical situation—although I really don't see them doing much better."

It is like any spring afternoon spent debating issues on the quadrangle of a U.S. college. The difference between this and an American university is that here it's not theoretical. The discussants are living these particular issues. They talk about the horror of Third World countries as superpowers capable of apocalyptic destruction bait each other, daring the other to strike first. Then the poet turns to the American. He is especially anguished over nuclear fears. "Tell me," he demands. "How does it feel, really feel, to be a gringo?"

It feels, the writer thinks, like being guilty for something he really doesn't remember doing. "It's an accident of birth," he answers finally. "How is it you chose to be born here, instead of five miles north of here? You or I could just as easily have been each other." They both know he hasn't answered the question. The poet's reply, distorted as it is by the clench of his passions, explains the difference:

"Ours is an aesthetic of desperation. We are up against all that annihilates humanity. The U.S.'s is an aesthetic of hope. We see it in your products, in the movies you distribute around the planet. You believe that humanity will survive. You don't realize that you are destroying it."

.   .   .

"It was an accident, a big accident," Tony Clark swears, hauling himself up the sixty-foot ladder anchored to the perpendicular innards of the square brick bell tower. Father Tony Clark, the youth director at Sacred Heart Church in Nogales, Arizona, likes to view the border from up high. In his enthusiasm, he has forgotten that forty children are celebrating their first communion today. To the strains of "Cordero de Dios," his entourage has to thread past the choir, whose loft is the only route to the tower.

With him are three of his prize pupils. Not from catechism. From his boxing team. Tony Clark's handsome Irish countenance rests on a stocky welterweight frame, which he once put to good use as an amateur. When he came to this border parish two years ago, he found himself working with kids who regard the international fence as a minor territorial division in the streets they freely roam. "Let's say they relied on physical rather than social skills to solve their problems," is how he puts it. Boxing was a way to forge discipline from their violence. He staked claim to the abandoned upstairs of an elementary school, put his boys to work building a ring and started teaching them what to do in it. The respectful way they defer to him indicates they have learned some other things as well.

The belfry contains several active pigeon nests. Excited mother pigeons rapidly circumnavigate the tower, frantic to return to their eggs. Tony and his boys pick their way to the edge and look. Like a cornucopia of the eclectic, Ambos Nogales spills over the sides of its pass. There is no sign of the namesake walnut trees, but the extremes of border architecture—adobe, Victorian, thin-shell reinforced concrete, even some caves—form a satisfying jumble below. At the Mexican customs house, flags of all the American nations ripple in a splashy oval. Someone points out that the United States and Cuba are next to each other.

At that moment the bells go off. They're not even real bells, but bell-shaped speakers, connected to synthesizer tapes of church bells. Loud church bells. Fingers jam into ears. Father Tony thinks this is pretty funny.

Father Tony is under indictment, facing twenty-five years in prison—five each for "conspiring, aiding, sheltering, transporting, and abiding" illegal aliens.

He becomes quickly serious whenever he's reminded. How did this blue-eyed kid from York, Pennsylvania, get himself into this, he often asks the mirror. Even when he speaks in Spanish to his boys, home roots wrap tightly around his speech. "I knew nothing about underground movements. Nothing about Central Americans. I was at Sacred Heart, organizing and evangelizing in the good Christian tradition. It just happens that when people without any resources cross the border, they sometimes look to the church to help. Me, I'm gregarious. I'm interested in marginal types who don't have any shoes, who are hungry. But then I start listening to these Central Americans. They don't just need shelter. They are far beyond, say, your normal starving human being.

"I'm no bleeding heart. But they keep telling about everybody they love being massacred. So we say, it's okay, no one will hurt you here, and they kind of totally collapse in a puddle of relief and emotion. When you see this, that tends to add validity to their little horror stories."

So Tony Clark became part of the sanctuary movement, providing succor to refugees from the ravaged isthmus that connects North and South America like a flawed, exposed nerve. The indictment against him and eleven others concerns interpretation of who is protected under the 1980 Refugee Act.

". . . any refugee demonstrating a 'well-founded fear of persecution on account of race, religion, nationality, membership in a particular social group, or political opinion' qualifies, according to how the law reads. But the State Department has a problem applying that to governments it props up. Really just looking for jobs, they say. Anyway, my reading is that these people are refugees until proven otherwise."

During pretrial hearings in Phoenix, sanctuary lawyers asked for dismissal of charges because, among other things, the United States admitted infiltrating church groups with spies equipped with electronic bugs—the sort of behavior it denounces in totalitar-

ian regimes. Besides obvious concerns about separation of church and state, the government's informants turned out to be an active pair of coyotes with an admitted history of smuggling aliens. And not just mojados: One of these ambitious federal employees who earned tax dollars for busting priests was widely accused of trafficking prostitutes in illegal labor camps.

District Judge Earl Carroll agreed that the United States's employment of such tactics and personnel was "not an acceptable practice." But he ruled that it was "not outrageous," as defense attorneys had protested, and quashed their motion for dismissal. He also disallowed religious convictions as grounds for defense.

"It's just harrassment," Tony says, peering gloomily down the ladder, fingering the wooden cross dangling from a thong about his neck. "They're trying to frighten us into quitting. Let them arrest as many as they want. Do they honestly think that's going to stop these people from coming? Reagan claims that 'foot people' are overwhelming our borders. I agree: We should do something to stop them. Stop sending arms. Stop bombing their villages."

He recently visited Guatemala and refugee camps in southern Mexico. When he asked people why they left their homes, they didn't talk about the wrong guy winning the election.

"They found daddy drowned in the well. Or somebody came and took their son and all other males fourteen or older in their village. Or somebody's ordering them to move. And when they say they just want to live by the river, like they always have, they're told they're resisting, not cooperating. Stuff like that."

The United States and Mexico may wrangle over the border they share, but they agree about the one between Mexico and Guatemala. In Chiapas, Father Tony found earth-moving equipment everywhere; he was told that the United States was financing road construction in appreciation for Mexico holding Central Americans in refugee camps. The roads will be of great military benefit to both countries, should the need ever arise. "Central Americans don't have many nice things to say about Mexico these days, either." He stares off across the line, into teeming Latin America. "Vamos al otro lado," he tells his boys.

They drive his van into Nogales, Sonora, where intense Sunday evening cruising turns normal streets into one-ways. A basketball tournament parade appears. The queen rides by in a convertible; her princesses follow atop the hoods of Trans-Ams. Traffic crawls, the Trans-Ams engines bake, and the girls squirm. Indian women from Oaxaca, who have come two thousand miles to beg coins from Americans in front of the Hotel Fray San Marcos de Niza, converse in Mixteco on the curb, looking defeated. Easter is usually a strong tourist season, but with the bad rap Mexico has been taking in the U.S. press, this year hardly anyone came.

Past the Niños Héroes monument, Tony heads for the parish of Padre Ramón Dagoberto Quiñones. Quiñones, a mild, olive-skinned man with dark-rimmed glasses, is also under indictment, for conspiring to sneak Central Americans into North America. He finds it hard to understand how he, a Mexican, can be accused of violating U.S. laws for something he supposedly did in his own country. "Christ came to remove borders," he notes, and that seems to be how the United States sees it too, because for a change it has ignored this one to press charges against him.

Quiñones's case has created discomfort for Mexican officials who are asked why they don't protest what the United States is doing to a Mexican citizen. Despite questioning the legality of his indictment, Quiñones has decided to stand trial. "I have to show my parishioners that I don't fear. I am fulfilling a ministry that can't be limited by any judge. If los Estados Unidos jails me illegally, another priest will come to take my place."

Something must be happening in Central America, he thinks, because lately the numbers have increased. Several busloads have been apprehended by Mexican immigration officials a few miles below the border.

He takes food to refugees herded into Nogales's Centro de Readaptación until arrangements are made to ship them back. Every week, he has to bring more.

The cell behind the barred door measures twenty by twenty feet. Its gray walls, painted with a swath of orange wainscoting, have grown smooth and oily from evaporated human perspiration. Overhead, the fluorescent light fixture on the flaking ceiling is empty of tubes.

The room connects to a slightly larger concrete courtyard. Atop its surrounding wall, bored guards with automatic rifles look down, sit, dangle their feet. They wear street clothes, and without their weapons they could be mistaken for the prisoners.

Ragged mattresses and blankets are spread on the floor of the cell and along the courtyard wall. There is not enough room for everyone to sleep inside. The temperature drops below fifty degrees at night; they have all been here for at least eight days and a virus is making the rounds. A single, nonfunctioning latrine serves the needs of the 52 men locked up here. Until a few days ago, they numbered 175.

Detailed graffiti attest to how many have been here. Names and dates are listed by countries—Guatemala, Honduras, Nicaragua, El Salvador. El Salvador and Guatemala are way ahead, practically in a dead heat.

Nearly all the current detainees are in their twenties. Most wear sneakers; a few are barefoot. Their clothes reflect the brisk Latin trade in t-shirts printed with English language ads and clichés. The blaring distraction of "Stayin' Alive" and "Club Med" tends to diminish tragedy to the level of irony. They look exceedingly young, and so ordinary.

Padre Quiñones has invited some American observers. "*This* is the terrible threat to our security?" one whispers. While church women prepare to serve a lunch of pork in tomato sauce, hotdog buns, and rice, Quiñones forms a prayer circle. Nicaragua, Guatemala, and El Salvador join hands with Mexico and the United States. Quiñones prays that they may find their way safely; that the power to the north might allow Central America to live in peace. They recite the Lord's Prayer.

The prisoners are hungry. Their daily soup comes laced with chile, which Central Americans aren't accustomed to, to discourage them from consuming very much. Quiñones asks all who left home because their lives were endangered to raise their hands. About half do, and he directs them to talk to the Americans while they eat. One Salvadoran found pieces of his brother's body in the yard. Another, a farmer with tiny, precise features, tells how the rebels came and ate one of his two oxen. Then government soldiers appeared and accused him of helping the rebels. To prove his loyalty, he had to let them eat the other one. With nothing left to buy his safety, he fled.

"After awhile," remarks a red-haired Nicaraguan, "we can't remember who is the enemy. No one trusts us. We live in fear, because we trust no one."

They eat, standing, squatting, sharing plates. Padre Quiñones passes out slips on which they write messages to be transmitted to their families. He permits them to receive mail in care of him. The reason why Nogales is a main conduit for refugees becomes apparent, and why the United States is so bent on stopping Padre Quiñones: Thousands of people throughout Central America have his address.

There are fewer incarcerated women, and they have beds, but their cell is a horror of flies. They paid 900 quetzales—$450—apiece for the bus ride that began in Guatemala City. When they were caught, they were strip-searched and their money was taken. Afterward, the police told them that for 25,000 pesos, they could go free.

A young guatemalteca, with the timid, rosy quality of the Caribbean, tells of a year during which, one by one, her father, brother, and husband simply vanished. She was alone on the small family plot with her four children, knowing that now she couldn't feed them and that somebody was coming for her next. She went to an aunt in Guatemala City, borrowed

bus fare and $200, and said she'd send for her children. "Now," she weeps, "the money is gone. The Mexicans will drop us off in the middle of the bridge at Tapachula. I'll have to walk into Guatemala and hitchhike on roads where soldiers rape every woman they see. If I make it home, I'll be poorer than when I left. All this will have been for nothing."

Swaying forward, she crumples, sobbing, into the arms of one of the American men. When she regains her composure, she and subsequently two other women pull him close to whisper in his ear. She tells him what she will do for him if he only smuggles her to Los Angeles: "Anything."

Bobby Bracker addresses a Nogales interfaith meeting of Catholics and his fellow Jews. Publicly, he challenges the selective enforcement of the Refugee Act. His parents and thousands more once fled European terrors; what he's heard about the Central Americans sounds too familiar. But the government, churches, sanctuary, and all their lawyers argue over who is an "economic" and who is a "political" refugee. The official line seems to be that Eastern bloc dissidents are political and Central Americans are the other.

That afternoon in the Centro de Readaptación, enough dread is recounted to know differently. But the testimony of those who did not raise their hands in response to Quiñones's question—the alleged economic refugees—disturbs as deeply as recollections of dismembered fathers and husbands. "No hay trabajo," each of them said: There is no work. No hay trabajo. No hay trabajo. "We get up at three in the morning and wait hours in line for a job that never existed in the first place." No hay trabajo; no hay trabajo.

No hay trabajo. It is a Third World mantra, repeated by rote in millions—so many millions—of stuck lives, a prayer wheel spun backward. With wars, even tragic, incessant Central American wars, there is always a hope for a cease-fire to end the immediate mortal danger. But the economics of no hay trabajo is the real struggle, and it is North America's too. For whatever historic and current reasons, economic systems that do not support their populations proliferate in the hemisphere. At this point, ecology, not ideology, takes over, because organisms seek and move toward resources that will sustain them.

"For us," says Tony Clark, "it would be like having to leave the U.S. to look for work. We can't imagine that. We grow up thinking that most of the world is like us. It's not. It's like them."

· · ·

Mother's Day.

In a concrete ditch running between the street in front of the Hotel San Carlos and the Nogales, Sonora, border fence, four families are hiding. Their coyotes lean on cars, pitch coins, watch the Dodgers on TV through the San Carlos lobby window, and wait for a mirror flash from the other side to let them know when to pass their little pollos over the line.

Elsewhere, Harold Swyers of the Eyelid Unit of the Arizona Department of Safety pulls up behind a red Chrysler with a flat tire, parked on the northbound shoulder of U.S. 89. A confused-looking Hispanic man and a woman with a baby are inside, arguing. There's no spare tire, and there's no registration, either. The car, the driver says in Spanish, belongs to a friend, who loaned it to him to take his family out on Mother's Day.

"Your friend's name?"

The driver hesitates too long. That, plus the missing registration, add up to probable cause. Lucky, Swyers finds at least fifty pounds taped inside the fenders. If it were twenty or under, no case. The costs of prisoner maintenance, county attorney's time, and a court-appointed defender can't be justified for lesser amounts.

The mule is fresh. He speaks no English, but he at least knew to use a cover. The car was waiting in the K Mart parking lot with the keys in the ashtray. All he had to do for $2,000 was drive it to Tucson. One

of two things happens now: either he goes free in exchange for informing on three other upcoming shipments or he ends up in jail for a year or two, where he'll learn English and come out a more valuable, higher paid mule.

The woman knows nothing. Seeing that it's Día de Las Madres, Swyers lets her go home, but takes daddy in. His bust is part of the maybe 3 or 4 percent of the total drug traffic they actually catch. About that frustrating reality he is philosophical, especially lately since he knows he has cancer. His wife, once the mayor of Patagonia, passed on a while back; the family ranch is gone; he's been working for either the DPS or the county sheriff's department for enough years to know that the narcotics battle was lost long ago.

It's Mother's Day. His friend Teresa Leal doesn't celebrate it, because she believes it's a macho hoax to honor mothers once a year and step on them the rest of the time. But he is sentimental and still wants to take her to lunch.

They meet at Chuy Machaca, Nogales's oldest restaurant, a tiny but major culinary border landmark. Especially during winter, customers come not only for shredded beef and rellenos but also for its two cozy wood cookstoves. The aroma of mesquite and condiments settles like a blessing on hearts and senses.

Teresa shows up looking like a lush California matron, wearing an orange cotton jump suit, a Mother's Day surprise from her daughters. "If I can't cure my own children of bourgeois tastes, how can I save Mexico?" she worries.

Swyers and Teresa met back when she was muckraking for the *Nogales International*, pursuing improprieties in the economics of drug enforcement. "When Arizona adds up what it costs to send five agents who earn $30,000 a year plus overtime on a four day stake-out, economics favor the smugglers," Swyers had told her. "What else is there to know?"

Teresa, seeking corruption, instead found affection. She and this oversized, grandfatherly officer with the fine waxed mustache eventually became confidants, she hearing of his private physical suffering, he learning about her one-woman stand against the pain of her people.

Fronterizos continually say that if they were handling American-Mexican relations, diplomacy would be a breeze. Person to person, not bureau to bureau; dinner and drinks, not dry memoranda, is how it's done. In the adobe warmth of Chuy Machaca, the incongruous friendship between a Mexican radical and an American narc suggests it may all be true. Swyers's charge of upholding the law squares with consorting with an anarchist, because he remembers that he doesn't hold up Mexico's laws. "We Americans have no right to tell another country how to live. Mexico has problems, but it's up to people like Teri to solve them. Not us."

He worries about her, though. Last year, over her reluctance, he trained her in small weapons defense. The incongruity grows—but it thins and dissolves away in the humanity of this cross-cultural alliance.

They talk shop. Drugs won't end, Harold Swyers fears. It would just put him and a lot of attorneys and judges out of work. "Towns in California that were dying before are cleaning up on fertilizer and farm equipment. People won't let laws stop them when their survival is at stake. Do the wets let the fence stop them?"

Two large families arrive; their chatter reveals they've saved to go out for Mother's Day. Chuy Machaca is suddenly saturated with children, and Teresa is enchanted. Swyers has already heard her defend giving birth to eight children in this overpopulated, underemployed country.

"It's the same as in an underpopulated country. I'm proud of my responsibility. When people are allowed to live responsibly, they make responsible choices whether to have children or not. Or how many."

Her justification is not entirely convincing, but it is interesting. Catholic priest Tony Clark, grieving for the increasing numbers of devastated people he sees, also has his answer ready:

"Reducing population is only a quantitative response to human problems. The real question about birth control is, what exactly is out of control? It makes us very anxious to see a country like Mexico outnumbering us. Is that because we plan responsibly—or because we've lost the humanness to be responsible?"

. . .

In the Americana Motel on the Arizona side, Art Doan and Abe Rochlin meet for breakfast, as they have for more than half their sixty years of friendship. Both Doan, a Mexican American with swept-back gray hair and a pencil mustache, and Rochlin, a dapper Jew in a bow tie, have served as mayor of Nogales.

They are proud of the two-thousand-year tradition of harmonious border relations, begun when the Hohokam of what is now Arizona and the Trinchera of what is now Sonora would meet and trade peacefully in Nogales Pass. They have compadres and godchildren across the line; theirs is the only border town with ties close enough to its Mexican twin to build a joint, gravity-fed international sewage treatment facility, in accordance with the shared Santa Cruz Valley topography. They cluck sympathetically over places like Douglas and even San Diego that lack such happy, useful relationships with their Mexican counterparts.

In recent years, though, life here has grown more complicated. Doan's daughter is Tony Clark's secretary, and has also been indicted. Maquiladoras have enriched the economy but strained the life style. At least one mayor of Nogales, Sonora, has been linked in print to the drug trade.

Rochlin believes there's a solution to drugs, albeit a less than perfect one. "Someday, we'll legalize and subsidize them. That will at least wipe out the criminal aspect. They're de facto legal already, because the government ignores small amounts."

The previous day, American and Mexican congressmen met in southern Mexico to discuss mutual concerns. No one from Arizona was in the delegation. "They send them from Rhode Island," Doan says scornfully. "Mexico is now a matter of life or death, and the decisions are being made by people away from where the action is."

Rochlin, sipping his coffee, agrees. "Within fifteen years, Spanish will be a principal language in the U.S., no matter what they try to legislate in Washington. If you removed the Latins, Los Angeles would collapse. The same thing is spreading everywhere, and fast."

————

"When you live on an edge," Nogales novelist Neil Claremon has noted, "anything is possible." The two ex-mayors believe that Ambos Nogales will find a way, even as population keeps growing and the economy remains poised in perpetual imbalance. "Mexico's not worried about its debt," says Abe Rochlin, "because it won't pay it anyway. And, besides, the banks won't stop doing business with them. They owe us $90 billion, but we owe ourselves $1 trillion. Business and the show just go on."

————

On May 1, 1986, Padre Ramón Dagoberto Quiñones was convicted of one felony count of conspiracy and one misdemeanor count of unlawful entry, eluding examination or inspection.

Father Tony Clark was found guilty of one felony count of concealing, harboring or shielding illegal aliens.

Mary K. Doan Espinoza, daughter of the former mayor, was acquitted of all charges.

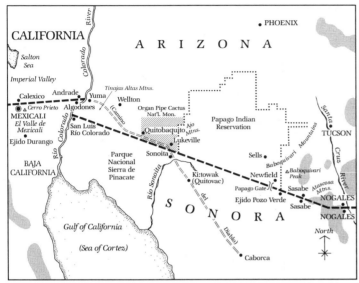

CHAPTER EIGHT

DESERT AND DELTA

The movies have yet to discover Sasabe the way they found Colonel Greene's San Rafael Valley. Or, if they have, they've decided it's easier to fake it on a studio back lot. Sasabe is prone to power outages; the telephones die during the summer monsoons, and flash floods in the arroyos assure that no one enters or leaves. Some government agents who have been shell-shocked in El Paso or Rio Grande City request transfers to tiny Sasabe, believing they will lead more peaceful, possibly longer, lives. Being trapped in the customs shed while waiting for a deluge to recede, with satellite-dish TV but no electricity to work it, could conceivably be restful.

Sasabe is only forty miles west of Nogales, but those miles are full of the Atascosa Mountains. *Atascosa* is an economical Spanish term implying all the following in English: *mired, stuck, bogged, blockage,* and *obstacle.* To drive to Sasabe via the jeep trails of the Atascosas is to enter a landscape jammed with decomposed granitic domes, eroding rims, sinuous washes, thorn forests, pale fields of large white thistles—and to emerge nearly three hours later.

On Sasabe's other flank rise the Baboquivari Mountains, which cannot be driven at all. To the north, Highway 286 runs straight up the Altar Valley to Tucson, and that is Sasabe's lifeline. Lately, that lifeline has been shortened. Sasabe's gate, formerly passable until midnight, was sealed following the Camarena assassination. Since reopening, it now shuts at 8:00 P.M. One-hundred-and-ten-mile-per-hour, early evening dashes for the border by Mexicans who go shopping in Tucson have become common local perils.

For all the possibilities inherent in a town of fifty, the American side is a shapeless disappointment of metal trailers and undistinguished brick. But Sasabe, Sonora, potentially the object of Hollywood's interest, is the Mexico that everyone who's never been there pictures when they think of Mexico. No pavement. Little chinked houses on cactus-covered hills. Burros, sloppy cantinas, sombreros, wooden saddles—la enchilada completa.

Dr. Rubén Pérez was working in Ciudad del Carmen on the Gulf of Mexico when a petroleum engineer from Tucson told him that Americans were donating an entire clinic to a border town and they needed a doctor to run it.

"¿Dónde está la clínica?" he inquired when he arrived in Sasabe.

"Pobre médico," was the reply. The village cacique had sold all the equipment and donated the proceeds to his own retirement fund. But before Dr. Pérez could flee, he had fallen in love with a doe-eyed norteña señorita.

Sixteen years later, their life revolves around trips to Tucson to buy groceries. Sasabe has a Conasupo, but its produce also comes from Tucson. When the United States closed the garita, everyone lost weight. Sasabe, Sonora, lacks a Pemex station, so its residents purchase gasoline on the American side at Knagge's General Store, which depends almost exclusively on Mexican business. Since the gas pump hose doesn't quite reach through the fence, vehicular movement and Knagge's income both vanished for a while.

"Things got pretty quiet here," Dr. Pérez remembers. "Quieter, I mean."

Sasabe has no truly level surfaces, let alone anything the length of a runway, so the junkyard full of airplanes on the red dirt slope behind the Mexican customs house requires some explaining. A decade ago, an American remembered locally as The Drunk hauled in several aircraft carcasses, many with bullet holes, with the declared intention of restoring them. He hired thirty workers, but the scheme died before the first payroll. His labor force returned to the brickworks south of town, to the ranches on the U.S. side, or to early retirement. "Sasabe," explains Mexican customs agent Antonio Barrajas, "has lazy people, no land, and scarce water. We are happy here because nothing can embarrass us."

The sole reason for a border crossing here is to provide access to water for the Mexican side. Sasabe, Arizona, is owned entirely by a Mexican, as are nearby ranches. A recent commotion concerned the sale of the biggest, the Buenos Aires, to the U.S. Fish and Wildlife Service as a refuge for the Sonoran masked bobwhite quail. Because quail don't require the attention of cowboys, local jobs were sacrificed in the name of conservation. Most of the vaqueros were Mexican, who protest that the whole thing was a migra plot.

Contraband, the other steady employer, has also ebbed. During the 1920s, a tent city here of several hundred smugglers pulled Tucson through the trauma of Prohibition. But with now-paved Highway 186 such an easily patrollable funnel, the action has moved west, across the Baboquivaris. And some of Sasabe, Mexico's entrepreneurs move right along with it.

A primitive road out of Sasabe, Sonora, feels its way around the Sierra Pozo Verde, the lower extension of the Baboquivaris. It is mostly sand, with archipelagos of bedrock that scrape the undercarriages of the Sasabe traders' pickups. Saguaro cacti, the pleading, arms-uplifted cruciforms of the Sonoran desert, alternate along the trail with dense mesquite clusters. Cooper's hawks prowl at treetop level, scattering the ravens as they swoop for rodents. After twenty miles, small bogs appear, sucking at the truck tires.

Cattle hoofprints lead to the moisture's source. It is Pozo Verde, a three-hundred-gallons-per-minute oasis. So rare is water here that the very vegetation turns aggressive; bamboo growing around the well must constantly be hacked back so other life forms may drink. Papago Indians, called O'odham in their own language, believe they have inhabited Pozo Verde since the world began.

Twenty minutes more and the traders pull over at a cattleguard spanning a breach in the border fence. Beyond it is the Papago Indian Reservation, the second largest in the United States, occupying 4,300 square miles of Arizona. The part of Sonora where the traders park is also on the reserve of the O'odham, but its size is a matter of dispute.

The trucks come on weekends, with cargos of cabbage, watermelon, lard, soda pop, cookies, fresh cheese, hunks of sugar cane, Budweiser, and José Cuervo. Their customers are Papagos from Arizona, like the family of George Juan who lives just over the line in Wecij Oidak, or Newfields. For the Juans, buying groceries a few hundred yards from home is simpler than driving twenty-five miles to the reservation trading post at Sells. Other Papagos come to drink. Reservation laws forbid liquor, but enforcement can't extend to Mexico, even though the O'odham recognize no border across the land Padre Kino called Papaguería.

In the mesquite shade, thirty Papagos chug tequila and beer and dance to "Te Vas, Angel Mío" as performed on an accordion, a plywood bass, and a Suzuki twelve-string. The three-piece conjunto has traveled six hours across the desert from Hermosillo. Few of the Indians understand the words to their songs, which cost them $2.00 apiece. The Papago have been bilingual for generations, but by the 1930s English began to replace Spanish as the companion language to the O'odham tongue. All the land was O'odham, but the advantages of living on the American half of it were difficult to resist. Fewer than one thousand remain in Mexico. Fifteen times that number live across the line.

Many of the dancers are overweight or actually obese. In less than a century, packaged foods have replaced the Papago's diet of seasonal desert selections, and diabetes and gallbladder disease now plague the tribe. Naturalist Gary Paul Nabhan, a gourmet of edible desert plants, is especially concerned about these people, the only remaining aboriginal population of the borderlands. He believes the O'odham—Desert People—evolved a metabolism in equilibrium with the desert's own rhythms. Besides the animals they hunted, they lived on saguaro fruit, mesquite pods, chiltepines, cholla buds, and iron-rich lambsquarter and pigweed. Like the mice and coyotes, they gorged themselves when weather cycles permitted and lived off their fat during the lean periods.

They farmed as well as gathered, watering their crops with the natural sheet flooding that occurs when it rains in the desert. Their native crops included tepary beans, squash, amaranth, and devil's claw for their baskets. Later they introduced wheat, but then white men introduced well drilling. A constant supply of water (at least until the aquifer is pumped dry) seems to have disrupted the Papago's agreement with their environment. In the long run, the hundreds of wells the U.S. government has provided since 1912 have only made water scarcer.

Seven hundred meters from the United States and just east of the market, straw-hatted Francisco Valenzuela, a compact man with close-cropped hair and mustache, broadcasts seed from a galvanized bucket. It is a bright day in early winter. The sandy soil here has been enriched with nutrients deposited by centuries of flood irrigation. Francisco Valenzuela's wheat field occupies a few of the hundred acres in all of Papaguería still farmed by traditional methods.

"One or two good December rains, then let the dew bring up the wheat," Francisco says. He knew how to do this before he was born.

Sounds of cumbia music float over from the mercado. Valenzuela's helpers chop overhead limbs from a giant mesquite that has been allowed to remain in the field, drinking part of the water but providing shade, firewood, and beauty. Just across the border is Baboquivari Peak, which hovers above the sierra like a bishop's mitre. To the O'odham, it denotes the center of the universe. Behind it is Kitt Peak, half on the reservation, half off, where the University of Arizona maintains an astronomical observatory. Some Papago are proud of Kitt Peak's international reputation; others call it a bunch of tin cans.

Francisco Valenzuela, born on this farm, is a trilingual O'odham. A few months ago, for the first time in his thirty-six years, he was apprehended by the INS while taking a load of firewood up to Tucson. Dumped by the migra in Nogales, he had to hitchhike several hundred roundabout miles home. His wife, a U.S. citizen, went to the city to redeem his confiscated truck.

The awkward part was that Francisco has been employed for years by the United States government, most recently as a caseworker for the Department of Economic Security. Before that he was the assistant director of a commodities distribution program for the Department of Agriculture. Nobody ever bothered to check his citizenship.

He's not even sure himself what it is. His mother, born in Tucson, gave birth to him on Mexican soil. No one recorded the event. At one point, he acquired a birth certificate in Sasabe, Sonora, but this is a casual procedure of selecting a place and date in exchange for a sufficient gratuity. Francisco is now on administrative leave until his nationality is determined.

The U.S. Federal Code permits American Indians born in Canada to cross freely into the United States, but no similar travel exemptions are granted to a tribe straddling the U.S.–Mexican border. Tacitly, the same policy is observed here. Papago living in either country pass onto reservation lands of the other without notifying immigration services.

Not that they ever would. The notion of a third country emerging along la frontera will remain a fiction as long as Washington and Mexico City control the borderlands more than the fronterizos themselves. But the Papago have always considered themselves a separate nation between the other two, and one far older than they are.

Papaguería was claimed by Spain more than four hundred years ago, an event that influenced the O'odham's language and religion. It even affected their name—*Papago* was adapted by Spaniards from the Pima word *papah*, meaning bean, because they ate the fruit of the mesquite. But as far as the O'odham were concerned, it did not alter their sovereignty. When the land became Mexico's, a few non-Indians received grants in their territory. But the real trouble began with the United States.

The 1848 Treaty of Guadalupe Hidalgo granted citizenship to Mexicans who suddenly found themselves living in the United States, and preserved their rights and titles. Both Spain and Mexico considered Indians citizens, a fact recognized in subsequent U.S. court decisions concerning Mexican Indians now in the United States.

But when the Gadsden Purchase cut right down the middle of Papaguería in 1853, neither the United States nor Mexico bothered to inform the Papago. Only when homesteaders began to move in did they understand what had happened. Their Mexican titles weren't in writing. Without actual grants, the United States became their unwanted guardian, eventually apportioning them scattered pieces of their own lands.

Then it was Mexico's turn. In the 1890s, Mexican trespassers started bringing in cattle and have yet to cease. Papago like Francisco Valenzuela have returned to their ancestral lands to keep invaders at bay. But new barbed wire continually appears.

At the tribal headquarters in Sells, Arizona, Arturo García heads the O'odham in Mexico program from an office lined with maps of James Gadsden's $10 million's worth of real estate. Every so often he and some of the older Papago drive into Mexico and spend a day knocking down fences. García would earn the deepest sympathies of Chapo and Fupau Varela for his struggles with Mexico's reforma agraria. In 1928, Pozo Verde was granted to the Papago as an ejido. "With ejidos, there's no ownership of the land. We want communal property, like on the U.S. side."

Next to the spring at Pozo Verde, where he grows melons, tomatoes, and corn, wizened Joe Wilson reduces a mesquite stump to kindling. He wears a beaten windbreaker over a cotton shirt and is as brown as his woodpile. Around him, pomegranate, orange, and fig trees thrive on the sweet irrigation water. "This spring," he says, "has flowed since before Jesus Christ," and he figures his ancestors farmed here back then too. Joe was born here, on land that Mexico considers its own, but he is oblivious to nationality. His father attended Carlisle, the old Pennsylvania Indian college, where his name was Anglicized. Four days after Pearl Harbor, Joe enlisted in the U.S. Army. He landed at Anzio beach and ended up in a Naples hospital, full of shrapnel. He is proud to have fought against evil; his brother died in the South Pacific for the same cause.

People like the Wilsons confuse Arturo García's issue, because their citizenship is so convoluted that Mexico could decide to deny them ejidos. "We're fighting to let dual citizens be ejidatarios. We don't know how it will come out legally. It should be solved by the U.S. and Mexico. They're the ones who drew the line without asking the Papago."

Each August, O'odham travel to the village of Ki:towak—Quitovac, Sonora—for the wi'igita prayer stick rain ceremony. Cornmeal is sprinkled, corn dancers perform, and clowns act out cycles of planting, harvesting, and rainmaking. To lose Ki:towak to usurping Mexicans is unfathomable. But it is already going. One of the largest oases in the Sonoran Desert, the wash surrounding Quitovac's tule-lined spring was recently bulldozed, and pumps were installed. Most of the Papagos here have intermarried with Mexicans, who now control the ejido.

Ernestina Noriega, one of the last of the purebloods, is the daughter of Quitovac's remaining traditional farmer. "Before, everyone just grew food for themselves. Now they want to export crops," translates Ernestina's mestiza daughter Aurora in unaccented Spanish. The primary school Aurora attends offers bilingual education to preserve the O'odham tongue. She lives in a Papago ramada made from saguaro cactus ribs. "But," says her mother, "she is growing up Mexican."

At dusk along the border in Papaguería, heaven goes up in flames. The exhausted sun tugs at the light, but cirrocumulus clouds with charred gray edges continue to glow like coals. As though heated from within, the bluffs surrounding Baboquivari Peak turn scarlet, until they are as crimson as the chiltepin and the flocks of cardinals nesting in the oak washes. The radiance intensifies and then withdraws. One by one, the lights in the pinnacles go out until only Baboquivari remains, pyramidal and shining, attended by arcing golden eagles and exchanging solar reflections with the rising moon.

Through the mesquite and hackberry, a pair of jerking headlight beams appear on the Mexican side. They approach the cattleguard that marks the boundary between the two nations that have torn apart a third. As the white truck crosses into the United States, a Border Patrol Suburban wagon pulls out of the bushes, blocking its path. The two patrolmen, carrying .30 caliber carbines, are Anglo. The driver and passenger are instructed to place their hands atop the dashboard.

After a half hour, the patrolmen are satisfied that this vehicle is clean. They had watched it depart the Valenzuela farm, which they suspect is a clearinghouse for drugs. They ask about Valenzuela; it turns out that their description of the pusher isn't him.

A few miles up, two U.S. Customs patrol officers again stop the vehicle. Same routine, except these officials are Papago. One of them, a small, courteous man in a fatigue jacket, checks behind the front seat while another, a big man wearing a camouflage vest, waits silently in the shadows.

"We were just checked by the migra," the driver says.

"Lots of drugs these days," the short officer apologizes. "Most of the Sasabe vendors are dealing."

The driver and his passenger, exasperated from an hour of this, are not mollified by the explanation. U.S. law enforcement agents, Papago or not, aren't popular here. They drive off, and the CPOs head back to scout the border. The short officer will not live to see the spring. A month later, he will radio that he is trailing three mules he knows to be carrying. Then, nothing. His partner will find his body just north of the cattleguard, a lead slug in his brain.

George Juan and his family return through the fence opening to their neat adobe compound in Wecij Oidak. They've been to Carmelo, a tiny chapel in a pastureland known as the Bajío, four kilometers below the line. Two days before, an uncle, Vicente López, died in a Phoenix rest home. They brought the body down and broke laws they don't know exist, by carrying Vicente into Mexico for burial in an ageless family plot.

Afterward, George Juan sits in his wheelchair watching the Dallas Cowboys on a nine-inch black-and-white TV. Years ago, when he was still in his seventies, George wrecked his shoulder in a spill from the pinto in his corral, and he has virtually no bones left in his legs. Only one arm works, stretching just enough to carry meat and tortillas from his bowl to his mouth. Once he ran cattle up in the Sierra Pozo Verde and down in the Bajío. Today in the cemetery they found barbed wire. Mexicans are actually trying to fence away the camposanto.

And it had fallen into neglect. Coyotes had dug up some of the graves. George is too old to do anything about it, but one of the boys, Frank Juan López, has decided that he must. He will resurrect the old family brand and move down into Mexico, to the Bajío. O'odham were always there; O'odham are buried there, in the long shadow of Baboquivari. O'odham will stay there. Mexico and the United States can tend to the rest.

.   .   .

The empty, sometimes awesomely hostile border, James Gadsden noted in 1853, would serve as a substantial buffer between Mexico and the United States. It hasn't, however, because their economic polarities build up such a charge that each country attracts its opposite. Add to that the invention of air conditioning, and mere environments are no obstacle.

Only a few wild tatters remain of that barrier Gadsden described: Big Bend; Texas between Candelaria and El Paso; New Mexico in general—although ranchers have that under their kind of control—and the one that begins with Papaguería and ends at the Colorado River. From the Papago's gate in the fence to the next border town is eighty miles, but neither country provides a direct route. Four-wheel-drive trails on the Mexico side eventually arrive there, but must be navigated by sun or compass. A combination of U.S. roads veers well away from the border's waterless stretches before dropping down to Lukeville, opposite Sonoita. There the Sonoita River and la frontera intersect, creating more beauty and trouble for the two countries.

.   .   .

"Russians?"

"Sí, Rusos."

Harold Smith, superintendent of Organ Pipe Cactus National Monument, has correctly understood Fernando Lizárraga, superintendent of the Parque Nacional Sierra de Pinacate. The two speak only fragments of each other's language, but their adjoining parks share an ecosystem, so they understand a lot about each other. The reason for Fernando's visit emerges. Russian scientists have appeared in the nearby Sierra Blanca, doing studies on mice, rats, coyotes, foxes, and bobcat, because the region is similar to parts of the Gobi near the Soviet-Mongolian border.

Of course, they would love to see Organ Pipe, but have no permits to enter because of the sticky little detail that it's in the United States. It would be so

PLATE 45
EL CAMINO DEL DIABLO, ARIZONA

PLATE 46
Trébol Crater, Parque Nacional Sierra de Pinacate, Sonora

PLATE 47
COLORADO RIVER DELTA, BAJA CALIFORNIA

PLATE 48
EDUARDO AUYÓN GERARDO, JARDÍN DE CHUNG SHAN YUAN, MEXICALI, BAJA CALIFORNIA

PLATE 49
CARRETERA 2, LA RUMOROSA, BAJA CALIFORNIA

PLATE 50
CHICANO PARK, SAN DIEGO, CALIFORNIA

PLATE 51

América, Minerva, and Andrómeda Martín, Tijuana, Baja California

PLATE 52
HOTEL INTER-CONTINENTAL, SAN DIEGO, CALIFORNIA

PLATE 53
Mariachis Aztecas, Caesar's Palace, Tijuana, Baja California

PLATE 54
BORDER ART WORKSHOP/TALLER DE ARTE FRONTERIZO, END OF THE U.S.-MEXICO BORDER
CALIFORNIA / BAJA CALIFORNIA

PLATE 55
INDOCUMENTADOS, SAN DIEGO COUNTY/
MUNICIPIO DE TIJUANA

PLATE 56
ENRIQUE, DANIEL, AND ELSPETH CLEGHORN MEDINA, SAN DIEGO

easy too, and no one would ever know. Quitobaquito, a famous Organ Pipe spring, is right up against the edge of the country. A gate there hasn't been locked for years. Mexicans open it all the time to go swimming in the duck pond. The Russians could just . . . but no one dares.

So Harold Smith sends a delegation across the line to meet them, headed by Dick Anderson, Organ Pipe's lanky resource manager. The Russians speak English, and have been using a Spanish-English interpreter, talking to Mexicans in the language of America. In Fernando's mobile home, environmentalists of three very different countries with many similar natural characteristics share dinner and knowledge long into the evening.

The following day, although there's really no reason, Fernando goes back to tell Harold about it. He just can't resist Organ Pipe. Whenever he comes to see his friend, Fernando Lizárraga's heart gives a great sigh. The monument is so perfect. It has pavement and curbs, restrooms and visitors' centers, naturalists, rangers, laboratories, and rules that get respected.

In the Sierra de Pinacate, Fernando is the superintendent and also the ranger, custodian, and security force. His park is not even really a park yet, just a wildlife reserve, although the maps all say "Parque Nacional." His headquarters didn't even have a sign until Organ Pipe donated one. The necessary paperwork has curled and yellowed in some Mexico City office.

Fernando, a pale, bushy-haired man in a baseball cap with an embroidered emblem of the black beetle known locally as the pinacate, admits he is just a bureaucrat sent from Mexico City to run the place from a trailer in Sonoita. But anyone who sees the Pinacate would know why it's important. Less often than he would like, because his gas ration is so low, he takes his boy, Fernando Junior, to show him sights that Organ Pipe, lovely as it is, can't touch.

The Sierra de Pinacate is all basalt malpais—exposed volcanic lava that hardened near what became a boundary a million years later. This is tierra negra, where layers of black ash cover the desert floor. The cinder roads are impossible, and Fernando Lizárraga wants them that way for now—not that there's any money for improvements. Otherwise, more hunters would come to plunder the bighorn sheep and javelina. At least this way he discourages them a little.

The Mexicans who throw things everywhere and leave broken glass are one problem. Another, he tells Harold Smith, "are Americans who come to Organ Pipe, follow the rules, don't litter, and then go to México where they toss everything and shoot everything else." Harold can't tell him why Americans are like that. He agrees they sometimes are.

All the wonders found in Organ Pipe are here: tall creosote bushes, taller saguaros, jumping cholla, ironwood and elephant trees, senita, palo verde, yellow brick caminos of brittlebush, and the parabolic organ pipe cactus itself, called pitahaya dulce by the Mexican Papago who render its fruit into sweet red jelly. The Sonoran is the salad bar of deserts, its sheer plant mass mocking the assumption that prolific growth implies abundant water. But the shock of the Pinacate is seeing these flora set against desert pavement as black and sparkling as new asphalt. Blue lupine, yellow Mexican poppies, orange yerba del negro, and scarlet chuparosa become jewels displayed on velvet. A scorpion is beautiful after all.

Fernando stops at a place where the liquid earth swirled and folded and rose like batter to form small peaks. He locks the hubs of his four-wheel-drive Ford pickup and descends to a black river of powdered lava. "Es mi favorito," he has been telling his son, because deep in the arroyo they might see whitetail deer or Gila monsters. Instead, what they find is a school bus, orange and glaring against the obsidian sand.

Lettering that runs its entire length reveals it belongs to the Secundaria Técnica No. 4, Secretaría de Educación Pública de San Luis Río Colorado, Sonora. Sleeping bags hang from windows; the hood is open and the battery is dead. They've been here a day now; neither the driver nor the teacher, a cheery woman with pencils stuck in her hair, are sure what they would've done had Fernando not come along, but they weren't especially concerned. The students, who hiked up ahead, are having a very educational time.

How the fifty-foot school bus got so far over these roads is a mystery. "Dios mío," Fernando says, and digs out his jumper cables. They form a caravan and creep onward like a preternatural termite with a black Ford for a head and an elongated, orange abdomen. Finally, atop a long, even slope, they arrive at Pinacate's best.

Cráter Elegante, three thousand feet across and several hundred deep, is round and pocked as the moon. To accustom themselves to lunar landforms, Apollo astronauts rode around here in a space buggy. The Pinacate has at least five hundred more of these cinder cones, many with perfect interior funnels. Porridge once simmered beneath the park's surface, blowing bubbles that spattered the surroundings. The ooze pushed up hills that cracked under pressure. Melted rock overflowed, coating their sides and stiffening in the atmosphere. In places, craters formed within craters.

Patches of light move across Elegante's broad, flat bottom. Rock and roll from cassette players drifts up from the crater floor, where the secundaria kids have descended. Anthills a foot across, minicraters themselves, dot the saguaro-creosote ridge. Straight head, the highest point in the Sierra de Pinacate is actually the rim of another crater; standing at its top, Fernando has seen the Colorado River, a hundred miles to the west.

One of the Pinacate's loveliest cones is also called Colorado, meaning red, because here the original tuff and breccia escaped burial. Cerro Colorado is a fiery ring amidst ashes, whose lava never spilled over to blacken its soft, salmon-colored escarpments. Instead, heat and wind have shaped them into honeycombs. If there are lunar surfaces this eccentric, four

Apollo missions did not encounter them. The greathorned lizards, rattlesnakes, and pinacate beetles here fritter away their lives spinning through labyrinths, meeting themselves returning along the curves of diabolic helixes. The land seems bewildered by some fundamental question.

Fernando Lizárraga has no answer, just a prayer. If there were only water, he would live here, move his family from that Sonoita trailer, sculpt them a cinder house and a park service center. Within human memory, Cerro Colorado briefly erupted and the course of the Río Sonoita shifted several miles south. A little stronger this time, and a little further west, is all it would take.

. . .

A year after the astronauts got far enough away to fit the entire earth into a snapshot, the United Nations began a project that pretends the only borders that matter are nature's. UNESCO scientists went around the world, identifying the essence of major ecosystems for special attention and protection. Because humans are arguably part of nature, the Man and the Biosphere program focuses on areas where civilization and conservation must coexist.

Selected to represent the Sonoran Desert were Organ Pipe Cactus National Monument and the Sierra de Pinacate.* UNESCO's ambitious vision is for countries to address in concert their common problems of water, land, pollution, forests, and urban systems.

Nonpolitical in theory, the Biosphere program smacks immediately into differences of sovereign opinion. Here, the biggest threat emanates from Mexico's side of the ecosystem. For centuries, Sonoita was a Papago garden irrigated by the intermittent Río Sonoita. Now, wells perforate the sands, watering everything from cotton to heat-resistant apples and peaches developed in the Israeli Negev. Organ Pipe

---

*The Chihuahuan reserves include Big Bend and Coahuila's Reserva de Mapimí, one hundred miles below the border.

long ago limited urbanity to customs and tourist services clustered at the border gate, and ran off cattle and mining operations. But it can't stop Sonoita from growing. The international water table is dropping; Sonoita's pesticides and herbicides blow though the fence, settling over Organ Pipe's pitahayas and wildflowers.

Mexico's participation in the Man and the Biosphere program is as urgent for Organ Pipe as for Pinacate, but Mexico's president has yet to formally sign the plan. Fernando Lizárraga and Harold Smith fantasize about shared training and research they would develop with joint Biosphere grants. Now, protocol is so stilted that to go into Mexico, Smith must remove his uniform and take annual leave time. Fernando is freer because nobody's watching, but on his budget he can only dream.

Which he does. Pinacate, designated as both a national park and a biosphere reserve, is still neither. Yet he already looks beyond it to the Sierra Cubabi, a granite range just east of Sonoita. In some unremembered past, angelic landscape crews were assigned to smooth out heaven, and Cubabi is where they dumped the rocks. Colossal boulders landed in heaps, cracked and strewn for miles through a forest of gray-green jojoba.

Here, chunks the size of planetoids appear so haphazardly poised that a random kick seems capable of bringing down two or three mountains. But ancient Papagos squeezed into the spaces between them, secure in the shelter of so much suspended tonnage. Many low caves here are scorched with the smoke of their cook fires. Charred dove and lizard bones lie in discreet piles. Spiral petroglyphs merely hint at the meaning of long-delivered messages. Fernando thinks the whorls must honor the wind, since nowhere else but inside a mountain could these people escape it. This too he must preserve, as new cotton gins, ejidos, and squatter's colonias swell toward the Cubabi.

On a December evening at Quitobaquito, Dick Anderson and other young park rangers gather in what was once, like Quitovac to the south, a Papago oasis. To attract more wildlife, the Park Service bulldozed away the old Indian adobes and enlarged the pond, but that has backfired. Without O'odham farming and its varieties of native seeds, half the bird species flew off and never returned. Man has his niche in the biosphere after all, they have learned at Organ Pipe.

A seasonal volunteer brings out her violin, and months later a mockingbird still whistles snatches of Bach's *Unaccompanied Partita in E Major*. In these dry borderlands, 120-degree temperatures are commonplace, but humans have found reasons to come for at least ten thousand years, and now more are arriving. Besides Quitobaquito's carpet of grama grass and cottonwood shade, those reasons involve desert miracles of orange globe mallow cups, fiddlenecks, blue chia, wolf berry, chicory, and wild onions—life delicate yet powerful in these juiceless reaches. The desert that was supposed to divide Mexico and the United States was a figment of an easterner's imagination. Both sides desire it, for the same coinciding and conflicting reasons they desire the river. If they claim it with care, a way may be found to accommodate both it and them. If not, the miracle at the far limits of tolerance will turn to a mirage and a memory, leaving the two countries with only the dust they kicked up and each other.

.   .   .

The skeleton of the intrepid Padre Kino lies on public display in a hexagonal glass vault in Magdalena, Sonora, an hour south of Nogales. Kino died there in 1711 while dedicating a mission. The Pima and Papago Indians he evangelized were awed by the mildness of this death, given the rigors he had survived in life.

For instance, El Camino del Diablo—the Devil's Highway. In 1698, Kino was probably the first white man to travel it, proving to other non-Indians who came after him that it could be done. The Camino began in Caborca, Sonora, entered what is now the United States at Quitobaquito, and continued a few miles north of the present Arizona-Sonora border until it reached the Colorado River. Except for Quitobaquito's springs, no flowing water was available for 120 miles. White men learned from Indians where the rain catches—tinajas—were that could save their lives. Indians learned from bighorned mountain sheep.

The Camino del Diablo has changed very little. It now crosses several invisible lines that designate wildlife refuges, gunnery ranges, and two republics. But the basic idea of a corridor through hell still applies. Too much of anything can overwhelm, and here the Sonoran Desert does exactly that.

There are other dangers. To travel the Camino del Diablo today requires an entry permit issued at the Cabeza Prieta National Wildlife Refuge headquarters in Ajo, Arizona. The form is a "hold harmless" agreement between travelers and the United States government. All along the Camino, including 95 percent of the wildlife refuge, they will be in an active U.S. armed forces bombing range, with "an inherent danger of falling missiles from gunnery, rocketry, strafing, and other related activities." The agreement goes on to mention live ordnance, dating back to World War II, that visitors might encounter with unfortunate results. As an afterthought, the use of four-wheel drive is urged, along with admonitions regarding several extra gallons of water and gasoline.

How could Kino and Juan Bautista de Anza, who came via the Camino on his way to found San Francisco, ever have dared to try this? Hundreds of deep washes cut across or turn and run concurrent with the gullied Camino. The land writhes, leaning north toward the watershed of the distant Gila River and then south toward Mexico. Spidery ocotillo, cholla, and leafless palo verde grow in shadowless clumps. Fingers of malpais shoot northward from the Pinacate, cutting at hooves or tires. As the day lengthens, so does the road.

Gusts of afternoon light sweep across the quilted desert floor. The Camino del Diablo is an incision in its surface that the sun-driven wind attempts to heal with a plaster of more sand. Bighorn sheep trails wander into oblivion. Phainopeplas, with cardinals' hats but dark underworld plumage, fade back, leaving an empty sky. This continues for ninety miles.

When it reaches the Tinajas Altas Mountains, the Camino divides into a series of rutty trails, and the sole road marker points to none of them. It is a twenty-foot arrow, formed of stones on the desert floor, pointing north into the indistinct waste known as Tacna Pass. The arrow is for the benefit of the undocumented. Forty deadly miles away are jobs in the vegetable fields of the Gila River Valley.

In 1978, thirteen El Salvadorans died between here and Organ Pipe. In the end, they drank bottles of aftershave, their urine, and mouthfuls of sand. Many others have perished over this route. Six miles south of the stone arrow, a truck stop called El Saguaro on Carretera 2 represents the starting line—and the payoff point for the coyotes who have taken them to the door to the United States. All they have to do is walk for a day. Ahí está. That's América, right over there. There won't even be a fence. The migra won't come near you here.

They are rarely told to pause at the dry waterfall as they pass by these white granite mountains. After only six miles, they should be still fresh enough for a short climb that dozens died trying to make. If they arrive between dusk and dawn, the unexpected occurrence of mosquitos might give them the clue of where to look, and for what.

Los Tinajas Altas, the High Tanks, are eight deep rain catches in a series of giant steps leading up the mountain. Forty years after the gold rush, boundary surveyors found the remains of forty-niners, some whose fingers had been worn away as they clawed to reach the water. On the gravel bench below the falls, fifty low mounds, some still marked by rock cairns, are their graves.

The tinajas are three to four feet long, with dark, mossy bottoms. So tortured is the rockface that they are not visible until a thirsty climber nearly tumbles into them. Travelers sometimes found the tanks fouled by the carcasses of desert bighorns that had slipped and drowned—or the lowest tinaja, the only one reached by a reasonably simple climb, drunk down to the sand by a previous party. Just twelve feet above, the twitter of orange-crowned warblers would indicate where there was more. But after ninety miles, twelve more feet was too far.

Around the uppermost tanks, bumblebees and purple-headed hummingbirds dogfight over yellow desert mariposa. Along the smooth wash, projectiles with their noses peeled back like banana skins attest to the presence of other, larger, flying objects.

It is not a necessary reminder. F-18 Hornets and F-4 Phantoms break the glassy silence and the sound barrier nearly every ten minutes, wheeling and diving within fifty feet of the saguaros. Restricted to U.S. airspace, they usually begin to bank over Tinajas Altas, but Fernando Lizárraga sometimes watches them arc over the empty Pinacate, clipping the edge of the Sea of Cortez perhaps to check on Soviet trawlers.

The perfect blackness of the Camino del Diablo nights brings the artificial heat lightning of flares illuminating ground targets. Hundreds of mojados walk north over this desert, sick with fright over the satanic terrain and heat, already awed by the immensity of an unknown country that both wants them and hunts them. And they are greeted by angry thunder, great flying triangles roaring overhead, kicking up staccato bursts of sound and sand all around them, dropping explosives and shattering granite faces next to their heads.

The desert, their risk, their poverty—how can they tolerate yet more fear? This has to be worth so much, the thing the United States jealously guards along its border with swift and terrible planes, lest some Russian try to take it.

Or some Mexican try to share it.

———

The road that Kino and the forty-niners followed from Tinajas Altas to what is now Yuma, Arizona, is closed. Access provided by the Luke Air Force Gunnery Range ends here, and the U.S. Marines take over. Nobody unauthorized enters their desert. The only North Americans are flying above it, testing weapons, so no one knows if alien lives have ended here, not by thirst or stroke, but by hellfire. On their way to the irrigated farms of Wellton and Tacna, the indocumentados don't fill out permits first.

With the road closed, today's visitors to the Camino turn around, backtrack fourteen hours in second gear, and hope there's enough gas. Or they can grope over an indistinct route south, around the Sierra Tinajas Altas. The road is filled with footprints, headed the opposite direction. The sandy, rocky washes are miserable, but the driver of a high-clearance, four-wheel drive vehicle is shamed into continuing by the unmistakable track of a bicycle, peddled by someone who passed here during the previous twelve broiling hours, wanting America that badly.

The track rolls by a rusted metal pole. Two miles later, the road disappears in a river of sand, but that bicycle came right down the middle. Several hundred meters beyond, the sound of airhorns and engine whine announce that blacktop is just ahead. Mexico's Carretera 2 runs parallel to the Camino del Diablo; motorists can cover in about an hour the distance that took Kino four days.

A little farther west, the road arrives at San Luis Río Colorado, Sonora, a border city of 225,000 people who work in cotton fields, in new maquiladoras, or in rows of vegetables stretching north from the boundary to Yuma. Arizona and Sonora's desert is over. Its terminus is a big, silt-laden river.

.　　.　　.

In theory, the Colorado River flows to the Gulf of California. Since 1950, that has been true only sometimes. Mariano Parra has given up trying to figure out when it will or won't, although it saddens him to think that someone actually knows, but doesn't tell.

From his bed, Mariano raises his brown head and watches the drizzle. His hair and beard are the color of the descending clouds. His roof of tules and arrowweed stops very little of the rain. Curled next to him, his sixteen-year-old son Esteban reaches a cold hand to adjust the hunks of cardboard deflecting the water from his blanket. Wires from a twelve-volt Delco battery slink up to a sixty-watt bulb suspended from the ramada. On three sides, the plywood walls are darkened from repeated soakings. The fourth wall is a fly made of plastic tablecloths pegged open to keep them from flapping.

The shack accommodates their mattress and a milk crate, on which Pablo Alvarado—"El Chato"— sits in his Epcot Center cap, weaving a monofilament gill net. He has a fire going in the doorway, boiling their coffee. Pablo, who lives in the tent next door, is mostly deaf, but speaks clearly through the few teeth protruding from his gums like the occasional cottonwood stumps rising from old, inundated levees. From outside, the steady pulse of a motor trying to pump floodwater to the correct side of a berm accompanies the sound of dripping.

They are on a low, muddy spit that three years earlier was a road leading between cotton and barley fields. Those fields are now submerged; for many kilometers in all directions, straight rows of drowned mesquite and salt cedar outline what were once the irrigation canals of Ejido Lerma, in the state of Baja California. Mariano, an ejidatario, is from nearby Ejido Zacatecas, which is also under water. Instead of a farmer, he is now a fisherman.

Another motor: A panel truck driven by one of the buyers from Mexicali glissades along the tractionless, waterlogged dike, an inch of slick gray bentonite sticking to his tires. He begins braking a hundred meters away, trying not to fishtail into the water. Gliding to a halt with a loud sucking noise, he jumps down into ankle-deep mud. His name is Israel. He is dark, in his twenties, and wears a transparent K Mart rainsuit. "¿Qué hay, muchachos?"

"Pues, hay bastante agua."

Right. There is rain. And what else? Nothing, they tell him. Yesterday they had no gas for their Evinrude, which lies in greasy disassembly in El Chato's tent, and today not even the birds are out in this cold lluvia. But Esteban awakens and reminds them that there's some lisa—mullet. The buyer has two old refrigerators lying in the truck bed, and one is already full of mullet. Since it's out of season this time of year, he's not giving much of a price. He only pays 150 pesos per kilo for lisa anyway—about fourteen cents per pound. "¿No hay bagre, bocón?

"Nada." The yellow flathead catfish have been spotty, and largemouth bass, which pay 400 pesos, are seriously scarce. Half as many as last year. "Mojarra, si quieres."

He definitely does not want mojarra, though they wish he would. It's everywhere, clogging their nets and eating everything else. During the winter, so many get trapped in the shallows and die when the temperature drops that these delta lands have turned into the continent's greatest smorgasbord for shorebirds. Green, black-crowned, and great blue herons; glossy ibises; and great white and snowy egrets do not merely gather—they riot, in airborne mobs numbering in the thousands. Gulls, terns, plovers, osprey, and whole squadrons of brown and white pelicans join them.

The principal object of their ecstasy is a fat, silvery cichlid: the mojarra, or tilapia. The fish has no business anywhere in the Americas, let alone these fields. It is a voracious, omnivorous African species, introduced in irrigation canals up in Arizona to eat the weeds. Prolific and hardy, it journeyed up ditches, through the locks of a few Colorado River dams, and poured with the floodwaters into Mexico, as have carp, catfish, and largemouth and striped bass. Some of these fish have provided a slender living for the ejidatarios whose farms now lie under one meter of unexpected water. But the unfamiliar tilapia hasn't developed much of a market, and it appears to be winning the waters on the strength of numbers.

"Oye, Chato, your net is illegal," Israel observes. Chato's handiwork in green monofilament has three-quarter-inch mesh, too small for fish but ideal for shrimp. Since the floods, Gulf shrimp, which spawn in freshwater estuaries, entered the submerged delta in huge numbers during late summer. Strictly off limits—and therefore valuable—during breeding season, the buyers were offering more than 1,000 pesos per kilo. Two summers ago, shrimp were jumping here like popcorn. Across the wide sheet of river, where the highway from Mexicali to San Felipe has become a causeway, fishermen hung nets over the culverts and snagged tons of them.

But this past year, nothing. Shrimping in the upper Gulf was dismal. No one knows if too many were poached or if invading aquatic species inadvertently introduced from the United States had preyed on them too heavily or if the growing demand up north for black-market shrimp had resulted in general over-fishing. El Chato and four hundred other fishermen like him are hoping that next year will improve. Something had better.

They make a deal with the buyer, trading lisa for gasoline they siphon out of his pickup. That afternoon, the rain stops. Esteban and Chato ride through channels resembling everglades more than ejidos, all laced together with gill nets. Esteban drives fast, keeping the bow high so the water from various leaks flows back to him, where he can bail without having to move. Back at camp, Mariano poles around the shallows in a wooden skiff, breaking off mesquite branches for firewood against the protest of birds who have appropriated them as roosts.

No one in Mexico knew that the water was coming. A half century ago, before Hoover and the rest of the dams were built on the Colorado, the river did this sometimes, reconfiguring its delta in the process. But by 1950, when Mexico built Morelos Dam at the bor-

der to divert the remaining flow into el Valle de Mexicali, the last hundred miles of the Colorado shriveled like a severed umbilical cord. Often it never reached the sea.

Then, in the early 1980s, more snow fell in the Rocky Mountains than skiers could believe. To the delight of the U.S. Bureau of Reclamation, snowmelt filled the big reservoirs behind Glen Canyon and Hoover dams to capacity—then well beyond capacity. Blame for what happened next flipped around as in a game of hot potato. No one had realized that the snowmass was going to be more than the dams could handle. A lot of water had to be released, and quickly. So it was, and it reached the delta farms long before any warning.

Ejidatarios like Mariano were given alternate lands to cultivate, but they weren't particularly good. So now he fishes. The government encourages this; fisheries agents come to talk about forming aquaculture cooperatives. Only everything depends on water from the United States. Rumors roil through the delta about snowpacks and drought reserves and men in Washington with access to a great spigot that either cuts them off or washes them away, whatever America wants. All that Mariano knows for certain is that the water is perceptibly dropping. Already some fields on the delta's periphery have emerged, white with alkaline sediments. Now that he's used to fishing, it looks like that will be taken from him. Can't the U.S. make up its mind? Or at least tell them?

"Pues, vas conmigo," Chato says to him. Chato has been a delta fisherman and hunting guide for thirty-five years. His old tourist camp fifteen kilometers south is completely under water just now, except for an island where a lonely bull has been trapped for three years. If the water does recede, Chato's going back. "You can cut off duck heads," he offers. Chato's North American hunting clientele were of two species: drunks who couldn't hit the sky with both barrels or cool sharpshooters who left bag limits behind at the border, blowing away 250 pintails, green-wing teals, and redheads in a morning, paying Chato a quarter apiece to decapitate and clean them.

To the west, the afternoon sun grazes the chiseled Sierra Mayor, and the swampy environs exude sudden color. Bands of mist rise from the water. The egrets and herons reappear, trapping huge wingfuls of air with their great strokes. Half-drowned, the delta looks magnificent. Mexico's historic plight has often been that as its troubles grow, strangely it becomes more beautiful.

Like the Nile, the Colorado River begins high in mountains and descends through desert. Rolling down its steep bed, it gains momentum and erosive power, leaving deep canyons in its wake. As the land levels near the U.S.–Mexican border, it decelerates, dropping its accumulated load of sediments. Before it was dammed, every year the Colorado would deposit 160 million more tons of suspended earth. A hole drilled a mile and a half here will not reach bedrock. Everything that once filled the Grand Canyon, as well as several other prominent gorges, has been reincarnated into the soft soil of the Colorado's delta.

James Gadsden knew a mistake had been made when the new border didn't reach down to the Gulf of California (also known as the Sea of Cortez). The United States would have had both a vital southern seaport and the entire length of the Colorado River—and, as it turned out, much less grief. During and after the Mexican-American War, President Polk and later Gadsden himself bargained for the Gulf, but Mexico was insistent on a land bridge between Sonora and Baja California. As victors, the Americans could have taken everything down to Guatemala had they chosen. But northerners feared that these newly acquired chunks of Mexico would end up as slave territory, and fought to limit the spoils of war to merely Texas, New Mexico, Arizona, and California.

Not long after, a Yale geologist named William Blake wandered into the Colorado Desert, an area just west of Yuma, Arizona, in extreme southern California. The region was known and feared by forty-niners who had hoped that the worst was over after surviving the Camino del Diablo. But here they found temperatures sometimes exceeding 140 degrees. Blake was scouting the eventual route of the Southern Pacific, and he realized that the desert here was below sea level. Examining its soil, he reconstructed a portion of prehistory that in the twentieth century would change America.

What he found were dehydrated river sediments. The Colorado River once flowed here. Eventually, he gathered that its delta was shaped like a giant T with 200-mile arms, one pointing to the Gulf and another to this depression that, at its nadir of 287 feet, was the lowest terrain in the Western Hemisphere. Blake named this most extreme basin the Salton Sink. Once this had been part of the sea, but the river deposited so much silt that over centuries it built a land barrier and diverted itself southward, leaving the water to evaporate. The process repeated itself regularly. Like a swishing garden hose, every few hundred years the Colorado undulated from one end of its delta to the other.

So all the torrid Colorado Desert needed was water to reconstitute its sediments into rich bottomland. A California doctor, Oliver Wozencraft, petitioned the legislature to let him develop an irrigation system, but the Civil War intervened. Others had more extravagant plans. Since all that stopped the sea from filling southeastern California's useless deserts was a geologically ephemeral berm of river silt, why not dynamite the thing, flood the Salton Sink, and create seaports and a wetter climate?

The plan to irrigate by gravity prevailed. The only obstacle was an inconvenient line of sand hills that ran from Yuma exactly to the border. A dry wash, the Alamo, showed how the Colorado once circumvented these dunes and followed a downhill path to the now-abandoned wing of its delta. The only thing needed was to redivert its flow. The sole sticking point was that the Alamo Wash was in Mexico, on land owned by a rancher named Guillermo Andrade.

It was not much of a problem. A group of investors calling themselves the California Development Company formed a Mexican subsidiary and purchased rights to the wash and options on potential irrigable land on the Baja side of the California border. This was 1900; the Porfiriato was in full flower. Investing in hitherto worthless land in Mexico was not terribly difficult.

With the mechanical aspects of their venture solved, now they had to sell it. Attracting farmers to a place called the Colorado Desert semed unlikely, so the same engineer who decided to use the Alamo Wash as their main channel thought up a new and tantalizing name. All over the United States, advertisements were soon luring people to the "Imperial Valley." By 1904, ten thousand had moved onto 100,000 acres irrigated by four hundred miles of canals branching from the Alamo Wash. Year round, they harvested melons, grapes, vegetables, and cotton such as the nation had never seen. Low humidity, high fertility, and profit made the heat bearable.

Now a new portion of the border was under development. Towns appeared in the Imperial Valley, named for associates and friends of the California Development Company. Border crossings where the Alamo Canal began were called Andrade on the California side and Los Algodones on the Mexican, celebrating the bountiful cotton crops and the man whose lands made them possible. Calexico and Mexicali, tiny villages of huts and ramadas whose names tangled their mirrored border localities, were outfitted with urban blueprints and hammered into towns.

The irrigation water flowed through more than fifty miles of Mexican territory, and by contract Mexico was entitled to half of it. Across the border from the Imperial Valley, the equally fecund Valle de Mexicali appeared. The establishment of its vast network of ditches was the work of American investors like Harry Chandler, publisher of the *Los Angeles Times*. His syndicate, the Colorado River Land Company, controlled 800,000 acres of Baja California. The Valle de Mexicali became Baja's equivalent of the American fiefdoms in Sonora and Chihuahua. The main difference was the labor: Instead of Mexican peons, Chandler and his partners used Chinese coolies.

But there was trouble. The inlet they had dug from the river to Alamo Wash was now a deltaic river channel, and it behaved like one by silting up repeatedly. At times, farmers in the Imperial Valley were not only deprived of water for crops but they were also in danger of dying of thirst. The company received permission in 1904 to cut a new inlet, but for reasons peculiar to the Mexican bureaucracy, separate authorization was necessary to build its headgate. That took nearly a year; by then it was too late.

Desperate to be back in business, they had cut the intake anyway, banking on the fact that the Colorado River had barely flooded for the past quarter century. But in the winter of 1904–05, unusual quantities of snow fell in the Rockies and the Arizona highlands. When it melted, it ran off through a West that had changed drastically in just fifty years. A quarter-million cattle in Arizona in 1883 had sextupled a decade later. Cows and sheep had so overgrazed the Colorado River drainage—one-twelfth the area of the lower forty-eight states—that natural erosion control was practically nil.

The Colorado had never flooded twice in one year. In 1905, it did that in February alone. Then came the March flood and then the second March flood, which smashed away every temporary brush dam they could devise. The river sought its lowest level, which was the Salton Sink. By June, the entire Colorado River was flowing through Alamo Wash and the parallel, aptly named New River, filling the Imperial Valley. Much of Mexicali's neat new street plan, buildings included, toppled into a wash running at ninety thousand cubic feet per second, and ended up at the bottom of the rapidly forming Salton Sea. Calexico dynamited the surrounding earth, frantically trying to match the pace at which the New River was gobbling it.

The gap defeated efforts to close it for two years. The United States, busy opening a canal in Panama, refused to get involved in the expensive business of closing one in Mexico. With no irony intended, Theodore Roosevelt stated that the United States couldn't fix a problem originating in a foreign country. Finally, the Southern Pacific Railroad, whose tracks were threatened by the rising inland sea, built a spur across the border to the intake and sent down a thousand cars loaded with rocks. From a bridge above the flow, they dumped riprap every ten minutes. Some cars fell in along with their loads. But the Colorado finally headed back to the Gulf, and then Mexico and the United States had issues to settle.

Everyone wanted the Colorado's water. Imperial Valley residents, angered over Mexico's refusal to pay its share of flood control, petitioned for a canal that would run entirely through the United States. When Mexico collapsed into revolution and bodies began washing up through the irrigation network, they grew more insistent.

Mexico didn't like that idea, because it realized that an all-American canal could capture the entire flow of the river, cutting it off completely. So it began to apply pressure. Of course, at this time, "Mexico" in the Valle de Mexicali meant Harry Chandler and friends, lobbying against their fellow Americans. But the idea for the All-American Canal gained momentum, and was lumped in with a plan to dam the Colorado at Boulder Canyon, Nevada.

This touched off new wars. States on the upper part of the river, like Colorado and Wyoming, feared that storage dams would soon monopolize water rights for lower basin states like Arizona and California. Arizona, with vital tributaries such as the Gila, was upset about all the water California was taking, seeing

as it didn't contribute a drop to the flow. The only thing the western U.S. states could agree on was that Mexico deserved none of it. The entire river came from rain that fell on the United States, and there it should stay.

Herbert Hoover negotiated a compact among all the states, apportioning the Colorado's water, with a vague reference stating that Mexico would receive the surplus. Plans for Boulder Dam and the All-American Canal were soon under way. And then Mexico played the card up its international sleeve.

With great topographical justice, what Mexico lacked in the Colorado River Valley it had in the lower Rio Grande. Except for the Pecos, all the major tributaries after El Paso came from the south. If the United States wanted to cut off el Valle de Mexicali, life could get very parched around McAllen.

Now both sides were building dams. Texas panicked and accused the Colorado basin states of undermining its agriculture. California and company were barely sympathetic. Back east in Washington, where more rain falls than anyone knows what to do with, no one could grasp what the fuss was about out west. But the State Department knew something about diplomatic issues and realized that it had one on its hands. Mexico and the United States were getting nowhere in their efforts to trade Colorado River water for Rio Grande water. A tough new Mexican president, Lázaro Cárdenas, had a big dam under way on the Río San Juan near Camargo. In 1936, on the centennial of Texas's independence, Cárdenas declared they could lose Baja California the same way unless Mexico took command of the situation.

Shortly thereafter, he expropriated the plantations of Harry Chandler and the rest of the Americans. He divided el Valle de Mexicali into ejidos named for Mexican cities and states, underscoring the nation's stake in his action. Now the two countries were truly squared off across the border, and each held yet one more card.

The United States's was a scheme for a long canal on the Texas side of the Rio Grande, to divert and store waters far enough upstream to nullify Mexico's stranglehold on the lower Texas valley. It was expensive, but it would ultimately work.

Mexico's was Europe. Germany was mobilizing, and German intrigue in Mexico just one war ago was a fresh enough memory around Washington. Cárdenas was doing nothing to contradict the rumors. Whether or not the United States shared the Colorado River with Mexico became an issue of intense interest throughout Latin America. The outcome would prove whether the United States was really their "Good Neighbor" as the current president, Roosevelt, would have them think.

At the same time the United States prepared to enter World War II, it began serious negotiations with Mexico over the rights to the shared surface waters of boundary rivers. Despite the opposition of western states, the two countries signed a treaty in 1944 guaranteeing Mexico enough water to develop its agriculture and supply its growing Baja California cities. The United States received critical allotments in the lower Rio Grande. The agreement included provisions for hydroelectric dams and international reservoirs on both rivers, schedules and locations of deliveries of water, and a jointly empowered International Boundary and Water Commission (IBWC) to carry it out and solve issues that might arise in the future.

The sharing of border waters has proved to be the most successful cooperation in the two nations' difficult mutual history, and the IBWC their most effective diplomatic channel. An occasion soon arose to test this, and the IBWC not only achieved a solution but also prevailed in spite of the State Department's blundering. The fact that the IBWC's U.S. and Mexican commissioners live in El Paso–Ciudad Juárez and lunch together weekly contributed in no small part to that solution, vindicating fronterizos' convic-

tions that the capitals might well leave diplomacy to those who live it every day.

Like everyone else in el Valle de Mexicali, Isidro Navarro remembers 1961. He was just a boy, but every day he would wake up to what looked like more snow in the fields of Ejido Durango.

At a foot above sea level, that was unlikely. Instead, these great fertile lands, the best-irrigated ejidos in all Mexico—courtesy of the American companies who lost them in the expropriation—were under chemical invasion.

The chemical was salt. One hundred miles away, near Wellton, Arizona, an aquifer of saline water underneath fields in the Gila River Valley was not allowing irrigation waters to drain away. The farmers' solution was to pump the contents of the fossil basin into the Gila.

The brackish water flowed down the Gila, entered the Colorado at Yuma, and continued into Mexico. Water that once averaged 800 parts-per-million of salt suddenly registered 2,700. When Mexico reported the change and the lustrous white coating that was destroying its soil, the U.S. State Department replied coldly that the treaty of '44 had determined the quantity of water Mexico would receive, but didn't specify the quality.

Isidro's family and all the other ejidatarios in the Valle picketed the U.S. consulate in Mexicali. And soon the IBWC was designing an annex to the treaty, guaranteeing that Mexico's water would have the same salinity as the Imperial Valley's. To accomplish this meant building a canal for Wellton's hypersaline discharge and the construction of the world's biggest reverse osmosis desalinization plant at Yuma to handle the increasingly salty irrigation waters returning to the river upstream.

The plant, scheduled for completion in the 1980s, is years over schedule, and will eventually cost at least a half-billion dollars. No one knows how well it will work, because no one has ever tried to desalt a river. In the meantime, the U.S. pumps water out of the Yuma Mesa into the bed of the Colorado, to comply with the quality standards it has promised Mexico. Right across the line, Mexico pumps out of the same aquifer. But an agreement is in effect, and even if logic is sometimes contorted a bit to fulfill it, an agreement between neighbors is better than none. "What else do we have?" Isidro asks.

But compared with people elsewhere in his struggling land, he is hardly complaining. The big ejidos of the Mexicali Valley have little in common with the dry-farmed plots of the south, where blank-faced children and campesinos dressed in white muslin trudge along highways behind pack burros, headed nowhere. The farms here enjoy some of the best features of both Mexico and the neighboring land that once sneaked across this border.

Isidro Navarro sits in pajamas, eating Gamesa cookies at his kitchen table with other ejido commission members. His house is brick, with a baby fussing in a second bedroom and the rest of the family grouped around a color television. There is a Christmas tree. Throughout the valley and delta, colored lights outline windows of neat ejido homes and encircle the trunks of palms and willows. Early December is rainy and cold, but there is more prosperity here than in most of Mexico, and there is gratitude.

Isidro has brown arms and shoulders like a sumo wrestler. He is named for his maternal grandfather, Tadajei Ishida, who stowed away on a ship from Japan when his family tried to make him marry a cousin. Disembarking at San Felipe, Ishida walked two hundred miles until he found work in what were then the cotton fields of the Anderson, Clayton Company, fields where his grandson is now the ejido secretary.

"Have they talked to you yet?" one of the men asks Isidro. They have not. The question refers to a group of Americans who are in the area. They are making interesting offers.

The salinity and the pink boll worm infestation that also entered Mexico from the United States eliminated three-fourths of the cotton industry here. It was once the world's biggest, with more gins in Mexicali than anywhere. That may have happened just in time, because China, once a cotton importer, now exports it. Even Mexico can't compete with Chinese prices.

The recent Colorado River floods flushed out enough salts that some farmers jumped back into cotton, only to have prices drop below production expenses. Many ended up grazing cattle in fields too costly to harvest. Others did much better, because instead of planting, they rented their hectares to Americans.

Vegetables involve risk and the assurance that they will make it to market before they rot. It's an investment a North American company can afford better than Mexicans. For years, Americans have farmed southern Sonora and Sinaloa. "Now they're here too," Isidro says, as though they've been expected back.

It's a hard deal to refuse. "You rent a field to the gringos. They come in with a laser and a Caterpillar and level the furrows perfectly and work the subsoil. They also hire a lot of people. You make three times what you would have, renting instead of growing, and when it's done you have a beautiful field that will have a better harvest next time you plant it."

If that ever happens. Here the ejidatarios grow wheat, white corn, barley, and seed sorghum. Baja California is a free zone, so they are able to import machinery and fertilizers unknown in the rest of the country. Their crops are for national consumption, but prices in Mexico can't touch what they make renting to Americans and their prestanombres who grow vegetables for export. In Ejido Durango, each family has twenty hectares, and some of them are now renting full time.

Isidro has watched this for a few years, and he has arrived at a conclusion. "The ejido system is sincerely not working well. Per field, they had better production back before '37. Even though I thank Lázaro Cárdenas for my twenty hectares, the country was better off then. More people worked. The only problem was, they didn't make enough."

But how many people do make enough in Mexico today?

"That's the point. Twenty-five years from now, there won't be ejidos. I don't know if there will be a revolution or what, but there is so much hunger. Not here at the border, but everywhere else. I don't want a revolt—I've got my land. I might end up with twice as much or none."

The Americans haven't approached him yet, but he is hoping they will. "Why not? They're great farmers. They employ a lot of people." Without any sense of disloyalty, he adds, "We can do a lot better if we turn the land back to them."

Despite the wonderful advantages here, these ejidatarios can see across into the Imperial Valley. Unavoidably, they compare. Because the government owns their land, they are limited to the value of their machinery for collateral on loans. Their members can list many other reasons why they can't compete with American farmers. But should that be their goal?

The enviable production of the old Harry Chandler days ended up feeding North America, not Mexico. The ejido system, for all its flaws, helps keep Mexico's birthright in Mexico. Isidro considers the history of foreign involvement here, and weighs that against what he has. Somewhere in this attempt at equation, he recalls his grandfather.

Tadajei Ishida worked the cotton fields here and became an ejidatario when Cárdenas took the land for his people. But during World War II, when his adoptive country signed a water treaty and a mutual defense pact with the United States, he was sent to Mexico City to wait out the fighting. The United States wanted no Japanese living near its borders. There were rumors of a radio station in the Mexicali area, receiving signals from Japan. Some people were known to maintain correspondence with Tokyo.

After the war, Ishida returned to Ejido Durango. In the post office, he found that the letters he had written to his family in Japan had also returned. His home town, Hiroshima, was no longer receiving mail.

Isidro Navarro honors his grandfather, who worked here until he died in 1966 at age seventy-five, who probably would not have turned the land over to Americans. The land was all he had, land that could not be bought nor sold, but land that could be left to sons and grandsons.

From the bedroom, Isidro's baby son starts to cry. He goes with his wife to check. Once, fathers raised their sons to continue what they did. What land or living awaits his boy in Mexico in the coming century, he can't imagine.

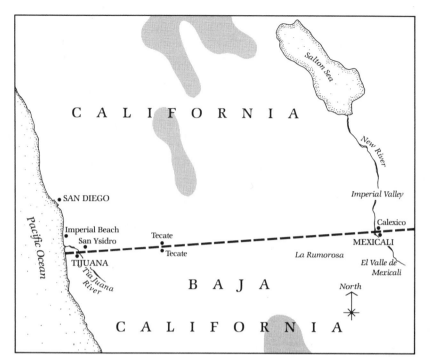

CHAPTER NINE

LAS

CALIFORNIAS

Eduardo Auyón, the Celestial Dragon, sits under a rubber tree in the Jardín de Chung Shan Yuan, sipping jasmine tea and smoking a Winston. Before becoming a garden, the Jardín was an alley; its trellised arches have transformed a brick tunnel between a clothing store and a hotel into an arbor of ficus and bougainvillea. Outside its iron portals, many of Mexicali's residents are absorbed with el Día de Nuestra Señora La Virgen de Guadalupe. But in the garden, the music and horns give way to the chirrup of blue and green parakeets that flutter in an airy white cage. Where the tunnel ends in a courtyard, old Chinese men circulate silently, as if shuffling on a pool of air.

Auyón finishes his tea. He is a thin man, with hair rising in dark swells from his brow. The emotions in his long face are obscured by a bewilderment of races. At fifty, he could pass for either much younger or much older. Crossing to a portico with dragon-entwined columns, he enters a room containing a table and desk. At one end, a round, gilded doorway frames an inner sanctum of low couches and Oriental rugs.

Over his street clothes he dons a black silk robe. Snuffing his cigarette, Auyón selects a cassette tape from a fabric-covered box. He spreads a sheet of translucent rice paper on the table, lights incense, and starts the tape player. Sounds of thunder and rain fill the chamber like smoke. He closes his eyes.

Like a sword flashing, the motion of Eduardo Auyón's arm pierces the shell of his own meditation, darting to a line of slim paintbrushes arranged on a wooden rack as precise as an abacus. His eyes are riveted to the rice paper, but his hand sees the exact width of bristle he needs, and in a single motion inks it and plunges its tip into the center of the paper.

A black smudge appears. The hand tilts, drawing the spattered ink along the surface. Nine times Auyón repeats this, spearing the whiteness with his brush until it gives way to the forms that emerge from his onslaughts.

They are horses, graceful and muscular, bulging with the power of the savage technique, revealing his mastery of the chaos he invokes with sound and gesture. His chiaroscuro conjures polarities of Tai-Chi, carried like a seed from Kwang Tung province to his Mexican alley, germinating into light and shadow, strength and weakness, simplicity and profundity.

"Celestial Horses," he announces, inking in this title in calligraphic columns. He signs his painting with two red-inked seals, square Chinese characters in the lower left and upper right. "Horses of motion and discipline, of beauty and service." The entire process—horses, mountains, chaparral at their precise hooves—has taken five minutes.

"No." He pointedly corrects that impression. "It has taken thirty years."

This far west, the consonant-laden Spanish of Texas and northeast Mexico softens to a song, but among Mexicali's Chinese it becomes an insistent drumming. Auyón, in languid tones clipped into calligraphic geometrics, describes how he erected this garden to honor the Kung Fu master who taught him to concentrate years into a breathless aesthetic burst. When he pleads for Mexico's Chinese, he nearly stammers as two cultures struggle for his voice.

Eduardo Auyón's father left Canton at age thirteen in 1893, in a wooden junk. The stormy voyage to Mexico took three months. When he waded ashore in Manzanillo, a grocer put him to work in exchange for Spanish lessons, drilling him until he mastered the *r* and then the double *rr*. His name, now forgotten, became Manuel. Within five years, Manuel Auyón was selling textiles and guns from his own dry goods market.

It was a time when human streams were leaking across the globe from the Orient. China's 1864 Tai-Ping Rebellion had presaged a dynastic decline into corruption and poverty. Thousands of hungry people set out for places like Jin-Shan, meaning Gold Mountain, their name for California. One route led through Mexico. Many never got any farther.

They came as laborers, working the mines of central Mexico and cane fields as far away as Cuba. They cut timber and laid railroad track. In the new century, they worked the oilfields of Veracruz. But nowhere did Chinese congregate in such numbers as in the Colorado River Land Company's Valle de Mexicali. For Harry Chandler, coolie labor was not only cheap, but it also kept Mexicans from establishing a presence in the portion of their country he wanted for himself.

Chinese like Manuel Auyón quickly moved into commerce. Their proficiency as entrepreneurs in Mexico led to jealousy and eventually to trouble—trouble that had its precedent in the United States. During the 1880s, having outlived their economic usefulness in California, Chinese were burned alive, disemboweled, and murdered in other memorable ways. Exclusion acts upheld by the Supreme Court denied them U.S. citizenship.

In Mexico, bayonet-wielding vigilantes slaughtered children and dragged adults by their queues through the streets. One hundred and sixty Chinese perished when a boat captain abandoned them on a fork of the Colorado River, with forty miles of desert between them and Mexicali. As President Plutarco Calles consolidated his institutionalized revolution in the late 1920s, anti-Chinese sentiment spread from his home state of Sonora. Former coolies who were now successful businessmen were shot; the homes of others were expropriated and their marriages with Mexican wives dissolved.

Many took refuge in Mexicali. This far-northwestern corner of the country was isolated enough to escape the worst of el movimiento anti-chino, and it was already a Chinese stronghold too powerful to defy. For a while, the chinos here outnumbered mexicanos three to one. Mexicali was headquarters to a chapter of Sun Yat-sen's Kuo Min Tang party and to the Asociación China, founded by five thousand single Chinese men. Both its theaters were Chinese; they had to build an insane asylum for lonely Chinese bachelors who went mad from the sight of a female on stage.

During Prohibition, the Chinesca district housed Mexicali's casinos. Beneath them, a series of tunnels led to opium dens and brothels. For the convenience of bootleggers, one burrowed under the frontera and surfaced in Calexico. Efforts to control this subterranean vice in 1927 erupted into the bloody Tong wars, with shootouts reverberating under the city. Not altogether coincidentally, Mexico's anti-Chinese movement began shortly after.

When it reached Manuel Auyón in 1935, he took his pregnant Mexican wife and left for a tranquil retirement in China—the dream of millions of expatriate Chinese. But he left without knowing what Japan, and later Mao Tse-tung, were planning for his country. By the early 1950s, the Auyóns were refugees in Macao. Eduardo, born in Canton the year his father had returned, studied in Macao's Academy for the Plastic Arts, while Manuel waited for the gears of the universe to cycle them a homeland.

With other wistful families like themselves they formed a Latin American Association in Macao, and wrote imploring letters to Mexico. In 1958, President Adolfo López Mateos, at his wife's urging, sent three old cargo planes across the Pacific. They hauled back five hundred grateful Chinese.

Eduardo Auyón emerges from his garden into Mexicali's streaming Chinesca. Clutching a notebook, he hurries through streets hung with Christmas bunting, fluttering banners of the Virgin of Guadalupe, and paper Chinese lamps. From the doorways of eateries selling shark's fin tacos and from the elaborate entrances to palatial restaurants like Chu Lim's, everyone bows to Maestro Auyón, who has brought honor to the Chinese colony with medals from both Mexico and China for his art.

On Calle Altamirano he enters MEXburger, a cafe owned by Julio Gee, president of the Asociación China.

The counter is filled with men eating hamburgers and drinking green tea. Teen-aged waitresses, embodying the beguiling combination of Oriental and mestizo characteristics, greet him in unison. "Hola, maestro," they call, and the men nod.

Gee, a spare man with a flat-top haircut, sits at a formica table with Antonio Wong, owner of Cafe Wong's across the street. Eduardo joins them, and soon the table is littered with napkins on which they make notes in Cantonese and Spanish.

"Tea, maestro?" Pouring is thirty-four-year-old Ham Lu Chan, recently arrived from Canton via a circuitous journey through Hong Kong, Tokyo, Vancouver, and Mexico City. It is no longer easy to enter Mexico. Once, Chinese came as tourists and then changed their visas, but with its deepening economic crisis, Mexico has stopped letting them in. Unofficially, visas can be arranged for a price in the Mexican consulate in Hong Kong; failing that, a well-timed bribe at a port of entry has been known to succeed.

A Mexicali legend once had it that no Chinese ever died; since they all look alike to Mexican officials, a dead man's papers would be passed along to someone else. Now, with the United States preoccupied over illegal aliens from Mexico, the Chinesca waits nervously to see if Mexico develops a corresponding attitude to aliens from China. This week, Calexico has invited a Mexican Chinese dance ensemble to its Christmas parade. Not knowing each dancer's current status, in MEXburger they wonder if they send performers to Calexico whether everyone could get back into Mexicali.

Confusion has ruled here ever since the United States severed relations with Taiwan and established them with the People's Republic of China. Formerly, Chinese with Taiwanese passports received free five-year visas. When the United States shifted recognition to mainland China, Chinese residents of Mexico went to the People's Republic's consulate in Tijuana and changed their allegiance, assuming this would be required to visit the United States. Instead, they found that only solo transit visas are available, at $5.00 each time.

"The U. S.," they were told in Tijuana, "is guarding against communist spies."

Mexico had broken relations with Nationalist China years earlier, when President Luis Echeverría was trying to cultivate a socialist image in his unsuccessful quest for the secretary generalship of the United Nations. Along with many of the richest Chinese, Mexicali's Taiwanese consulate moved to Calexico. Without U.S. recognition, it still operates, but no longer calls itself a consulate. Bearers of unrecognized Taiwanese passports get waved into the United States as easily as ever, whereas official People's Republic credentials evoke minute scrutiny and extra charges.

For Eduardo Auyón, born in Canton to a naturalized Mexican father, Mexico is his legal home, even though he neither saw it nor spoke its language until he was twenty-five. To the children of Antonio Wong and his Mexican wife, Graciela, Mexico and Spanish are all they know. An older generation keeps one form of Chinese nationality or another, in hopes of visiting the homeland before they die. Auyón too might soon be able to exhibit in Communist China. But China's numbers, like Mexico's, still outdistance its economy. Harsh penalties for families with more than one child may one day reduce its poverty, but until then, immigrants will challenge China's sealed borders, trying to reach where others have gone before them. For the same reason, taking advantage of an unsealed border, Mexico's unregulated population will do likewise.

A block from the Chinesca, a carnival is swaying in front of the cathedral. A barrel-chested youth hand cranks a carousel for little girls wearing embroidered skirts and boys in sombreros and lamp-blacked mustaches. Their costumes honor the Indian Juan Diego, to whom the Virgin appeared during the snowy winter of 1531 with a gift of roses. He had gathered them in his cloak, and when he later unfurled it to show a doubting bishop, her brown-skinned image, encircled in a golden aura, was embedded in the rough

cloth. They framed the miracle and hung it in the basilica they built for her, north of Mexico City. God's mother had personally shepherded los indios, the aborigines of the New World, into the Spanish church's flock.

The portrait is still there, its origins inexplicable to chemists who have analyzed the impregnated fibers, but indisputable to Mexico's indigenous faithful. Their descendants, hybridized with various Europeans, still celebrate December 12, the anniversary of the vision. But among the exuberant children of Mexicali are tiny señoritas and señoritos whose cheekbones and almond eyes represent a different hybridization, a reinfusion from the parent stock that gave rise to human life in America.

From somewhere in the Orient, hunters pursued game that led them over a Siberian bridge to the other side of the world. When the bridge disappeared under seas, the Western Hemisphere branch of the Mongolian race was sealed from the flow of its genetic source. As it adapted to new environments, it bred its own qualities.

Over the past century, Chinese again arrived here in pursuit of sustenance. Along this frontera, the family has begun to reunite.

.　　.　　.

Mexicali was born with the century—and sometime before the century gives out, it will join that once elite order of cities containing more than one million residents. By then, barring several potential environmental disasters, Mexico City will have around thirty million. But for the rest of the continent, one million people in one hundred years is a record not likely to be matched until . . . until Tijuana, another 184 kilometers to the west. But Tijuana grew in spite of itself, trapped in geographic complicity with California—the southern conclusion of an urban corridor comparable to Bos-Wash and the metropolitan Rhine, swooping down across the U.S.–Mexican border from San Francisco.

Mexicali, by comparison, grew alone in a desert—or so it would seem from an airplane. But the aerial view also reveals that Mexicali, flattened along its northern edge like a snail pressed against an aquarium wall, owes its very existence to the border. Before the boundary was there, Mexicali wasn't. Now it slams its urbanity against the fence and the cultivated Imperial Valley. Calexico, with fifteen thousand people, is a mere nub on its northwest flank.

Calexico can never grow much, as the Imperial Valley is controlled by agri-empires like Holly Sugar that have no interest in losing cropland to urban sprawl. Calexico is Mexicali's convenience mart; in predevaluation times, a floating population of forty thousand Mexicali citizens wafted daily through its blocky little mercantile district. More than half of Calexico's police budget deals with matters concerning not its residents but the border. On the other hand, fines levied against Mexican motorists who forget that a stoplight in the United States has other than an ornamental function account for a vital portion of Calexico's revenues.

In Mexicali, drivers habitually turn right on red lights, although the law permitting them to do so is really Upper, not Lower, California's. Unlike Calexico, the city has engulfed entire agricultural ejidos as it grows, resulting in struggles over which government agency, urban or agrarian, provides services to the residents. With its arachnoid glorietas flinging boulevards in all directions, Mexicali is better suited for vehicles than humans. Some families without houses have multiple cars. At a foot below sea level, it is also one of the world's hottest, driest cities, hooked by tubes like a dialysis patient to the Colorado River.

Yet Mexicali exudes a civic confidence unknown in border cities in places like Tamaulipas. Although everyone shops in Calexico and upward of fifteen Mexicalenses work in agriculture across the line, few people here are on their way to the United States. That kind of transience is for Tijuana, where a string of employment opportunities stretches to British Colum-

bia. Here an indocumentado would just be stepping into a large, empty void. More residents belong to Mexicali than dream of leaving it, a uniquely stable situation along the border.

It is also the only border town that is a state capital. At the onset of the Mexican Revolution, an armed contingent briefly occupied Mexicali and Tijuana, professing to be Baja California's protectors. They were actually filibusterers, intent on separating the peninsula from Mexico and possibly annexing it to the United States. Federal troops soon chased them away; in 1920, the old territorial capital was moved from Ensenada up to the border, lest the United States mistakenly assume that the area was not really Mexico.

Besides extra government services and payrolls, being the capital means having one of Mexico's finer state universities, the Universidad Autónoma de Baja California. Culture, political power, the wealth of el Valle de Mexicali, and a free zone have made Mexicali one of Mexico's most middle-class cities. More than any other Mexican border community, it looks inward, rather than over its shoulder at North America.

Fernando Medina was an accountant for the Mexican Treasury Department in Ciudad Juárez when he was transferred here in 1924. In his nineties, he still works as an accountant and, like most Mexicalenses, still drives a car. When he first arrived, Mexicali was becoming the world's capital of cotton, with so many gins that the Chinese even had one to themselves. Medina represented the Chinese community in fiscal affairs; Chinese became godparents to his children. During his early career, he saw not just gins but also oil presses, soap factories, paper companies, mattress fabricators, and cattle-feed industries develop as outgrowths of the monoculture of fibrous white plants. Later, salinity, polyester, and insects would demolish three-fourths of the cotton business, but by then Mexicali was too large and established not to be able to diversify.

Just southeast of the agricultural valley, hissing mud

volcanos and sulfurous fumaroles near a squat mountain known as Cerro Prieto were tapped for steam. The ground roared like humid hell, and Cerro Prieto proved a geothermal prodigy, with enough boiling force to light every bulb in northwestern Mexico and have wattage left to sell to the United States. Its development coincided with the arrival of the maquiladoras. Within a decade, industry became Mexicali's chief business, producing everything from cassette tapes to shuttle parts for NASA. The new plants, and some older firms that made substances like fertilizers, contributed unusual, toxic residues to the northward-flowing New River, where they passed through the Imperial Valley and collected in the Salton Sea. U.S. farmers objected. Mexican farmers pointed to the white, salty crust on their own fields and objected back. And Mexicali grew on.

Fernando Medina's son, Fernando Junior, was by now a state planner. Gray and cherubic, urbane in two languages and a PRIista, Fernando Medina lives in a home on Avenida Madero that has acquired several new additions since 1924. Behind the house is another, where his father pores over account ledgers. Twenty meters farther is the tall mesh fence separating Mexicali from American lettuce fields. Except for when a son's baseball would bounce irretrievably over it, the Medinas have rarely noticed it.

What does command Fernando Medina's attention is the emergency in his country. For twenty-two years, while the peso was stable and markets were secure, Baja California tingled with growth. It was a fine place to be a professional planner and to raise a family—all the benefits of the United States next door and a life style at one-third the price, with none of the chaos of a Tijuana.

"But you can't plan in a crisis," he keeps telling his wife, Martha, over breakfast in their blue-tiled kitchen. "At best, you can manage a crisis. How can you make recommendations if you don't know what prices will be in six months—or six days?"

The Medinas have a son in the attorney general's office and one who is a radiologist, both graduates of the university here, and another who received a scholarship to San Diego State and eventually settled there. It distresses Fernando to think that this emigrant son, who has taken the risk of becoming an entrepreneur with nothing but his wits to invest, may be more secure than the two professionals, simply because of a fence. In black moments, he wonders if they all shouldn't just go to the States and join their boy Enrique in San Diego. But their lives are here. Must Mexico, this fine, big nation drenched in beauty and resources, collapse under the weight of its political history?

The United States hasn't helped much, but now it is frightened by the specter of a Mexican default that could pull down its banking system. Fernando Medina sees that a plan it has urged, one that Mexico has finally agreed to accept, may be the last hope. Critics predict that with Mexico's decision to enter GATT, the General Agreement on Trades and Tariffs, half of its industries will go bankrupt in the face of U.S. and Canadian competition.

"So what if some businesses close—money is leaving the country anyway. Fifty billion dollars belonging to Mexican nationals is already in U.S. banks. We can't depend on oil now. We have to manufacture. Mexican products will learn to hold their own and take advantage of lower production costs. Rhetoric about wages is one thing. Reality is another. We'll never catch up to the U. S. with the obsolete machines they send us, but we'll produce jobs. In today's Mexico, that is ethically justifiable."

Ethics of a crisis: Fernando Medina watches the government he has served increasingly resort to authoritarianism to keep the peace. Soldiers and federal police are stopping cars on the highways, checking for arms. He predicts trouble as Mexico's eighty-six-year-old labor czar, Fidel Velázquez, finally relinquishes his near omnipotent control over Mexico's work force. Velázquez, who dates back to the founding of the PRI, has been accused of many deals with the devil, but his passing will mean confusion as successors vie for his crown. "It's a perfectly Mexican opportunity. Oil workers and teachers will fight it out until an authoritarian government steps in to restore order."

Or this dire scenario: Labor unrest is allowed to fester until enough violence justifies martial law. The government will have to protect the people from themselves. As police become overwhelmed, soldiers will step in and take over. Fernando Medina wonders about this. Each time the peso budges a little farther, he wonders what could keep it from happening.

"When a government becomes authoritarian," he often finds himself saying lately, "a linear policy establishes itself. Stick to the line, regardless of the consequences. We may see more of that. From there to a dictatorship is a very small jump."

In an automotive repair terminal in Mexicali, a fleet of yellow school buses submits to the necessities of lubrication. The radio inside each turns them into huge bass speakers booming out Christmas salsa, while graying tumbleweeds, valiant and unheralded, struggle to produce oxygen from their exhaust. To the west, La Rumorosa, the awesome rockpile named for the constant whisper of winds through its passes, sparkles with a rare snowfall, the first in eighteen years, that has closed Carretera 2 near its summit. By noon, cars are skidding hilariously down its icy skirts, racing home before the snowmen on their hoods melt under the reality of sea level. On XHBA, the university's cultural FM station, a discussion about whether Mexicans on the border are more influenced by Americans than vice versa gives way to a recording of Les Paul and Mary Ford's "Vaya Con Dios."

At the border itself, fantastic lines form. The wait for a car to enter Calexico approaches two hours. Even pedestrians queue up for twenty minutes, unconvinced by signs claiming that the Christmas gifts they seek can all be found in downtown Mexicali. They know better; the supply of toys manufactured in Mex-

ico City gives out long before it reaches la frontera.

Public address systems aimed from Calexico entice them in Spanish to where they can fill the plastic shopping bags they bring from Mexico. Spurred by the incipient decision to enter the GATT, the peso has actually improved slightly against the dollar, and everyone wants to spend theirs while they're still worth something, however little.

With the unseasonal weather, army surplus jackets are especially popular, and many Mexican shoppers wear crackling new olive drab. Niños make requests and promises to bilingual Santa Clauses. The Christmas parade goes by, minus the Chinese dancers. The border fence, festooned with red and green, combines with the improbable pure white snow on the mountains to the west to complete Mexico's national colors. A nice sign, people agree, even if it's a little cold.

"Próspero año nuevo," they hope for each other.

"Si Dios quiere," they reply. It's in God's hands.

· · · ·

Since the completion of Interstate 8 just ten miles above the border, anyone from Mexicali with a crossing card uses it to go to Tijuana, rather than risk sliding off La Rumorosa. For U.S. citizens, four concrete lanes are nearly always a foregone choice over whatever they've replaced.

For either nationality, the decision is expedient but regrettable, because of two lovely alternatives that dangle like wild streamers on either side of the broad, mountainous spine along the border's final western flourish. The summit village of Rumorosa is just a few miles from Jacumba, California, but a moon's worth of granite separates them. On the northern side, State Highway 94 pours around a mountain like a black river seeking the coast, passing through groves of lollipop oaks and sycamores, entering hamlets whose Spanish names are the only suggestion that Mexico is nearby: Campo, Potrero, Dulzura—which, meaning sweetness, describes the region.

This mostly forgotten route to San Diego bears little

resemblance to the portion of Carretera 2 just to the south. That road is exceptionally Mexican, with agriculture marching up powerful hills and human habitations glued to precipitous inclines, whereas Highway 94 is a confident tour through the quiet assurance of southern California. Together they form a refrain to the extended beauty of the borderlands.

At Tecate—spa and brewery on the Mexico side; store and customs house in the United States—the two roads nearly touch. Then they break away, each toward its own country's living dream of an urban future. On the way to Tijuana, Carretera 2 dips through rolling dairy farms and olive groves. Highway 94 sweeps around a lake—and suddenly vanishes into condominia.

Somewhere within a jangle of people, pavement, and plaster, the border continues threading its way to the sea. But before it dissolves away to meaninglessness in the Pacific tides, San Diego and Tijuana tie that thread into several elaborate knots.

San Diego and Tijuana's location isn't particularly suitable for a large city—let alone two. The terrain is erratic, with deep gulches separating eroding bluffs, and water is scarce. The largest river, the Tía Juana, alternately floods and dries up. The only groundwater is the undependable subsurface alluvial flow of intermittent washes. So the gardens and greenery that make San Diego an oasis are artificial, because the water that supports them is imported from distant sources, chiefly the overtaxed Colorado River.

A jam-packed bandwagon of hydrologists points out that if the law of supply and demand were truly in effect regarding water, San Diego couldn't afford all those lawns and eucalyptus. With new canals funneling the Colorado away to Tucson, Phoenix, and Tijuana, if the shale oil companies and Indian tribes upstream ever claim their allotments, perhaps someday it won't be able to.

Should that occur, San Diego would be plagued with dust. Unlovely concrete patios would replace sod

and herbaceous ground cover. The city would suffer chronic hillside erosion, exposing sewer lines that would periodically crack and spill their contents. In short, it would look a great deal like Tijuana.

Tijuana, which has never been able to afford the luxury of much foliage, is grateful for the new pipeline from the Colorado—not for landscaping but to give its geometrically increasing population something to drink. Between 1950 and 1970, the number of Tijuana residents sextupled, and doubled again during the last decade. More water and people means more strain on its beleaguered sewage system. This would be a problem for any city, but in Tijuana's case, it's two problems. San Diego, downslope from Tijuana, gets upset about being on the receiving end.

Although it doesn't grow at quite Tijuana's breakneck pace, every year metropolitan San Diego adds about forty-two thousand more inhabitants. Were it not for a fortuitous loop in the shoreline, people might not have amassed along this particular junction of desert and ocean. But alluvial gravel created landspits, connecting former islands with the mainland. The results were Coronado, Point Loma, and the harbor sheltered between them. Spain and Mexico established only minor colonies here, but in 1867 an empresario named Alonzo Erastus Horton saw the empty brown spaces around the great bay and knew they could make him rich.

In one of California's most successful real estate speculations, they did. For several decades, few others profited like Horton, because after the initial boom the city's financial base was uncertain. A sprawling Victorian resort built in 1887, the Hotel del Coronado, advertised San Diego's climate, which had attracted Horton in the first place. But the best promoter for San Diego's development turned out to be the War Department. Beginning with the Spanish-American War, the U.S. Navy brought military personnel who liked the weather and stayed on after active duty. And they told their relatives.

Tijuana sprang up, partly because Mexico wanted

to defend the sparsely settled Baja California peninsula, but mainly to service thirsty gringos during Prohibition. That, of course, happened all along the frontera, but no other stretch had Hollywood three hours away. Along with Clark Gable and Rita Hayworth, astonishing amounts of money poured into Tijuana, building racetracks, casinos, hotels, and swank bordellos. From prostitutes to parlor entertainers, Tijuana's employment needs sucked Mexicans up from the interior like a vacuum.

When Prohibition ended, there was the bracero program in California, to which a Tijuanense could commute much easier than someone from Guadalajara. There were also U.S. sailors with their paychecks. The Tijuana legend of money in the streets derived from inebriated Americans dropping change and greenbacks into the gutters as they tumbled into taxis. More Mexicans moved here, just to see for themselves.

Today, 270 maquiladoras strong and with all of California beckoning, Tijuana grows even faster, and is on its way to becoming Mexico's second most important city. It's surprising how San Diego has ignored that. "For too many years," opines Jorge Bustamante, Mexico's intellectual laureate of the border, "San Diego viewed Tijuana as one of those backyards that everyone knows is there but is kind of embarrassed about." The city has modernized, sanitized its tourist district, built one of the hemisphere's most visually arresting museum complexes—the Centro Cultural, with one building in the form of an egg giving birth to a planet—and has practically zero unemployment. Because it is a cultural crossroads for the two Americas, Mexico's artistic vanguard now makes obligatory pilgrimages here, filling the Centro Cultural with a continuous dazzle of exhibitions, ballets, and concerts.

San Diego is largely oblivious. What San Diego did notice, though, was the garbage. Especially unpleasant was 1983, during which a collapsing hill ruptured a pipe and five million gallons of raw sewage flowed each day into the United States. There it joined the Tía Juana River, which crosses the border just to the east and continues through San Diego County until it reaches the Pacific. Soon Imperial Beach was closed to swimming, and when Tijuana refused San Diego's offer of equipment to repair the break, San Diegans grew livid. "Only the federal government can arrange that," Tijuana Mayor René Treviño explained.

The editorial reaction of San Diego newspapers did not endear the two cities to each other. San Diego wanted Tijuana to share in a joint $750 million waste treatment plant. Mexicans calculated that this would probably wipe out the country's annual environmental budget, just to keep some California surfers happy. Tijuana's own papers began recalling some North American environmental indiscretions, again bringing up the layer of frosting on the Mexicali Valley— and the so-called joint flood control project on the Tía Juana River.

That program actually started harmoniously. The river periodically washed away the hovels of Tijuana squatters, drowning occupants and creating messes on the U.S. side. With the guidance of the IBWC, both countries agreed to channelize the river, in the manner of El Paso–Ciudad Juárez's concrete Rio Grande. At considerable expense, Mexico complied. The United States planned a recreation area along its five miles of cemented Río Tía Juana, but then environmentalists raved over the certain destruction of a unique salt water estuary.

Today, the concrete ends as the Tía Juana rolls under the border fence. A system of earthen dikes retards the flow on the U.S. side, but on at least one occasion the water backed up into Mexico, forcing the relocation of several flooded neighborhoods.

So Tijuana was not thrilled by the prospect of a joint sewage disposal system, because topography would logically locate such a plant on the U.S. side. If the United States changed its mind someday, as it already once had done, it would leave Tijuana helpless, drowning in its own aguas negras. A plant on the American side only meant increased dependence on the United States.

Since San Diego was already treating thirteen million gallons of Tijuana's wastes a day, it was not impressed by this argument. The arrangement was for emergencies, but for the past five years the emergency was constant. Tijuana's payments were two years behind, and San Diego hadn't cut them off yet. Even without accidental spills, Tijuana was dumping eight million more gallons into the ocean. The EPA and county health officials estimated that within ten years, posh Coronado and San Diego Bay would be quarantined.

So San Diego Mayor Roger Hedgecock went to Washington to lobby for a joint plant. The summer before, presidents Ronald Reagan and Miguel de la Madrid signed an agreement to preserve the environment along their mutual border. It was the only benign result of a meeting during which they disagreed on everything else, from tuna embargos to Nicaragua. But Hedgecock was told that the United States would not pay for any problem originating in Mexico.

"The federal government," he argued, "has to protect citizens along its borders. This is a foreign invasion, even if it's sewage and not soldiers."

Mexico is proceeding with plans to pump Tijuana's sewage over hills, to plants that eventually will discharge it into the ocean or into a tributary of the Tía Juana River. Yet if no border existed, there is no question where the treatment plant for the San Diego-Tijuana metropolitan area would be. Instead, Mexico will incur potentially exorbitant pumping and maintenance costs. And, EPA officials point out, the system will not meet U.S. treatment standards. With tourism and life style among San Diego's greatest assets, many wonder if the excesses of a Tijuana that can't clean up after itself will spoil one of North America's truly graceful cities.

It's a touchy issue. It suggests that Mexico is in-

capable of developing and maintaining adequate sanitation. It reminds Mexico that it is a poor nation sharing space with a wealthy one. Mexico counters by pointing at the windborne excretions from Los Angeles that sometimes foul Tijuana's air so badly that its hills appear as though viewed through waxed paper. Whose standards apply there? And if U.S. interest rates dropped a point or two, the difference in Mexico's insatiable debt payments could cover sewage disposal costs. A trashed border, Mexicans say, is the price the United States pays for huge defense outlays that force up interest rates.

The border, with its lean and exceptionally beautiful environment, is populating faster than nearly any other region on the continent. The ecological problems this poses will become permanent diplomatic irritants, especially if Washington and Mexico City insist on an adversarial, rather than a technically sensible, approach to them. Regional planning challenges both nations' strong senses of sovereignty, but the shared environment, whether involving contamination or international biosphere parks, presents tangible opportunities for enlightened cooperation.

Otherwise, the border could deteriorate into a refuse heap, with each side blaming the other for what inevitably occurs wherever man draws lines without regard for the topographical cleavages of nature.

. . .

Alan Eliason, the tall, ruddy chief of the San Diego sector of the Border Patrol, has spent the morning reading a study just released by the Rand Corporation, which concludes that Mexican immigration does not pose a crisis for California. Rather, it states that the influx has "provided strong economic benefits" and that the undocumented immigrants' "use of public services is not generally a problem."

Eliason has heard this before. He has also heard the scholarly theories that most aliens prefer to be in their own country and intend to return there after working a while. He doesn't buy it. He tosses the report on his desk. Resignation and contempt commingling in his voice, he tells Mike Williams and Arnie Murray, the two agents sitting in his office, that "we are no longer determining the composition of U.S. society. It is determined for us by alien smugglers and people in remote villages all over the world."

Eliason has been at this thirty years. After the Marine Corps, he tried a little college, and then, at the suggestion of the police chief in his San Joaquin Valley hometown, he applied to the Border Patrol. His first decade made sense: apprehend aliens, send them back. In 1965, they caught 6,500 in San Diego. It seemed a reasonable figure.

In 1985, they caught 427,000. In twenty years, the problem they were supposed to be controlling was sixty-six times worse. "How long," Eliason asks, "can we let this unmitigated disaster go on? The strength of the United States is a viable middle class. What's developing here is a poor class living outside society, a subculture of illegal status."

Bright sunlight enters his office windows, which look out at Tijuana beyond layers of chain-link fence. The sector headquarters is on a hill in San Ysidro, a community San Diego annexed back when this land was still in orchards, guessing correctly that one day the city would grow along the border. The fences here encircle a corralón, so crowded during the busy summer season that the INS has to rent the San Ysidro Travelodge to house the overflow of aliens.

The seventeen miles from the Otay Mountains to the Pacific Ocean compose the busiest stretch of human traffic across a political border anywhere in the world. Ninety percent of illegal entries occur at Otay Mesa, adjacent to the industrial park on Tijuana's Mesa de Otay. San Diego has annexed Otay Mesa, and envisions nearly fifty thousand people living there. How jobs for them will materialize is uncertain; San Ysidro, mainly Hispanic, suffers from high unemployment, and San Diego hopes that some American version of the twin plants might be induced to locate here in a free trade zone.

Eliason has nightmares about how a new residential area right against the border will complicate his life. An environmental impact statement for the development concerned itself with saving the Otay tarweed, but neglected to mention the herds of aliens that would trample it. But what has him most upset are plans for a San Diego International Grand Prix Racetrack, which would draw up to seventy thousand spectators on weekends.

Track developers expect traffic jams of three to five hours on race days. "Now how do we get a patrol car into that? What are immigration officers walking down the rows of cars supposed to do when a van with thirty people bails out and it sits there, abandoned and blocking traffic, with aliens running all over the freeway?"

A century ago, he is sometimes reminded, the Statue of Liberty in New York Harbor began inviting the world to send its poor, huddled masses. "There were only fifty-eight million in America then," Eliason replies. He talks about healthy, controlled immigration, about the water crisis in the West and how the land can take only so many people. He believes that what the patrol is doing is good for the United States. Hurt and bewilderment pervade its ranks over why the public often regards them as ogres and why the government asks them to do a job but never gives them enough funds or manpower. It charges them with reducing immigration, while at the same time it tells the world that population control is bad for economics. It welcomes the capital that rich Mexicans export to U.S. banks, failing to make the connection that thus, they are also exporting their unemployment here.

Alan Eliason tries to ignore these contradictions, and accepts the proposition of protecting his country's borders at the sacrifice of personal popularity. Los Angeles is the latest American city to be declared a sanctuary for undocumented Central Americans by its city council. The mayor of New York, a city with 400,000 to 700,000 aliens, states he will not cooperate with the INS. "We are the bad guys. Most Americans believe there's an immigration problem, but then an individual alien comes along with a heartrending story, and the media wail that the nasty migra is going to deport that nice guy, that poor, churchgoing underdog. Schoolkids send money to help him hire a lawyer."

Eliason sympathizes with the aliens, extends them their rights when apprehended, weeds out corrupt and sadistic patrol officers. But he questions why he must take as his personal burden the discontent that aliens have with their own countries. "I look at the growing number of Central Americans, Chinese, Indian Punjabs, and Yugoslavs we're getting. I look at the past twenty years with Mexico. I think that in twenty more years we will be like the rest of the world. If we can't slow this down, we will be just like those sending countries. Our middle class will dwindle. We will fall to Third World status.

"If somebody takes over your country, does it matter how they do it?"

"It's a fun job, but someone's got to do it," reads a sign in the Border Patrol flight room at Brown Field on Otay Mesa. Remnants of a Christmas party buffet of machaca burritos and vegetable dip cover a map table. As twilight deepens outside, patrolman Ray Ortega drives up in a Ram Charger and chats with pilots Dave Quick and Jim Smith about his interesting afternoon spent catching some wets who frequently work on his father's tomato farm up in the Salinas Valley. He's known these guys since he was a kid.

Quick, his crew-cut mashed from two hours in his radio helmet, has just landed and is still in his flame-retardant flight suit. Smith, a short, quiet man in his thirties, is about to take off. "Only a few hundred out there tonight," Dave tells him. With Christmas coming, most of the aliens are headed the other direction.

The Border Patrol's San Diego sector uses Hughes Aircraft OH6-Alpha helicopters, relics that were each shot down at least twice in Vietnam. Here in San Ysidro, one crashed when a well-aimed rock hit a rear propeller, tearing off the gearbox. They are hot goldfish bowls, the approximate size of a VW beetle, but comfortable on a chilly December evening. Two pilots fly together, one aiming a bank of quartz halogen lights controlled from within by an adapted motorcycle throttle cable and joystick.

"Just a glorified flashlight." Quick finds some similarities between here and Vietnam. The terrain is erratic, the quarry elusive, and the mission sometimes seems futile when a single chopper, some ground vehicles, and agents manning starlight scopes are trying to contain a thousand scattering aliens. Often, the most a pilot can do is herd people down one trail like a flying sheepdog, then zip across the mesa to head off more going up five other routes.

"Up there," says Smith, "you get the larger picture. You see how many are getting away."

Minutes later, he is looking down at Wruck Canyon, which drops off Otay Mesa into a snakepit of gulches and trails that lie between swollen Colonia Libertad in Tijuana and Horatio Alger's land of opportunity. Below is brush, mesquite, and tamarisk. The helicopter darts across the sky like a nocturnal dragonfly, responding to radio requests from four-wheel-drive ground patrols.

These include the Border Crime Prevention Unit, San Diego city policemen who accompany the Border Patrol in search of gangs that prey on the hapless undocumented migrants. The unit has been effective, something that both pleases and annoys San Diego Police Chief William Kolender. "We've gotta be the only police department in the business of protecting illegal aliens," he often growls. Some of the bandits doing the looting and raping turn out to be Tijuana police. The previous December, Kolender was interviewed on radio with the new anticorruption Tijuana police chief, who didn't even last the year. "They change 'em like underwear, they're so unstable and corrupt. Every time there's an incident, they just fire the chief. Stupid."

Kolender has been at his own job for ten years. In 1981, Ronald Reagan offered him the directorship of the INS. He refused, not wishing to leave San Diego—although he considers this a war zone. "Congressmen think that no immigration policy is a policy. 'Let Mexico use the U.S. as a safety valve so it won't go communist.' That's bullshit. I don't blame the aliens—we'd all be busting our fannies to get over here. But the Mexican government has no incentive to get off its ass. So we get millions of their people, and in order to survive they become criminals."

The helicopter loops around the quarter moon, playing its cone of light over the surfaces of hills scarred with deep ravines that began as foot trails. It circles over a bush that appears to have arms and legs, the wind from its throbbing rotors whipping the foliage. William Kolender believes that terrorists bent on committing acts against the United States will soon pour over the border. Alan Eliason perceives the United States's fate being decided by foreign refugees, forgetting that it's always been like that. The poor devil Smith has pinned with his beam might be a terrorist, or he might change America's destiny. Probably, though, he is merely hungry or ambitious or both. He is also temporarily expensive. Gas for the helicopter and the ATV pulling up to nail him, processing at sector headquarters, a meal or two, deportation—these things add up. And he will keep coming back, until he makes it.

On the edge of Colonia Libertad, Alejandro Lara sits on a rock, hands dug inside the pockets of a hooded gray sweatshirt, waiting for 8:00 P.M. Around that time, the helicopter pilots change shifts, and he will take his group up one of the crisscrossing paths into North America. Every third day he guides pollitos, his little chicks, through canyon switchbacks to houses in San Ysidro. Later, cars will shuttle them up to Los Angeles, after phoning ahead to make sure the Border Patrol checkpoints north of San Diego are clear.

Lara has been a pollero, a coyote, for three months. Before, he harvested peaches for two years outside of Fresno until the migra escorted him home. Picking paid $50 on an exceptionally good day. As a coyote, he charges $300 per Mexican and $400 to $500 per Central American. Kids come for free.

He prefers to take no more than seven at a time. Groups of forty were once not uncommon here, but the migra has increased its vigilance in the canyons because the cholos were robbing and killing. The same numbers are still getting through, but in smaller batches. Alejandro gets paid in dollars, usually by relatives, when he delivers them in L.A. His expenses are bus fare back from Los Angeles and the cuts he pays to safe houses and drivers. As long as he avoids being ambushed by the cholos, twenty-two-year-old Alejandro makes a very decent living.

About four hundred people, half the usual amount, warm themselves around burning tires on the plateau known locally as el campito de fut—the little soccer field. Several carry suitcases, and many groups include children. There is no fence here, and the campito is actually in the United States. It is tierra de nadie that the migra tacitly relinquishes to them, because otherwise there would be no place for anyone to stand. Colonia Libertad, one of the world's densest human concentrations, crowds the invisible line, apparent only because the shacks abruptly stop and naked yellow soil begins.

Evening and temperature have fallen, and business picks up around los canelos, pushcart vendors who sell cinnamon tea strengthened with tequila to give warmth and courage for the journey ahead. Others fry sizzling carnitas over grills made from hunks of fencing appropriated from the bedraggled Tortilla Curtain down near the customs area. Clothing is also for sale; many people from the south did not expect golden California to be so cold in December. Every so often an Aeroméxico jet fills the sky overhead, stenciled against the night by its running lights, taking off from the Tijuana Airport on Mesa de Otay just two kilometers up la frontera. At first, the planes are virtually silent, but so close that their undersides reflect the amber bonfires. A whiff of jet fuel blends with aromas of cinnamon, sewage, cooking grease, and Goodyear.

"¿Ya te vas?"

"Ya merito." Alejandro is almost ready to go, he tells his sister Lourdes, who sits nearby. For the past month, Lourdes has been varnishing furniture at Amex de México, a maquiladora up on Mesa de Otay. The work is all right, but she can't get the stains off her hands and clothes. Before, she was at a Japanese TV parts maquila employing a thousand women. The Japanese have lately discovered a way to counter the Americans who compete with them by putting assembly plants across the Mexican border: Japan is now putting them here too. Lourdes left because her Japanese manager kept fondling her. So far, the gringos have been more respectful, but with her hair all sticky with varnish, this is no great surprise.

"¿Cuántos tienes?" she asks. He has only four tonight, three men and a woman from the state of Michoacán. He and Lourdes are also from Michoacán; they are two of seventeen children. Their father has an ejido near La Piedad, but came to Colonia Libertad, where carpentry pays better than sorghum, the year Alejandro was born. With his coyote profits, Alejandro intends to go back to claim the family farm. All his life, his father has talked of Michoacán's pines and lakes.

"Que tengas cuidado," Lourdes warns him. She worries about his safety, and wonders lately about his motives. He has promised to quit this when there's enough money, but when will that be? He is making so much.

He stands and looks around for the frightened little group upon whom he will now bestow residence in the United States. Just this past week, his own family was down in Cañon del Muerto just below, cutting firewood, when the migra appeared. Usually, they allow locals to gather mesquite, but this time they were muy bravo and locked them in the corralón. Their father was so humiliated—he had never cared about going to the United States.

"Don't worry," he tells her, kissing her cheek. He heads toward a northbound path and disappears into the gloom.

Lourdes walks back into the colonia. The radios that earlier were blaring Madonna's "Like a Virgin" are now hushed. Children in twos and threes walk along the wet cobbles of the colonia, singing Christmas carols. Several houses have strings of colored lights. Far across the canyons, more of these can be discerned, blinking from a Christmas tree at the chile farm where, si Dios quiere, Alejandro will soon safely pass, leading his paisanos to a new hope.

"Feliz Navidad," she is greeted by two tiny girls carrying large schoolbooks.

"Feliz Navidad, mis hijas. Próspero año nuevo."

.   .   .

At its end, the border is practically frictionless. Some twenty-five million legal crossings, more than anywhere, occur at San Ysidro each year. Twenty-four lanes of cars and five of pedestrians enter the United States, and still that isn't enough. A second port of entry, recently opened on Otay Mesa, is already mobbed. People pour north through every conceivable opening. Although narcotics are less significant here than along the Rio Grande, the estimated $200 million annual drug trade is one more contribution to the flow.

The suitcases full of bills that arrive in the currency exchanges lining San Ysidro Boulevard are another. Surrounded by bulletproof glass and closed circuitry, speculators recalibrate dollar-to-peso-and-back-again margins every half-hour, sometimes every half-minute when the peso is hyperactive. Fleet-footed couriers trading plata for oro ("silver" pesos for "gold" dollars) make dozens of trips across the line. Other dealers operate from stationwagon tailgates in parking lots, buying dollars for 692 pesos and selling for 701.* No one knows how much of Mexico's net national profit has been laundered here on its way to Bank of America. Insiders on San Ysidro Boulevard, which lately resembles a fast food stock exchange, hint that published estimates of $5 million a day reek of disinformation.

The cross-boundary conveyor is an endless loop running both ways. In 1980, the machinery behind a luxury car theft ring was traced to the chief of Mexico's security police. Thieves would take cars for test drives from California auto dealerships and head across the border for Mexico City. A U.S. attorney in San Diego kept trying to prosecute the ringleader, who turned out to be the Central Intelligence Agency's prize Mexican informant. The CIA, aware of the car scam, wasn't about to let a loyal stooge be indicted. The U.S. attorney who tried lost his job.

There are other lucrative items. According to the San Diego office of the Bureau of Alcohol, Tobacco, and Firearms, a semiautomatic AR-15 selling for $400 in San Diego brings at least $1,200 in Tijuana. Regardless of their attitude toward guns, many find the idea of tripling their money in only sixteen miles irresistible. A federal license to deal in firearms costs $10. In San Diego, a thousand or more citizens do it, the majority right from their homes.

Agents at ATF guess that 35–40 percent of these sales end up in Mexico, which has no sporting goods stores or any other legal place to acquire such weapons. In the United States, selling firearms to a nonresident is forbidden. But in the neighborly, prestanombre spirit that has allowed Americans to own estates and agribusinesses in Mexico, for $25 obliging San Diegans will sign their name to registration forms

---

*At the time of publication, the peso's value was changing so rapidly that rumors of its disappearance and the emergence of a new currency called the azteca once again became common gossip.

so a Mexican can buy an Uzi in California. If the Mexican doesn't know any such person, gun shops arrange friendly introductions.

For a while, the ATF tried working with Mexico, using army officers to pose as customers in stores suspected of selling to Mexicans. It was not an auspicious collaboration. "They're a pain in the ass to work with," complains one agent. "They shake you down for money for a new tire, for the baby-sitter, for the lieutenant and the driver. Then, after paying everyone off, you can't depend on them to come to trial."

Hot items like fully automatic weapons can't be purchased over the counter. But in magazines such as *Shotgun News*, separate ads will sell parts that, when combined, add up to an automatic conversion kit. Or a silencer: Last year, Tijuana police officials were suddenly buying a lot of silencers. "It scared the hell out of us. Why would police need a silencer? You don't shoot ducks with them. You kill someone quietly."

Nervous about their jobs, ATF agents don't like being quoted by name. At the urging of the National Rifle Association, the current administration at times has tried to abolish the bureau.

"There is a point where the right to bear arms gets a little ridiculous. In December, we caught two Mexican drug traffickers ordering M-16 machine guns with M-203 grenade launchers. The NRA is worried that if we control this stuff, the next thing they know we'll be trying to control something else. Meanwhile, our Drug Task Force goes in with .38s, and the pushers come back at us with fully automatic Uzis."

The Israeli Uzi is currently the automatic weapon of choice among drug runners. It converts easily from semi- to full auto, looks evil, and conveys the macho mystique of an Entebbe raid. No one knows how many of them and the competitive American models like the Colt AR-15 are in Mexico. Since la crisis económica, narcotic and other sinister armies are growing. While the United States sees Soviets and Cubans fomenting Latin American uprisings, it and Israel profit by arming them.

"As long as Mexico is comprised of two classes, one rich and one poor, the threat of revolution will keep guns flowing south," says the ATF agent, who's watched the arsenal grow for twelve years.

Along the border, everyone wonders whether revolution can occur again. The hunger and corruption are familiar to historians. The last time around, despite neutrality laws, the outgunned Villas and Carranzas found a way to get weapons, and that way was from the United States. Someday, someone may write that in the 1980s or '90s, it happened again.

. . .

Wooden donkey carts are found in every border town from Juárez to the Pacific. Once a means of transportation, they are now immobile, bedecked with images of Aztec kings in heroic landscapes that display all the taste and energy of a velvet painting. Sometimes the burros are dyed to resemble zebras. Tourists climb aboard, don serapes and sombreros, and pose for $2.00 Polaroid mementos beneath signs reading "Bienvenidos a Tijuana."

In 1985, David Avalos, artist-in-residence at the Centro Cultural de la Raza in San Diego's Balboa Park, was invited to participate in "Streetworks," an outdoor exhibition funded by the National Endowment for the Arts. Avalos, from National City, a working-class district between San Diego and the border, submitted a sculpture of a life-size donkey cart. Instead of Cuauhtémoc, its backdrop depicted a Hispanic, his face contorted and arms upraised to suggest a crucifixion, being frisked by la migra. Like a Mexican roadside shrine, the cart was trimmed with relics and images, including the photograph of an undocumented alien who was fatally shot by border patrolmen in 1980. Avalos surrounded his work with a wire fence and entitled it, "San Diego Donkey Cart."

His cart art was reviewed and a permit was issued by the General Services Administration to install it in the Federal Building plaza in San Diego. The next day, without a hearing, Chief District Judge Gordon Thompson had it removed, "for security reasons." Some kook, he explained, might decide to blow it up.

Suddenly, Judge Thompson found himself an unwitting patron of Latin protest art. The attention immediately surrounding David Avalos was a kind of golden spotlight that artists might kill for. Newspapers nationwide noted that kooks generally don't determine who is allowed to exercise their First Amendment right of expression. Art critics began to look more carefully at Avalos and his group of San Diego and Tijuana colleagues, known as the Border Art Workshop/Taller del Arte Fronterizo. Outraged by the censorship, the reviewers concluded that these people are not just political advocates but also sophisticated artists who reject abstraction in favor of political forms.

"I don't see the characterization of art as political as being valid," argues David Avalos. He and Guillermo Gómez-Peña, a writer and performer, are driving down Interstate 5, to meet the rest of their colleagues at the sandy intersection of Mexico, the United States, and the Pacific. He is slightly uncomfortable about his work receiving its greatest attention after it was removed from public view. "It's social: a social creation that connects me, a social animal, with the rest of the community. Noncontextual expressions of art as pure ideal have reached a dead end."

Avalos is a burly mestizo, wearing steel-rimmed glasses and a stretched gray sweatshirt, with his long hair tied back in a ponytail. What grips him about the border is that everyone is in this together. Not just Caucasians, Chicanos, and Mexicans: The border is also a symbol for blacks, who are North America's mestizos, and for Orientals, who have been called a yellow peril by both countries—the ultimate aliens. The aesthetic challenge is to convey this unification and take advantage of the cross-pollination.

Gómez-Peña is from Mexico City, but now roams

between Tijuana and San Diego. His sonorous actor's baritone turns his thoughts into a musical incantation of the energy being released through cultural nuclear fusion along the border. When he and David converse, it is like Greek monologues and answering choruses.

"We have to be mapmakers, man," he sings, "topographers, redefiners of the parameters of reality, reinventors of landscapes to redraw the borders of the world. This is terra incognita. There's a world to be renamed, its real borders to be discovered. We are creating artistic, political, and anthropological cartography."

David ponders the tierra incognita. They are in the Dodge van belonging to dancer-choreographer Sara-Jo Berman, hauling props and a portable generator down to the beach. The tableau they are about to enact is largely the creation of Avalos and Michael Schnorr, a printmaker and art professor at San Diego's Southwest College. "Yeah," Avalos finally replies, "but western aesthetics always exalts the weird. If we present the border as strange, people will put it up on the shelf with the African masks. It's like the Third World is okay, as long as it stays in museums. It has to be made both beautiful *and* everyday."

It is a delicious task, Guillermo thinks, to resolve the intersection of two pop cultures that superimpose Clint Eastwood and Pancho Villa, punk and salsa, Jesus and E. T., disco and mambo. The border is priceless for exploring relationships. Artists here can feed off the vigor of two new cities unencumbered by an artistic tradition, with an ear to both North and South America. They can experiment and watch the gears of two societies begin to mesh within the machinery of the future.

"This will be a mecca one day," he predicts. "A new culture in creation, like New York after World War I. Not a regional culture, like western painting, but culture with something to show the world about how rich and poor will merge like two continental plates. The border is finding its own voice. It's learn-

ing how to sing, to write, to act. Once it can explain itself, this will be Mecca."

Two miles above the border, they leave the interstate and follow a road that cuts across the ripe-smelling Tía Juana River estuary. It leads to Border Field State Park, a manicured lawn set like a green toupée on a bluff overlooking the ocean. Except for the helicopters buzzing overhead, it is empty. On one end, a fence rolls in from the canyons and hills to the east. Just beyond it are a lighthouse and Tijuana's Bullring-by-the-Sea.

At the bluff's edge, the rigid mesh is cut to fit around a marble pagoda, the marker established by the first boundary survey in 1849. Just below, the fence stops thirty feet short of the water. Beachcombers and joggers casually pass beyond it, wandering between the Americas.

The other artists are waiting. With Michael Schnorr's students manning the props, they begin the tableau. It is part theater, part sculpture, part representational art, and part political cartoon. On the Mexican side, puzzled onlookers gather at the fence. A border patrolman, cruising the park, sits on the stone retaining wall and watches, although from behind he cannot tell what they are doing.

He would probably not be pleased. They have positioned three large masonite caricatures in the sand, depicting a terrified Hispanic youth, a demonic border patrolman gunning him down, and a black silhouette of a helicopter that has nose-dived into the beach. Sara-Jo Berman is dressed like a Tijuana whore and is flirting with the cutout of the migra. David Avalos is on his knees with his hands behind his head, in submission to a knife-wielding cholo portrayed by Guillermo Gómez-Peña. Behind them, a stepladder appears to span the fence; filmmakers Isaac Artenstein and Jude Eberhard confront each other at the top in impenetrable leather masks. Artenstein, a Mexican, and Eberhard, a native of Trinidad, have teamed up on documentaries that have earned a blue ribbon at the American Film Festival and an Academy Award nomination.

Hanging from the ladder in tortured suspension is Schnorr. In front of him, two-foot letters outlined in blinking light bulbs spell out the word *hell*. Amidst all the psychological violence, Victor Ochoa sits impassively on a folding chair, engrossed in the static coming over a portable television. Ochoa is responsible for much of the art in San Diego's Chicano Park, a drive-in museum created by muralists on pillars under the Coronado bridge. When he was a boy in Los Angeles in 1955, his father was thrown back into Mexico during Operation Wetback. Victor helped support the family by selling seat cushions in the bullring that looms over the wicked scenario he and his colleagues have created at the end of the border.

It is hardly an attempt to build bridges of understanding between the protagonists of border life. But neither is the clipping that David Avalos has been steaming over all week: a photograph in the *San Diego Union* showing a silhouetted horseback border patrolman in a cowboy hat and three wets with their hands behind their heads, walking in front of him. "The simple, nineteenth-century solution to the problem. The hunter stalks the lawbreakers and brings them to justice. The law they broke was merely wanting to live."

The border snaps like a taut band. Its ends fly together and converge into this single issue. Aliens are guilty for invading the United States to earn dollars. Employers are guilty for encouraging them. Congressmen are guilty for failing to pass laws that punish employers for doing this. And everybody is guilty for wanting cheaper vegetables.

Mexico, too corrupt to share its wealth among its own people, is perhaps guiltiest of all. But Mexico blames a legacy contaminated by dictators, churches, kings, viceroys, and Aztec emperors, whose centuries of behavior aren't easily eradicated overnight. Besides,

it reminds critics, American corporations and U. S. Marines created the same kind of plutocracies in a chain of banana republics, which in turn produce more hungry, invading aliens. The United States inherited this disregard for native populations from its own brutal history of manifest destiny.

Everyone—our ancestors and ourselves—is guilty. No law or fence will contain the hungry, devastated people we bring into this world, if there are too many of them to subdue. Blaming this on the communists will not help. It is equally doubtful that visions of nineteenth-century cowboys will solve things, either.

.   .   .

Early evening: The harbor reflects queenly San Diego, with its Old Town and pastel Horton Plaza and glass-and-steel buildings resembling twenty-story filing cabinets. The last surfaces touched by the waning sun are the Spanish colonial walls in Balboa Park, where families are gathering for caroling at the Organ Pavilion.

In Tijuana, the posadas have begun, candlelit processions where children reenact the journey in search of an inn. At the Centro del Desarrollo Infantil Mariana, 112 orphans are happily smeared with a rare treat of chocolate cake. Some were so limp with malnutrition when they arrived that they were unable to walk. Revived with regimens of six meals a day, they play on the floor around the tree, while new ones too weak to move lie in the nursery, oblivious to Christmas.

Some of the little ones here are Central American, their parents detained in a Tijuana jail or already deported without being able to reclaim their babies. Others were simply abandoned. Baja California has many orphanages; homeless Mexican children often end up in prostitution in Los Angeles. The border was shocked recently when an American-run orphanage in Tecate was discovered making child pornography films.

This state facility has no official adoption program, and few Mexicans can afford to adopt. Mexican Americans sometimes pay an unwed mother's labor expenses, buy a birth certificate naming themselves as the parents, and tell immigration officials they had their baby in a Mexican hospital to save money.

For other North Americans, adoption in Mexico can mean a prohibitive bureaucratic tangle in a country that does not like to admit it cannot look after its own. "But if it could be arranged so Americans could take some of these kids," says Guadalupe Morales, the psychologist here at the centro, "that would not be bad. What difference does it make which side they live on," she asks, indicating the fence at the end of the block, "if they have a chance to be happy?"

On the south edge of town, several hundred people crowd into a drafty palenque. The cockfights have been going on all day and will last until dawn. From mother-of-pearl inlaid boxes, handlers in white guayaberas select two-inch bayonet gaffs or the favored one-inch Mexican knives. The long Filipino blades are eschewed here, but in the Escondido hills above San Diego, the Filipinos themselves are at it with their own gamecocks.

The handlers caress and whisper to their gallos as they arm their spurs. These are beautiful roosters, two year-old Yellowleg MacClean Hatches, Straight Combs, Kelsos, and a few Minor Blues. At least a thousand cockers are raising fighting stock in Tijuana and San Diego, but the best birds around come from places like Jasper, Alabama, and Henrietta, North Carolina. Many men here save for years to fly to the Southeast to buy breeding trios, and speak warmly of their amigos in Dixie.

Their blades annointed with a fresh lime, a Blueface Hatch and a Kelso are held face to face in the circle until they are locked in hatred. Released a few feet apart, they merge in midair and descend kicking. Stray feathers settle around them, and presently a fine spray of blood stains the dirt circle. Even as the crowd comes to its feet, the roosters fight in silence. A buzzer sounds; knives are inspected, and la pelea resumes, although dark fluid pumps from the Kelso's russet breast.

The buzzer does not sound again. Granted once again the satisfaction many humans derive from watching something die, the crowd settles back. Children inspect the defeated carcass, while their parents stand in line for tamales and beer. The public address system announces free admission on Christmas Day.

. . . .

Night.

There are elites in Tijuana, but the city is too young to have aristocracies. Once its scattered inhabitants were Diegueño Indians who called it Teguan, a place by the sea. The Diegueños interbred and long ago vanished within the beige spectrum of mestizaje. Tijuana is now a city of migrants, of nuclear rather than extended families, a suitcase society ready to go back to the interior of Mexico or on to the United States. Everyone is working or on their way to work. The border becomes increasingly dynamic as it goes from east to west. The stagnant Brownsville-Matamoros economy has no equivalent in the Californias.

Americans came here to lose themselves during Prohibition at the fabulous Agua Caliente resort, begun by General (later Presidente) Abelardo Rodríguez and his American partners and finally closed by Presidente Lázaro Cárdenas. El Casino de Agua Caliente invoked all creeds of lavishness, its interiors a medley of art deco, Spanish colonial, Moorish, and French provincial designs that only excess wealth could justify under a single roof. Beneath the Louis XV gold chandeliers, Douglas Fairbanks, Jean Harlow, Dolores del Río, and the Aga Khan danced on its marble floors.

Only the racetrack remains today; the stripped cabañas house a preparatory school. But on Tijuana's Calle Revolución, Americans still seek an outrageous night world they cannot find on their own side of the border. From Coronado and La Jolla, men and women around thirty, coming out of their youth but coming into their own, are in the Ballena, the longest bar in the city. As long as they don't kill, here they can break bottles, scream, spin from table to table, drink themselves to paralysis, and suspend their hard-won beliefs in the long, smoky hall.

A truce forms in the Tijuana night between worlds that normally don't meet by day—yet. The cholos are out, hybridized with North American punk, their hair sculptures both lubed and chiseled, with tattoos over their hearts and leather over their tank tops. They ooze into the Ballena like an oil slick, and the music skitters back and forth between Costello and cumbia. "Vaya, asshole," mutter dazed cholitos in spiky paraphernalia, stumbling over the slant-heeled boots of a couple of norteños from Sinaloa, landing in the laps of incipient Junior Leaguers or getting shoved back by off-duty federales. A few whores, not yet punched in, wander by for a drink before heading to work, nodding lewdly at everybody.

Cultures ensnarl further at El Diamante, where tropical and salsa are the back- and foreground music for nonstop, soundless American science fiction projected on the sensorial, dominating video screen. Yet the bar here is full of Mexican construction workers, who stare unsteadily at Spock, at invading body snatchers and the Blob, and swallow shots of Hornitos.

In the smoke-lit basement called the Unicornio, a grimy Tijuana legend persists. The touring U.S. Navy has the floor show surrounded on every flank, breaking ranks only to slip into back rooms where las cabronas giving them head are mostly transvestites. On the stage, beefy mestizo transsexuals ripple up to the sea of pale, perspiring faces, telling them where to tuck their bids. A hand shoves in a twenty. Two twenties. A sailor dives between her legs as she leans over to give $5.00 chances to suck, left and right, to his mate while bored musicians doze over their instruments and the circle of boy-men is chanting "Go Jock! Go Jock!" The secretive and curious wander in from the street: Mixteco Indians, gays, narcs, grave intellectuals from the University of California-San Diego and el Colegio de la Frontera Norte, tourists who don't know why they're here at all. They stay.

Beyond the legend is the Zona Norte, where Tijuana refused to change its image for the Secretaría de Turismo. The sidewalks are pressurized arroyos cutting between norteño saloons and redundant barbeques of goat and carnitas, offering smells both wonderful and horrifying. The arroyos surge with cholos, vatos, jotas, putas, albinos, Vietnamese, American blacks, vaqueros, Salvadorans, Santa Claus, and whomever else is churned up from the fertile murk of Tijuana.

At a benefit for La Casa de la Cultura, a Tijuana fine arts institute, a punk band from San Francisco named the Dead Kennedys is double-billed with Tijuana's La Solución Mental in a gesture toward transborder exchange. It is bedlam. Barrio Logan and other San Diego cholo enclaves have swarmed into Tijuana. Everybody gleams with ornamental chain. The auditorium is incandescent with racial tension. Jello Biafra, lead singer for the Dead Kennedys, begins yelling "PRI no! PRI no! How many of you culeros voted for the PRI?" Slam dancers, skinheads, suburban punks, cholos, border hybrids, and a couple of misplaced surfers roar an unintelligible reply.

All over Tijuana, across in San Diego, at the pedestrian bridge where coyotes murmur "a Los Angeles, a Los Angeles" from the shadows and alcohol-doused gringos who usually know better trudge toward their cars over the twenty-four lanes joining Mexico and the United States—all over the world's most energized cultural confluence, social gases are swirling, starting to coalesce, to form something. Cardinal points collapse. North becomes south; the east-west border oscillates like the graph of a racing heartbeat, the compass yaws wildly, attempting to reposition itself, pointing toward incredible strength in all directions.

Out in the universe, planets have taken shape around less.

·   ·   ·

After earning his master's degree in aquatic biology from San Diego State, Fernando Medina's son Enrique tried for two years to find work in Mexico. He trimmed his beard and his halo of wiry hair, and presented himself and his título from an American university at the fisheries subministry in Mexico City.

They sent him to a marine biology center at a Mexican naval installation in Manzanillo. It had no budget or equipment. The director suggested Guaymas or Ensenada. He went to those places and to the Instituto Nacional de Pesca and back to Mexico City. Everyone greeted him with enthusiasm. He encountered many bureaucrats, but no jobs. At one point, after learning that Chilean exiles were being hired over Mexicans, he wrote to Presidente López Portillo, protesting that he was trying to repatriate with his skills and not be part of the brain drain northward. Mexico was supposedly expanding its fisheries, yet he couldn't get work while foreigners could. The president did not reply.

He found a temporary stint in Baja California, counting gray whales. Many scientists from the United States were there, and it was a relief to talk to working colleagues. He was invited to San Diego. He went.

He didn't seriously think about living in the United States, but Mexico had been depressing. He had some time left on his visa. On a trip in 1978 to Santa Cruz, a tutoring opportunity turned up. Within a year, Enrique Medina was directing a Santa Cruz nonprofit nutrition program, delivering meals to Mexican American farmworkers.

When he had first left Mexicali for college, his father discouraged him from associating too much with Chicanos. "They have the mentality of a minority. You are from a majority." Santa Cruz County and his food bank were heavily Chicano. Enrique felt accepted, but he also felt the difference. Mexicans who were U.S. citizens were two minds occupying one body.

His own life was becoming more complicated. There was the matter of his student visa. He was not study-ing; it was about to expire and he had no grounds for an extension. He was sharing a house with several people of both sexes whom he liked; it was comfortable in the United States, and Enrique was uneasy about returning to joyless prospects in Mexico. He and his housemates discussed it over dinner.

"Why can't one of us just marry you?" suggested one of the women.

"Huh?"

It would work, they realized. An American wife would qualify him for legal residency. But who would . . . ? The woman named Ellen volunteered herself; it was a purely platonic arrangement to help a friend that would not otherwise interfere with her life. Touched by this generosity and struck by finding so simple a solution, Enrique decided the idea appealed to him.

But right when he faced a series of interrogations with the INS, Ellen got a chance to visit China.

"Well, Enrique," said her roommate, Elspeth, "I guess I'll have to marry you."

Elspeth Cleghorn grew up in Menlo Park. In Santa Cruz, she drove a forklift in a cannery. Though she complained about always smelling like brussels sprouts, she had sunlit hair and clear sky for eyes, and Enrique greatly admired her. She also had a boyfriend, but a few months before Enrique either had to be married or in Mexico, they began dating. Elspeth wasn't planning to be wed to him for life—although she'd had a crush on him and she didn't consider this strictly a business proposition.

"I can't," she told her boyfriend when he mentioned a camping trip. "I'm, uh, getting married in a couple of days."

During the brief ceremony, Enrique produced a ring.

"You're kidding."

"Hey," he said, embarrassed. "I love you."

They passed the INS's quiz, concurring on what they'd

had for dinner the night before and what each other's parents' names were. Enrique got his green card and found work with an aquaculture firm that sent him to Mexico to develop a hatchery program for the government, the kind of position he had tried so hard earlier to get as a Mexican citizen. He and Elspeth discussed it; she was willing to learn Spanish and live in his country. But then the peso caved in and the hatcheries folded with it. Enrique took a job with a San Diego seafood firm that needed help to import sea bass and corvina from Baja California.

Born to the border and bilingual, Enrique Medina congenitally knew how to slip through the morass of Mexican and American customs, offering exactly the right amount of a gratuity here, leaving a few smoked flounder there, to get a load of perishable yellowfin or rock cod across the line. Soon he was in business for himself in both San Diego and in Tijuana, employing fishermen with a Mexican partner and exporting their catch to his own company to supply California restaurants. Now he plans to start a maquiladora to process fish, before some other immigrant entrepreneur like himself does so.

A few days before Christmas, Enrique and Elspeth take their son, Daniel, to play on the slides and swings in Balboa Park. The afternoon is warm; many families are picnicking under the pepper trees. Balloons are everywhere, and soon one is tied to Daniel's wrist.

He has Enrique's coloring and curls, but his blond hair traces back to Elspeth's childhood. In a few years, they will send him, at least for a while, to school in Tijuana so he can learn the Mexican half of his heritage. Enrique wants this, although he worries about the confusion his border child will unavoidably feel. Right now, he has to contend with his own ambivalence. With oil prices draining away faster than Mexico can plug the leaks, he knows he is fortunate to be in the United States. Since there is no assurance that the United States will never expel resident aliens,

he may someday break down and apply for citizenship. It's hard, because he still feels Mexican.

"I have a great deal of trouble saying 'our boys in Grenada,' " he tells Elspeth.

"So what? I do too. You talk about 'our taxes,' don't you?"

Daniel is on the merry-go-round, the kind that children run alongside and push. Playing with him are three girls and two boys. One girl is black, one is Korean, and the other is as Caucasian as Elspeth. The older of the two boys is Japanese; the other, Enrique perceives, is the son of the undocumented couple sitting unobtrusively in the eucalyptus shade. Neither he nor Elspeth could have witnessed such a scene when they were growing up a generation earlier. But here it is.

"Tú estás pushing too hard," Daniel tells the Korean girl, placing Enrique and Elspeth among the ranks of thousands of parents living along this cradle of a new American civilization who cringe over the imagined destruction of their respective languages. Centuries ago, the same complaint was heard in the Roman Empire, but the mongrelized version of Latin that was the Tex-Mex and Spanglish of its day eventually became the beautifully liquid Italian.

A memorial in Mexico City's Plaza of the Three Cultures in Tlaltelolco recalls that the final battle of la conquista "was neither triumph nor defeat, but the painful birth of the mestizo people that are Mexico today." Along the United States–Mexico border, the further coupling of New World societies is now in progress. No similar plaque yet announces the birth of a new people; instead, Niños Héroes monuments and tortilla curtains of two dominant cultures still face each other warily. To say that the borderlands are already a third country between the other two is to ignore the pain and excitement of creation that await us.

Yet the border is not a line, but a full circle. Centuries ago, with the encouragement of Rome, Spain expelled the Moors who had already changed its life and language. Together, Rome and the southern European nations of Iberia forged a religious imperialism that contradicted the growing reformation in northern Europe.

The descendants of these two adversaries confront each other today along another frontier. Enriched by the hues of native Americans, resilient Africans, and venturesome Asians, they meet at a border established by two countries, the United States and Mexico, and pull the world along behind them.

Except for outer space, there are no other frontiers. No place to go to escape the problems or ignore the potential. This frontera is the border between the present and the future: Along it, its people must eventually create yet a newer world.

ACKNOWLEDGMENTS

During our travels, professional and independent scholars continually helped us to understand the borderlands. In addition to their works that appear in the bibliography, many took time to personally share their wisdom, research, and enthusiasm.

We especially thank Eliseo Paredes, Matamoros; Antonio Noé Zavaleta, Texas Southmost College; Rodolfo Rocha, Pan American University; Ernesto Garza, Camargo, Tamaulipas; Jerry Don Thompson, Laredo Junior College; John Stockley, Quemado, Texas; Macedonio Aguilar Aldama, Ciudad Acuña; Enrique Madrid, Redford, Texas; Alan Brenner, Chihuahuan Desert Research Institute, Alpine, Texas; Guillermina Valdés-Villalva, Colegio de la Frontera Norte, Ciudad Juárez; C. Richard Bath, Howard Applegate and Oscar J. Martínez of the University of Texas at El Paso; Stephen P. Mumme, Colorado State University; Gary Paul Nabhan, Office of Arid Lands Studies, University of Arizona; Susan Clarke Spater, Pimería Alta Historical Society, Nogales, Arizona; Fernando Medina Robles, Mexicali; Jorge A. Bustamante, Colegio de la Frontera Norte, Tijuana; and Joseph Nalven, San Diego State University.

We are also indebted to library collections at the Center for Inter-American and Border Studies, University of Texas at El Paso; at Arizona State University; and at Colegio de la Frontera Norte, Tijuana.

Change along the border is so dynamic that everyone's writings would be obsolete by the time the ink dried, were it not for the relentless bicultural coverage of frontera journalists. For risking deadlines on our behalf, we thank Dan Bus, *Del Rio Guide*; Keoki Skinner, *Arizona Republic*; Heleodoro Pacheco, *La Voz del Norte*; Raul Guerra, *The South Texas Reporter*; Marco Vinicio, *Uno Más Uno*; Guillermo Gómez-Peña, *La Opinión*; Juanita Contreras, *La Controversia*, and especially Carmina Danini, *Laredo Morning Times*; Debbie Nathan, *El Paso Times*; and Marjorie Miller, *Los Angeles Times*.

Editor John Boynton at Harcourt Brace Jovanovich made everyone, including us, believe in the importance of this book. Throughout, it has been reassuring to work with people like him and his colleagues: editor Martha Lawrence, designer Joy Chu, and production director Warren Wallerstein.

Back home, we are obliged to Prescott College librarian Susan Burton and student Andrea Arel for eleventh-hour research; professors Carl Tomoff and Pedro Angel Aísa, and Ann-Lawrie Aísa, for verifying details about the natural environment and the Spanish language; and to Paul McKee for countless hours of expert and dedicated assistance in the darkroom.

Thank you, Kathie Dusard, for taking such good care of us both.

And muchísimas gracias, fronterizos, people of the border, for your hospitality and candor, and for standing watch at the brink of change on behalf of us all. Dios les bendiga—God bless.

PHOTOGRAPHING

THE BORDER

Alan Weisman and I went down the road together, making the several trips in alternating King Cabs— his Nissan, my Datsun. That meant traveling light; no room for his guitar or my cornet (no time to make music), but we wouldn't have gone the distance without our stash of cassette tapes: Guy Clark, Little Joe y La Familia, Gershwin, Mary McCaslin, Townes Van Zandt, vintage Miles, and plenty of corridos.

For a view camera shooter, my photographic outfit for this project was pretty compact: a stripped-down 4x5-inch Busch Pressman folding camera and six lenses, in focal lengths of 100, 135, 180, 240, 260, and 335 millimeters. The latter three lenses are small apochromats, and the entire layout, including a Pentax Spotmeter V, fit into one medium-sized case, except for my indispensable old wooden Ries tripod.

Throughout, I used the Ansel Adams Zone System for coordinating exposure and film development. My exposures ranged from ⅟₂₅ second to 23 seconds. Kodak Tri-X film-pack was rated at ASA 250 and developed in Kodak HC-110, dilution B.

The conditions of light ranged from glaring sand and sky to the feeble glow of miners' lamps focused on my portrait subjects, 350 feet below the surface. For the book's reproduction prints, using a cold-light enlarger, Pal Print chlorobromide paper and Kodak

Selectol developer produced the richest results. Selective reduction with a solution of potassium ferricyanide and sodium thiosulfate was done on most of these prints. An integral step in my printing procedure, the bleaching was used to achieve degrees of tonal adjustment and balance too subtle for the conventional exposure controls of dodging and burning-in, which I also employed extensively.

Before this project got started, my vision of the border was lots and lots of virtually unpopulated miles of desert and mountain cattle range with a seven-strand barbed-wire fence running down the middle of it— not a bad vision at all. When I had cowboyed for the old John Slaughter Ranch in southeastern Arizona back in 1963, I had ridden that very fence, fixing the loose and busted wires. Given two thousand miles of border, I assumed there would be plenty of time spent in such places—punctuated, of course, by visits to a few border towns. I just didn't click in to border cities.

Even though I was born in St. Louis and had done time on Florida's Gold Coast and in Tucson, I had still pretty much managed to steer clear of urban areas, preferring to consider them only in terms of rare and abbreviated binges of art and live jazz.

Sure, I knew about border cities: El Paso/Juárez, San Diego/Tijuana—even Brownsville/Matamoros. But I hadn't done my homework; I wasn't prepared for Mexicali, the Nogales twins, Reynosa, los Laredos, and the Sunbelt sprawl of the Lower Rio Grande Valley in Texas. There are plenty of cities on la frontera. Not all big ones, but cities nonetheless. And growing. And it's in these cities that most of the dynamism, frustration, and human stories of the border are to be found.

And that's where we ended up. It turns out that the only classic border towns left are Los Ebanos, Boquillas, Santa Elena, Candelaria, Columbus, Palomas, a couple of Nacos, and a pair of Sasabes.

In our year on the road, I didn't learn much Spanish. I know a lot of the words and can sometimes get the drift of things, but when I hear it coming at *me*—even from a five-year-old—I freeze up and am useless. Alan was too good, too fluent, and I leaned on him like a crutch. Given our pace, it was expeditious for him to let me do so. I'm not exactly proud of this.

This project split me right down the middle—like the border splits a continent. Thus laid open, my two halves seemed polarized, irreconcilable. One just wanted to be somewhere else, preferably horseback—but then there was that part of me receptive to all the surprises and the consistent warmth of humankind that wouldn't have missed this for the world.

Jay Dusard
Prescott, Arizona
May 1986

BIBLIOGRAPHY

GENERAL

Books

Barnes, Will C. *Arizona Place Names*. Revised and enlarged by Byrd H. Granger. Tucson: University of Arizona Press, 1960.

Bartlett, John Russell. *Personal Narrative of Explorations and Incidents in Texas, New Mexico, California, Sonora and Chihuahua Connected with the United States and Mexican Boundary Commission During the Years 1850, '51, '52, '53*. 2 vols. New York: D. Appleton, 1854.

Bustamante, Jorge A., y Francisco Malagamba. *México-Estados Unidos: Bibliografía General Sobre Estudios Fronterizos*. México: El Colegio de México, 1980.

Coerver, Don M., and Linda B. Hall. *Texas and the Mexican Revolution: A Study in State and National Border Policy, 1910–1920*. San Antonio: Trinity University Press, 1981.

Crewdson, John. *The Tarnished Door*. New York: Times Books, 1983.

Demaris, Ovid. *Poso del Mundo*. Boston: Little, Brown, 1970.

Ehrlich, Paul R., with Loy Bilderback and Anne H. Ehrlich. *The Golden Door: International Migration, Mexico and the United States*. New York: Ballantine Books, 1979.

Emory, William H. *Report of the United States and Mexican Boundary Survey*. 3 vols. Washington, D.C.: U.S. Department of the Interior, 1857–1859.

Garreau, Joel. *The Nine Nations of North America*. Boston: Houghton Mifflin, 1981.

Gehlbach, Frederick R. *Mountain Islands and Desert Seas: A Natural History of the U.S.-Mexican Borderlands*. College Station: Texas A&M University Press, 1981.

González Salazar, Roque, ed. *La Frontera del Norte: Integración y Desarrollo*. México: El Colegio de México, 1981.

Hansen, Niles. *The Border Economy: Regional Development in the Southwest*. Austin: University of Texas Press, 1980.

Hine, Robert V. *Bartlett's West: Drawing the Mexican Boundary*. New Haven: Yale University Press, 1968.

Horgan, Paul. *Great River*. New York: Holt, Rinehart and Winston, 1954. Reprinted by *Texas Monthly Press*, 1984.

Jamail, Milton H. *The United States-Mexico Border: A Guide to Institutions, Organizations and Scholars*. Tucson: University of Arizona Latin American Study Center, 1980.

Johnson, William Weber. *Heroic Mexico*. Rev. ed. San Diego, New York, London: Harcourt Brace Jovanovich, 1984.

Kingston, Michael T., ed. *The Texas Almanac*. Dallas: Dallas Morning News, 1984.

Meyer, Michael C., and William L. Sherman. *The Course of Mexican History*, 2d ed. New York and Oxford: Oxford University Press, 1983.

Miller, Robert Ryal. *Mexico: A History*. Norman: University of Oklahoma Press, 1985.

Miller, Tom. *On the Border*. New York: Harper & Row, 1981.

Newsome, C. M. "Buck." *Shod with Iron: Life on the Mexican Border with the United States Border Patrol*. Marfa, Texas: n.p., 1975.

Nostrand, Richard L., Ellwyn R. Stoddard, and Jonathan P. West, eds. *Borderlands Sourcebook*. Norman: University of Oklahoma Press, 1983.

Paredes, Américo. *With His Pistol in His Hand*. Austin: University of Texas Press, 1958.

Riding, Alan. *Distant Neighbors: A Portrait of the Mexicans*. New York: Alfred A. Knopf, 1985.

Ruff, Ann. *Traveling Texas Borders: A Guide to the Best of Both Sides*. Houston: Gulf Publishing Company, 1983.

Russell, Phillip. *Mexico in Transition*. Austin: Colorado River Press, 1977.

Stoddard, Ellwyn R. *Patterns of Poverty Along the U.S.-Mexican Border*. El Paso: Center for Inter-American Studies at the University of Texas at El Paso, 1978.

Womack, John Jr. *Zapata and the Mexican Revolution*. New York: Alfred A. Knopf, 1969.

Articles

George, Edward Y., and Robert D. Tollen. "The Economic Impact of the Mexican Border Industrialization Program." *Center for Inter-American and Border Studies-Border Issues and Public Policy No. 20*, University of Texas at El Paso (February 1985).

"Hit and Run: U.S. Runaway Shops on the Mexican Border." Special issue of *NACLA's Latin American and Empire Reports 9* (July–August 1975).

Sánchez, Vicente, and Ing. Fernando Ortiz Monasterio. "Considering Environmental Aspects in the Development Process along the Mexico-United States Border." Discussion Draft, Symposium on Bioresources and Environmental Hazards of the United States-Mexico Border, UCLA (September 1983).

Tiano, Susan B. "Export Processing, Women's Work, and the Employment Problem in Developing Countries: The Case of the Maquiladora Program in Northern Mexico." *Center for Inter-American and Border Studies-Border Issues and Public Policy No. 22*, University of Texas at El Paso (April 1985).

CHAPTER ONE

Books

Chatfield, W. H. *The Twin Cities of the Border and the Country of the Lower Rio Grande*. New Orleans: E. P. Brandao, 1893.

Cruz, Gilberto Rafael, and Martha Oppert Cruz. *A Century of Service: The History of the Catholic Church in the Lower Rio Grande Valley*. Harlingen, Texas: United Printers and Publishers, 1979.

Paredes Manzano, Eliseo. *Homenaje a los Fundadores de la Heróica, Leal e Invicta Matamoros en el Sesquicentennial de su Nuevo Nombre*. Matamoros: Impresos Alta, 1976.

Thompson, Jerry Don. *Vaqueros in Blue & Gray*. Austin: Presidial Press, 1976.

Zavaleta, Tony. *Brownsville Health Needs Assessment Survey: a U.S.-Mexico Border Case Study 1984–85*. Brownsville: South Texas Institute of Latin and Mexican-American Research, Texas Southmost College, 1985.

Articles

Miller, Huber J. "Mexican Migrations to the U.S. 1900–1920, with a focus on the Texas Rio Grande Valley." *Borderlands 7, No. 2* (Spring 1984): 165-205.

Southwest Region of U.S. Fish and Wildlife Service. "Land Protection Plan for Lower Rio Grande Valley National Wildlife Refuge in Cameron, Hidalgo, Starr, and Willacy Counties, Texas." U.S. Department of the Interior (January 1985).

CHAPTER TWO

Books

Del Cántaro, Juan, y Tomás Hinojosa Rodríguez. *2 Poetas de Ciudad Mier*. Ciudad Mier, Tamaulipas: Editorial Arana, 1970.

Lindheim, Milton. *The Republic of the Rio Grande* (booklet). Waco: W. M. Morrison, 1964.

Thompson, Jerry. *Sabers on the Rio Grande*. Austin: Presidial Press, 1974.

Articles

Green, Stanley. "Laredo 1755–1920: An Overview." *Nuevo Santander Museum Complex Occasional Papers* (October 1, 1975).

Thompson, Jerry. "Blood on the Border: The 1886 Laredo Election Riot and the Formation of the Independent Club." Manuscript in preparation.

CHAPTER THREE

Books

Amada Solís, Luisa, ed. *Cien Poetas Mexicanos*. México: Libro-Mex Editores, S. de R.L., 1980.

Arreola Pérez, Jesús Alfonso. *Coahuila*. Monografía Estatal. México D.F.: Secretaría de Educación Pública, 1983.

Calderón, Roberto R., ed. *South Texas Coal Mining: A Community History*. Eagle Pass, Texas: n.p., 1984.

Canales Herrán. *Narraciones Monográficas de Cd. Acuña*. Ciudad Acuña, Coahuila: Editora Fronteriza, S.A., 1962.

Gutiérrez, A. E. *A History of San Felipe*. Del Rio, Texas: Whitehead Memorial Museum, 1978.

Kerig, Dorothy Pierson. *Luther T. Ellsworth: U.S. Consul on the Border During the Mexican Revolution*. Southwest Studies Monograph 47. El Paso: Texas Western Press, 1975.

Navarrete, Carlos. *Carbón Mineral y Electricidad en México*. México: Grupo Proyección Integral, 1982.

Articles

Aguilar Aldama, Macedonio. "Monografía del Municipio de Acuña, Coahuila." Obra inédita.

Goodyear, Russell H. "Historians Hear Paper on Dr. Brinkley." *Del Rio Guide 4, No. 1* (April 1984): 5.

Pingenot, Ben E. *Historical Highlights of Eagle Pass and Maverick County*. Eagle Pass, Texas: Eagle Pass Chamber of Commerce, 1971.

CHAPTER FOUR

Books

Applegate, Howard G. *The Demography of La Junta de los Rios Del Norte y Conchos*. San Francisco: Anduin Institute, n.d.

Gallegos Landeros, Dr. Artemio. *Semblanzas Políticas*. Ojinaga, Chihuahua: Imprenta Reysa, 1983.

Maxwell, Ross A. *The Big Bend of the Rio Grande: A Guide to the Rocks, Landscape, Geologic History, and Settlers of the Area of Big Bend National Park, Guidebook 7*. Austin: University of Texas at Austin, 1979.

Riskind, David H., and Roland H. Wauer, eds. *Transactions of the Symposium on the Biological Resources of the Chihuahuan Desert Region, United States and Mexico, Sul Ross State University, Alpine, Texas*. Washington, D.C.: U.S. Department of the Interior National Park Service Transactions and Proceedings Series/No. 3, 1977.

Torres, Eliseo. *The Folk Healer: The Mexican-American Tradition of Curanderismo*. Kingsville, Texas: Nieves Press, n.d.

Tyler, Ronnie C. *The Big Bend, A History of the Last Texas Frontier*. Washington, D.C.: U.S. Department of Interior, 1975.

Wauer, Roland H. *Birds of Big Bend National Park and Vicinity*. Austin: University of Texas Press, 1973.

Articles

Girón García, Marco A. "Sierra del Carmen, Coahuila: Alternativas de Protección de la Zona Fronteriza." Presented at the First Regional Conference of the Rio Grande Border States on Parks and Wildlife, Laredo, Texas, November 5–8, 1985.

CHAPTER FIVE
Books

Bath, C. Richard, ed. *Vehicles and Air Pollution in El Paso-Ciudad Juárez*. El Paso: Center For Inter-American and Border Studies, University of Texas at El Paso, n.d.

Martínez, Oscar J. *Border Boom Town—Ciudad Juárez Since 1848*. Austin: University of Texas Press, 1975.

———. *The Chicanos of El Paso: An Assessment of Progress*. Southwestern Studies Monograph No. 59. El Paso: Texas Western Press, 1980.

Moskos, Harry, ed. *Special Report: The Border*. El Paso: El Paso Herald-Post, 1983.

Sonnichsen, C. L. *Pass of the North: Four Centuries on the Rio Grande*. El Paso: Texas Western Press, 1968.

Articles

Applegate, Howard G. "A Discussion of U.S.-Mexico Experience in Managing Transboundary Air Resources: Problems, Prospects and Recommendations for the Future." *Natural Resources Journal* 22 (October 1982): 1169–1174.

———. "Transboundary Air Quality: Problems and Prospects from El Paso to Brownsville." *Natural Resources Journal* 22 (October 1982): 1133–1139.

———, and C. Richard Bath. "Bilateral Emissions Trading in an International Airshed." Cross-Cultural Center of the Southwest

and Department of Political Science, University of Texas at El Paso. n.d.

Barilleauz, Ryan J., and C. Richard Bath. "Groundwater Policy in the El Paso Region: Domestic and International Implications." Presented at the Annual Meeting of the Western Social Science Association, San Diego, April 26, 1984.

Gingerich, William P., ed. "Air Quality Issues in the El Paso/Cd. Juárez Border Region." *Center for Inter-American and Border Studies Occasional Papers 5*, University of Texas at El Paso, n.d.

Gorby, Earl W., M.D. "Emerging Tuberculosis Problems in El Paso/Juárez; Staff Study No. 2." *Region 3, Texas State Department of Health Resources* (January 1976).

Hidalgo, Margarita. "Language Attitudes and Language Use in Cd. Juárez, Mexico." *Center for Inter-American and Border Studies-Border Issues and Public Policy No. 17*. University of Texas at El Paso (October 1984).

Lloyd, William J., and Richard A. Marston. "Municipal and Industrial Water Supply in Ciudad Juárez, Mexico." *Water Resources Bulletin 21, No. 5*, American Water Resources Association (October 1985).

Magee, James R. "Life in the Juárez Dump." *Center for Inter-American and Border Studies-Border Perspectives No. 1*, University of Texas at El Paso (March 1983).

Martínez, Oscar J. "The Foreign Orientation of the Mexican Border Economy." *Center for Inter-American and Border Studies-Border Perspectives No. 2*, University of Texas at El Paso (May 1983).

CHAPTER SIX
Books

Faulk, Odie B. *The Geronimo Campaign*. New York: Oxford University Press, 1969.

Hadley, Drummond. *The Webbing*. San Francisco: Four Seasons Foundation/City of Lights Books, 1963.

———. *The Spirit by the Deep Well Tank*. Santa Fe: Goliard/Santa Fe, 1972.

Sonnichsen, C. L. *Colonel Greene and the Copper Skyrocket*. Tucson: University of Arizona Press, 1974.

CHAPTER SEVEN
Books

Baird, Peter, and Ed McCaughan. *Beyond the Border: Mexico and the U.S. Today*. New York: North American Congress on Latin America, 1979.

Claremon, Neil. *Borderland*. New York: Alfred A. Knopf, 1975.

———. *Easy Favors*. New York: McGraw-Hill, 1980.

Ready, Alma, ed. *Nogales, Arizona, 1880–1980 Centennial Anniversary*. Nogales, Arizona: Nogales Centennial Committee, 1980.

CHAPTER EIGHT
Books

Duke, Alton. *When the Colorado River Quit the Ocean.* Yuma: Southwest Printers, 1974.

Greene, Jerome A. *Historic Resource Study: Organ Pipe Cactus National Monument, Arizona.* Denver: Historic Preservation Division, National Park Service, United States Department of the Interior, 1977.

Hundley, Norris Jr. *Dividing the Waters: A Century of Controversy Between the United States and Mexico.* Berkeley and Los Angeles: University of California Press, 1966.

Kennan, George. *The Salton Sink: An Account of Harriman's Fight with the Colorado River.* New York: Macmillan, 1917.

Lumholtz, Carl. *New Trails in Mexico.* New York: Charles Scribner's Sons, 1912.

Minckley, W. L. *Aquatic Habitats and Fishes of the Lower Colorado River, Southwestern United States.* Boulder City, Nevada: U.S. Department of the Interior, Bureau of Reclamation, Lower Colorado Region, Contract No. 14-06-300-2529, 1979.

Nabhan, Gary Paul. *The Desert Smells Like Rain: A Naturalist in Papago Country.* San Francisco: North Point Press, 1982.

Sykes, Godfrey. *The Colorado Delta.* American Geographical Society Special Publication No. 19. Washington, D.C.: Carnegie Institute, 1937.

Tohono O'Odham: History of the Desert People. Salt Lake City: University of Utah Printing Services, 1985.

Tohono O'Odham: Lives of the Desert People. Salt Lake City: University of Utah Printing Services, 1984.

Articles

Cohen, Felix S. "The Spanish Origin of Indian Rights in the Law of the United States." *The Georgetown Law Journal 31* (November 1942): 1–21.

Dyer, Jon P. "The Rio Grande and Colorado Rivers as Factors in United States–Mexican Relations (1944–1964)." Master's Thesis in History, University of Southern California, August 1964.

Furnish, Dale Beck, and Jerry R. Ladman. "The Colorado River Salinity Agreement of 1973 and the Mexicali Valley." *Natural Resources Journal 15* (January 1975): 83–107.

Kirk, Bryan. "The Papago Country, Arizona." *U.S.G.S. Water Supply Paper No. 499* (1925).

Kniffen, Fred B. "The Natural Landscape of the Colorado Delta." *Lower California Studies III.* University of California Publications in Geography 5 (1932).

Mumme, Stephen P., and Helen M. Ingram. "Empowerment and the Papago Tribe: Water Politics in Southern Arizona." Paper presented at the 1984 Annual Meeting of the American Political Science Association, August 1984.

Nabhan, Gary P., et al. "Papago Influences on Habitat and Biotic Diversity: Quitovac Oasis Ethnoecology." *Journal of Ethnobiology* 2, No. 2 (December 1982): 124–143.

Rea, Amadeo M., Gary P. Nabhan, and Karen L. Reichardt. "Sonoran Desert Oases: Plants, Birds and People." *Environment Southwest 503* (Autumn 1983).

Sykes, Godfrey. "The Camino del Diablo: With Notes on a Journey in 1925." *Geographical Review* (1925): 62–74.

CHAPTER NINE
Books

Auyón, Eduardo Gerardo. *Los Chinos en Baja California Ayer y Hoy.* Hong Kong: n.p., 1971.

Christman, Florence. *The Romance of Balboa Park.* San Diego: The Committee of 1000, 1977.

Gómez-Peña, Guillermo. *Ocnoceni (In Some Other Place/En Algún Otro Lugar.)* San Diego: Poyeses Genética New Image Latino Theatre, 1985.

Herrera Carrillo, Pablo. *Colonización del Valle de Mexicali.* Mexicali: Universidad Autónoma de Baja California, 1976.

McKeever, Michael. *A Short History of San Diego.* San Francisco: Lexikos, 1985.

Medina Robles, Lic. Fernando. *Mexicali-Calexico: Estudio Descriptivo de su Desarrollo.* Mexicali: n.p., n.d.

Mills, James R. *San Diego: Where California Began.* 5th ed. San Diego: San Diego Historical Society, 1985.

Pinera Ramírez, David, ed. *Historia de Tijuana: Semblanza General.* Tijuana: Centro de Investigaciones Históricas UNAM-UABC, 1985.

Summers, June Nay. *Buenos Días Tijuana.* Ramona, California: Ballena Press, 1974.

Walther Meade, Adalberto. *Origen de Mexicali.* Mexicali: Universidad Autónoma de Baja California, 1983.

Warren, Gerald R., ed. *The Border Society.* San Diego: San Diego Union, 1984.

Articles

Burciaga Valdez, R., and Keith F. McCarthy, "Current and Future Effects of Mexican Immigration in California." Executive Summary. *Rand Publication Series* (November 1985).

Nalven, Joseph. "The Political Process in Regional Planning: The San Diego-Tijuana Sewage Disposal Problem." *Proceedings of the 1982 Meeting of the Rocky Mountain Council on Latin American Studies.* C. Richard Bath, ed. University of Texas at El Paso (1983).

Weisman, Alan. "A Matter of Jurisdiction." *Atlantic 254 No. 1* (July 1984): 16–24.

INDEX

ALAN WEISMAN, *born in Minneapolis, Minnesota,
is a 1974 graduate of the Medill School of
Journalism at Northwestern University, where he
was also an undergraduate. He spent four years in
the interior of Mexico in the late seventies and
early eighties, working with orphan children,
consultant to a fisheries project, and writing and
researching Latin American subjects. A 1986 John
Farrar fellow in nonfiction at the Bread Loaf
Writers Conference, he presently lives in Groom
Creek, Arizona.*

*Educated as an architect at the University of
Florida,* JAY DUSARD *forsook a brief career as a
cowpuncher for photography. He has been
creating black-and-white photography with
large-format cameras since 1965 and has won
wide respect for his portraits, landscapes, and
abstractions. A 1981 Guggenheim Fellowship led
to the publication of his acclaimed book,* The
North American Cowboy: A Portrait. *He and his
wife, Kathie, raise quarter horses near Prescott,
Arizona.*